kid THE power BOOK

FOR CARING ADULTS

*Personal Safety, Self-Protection, Confidence,
and Advocacy for Young People*

Irene Van der Zande

kid**power**
PRESS

Copyright And Use Information

Use of Kidpower Content. We encourage readers to use ideas from this book and other Kidpower Teenpower Fullpower educational materials to teach self-protection, confidence building, advocacy, and personal safety skills to the young people in their personal and professional lives. However, we ask that readers: 1) give clear acknowledgement to Kidpower and tell people how to find us when using examples, ideas, stories, language, or practices they learned from our program; 2) follow the *Permission to Use Requirements* on our website before reproducing any part of our materials in any online or printed form; and, 3) are careful NOT to promote themselves in a way that might give the impression they are certified by our organization or authorized to represent Kidpower unless they truly are. For any questions about acknowledgement or use, please e-mail safety@kidpower.org.

Restrictions. "Kidpower" and "Kidpower Teenpower Fullpower" are trademarked names. Individuals and groups must have an active certification or agreement with Kidpower Teenpower Fullpower International to be authorized to teach, promote, or organize workshops or other presentations using the Kidpower, Teenpower, or Fullpower program names or our workshop names, reputation, or credentials in their marketing. Please visit the Kidpower.org web site or call our office for information about our instructor certification, affiliate agreements, and center development programs.

Disclaimer. Each situation and individual is unique and neither the author nor Kidpower can make any guarantee about the safety or effectiveness of the content or techniques described in this book. We do not accept responsibility for any negative consequences from the use or misuse of this information.

Publisher. Kidpower Teenpower Fullpower International
P.O. Box 1212, Santa Cruz, CA, 95061, U.S.A; (o) 1-831-426-4407
safety@kidpower.org   www.kidpower.org

Graphic Design and Layout.
Thank you to Kristen Calcatera of Big Sky Creative for our Advance Reader's Copy edition cover and design. Thank you to Ian Price of www.pricewatkins.com for our First Edition cover and book design.

A Dedication to My Family

Kidpower would simply not exist without the love, generosity, and help of the members of my family, and this book is dedicated to them.

To my husband Ed who has given me and Kidpower constant unwavering support, our two children Chantal and Arend who brought me into this work, and our joyous granddaughter Svea who keeps me doing it.

To my parents Raim and Lily who taught me to do good in the world, put important things into writing, and be true to myself. To my sister Elaine and brother Ken, for every idea, phone call, email, and early morning walk.

This book is also in the honor of the memory of our longtime family friend, Eve, and of my friend and sister in this work, Annette. Eve, who passed away at the age of 95, provided endless cups of steaming tea and perfect soft- boiled eggs, as well as endless faith that Kidpower would flourish, even during the most challenging times. Annette was an inspiring teacher who helped thousands of women, men, teens and children to find power and belief in themselves and who supported my leadership in this work from the very beginning.

And, finally this book is also dedicated to the countless individuals who have made a commitment to become part of our growing Kidpower family for over two decades. To each of you, I give my deepest thanks for all you do to make our organization strong and our services exceptional.

Foreword by Gavin de Becker

Gavin de Becker is the bestselling author of *The Gift of Fear* and *Protecting the Gift*. He is the leading expert worldwide on the prediction and management of violence.

I've been fortunate to serve as an Advisor to Kidpower Teenpower Fullpower International for almost 20 years. That commitment began as I watched kids at a workshop, saw them joyfully and successfully taught to practice skills that can keep them safe, and I felt intuitively "This is right."

Since then I've raised eight children on these concepts (and two more to go, who are still toddlers). If you are reading these words, you are giving time and attention to protecting young people from bullying, abuse, abduction, assault, and other forms of violence. This action alone expresses leadership on your part, and I commend you.

Life's miseries fall disproportionately on children, told clearly and sadly by this statistic: Throughout history, half of all children failed to reach adulthood. Half. The odds are far better for children in America today, but the truth remains that childhood is safe only when adults make it so.

Among all the possible risks to our children, from the freak accident to the predictable accident, from the chemical under the sink to the chemical sold on a street corner, nothing is more frightening to us than the danger posed by people – danger committed consciously, purposefully, by design.

Though many people act as if it is invisible, the danger that is conscious is usually in plain view, disguised perhaps, but in plain view nonetheless. Some of the behaviors that precede this kind of danger are designed to distract, confuse, or reassure us, but those behaviors are themselves signals. There is a universal code of violence, and Kidpower teaches parents and other caring adults how to understand that code so they can protect and educate their kids and teens.

Though parents are the primary safety resource for children, there does come a day when the people initially responsible for a child's safety welcome a new member to the team: the child. Parents may agonize over whether their child is ready; they may even delay the day, but the day will come. Though it's at the end of a gradual process, your son or daughter will make that walk to school, or to a friend's house, or to the market, and the eyes that used to casually take in the sights will have to detect, assess, perhaps even deter danger.

In my book *Protecting the Gift*, I presented *The Test of Twelve*, which is a list of skills that children would ideally know before they are ever alone in public or on their own without the protection of their adults.

The Test of Twelve

Do your children know...

1. How to honor their feelings – if someone makes them uncomfortable, that's an important signal;
2. You (the parents) are strong enough to hear about any experience they've had, no matter how unpleasant;
3. It's Okay to rebuff and defy adults;
4. It's Okay to be assertive;
5. How to ask for assistance or help;
6. How to choose *whom* to ask for help;
7. How to describe their peril;
8. It's Okay to strike, even to injure, someone if they believe they are in danger, and that you'll support any action they take as a result of feeling uncomfortable or afraid;
9. It's Okay to make noise, to scream, to yell, to run;
10. If someone ever tries to force them to go somewhere, what they scream should include, "This is not my father" (because onlookers seeing a child scream or even struggle are likely to assume the adult is a parent);
11. If someone says "Don't yell," the thing to do *is* yell (and the corollary: If someone says "Don't tell," the thing to do *is* tell);
12. To fully resist ever going anywhere out of public view with someone they don't know, and particularly to resist going anywhere with someone who tries to persuade them.

Kidpower provides extensive tools that further the ability of parents and other caring adults to prepare children to pass each of the milestones on this test.

Item number 12 can take the most courage to apply. To resist fully is not easy, but if a predator orders a child or teen to go somewhere with him, he is really saying that staying here is to the child's advantage and to the predator's disadvantage. He wants to take the child to a place where he'll be able to do whatever it is he can't do here. Since people often cooperate out of fear of being injured, it is essential to remember that initial injury is far from the worst consequence of a violent crime.

Item number 8 of the Test of Twelve requires a child to know that it's okay to strike, even to injure someone when that's appropriate. Though many people believe that fight or flight are the only available responses to danger, that's true for animals more than it is for human beings. People have many resources, including: dexterity, agility, guile, negotiation, speed, cleverness, noise, strength, alliance, and the keen ability to predict behavior.

Adults who know how to protect their kids and young people who are prepared with the skills and knowledge to protect themselves have a more effective defense system than lions or tigers or bears – and this book provides a valuable resource in making that true for your children. I recommend Kidpower as a strong foundation for every family's personal safety training.

Gavin de Becker

Contents

Irene van der Zande

Introduction

This book is the very long conversation we would have if I had the time to sit down and meet with each of you personally to discuss your concerns about the emotional and physical safety of the children and teens in your life.

When a story about Kidpower first appeared on national television in the United States in 1989, I received hundreds of letters from people, many of them with newspaper clippings about tragic abductions, abuse, and bullying. People told stories like, "We moved our family to this small town to be safe. Now this awful situation has happened, and we don't know how to protect our children." A few years later, as soon as we launched our kidpower.org website, we started receiving the same anxious questions from worried adults all over the world.

The purpose of this book is to share with you the fundamentals of the Kidpower program and our method for making the learning of "People Safety" skills empowering, effective, and fun. Our goal is that this kind of skills-based social-emotional education will someday become ordinary in families, schools, organizations, and communities everywhere.

One of Kidpower's values is to be inclusive. This means that we welcome people of any age, culture, religion, race, gender, political belief, sexual orientation or identity, marital status, any kind of disability, or level of income who share our values of integrity and safety for everyone. The writing in this book reflects the diversity of the people we serve.

All of the stories used here are true. When necessary to protect confidentiality, names and details have often been altered. The names of our students are all changed, unless these are adults who have given permission to use their real names. However, because so many people whom we have served have similar experiences, it is possible that someone with the same name and age might have a similar story. If so, this is a coincidence.

The safety of kids is everybody's business, and this book is for any adult who cares about the well-being of young people. For the purpose of this book, whether or not you are a parent, teacher, or other concerned adult, the children and teens important to you are "your" kids. When you are helping them learn, you are their teacher and they are your students.

Mahatma Gandhi said, "Be the change you wish to see in the world." The change that we at Kidpower wish to see is the creation of cultures of caring, respect, and safety for everyone, everywhere, starting from the time they are born and continuing throughout their lives. We want to protect people of all ages and abilities from the suffering caused by preventable violence and give them tools for creating healthy relationships and exploring their world with safety, confidence, and joy. We believe that the ideas, actions, values, passion, and skills that combine to create what we call "Kidpower" truly help to make this possible. respect, and safety for everyone.

Irene

Irene van der Zande
Kidpower Executive Director/Co-Founder

Drawing by 10 year-old student

The Kidpower Story

Chapter One

The Kidpower Story: A Wake-Up Call

I shouted, "You are not allowed to scare children!"

Why Kidpower Began

The inspiration for starting Kidpower happened in 1985 when, in a public place, in the middle of the day, with people standing all around, a man threatened to kidnap my children. I was on a field trip with my seven-year-old daughter, Chantal, six of her friends from school, and my four-year-old son, Arend. I had taken the children to visit an exhibit of merry-go-round animals at the city library. It was a typical day in my life as a mother. Arend kept asking why he could climb on the merry-go-round animals at the amusement park, but not in the library. When one child wanted a drink of water, all of them became desperately thirsty.

As we left the library, a man on the street started following us, leering and muttering that I had all the cute little girls and he had no one. The children, who had been cheerfully talking and moving around, suddenly became silent and clustered next to me. Even though the man's behavior was creepy, I was used to people with problems, so I stayed calm. "It's okay," I said reassuringly. "He doesn't mean any harm." The children didn't look convinced, so I added, "Anybody who's scared can hang on to me." I crossed the next street looking like an octopus, with eight small hands clutching my body.

I glanced back toward where the man had been, but he'd disappeared. Despite a nagging sense of worry, I cheerfully got the children back into the fun of our downtown adventure. Part of our field trip included riding the bus. When we got into the lobby of the bus station, one of the girls said in a worried voice, "Here he comes again!"

This time, I turned around to see this man charging towards us with his arms outstretched. He was shouting, "I'm going to take one of these girls to be my bride!"

Although the lobby was full of people, everybody froze – except for me. This reaction was not because they were bad people, but because of what is called "the bystander effect." In an emergency, people watching often freeze because they don't understand what is happening, because they are afraid, or because they don't know what to do.

To this day, even after more than 25 years, I still have a vivid image of the blank faces of the bystanders, the contorted face of the man attacking us and of that terrified huddle of children, with my little boy trying to hide behind his big sister because he was so scared.

I did what I bet you would have done. I put myself between the man and the kids, and started yelling. "You are not allowed to scare children!" I shouted. Later, I thought that this was not the most intelligent thing I had ever said in my life, but it was all I could think of at the time.

The man yelled back, "I can do anything I want! I can say anything I want!"

"Go away!!!! Leave us alone!!!!" I kept shouting over and over, afraid that at any instant, the man might knock me down and try to grab one of the kids. The two of us stood there for what seemed like an endless time, locked into a face-to-face shouting match, with people standing motionless and silent all around. Finally, I ordered a man who was watching from a few feet away with his mouth dropped open, to, "Get over here and help me! Can't you see these kids are scared?"

Somewhat embarrassed, the man watching wandered reluctantly over to my side. As soon as I had another man standing next to me, the man who had been attacking us ran away, leaping out the door and down the street.

The children were fine. From their point of view, when I yelled, the bad guy ran! But I wasn't fine. I kept worrying, "What if that man had knocked me down? What if he had even touched one of the children?" I knew I'd have tried to fight him if need be, but I wasn't sure that I knew how. I kept imagining the unprotected children that this man might have gone on to frighten or hurt.

Looking for Answers

A friend of mine, Ellen Bass, who was the mother of one of the girls, recommended that I take a Model Mugging class, because it had been a great help to her. The Model Mugging program was started by a martial artist named Matt Thomas, who wanted women with no prior martial arts training to know how to defend themselves.[1] The program gives students the opportunity to escape from a simulated assault by practicing self-defense techniques using full force with a head-to-toe padded instructor.

I took the class and got to practice stopping someone who might try to harm my children. I then became very involved in helping people who were teaching full-force programs for adults, because I wanted to make sure that this kind of training would still be around for my daughter and son when they grew up.

Through this work, I kept meeting women and men who wistfully told stories that began with "If only!" For example, "*If only* I had known what to do when my youth group leader dropped everybody off except for me and he touched me in a way that my parents told me never to let someone touch me. *If only* I had known the words to say to stop him! *If only* I had known how to tell my parents what happened. My whole life would have been so different!"

The widely quoted statistic at that time was that one in three to four girls and one in four boys would be sexually assaulted before they are eighteen years old. This statistic stopped being numbers for me and became real people with real stories. All of the girls that had been with me on that field trip later ended up in my Girl Scout troop. There were fifteen girls in all. I kept looking at them and thinking, "One in three assaulted means *five* of them! *Which* five girls is it okay with me that this happens to?" And the answer, of course, was, "*None* of them!"

One day, I overheard my daughter talking to her friends. Two years after the attack, it occurred to them to wonder, "Remember that guy who tried to grab us? What if that man had knocked your mom down?"

At age nine, Chantal, who had seen me practice my self-defense training, said, "Oh, well. If some guy tried to knock my mom down, he'd be sorry!" And then I heard my daughter add wistfully, "I wish I could do that too."

That was it. I wanted to keep my children safe, but I knew that I couldn't be with them all the time, so I decided I would have to figure out how to teach them to protect themselves.

During this same time, there had been a series of abductions near my home. I watched the anguished parents on television who said things like, "I told my daughter, and I told her, and I told her not to go anywhere with a stranger. But when a friendly man said he would help her with her bicycle, she got tricked into following him to his van. And now she is gone."

As I grieved for these heart-broken parents, I realized that in addition to teaching my own children, I wanted to help all children be safe.

A Passionate Child Advocate + a Talented Martial Artist
If you had told me in 1985 that I would someday be leading an international organization teaching self-defense and personal safety, I would have told you that you were out of your mind. My entire career up until then had been in program development and management with nonprofit organizations, especially those serving children. I had just written a book called *1, 2, 3 ... The Toddler Years*, which is still used in many early childhood education programs.[2] By now, I'd probably be writing *19, 20, 21 ... The Letting Go Years*, but Kidpower happened instead.

Like any good community organizer, I asked everyone I could find to help me figure out what to teach. We paced the floor of my living room wanting to make sure that whatever we taught would truly empower children instead of traumatizing them. One of these people, Timothy Dunphy, is now a seventh

*I asked myself, "Which five girls is it okay with me that getting assaulted happens to?" The answer, of course, was, "**None** of them!"*

Kidpower Co-Founders Irene van der Zande and Timothy Dunphy

> *"The safety and self-esteem of a child are more important than **anyone's** embarrassment, inconvenience, or offense."*
>
> Ellen Bass, Kidpower Founding Board President

degree Black Belt and international championship winner in Tae Kwon Do. At that time, Timothy was also the worried father of a three-year-old girl.

Kidpower is what happens when you take a talented martial artist like Timothy and put him together with a passionate child advocate like me. Timothy would tell a story about a master martial artist in Korea having enough power in the pitch of his voice to kill nearby chickens. I would argue that this joke was about killing rather than about protecting, so we had to make our point another way. Timothy then came up with our NO Game, where kids can build up the power in their own voices by yelling. Timothy was my partner in the development of the Kidpower program during our formative years and is my Kidpower program co-founder.

Inspiration at the Bank

When we decided to start a nonprofit organization in 1989, I asked my friend Ellen Bass if she would be the president of our Kidpower Board, giving us the credibility she had as the co-author of *The Courage to Heal*, which is known internationally as a groundbreaking book for survivors of childhood sexual abuse.[3] Ellen led the board for sixteen years and is our founding board president. She continues to walk with me on the bike path by the sea in Santa Cruz, California, where I have the great privilege of having Ellen listen to my worries and ideas and then having her capture the essence of what I am trying to teach or resolve in a few well-chosen words.

I remember when Ellen and I went to the bank to get our signatures notarized on the papers that would make Kidpower an official nonprofit organization. We were just two mothers chatting about the end of school and summer plans for our daughters, our work, and our daily lives. Ellen suddenly said, "What we are doing here is revolutionary. We are saying that the safety and self-esteem of a child are more important than *anyone's* embarrassment, inconvenience, or offense."

"Would you repeat that, please?" I asked and scribbled down on the back of an envelope what became Kidpower's underlying principle.

Family Stories

Kidpower is like part of our family, which has helped me raise this organizational child that I brought into our home. For the first twelve years, my husband Ed supported our family and covered all our expenses so that we could put most of Kidpower's income back into building the organization. Our children, Chantal and Arend, have assisted me in classes, helped me in the office, and given up their bedrooms for out-of-town guests. Over the years, countless people from close to home and far away have crowded around our kitchen table, curled up on our couch, overloaded our precarious plumbing, and helped us turn Kidpower from a good idea into a powerful reality.

It has been a lot of work, and many times I wondered whether it was worth it. I was often not the most organized mother. Once, a few years after Kidpower started, I was overwhelmed with guilt because I had forgotten to put the eggs into the batter when I was making a cake. I wrung my hands over the resulting crater in the cake and groaned that I was a bad mother.

My ten-year-old daughter Chantal tilted her head and gave me a knowing look. In a dry voice with a wry smile, she said, "It's true that some mothers cook everything from scratch, and the food looks beautiful and tastes perfect. Some mothers sew their children's Halloween costumes instead of pulling old clothes out of the dress-up box. Some mothers actually vacuum the house instead of running around like crazy to pick up the dust balls by hand when we have a guest. But you are the *only* mother I know who made a *whole* program just for *me*."

A few years later, at age sixteen, Chantal came home and took hold of both my hands as soon as she walked in the door. "I have been thinking," my daughter said, "About the fact that I would probably have already been hurt if I had not learned Kidpower. Today I was riding the bus, and a drunken man got on. I watched the whole bus get quiet as he started bothering a young woman. She looked really uncomfortable because he kept touching her and saying stuff, but she didn't do anything to stop him."

Chantal smiled at my anxious face and continued, "I glared at the man so he would know that somebody was watching. The woman got off the bus and the man turned towards me. I put up my hands and told him to leave me alone. He kept apologizing and saying he couldn't help himself because he was so drunk and I was so pretty. But he didn't try to come closer to me until I got off the bus. When he started to follow me, I got into ready position and I said in a big voice, 'you are not going to walk *this* way! You are going to turn around and walk the *other* way!' And he did!"

A bit teary, I clasped my daughter's hands and thought, if she is the *only* child who ever gets helped by Kidpower, it has been worth it!

About to leave on his first real journey to New York City, three thousand miles from home, my son Arend, grown tall and now seventeen years old, walked with me arm-in-arm through the airport. "Do you have any good advice for me, Mom?" Arend asked kindly, knowing that this separation was harder on me than it was on him.

Filled with an intense mixture of pride, sadness, joy, and worry, I said slowly, "Please remember to ... !" I paused to pick from the too many things I wanted to say and then sighed, "Please remember to look *both* ways before you cross the street!"

Arend grinned at hearing my constant reminder throughout his childhood. He straightened up tall and glanced around the airport. Still holding my arm tucked firmly into his, my son said, "In other words, Mom, you want me to Walk With Awareness, Calm and Confidence!" Walking With Awareness, Calm and Confidence is one of the first self-protection skills that we have children practice. As difficult as it was to let him go, I realized that our son was going out into the world far better prepared than his father or I had been.

Kidpower Today

Thanks to the dedication and commitment of our international community of leaders, Kidpower has reached over two million children, teens, and adults, including those with special needs. Our official name is Kidpower

*I clasped my daughter's hands and thought, if she is the **only** child who ever gets helped by Kidpower, it has been worth it!*

*Kidpower is an international community of leaders dedicated to empowering and protecting kids – and people who **used** to be kids!*

Kidpower 20 Year Anniversary Conference

Teenpower Fullpower International because our nonprofit organization serves people of all ages, though we still go mostly by just "Kidpower". We like to say that Kidpower is for kids - and everyone who *used* to be a kid!

Instead of using fear to talk about violence prevention, Kidpower makes it fun to learn to be safe. This is important because people learn better when they're having fun. Successful practice of the "People Safety" skills we teach can prepare individuals to build better relationships, develop confidence, and prevent most bullying, abuse, harassment, abduction, and other violence.

We are proud when we hear from caring adults living across the United States and around the world about how our workshops and educational resources have helped them to protect their children from danger and to empower them with skills. The Kidpower program has been taught in over fourteen different languages and adapted for many different cultures. Currently, we have centers and/or advocates in Argentina, Australia, Belgium, Brazil, Canada, Germany, India, Mexico, the Netherlands, New Zealand, Pakistan, Peru, Sweden, Switzerland, South Africa, the United Kingdom, Vietnam, and the United States in California, Colorado, Illinois, Maryland, New York, North Carolina, Texas, Vermont, and Washington, D.C.

Kidpower's vision is to work together with families, schools, organizations, and communities to create cultures of caring, respect, and safety for everyone, everywhere. You can join us by reading this book, using these ideas in your own life, and sharing this knowledge with others.

PART ONE

The Kidpower Method

Chapter Two

What Adults Need to Know About "People Safety" for Kids

Safety is a basic human need, and emotional and physical safety for children begins with their adults taking charge of their well-being. As adults, we are responsible for protecting our children from harm, treating them with respect, teaching them to behave respectfully, supervising what they are doing, and managing the people and places around them. When children become old enough, our job is to prepare them with the skills and understanding they need to be safe and effective in dealing with the difficult and potentially dangerous situations that they will face.

As caring adults, we are all teachers for the young people in our lives. We want to be sure that that the "People Safety" lessons we adults are teaching children and teens are the lessons that we truly want them to learn.

What is "People Safety"?

If we were to think of Fire Safety as just meaning "burning prevention" or Water Safety as just meaning "drowning prevention", we would limit our perceptions of the ways in which we can enjoy both fire and water safely. Because there is not a generally agreed-upon term about people being safe with and around people, at Kidpower we use the term "People Safety" to mean what individuals can do to keep themselves and others emotionally and physically safe. This is important because we don't only want to protect children from harmful interactions with others - we want to prepare them to have joyful, exciting, fun relationships and experiences.

At different times in our lives, we might find ourselves in different situations. We might need different kinds of help, and we might have different abilities, but what is important to our People Safety is the same from the time we are born until the time we die. In Kidpower, individuals of all ages, abilities, cultures, and walks of life have found that using People Safety tools prepares them to:

- Build healthy relationships
- Develop more confidence
- Advocate effectively for the well-being of themselves and others
- Act as powerful respectful leaders
- Protect themselves and others from most bullying, harassment, abuse, assault, abduction, and other kinds of violence

"People Safety" means what individuals can do to keep themselves and others emotionally and physically safe.

People Safety knowledge and skills include:

• Understanding that everyone has the right to be emotionally and physically safe – including ourselves.
• Knowing what behaviors and situations are more safe and less safe.
• Communicating effectively and appropriately about what we do want and what we do not want.
• Taking charge of safety in different situations;
• Being persistent in asking for help;
• Knowing how to protect our feelings and our bodies if others are thoughtless, mean, scary, or dangerous;
• Staying in charge of what we say and do so that we make safe, respectful choices.

NOW Is the Right Time to Teach– And YOU Are the Right Person to Do It

Often parents and other adults worry about not being "qualified" to teach self-protection skills to their children. They keep waiting for "the right time" or look for an "expert" to do the teaching for them. They worry about doing something "wrong" that will be harmful to their children. The problem is that, because they are imagining that this kind of teaching is hard, adults often wait too long to do it or don't do it at all. Children learn best when People Safety skills and ideas are an ordinary part of their daily lives.

The reality is that anyone responsible for the care of children is always teaching, including safety skills. We teach young children to wash their hands, hold our hands when they cross the street, and make their way down the stairs without falling. As they get older, we teach children how to stay safe as they ride a bike, use matches, and cook on the stove. The Kidpower People Safety skills described in this book are simpler than any of these activities. We often see children teach them to each other and adapt them to fit different situations.

If these important skills are so simple, then why aren't all adults teaching them all the time? Most adults are stopped by the complexity of their feelings about the issues of bullying, molestation, assault, and kidnapping. Most people did not learn how to set clear boundaries when they were growing up and are still not sure how to protect themselves now. Students in our adult classes are usually surprised at how easy it is to protect themselves once they stop worrying and start practicing. "This is not rocket science!" I tell them. "It is just People Safety!" As you are getting ready to teach, remember that the skills are simple and that you have already had a lot of experience in helping children learn to be safe.

"This is not rocket science! – It's just People Safety!"

Violence Against Children – All Kinds and Too Much

Even though research about exact numbers varies, we know that too many children and teens are harmed every day by bullying, abuse, harassment, abduction, and other violence.

In 2009, the U.S. Department of Justice released a study about violence against children entitled "Children's Violence: A Comprehensive National Study" According to the study director and director of the University of New

Hampshire Crimes Against Children Research Center, David Finkelhor, Pd.D., "Children experience far more violence, abuse and crime than do adults. If life were this dangerous for ordinary grown-ups, we'd never tolerate it." The study found that over 60% of the children surveyed were exposed either directly or indirectly to some form of violence in the last year.[1]

A Bureau of Justice statistics report predicts that, if current crime rates remain unchanged, about five out of six American twelve-year-olds will become victims of an attempted or completed violent crime in their lifetimes.[2]

In a study conducted by the National Incidence Studies of Missing, Abducted, Runaway, and Thrownaway Children, there were an estimated 58,000 child victims of non-family abductions in 1999, and approximately 100,000 attempted non-family abductions occur each year. Nearly half of those successful non-family abductions involved sexual assault. The average incident lasts from 3 to 24 hours and can cause psychological damage that persists throughout a victim's lifetime.[3]

Ellen Bass, co-author of *The Courage to Heal*, – an internationally renowned book for adult survivors of childhood sexual abuse – has worked with thousands of people who were abused as children. One significant finding of her work is that even what seems to be a "minor" molestation can have a lasting, harmful impact on someone's life.[4]

According to the Department of Justice in a 2008 study, 75% of sexual assaults against children happen with people they know. Of these, over 85% are acquaintances – neighbors, friends, teachers, religious leaders, youth group elders, health care professionals, babysitters, and other children. The rest are family members – parents, siblings, or other relatives. Contrary to popular belief, child molesters do not obviously stand out in society, and most child molesters are equivalent to average residents of U.S. households in terms of education, marital status, religious affiliation, and distribution of ethnic group.[5]

Bullying harms millions of young people throughout the world. According to a 2009 study of 15,000 schools in the United States published by the Centers for Disease Control, 29.9 percent of students are involved in bullying either as a bully (13.0 percent), a victim (10.6 percent), or as both a bully and a victim (6.3 percent). On any given school day, at least one child will be bullied in each classroom, and one in twenty students are afraid of being attacked or harmed at school.[6]

According to the Hostile Hallways study sponsored by the American Association of University Women, 83% of girls and 60% of boys in grades 8-11 reported experiencing sexual harassment at their school. A majority of reported cases happened in the hallway of their school. Nearly half of those students felt very or somewhat upset right afterward.[7]

Cyber bullying has increased substantially in recent years and has been identified as an emerging public health problem by the Center for Disease Control. In 2005 roughly one of out ten Internet users ages 10-17 had

"Children experience far more violence, abuse, and crime than do adults. If life were this dangerous for ordinary grown-ups, we'd never tolerate it!"

Dr David Finkelhor

The Dinosaur Story

been a victim of "on-line harassment". This adds a new dimension of powerlessness among victims since they can be targeted 24 hours a day, 7 days a week, even if they are in a safe place such as their home. Fifty percent of victims who were bullied off-line and on-line by the same people reported being distressed by the incidents.[8]

Our Children Do *Not* Need Our Fear

Thinking about information like this can be overwhelming. Children are so vulnerable, and the thought that something bad might happen to them is horrifying. Before we can be effective in teaching safety skills to children, we need to manage our own feelings.

Abduction. Assault. Abuse. Read these three words and think about children – yourself as a child, your own children, or other children in your life. What feelings come up for you? You might take a few minutes to write down your feelings. Across the boundaries of many different countries in many different languages, I have heard people give the same answers to describe their feelings: "Terror ... Rage ... Regret ... Hatred ... Denial ... Fear ... Anger ... Despair ... Disgust ... Revenge ... Sadness ... Disbelief ... Pain ... Horror ... Kill!" The words go on and on and on.

I have come to believe that caring adults throughout the world share a huge pool of grief about the terrible harm that people sometimes inflict on children. We have every right to these feelings. We deserve support for them in settings with other adults.

But, if we dump our load of upset feelings onto children when we are trying to teach them to protect themselves, it will be harder for them to learn. One risk is that children will take in our feelings and become overly anxious. They might start worrying all the time about "bad guys" hurting them or stealing them. Other children are likely to become so overwhelmed that they will go into complete denial or use magical thinking to make themselves feel safe. They might cover their ears and say, "This is so boring! You already told me that! I know! I know! I know!" They might say, "I don't need to worry about bad guys, because I'll just take my power sword and zap them."

Keep in mind that children experience the world in a different way than adults do. When I took my first self-defense course, I was filled with sorrow at all the stories of so many women who had survived terrible experiences. After a particularly hard class, I came home to my eight-year-old daughter Chantal, gathered her into my arms, and burst into tears.

Being used to her emotional mother, Chantal sat calmly on my lap as my tears dripped into her hair and asked, "What's the matter, Mommy?"

"It's just that you're such a wonderful kid," I said sadly, "and I wish I could give you a better world to live in."

"It's all right, Mommy," Chantal said cheerfully. "Look at it this way – if we were living in the time of the dinosaurs, we'd all have to worry about being eaten, all the time!" Suddenly I realized that my fantasy of a safe perfect world for my child was just that – a fantasy – and not her reality at all.

Children's favorite stories are often not about safe, perfect worlds. Even very young children love classics such as Maurice Sendak's *Where the Wild Things Are* [9] and Mercer Meyer's *There's a Nightmare in My Closet*.[10] Instead of being about safe, perfect worlds, these much-loved books are stories about children being powerful in the face of danger. Children do not need our terror about what might harm them, and they do not need our despair about the problems of the world. Instead, they need our belief that they can keep themselves safe most of the time, and our confidence that they can learn how.

Accept That There Are No Guarantees

In one parent education night, a mother asked me desperately, "How old is my daughter going to be before I get to stop worrying? I am so tired of being so afraid!" Her daughter was four.

With a great deal of sympathy, I had to give this worried mother some bad news, "My children are adults now and do a great job of taking care of themselves. But, I never stop feeling like their mom, and my heart still skips a beat any time I think of a possible threat to them!"

It helps me to regain my calm and keep my perspective when I can accept that there are no guarantees. Facing this reality can be painful, but uncertainty is part of life. To quote Sir Francis Bacon, a sixteenth century philosopher, "To have a child is to give a hostage to fortune."[11] To quote author Elizabeth Stone, "Making the decision to have a child is to decide forever to have your heart go walking outside your body."[12]

This means that those of us who are lucky enough to have children we love in our lives are all hostages to fortune, and our hearts are all walking around outside our bodies forever.

That's just the way life is, and letting our fear about this reality stop us from enjoying our own lives does not make our children safer. Being constantly anxious and restrictive can make our children's lives more stressful and less enjoyable, and won't make them safer.

As Ariel's mother told me, "I tried to protect Ariel from everything. I never let her climb up on a play structure for fear of falling. I didn't let her play in a swimming pool because of germs. And I kept her away from other kids and families who might stress her too much. "When she was almost eight, Ariel got terribly sick. As I sat in her hospital room, I thought about all the fun my fear had kept my child from having. When she thankfully got better, I decided to set my fear aside and take more risks. Ariel has broken her arm, gotten head lice, and coped with a bully. But her joy in doing new things has been worth it."

We want our children to see their lives as an adventure, with uncertainty not being a reason for worry and fear. When problems come up, we want them to see themselves as explorers of life overcoming challenges, not as victims of the unexpected

Children need our belief that they can keep themselves safe most of the time, and our confidence that they can learn how.

When problems come up, we want children to see themselves as explorers of life overcoming challenges, not as victims of the unexpected.

Resist the "Illusion of Safety"

Although the focus of this book is the prevention of emotional and physical violence and abuse, the same understanding and skills can also help to protect kids from many other kinds of harm. For example, thousands of kids get injured and killed every year through preventable accidents.

I once saw a three-year-old girl left alone sitting on a picnic table while her parents played with their other children in a river just out of sight. Signs nearby warned: "Do not leave valuables in your car." and "Do not feed the bears." I stayed near this little girl and finally yelled for her parents. When her mother reluctantly appeared, I said, "Your child is too young and too precious to be left alone even for a second!"

A friend of mine told me, "I was walking in the park when I saw two parents watch their nine-year-old son as he climbed onto the train track on a narrow bridge over the water. I was about to warn them when suddenly a train came by. Thank goodness, this boy got out of the way just in time. What on earth were they *thinking*?"

In both cases, these parents would have been devastated if anything bad had happened to their children, so indeed what was going on that caused them to fail to take sensible precautions? I believe that they were lulled into complacency by what we call the "Illusion of Safety".

The Illusion of Safety happens in settings or situations where people feel so relaxed, sheltered, or distracted that they stop focusing on ensuring that their children have adequate supervision, understanding, and skills to avoid potential dangers. Sadly, the Illusion of Safety can lead to children being traumatized, injured, or even killed from problems that could have been prevented. Kids lack experience and do not see the world the same way adults do. They need adult supervision until they are prepared to take care of themselves.

Be Prepared for Change

Although change is a reality at any stage of life, children tend to change more quickly and suddenly than adults. For parents and caregivers of children, this means that we are constantly readjusting our balance about the kind of supervision our children need for their well-being.

I will never forget when Chantal, at age one, had just started to pull herself up to a standing position. Both my husband Ed and I were sitting right next to her and talking. Suddenly, Chantal reached up to a table that had been out of her reach and pulled a just-poured cup of hot coffee onto her face. Thanks to good luck and the miracle of ice water, our toddler was fine, but Ed and I have never fully recovered.

The problem was that Ed and I were simply not prepared for the fact that our daughter could reach more from a standing position than she could when she was crawling on the floor. As soon as we understood, we moved some things out of her way, watched her as best we could, and worked hard at teaching her concepts like "Hot!" and "Don't touch!"

We can prevent many upsetting experiences by anticipating what is going to change when a child reaches a new level of development. Whether the issues are about People Safety or something else, each change in skill, awareness, and situation leads to a need for re-assessment. As children get older:

- *Their abilities increase.* This brings both more risks and more opportunities to learn.
- *Their understanding increases.* Children may worry about new situations or problems as they become more aware of them. As their understanding and knowledge of the world grows, our ability to discuss things with them also grows.
- *Their boundaries change.* The preschooler who sat for hours on our laps and told us everything becomes a pre-teenager with a great need for privacy and personal space.
- *They go to more places and meet more people.* Part of what makes life good is being able to do new things, but just assuming that each place and person will be okay or not okay is a mistake. Instead, our job as adults is to pay attention to potential problems and to give children tools both for telling us about their concerns and for finding solutions.
- *Their need for independence grows.* We do not want to abandon children before they are ready, but we do want to support their capacity for being able to take care of themselves and for fostering their independence.

Over time, children will eventually grow from being in our arms to holding our hands, from being within our reach to staying where we can see and hear them, from being close enough to get back to us quickly to being required to tell us what they are doing... and eventually going somewhere without any supervision at all. By being prepared for the results of the many changes that life brings, we can protect our children from most harm while teaching them how to protect themselves.

Set a Good Example
Children learn more from what their adults actually do, than from what we tell them to do, and often surprise us with what they've chosen to pick up from their observations. This means that we need to set a good example.

We are role models for all the children around us, even if they don't seem to be paying attention. As Michael, who has been a school teacher for over thirty years, says, "It isn't always true, of course, but so often I see the behavior of parents reflected in their children. I will see two impatient fathers arguing over a parking spot because they are both in a hurry – and their two impatient sons arguing over a toy because they both want it at the same time. I will see a mother who is letting people walk all over her at a school meeting by agreeing to take on projects that she really has no time for, and then I will see her daughter getting bossed around by other kids on the schoolyard."

Setting a good example also means being prepared to step in and speak up to stop unfair behavior. "I kept trying to follow the advice of letting children work things out for themselves," Gabriel's mother explained. "I would sit on the park bench gritting my teeth and feeling terribly uncomfortable when a couple of older kids would crowd in front of Gabriel on the slide and then make fun of him when he got upset. Not only that, but as soon as a smaller child started

Kids learn about safety from watching how their adults handle problems

*Children are more likely to trust that they have the right and the ability to protect themselves if we show them that **we** have the right and the ability to protect ourselves.*

trying to get onto the slide, Gabriel would be the one to crowd ahead."

Gabriel's mother gave a frustrated sigh and continued, "Suddenly I realized that by doing nothing, I was setting a poor example. Now I stand closer to Gabriel when we are at the park. Just the fact that I am nearby stops most problems. If a bigger child does try to push ahead of him, I encourage Gabriel to tell the child to wait. If this doesn't work, then I will say politely and loudly, 'Please wait! It is his turn now!' I can see that Gabriel is becoming less likely to crowd in front of smaller children and is getting more confident about speaking up for himself."

Self-protection skills are important for everybody. One of the most useful things we can do for our children's safety is to take a self-defense class for ourselves. Children are more likely to trust that they have the right and the ability to protect themselves if we show them that we have the right and the ability to protect ourselves. They are most likely to respect others if they see their adults doing the same.

For a mother, learning self-defense can give a whole new meaning to the term "Super Mom." Once when my family was young, we were hiking in the mountains. A large black bear suddenly strolled across the trail. Both Chantal and Arend immediately ran to stand next to me. Ed smiled and asked our kids, "Why are you running over to Mommy?"

"Because," Arend explained, "if that bear gets too close, then POW! Mommy will stop him!" Chantal nodded in agreement.

A little alarmed at their level of confidence, I said, "Daddy knows how to protect you, too. Besides, if we don't bother that bear, it's not going to bother us."

"Maybe," replied Arend, "But we've seen you practice fighting for your class, Mommy. We feel better standing next to you."

Ed smiled at me. "Hmmm," he said, "I think that this is where real change begins. And the next time we're walking down a dark, lonely street, I'll let you go first!"

Know WHY to Practice

Just telling or showing children what they need to know is not enough. As Teri's mom told me, "By the time Teri was ten, I had spent years explaining to her how to avoid every dangerous situation I could imagine. I read books to her when she was younger, and we watched videos on safety. But last week, a man who seemed confused approached Teri. Because she felt so sorry for him, she froze and forgot everything we'd ever talked about. She let him hug her even though it made her really uncomfortable. Fortunately, nothing worse happened."

Dr. Sherryll Kraizer is the author of *The Safe Child Book*, founder of The Safe Child Program, and one of Kidpower's early advisors. In a study funded by the U.S. Department of Health in 1976, Kraizer tested the ability of over 1,000 elementary school children to act on the safety rules they had been told to follow.[13] One part of the study had children walking one at a time down the hall of their school. A video from the study shows a nice-looking man approaching a child and saying something like, "Hi, I'm Joey's dad. Would you come with me to the car to get the puppets for our puppet show?"

Over half the kids agreed to go, even though they had never seen this man before. Their perception was, "That's not a stranger! That's a dad!"

Another part of the study had children sitting in a room with a researcher to whom they had been introduced. The video from the study shows a child squirming as the researcher pinches her cheeks. The researcher asks the child, "Do you like this?"

The child says, "No!"

The researcher then says something like, "But we are friends! If you like me, you will let me keep pinching your cheeks."

Over half the children in the study then agreed to let the cheek pinching continue. When these children were re-taught with an opportunity for each child to practice skills through role-play, over 90 percent of the children were able to make safer choices.

Children learn better by doing than by being told or shown what to do. Rehearsal can also help children be emotionally safer. I have heard from firefighters that children who are trapped in fires who have practiced how to stop, drop, and roll are often less traumatized than children who have not. Instead of feeling completely helpless in an emergency, children who have practiced what to do can keep thinking of their choices.

Like many activities we do or imagine doing, the practice of safety skills is

"I didn't have to worry. I felt as if my body just knew what to do."

It is never too early to build a foundation of People Safety Skills

stored in our minds and felt in our bodies. When something reminds us of an experience, good or bad, we can feel these memories in our nerves and muscles. For example, suppose you imagine right now that I am throwing a ball to you. You can probably feel the sensation of catching that ball. Now, think back to a time when you were really astonished. You can probably feel the sensations in your body of being breathless or full of wonder. Those feelings are what is meant by "body memories".

Children who have practiced how to respond appropriately in different situations are likely to do what they've practiced in real life. Many of our students who handled dangerous situations successfully told us later, "I didn't have to worry. I felt as if my body just knew what to do."

Find Teaching Moments – The Earlier, the Better!

Parents often ask, "So when should I start?" The most accurate answer would be, "Whether you realize it or not, you already have!" Building People Safety understanding and skills can begin from the time a child is born. Magda Gerber, founder of the organization Resources for Infant Educators and co-author of the book *Your Self-Confident Baby*, describes how each interaction with even a very young infant is a form of education.[14] Daily activities like crying, diaper changing, sleeping, and eating are all opportunities to show respect and build understanding.

I once watched a mother as she acknowledged her infant's feelings while putting safety first. At about two weeks old, this baby had decided that she hated her infant seat in their car. She'd scream and struggle. Her mother had tried picking different times of the day and nursing her first, but sometimes nothing helped and they just had to go. As this mother gently but firmly moved her daughter's flailing little arms to strap her in, she explained in a calm, loving voice, "It's okay to be angry. All of your feelings are okay, but some things are not your choice. Being in the car seat is for your safety." Even though this baby didn't understand the words, her mother's way of communicating that everything was okay helped to sooth her and make her feel safe.

When toddlers begin to learn to talk, their adults can look for opportunities to let them make safe choices, ask for help, move away from danger, discuss what a stranger is, check with an adult about possible problems, and set boundaries.

Suppose that you have a young child who is always asking, "But why?" Younger children simply need to know what they are supposed to do. They do not need the scary "why" reasons that put upsetting images into their minds. If a child asks, "Why?", you can get a better understanding of what the child is worrying about by asking, "What do you think?" If that doesn't work, the simplest answer is, "Because that's our safety plan. It's my job to make the safety plan because it is my job to keep you safe."

As children get older and more independent, they need enough information to make wise decisions for themselves. You can help develop judgment by asking them to think of as many choices as possible for handling different problems. Encourage them to come up with a long list of silly ideas as well as useful ones. Keep asking "What else? ... What else? ... What else?" Then discuss the pros and cons of different possibilities.

Tad's father, who had been badly bitten by a dog as a child, told me this story, "We live in the country. When Tad first started riding his bike to visit his friends, he was chased by our neighbor's large, aggressive dog. Because of my own bad experiences as a child, I was really upset. I knew it was wrong, but I fantasized going over to yell at my neighbor and even threatening to shoot his dog."

Tad's father laughed a little and said thoughtfully, "Instead, I thought about what I wanted Tad to learn from this experience. First of all, I told my son something that no one had ever known to tell me – that he had the right to be safe with dogs. We brainstormed dozens of different solutions for how to make this possible. Tad finally decided that what he really wanted to do was to go over to our neighbor and make friends with his dog, so that's what we did. This was his own idea, and it would never have occurred to me!"

Daily life gives us many teachable moments when we can introduce ideas, tell stories, discuss choices, and role-play solutions that prepare our children to develop their judgment and solve problems in ways that are relevant for them.

Learning Safety Through Fun and Successful Practice

When I was growing up long ago, some of my teachers meant well but taught in ways that made it much harder to learn. These teachers would get upset when their students made mistakes instead of trying to figure out what the roadblocks were. They would punish failure with sarcastic, critical remarks. They would present large amounts of information all at once instead of breaking activities or ideas into small, achievable steps. Often teaching was done almost exclusively by the adult telling and showing rather than by helping students be successful in actually performing an activity. If there was a safety concern, adults would often try to scare their students into being "good" instead of just being clear about what they wanted students to do and insisting that they do it.

For me, it has taken a great deal of conscious effort to overcome negative learning models and not teach my students the way that I was often taught. My goal with my own students is to make learning to keep themselves safe both easy and joyful. Thankfully, teacher trainings and educational models have evolved greatly since I was a child, and I've met many brilliant classroom teachers from whom I've learned a lot!

Learning safety skills is not a time for guesswork. Most of the time, encouraging children to experiment so they can discover how the world works on their own is very important. When a child tries to put a puzzle piece in the wrong spot, great learning takes place as the child moves the piece in different directions until she figures out how to make it fit. If she gets stuck, she can experience what it means to fail and to overcome frustration. If need be, an adult can offer suggestions or help a little, without taking over and doing the puzzle for her.

Look for teachable moments in daily life when you can introduce ideas, tell stories, discuss choices, and role-play solutions that would be relevant for your child or children.

***How** People Safety ideas are introduced and **How** the practices are handled are as important as **what** we want children to learn.*

Learning by doing step by step

When teaching safety skills, life provides enough challenges and opportunities for children to have to figure things out and to deal with the results. In some situations, the consequences of a child not knowing what to do can be harmful. As adults, part of our job is to supervise what is happening. If there is a problem or risk, we need to judge when a child needs the chance to find the solution, and when we need to step in and take over.

The Kidpower approach is focused on helping children to develop People Safety understanding and skills as quickly as possible. In real life, children tend to do what they've practiced. By using very positive, in-the-moment coaching, we give children opportunities to practice keeping themselves safe, rather than allowing them to practice behavior that is not safe. We lead children through a process to develop their understanding quickly, instead of risking that they might be confused about what their safety rules are and what they are supposed to do if something potentially dangerous starts to happen.

Kidpower's Positive Practice Teaching Method

In Kidpower, we have found that *how* People Safety ideas are introduced and *how* the practices are handled are as important as *what* we want our students to learn. Remember that, if you are an important adult to a child or teen, that young person is also your student. Here are 14 key steps for using our Positive Practice method:

1   *Be calm and positive.* Keep your focus on all the powerful actions that your student can take to be safe, not on all the awful things that might happen. Make sure that your tone of voice, facial expressions, body language, and choice of words convey enthusiasm rather than anxiety. A typical scene in a Kidpower parent-child workshop consists of a large circle of young children squirming and leaning into their anxious parents' laps. In a reassuring, cheerful voice, our instructor says, "Children, please take hold of the hand of the adult you brought to us today. Now, pat your grown-up's hand and say, 'Be calm. I learn better when you're calm!'" The children pat and repeat the instructor's words, looking earnestly up into their parents' faces. And everyone smiles.

2   *Demonstrate skills in the way that you want your students to use them in real life.* For example, if you don't sound respectful and firm when you model how to tell someone to stop bothering you, then kids are likely to copy your hesitant or irritated attitude rather than rehearsing effective boundary-setting. One of the great benefits of teaching safety skills to kids is that you will be improving these skills for yourself.

3   *Be specific.* When you are getting ready to do a role-play, make sure that you are clear about where you and the student each are, where safety is, what is happening, and whom you are pretending to be. Are you in the front yard? At school? In a store? Are you a stranger? Another child? An adult the child knows and trusts? Kids are used to playing games with imaginary props and characters. All you have to do is be clear on who is who, what is what, and where is where.

4   *Remember you are just pretending for the purpose of practice.* When you take on a role, act like someone who just does not know the safety rules or who is in a bad mood. If you pretend to be evil or very frightening, this can become stressful or distracting, and get in the way of focusing on the skill you want your student to learn.

5   *Go step-by-step.* Avoid the temptation to test kids by tricking them or to go too far, too fast. The Positive Practice approach starts with what children already understand and know how to do on a very basic level. From there, start to add new skills and ideas that slowly and simply build toward more complex

situations. Your goal with each practice is to help the child be successful. To ensure success, go step-by-step and tell the child what is going well, so that she is rewarded for her accomplishments each part of the way.

6 *Coach in the moment like the prompter in a play.* Rather than letting your student struggle or practice incorrectly, switch back and forth in the moment between you being the student's coach and you pretending to be the person breaking the safety rules. Most people will have no trouble as long as you are clear with your tone of voice and body language about which role you are in. If you listen while young children are playing imaginary games, you can hear how they shift roles all the time. "Now you are the baby lion and I am the mommy lion... Okay, now you can have a turn being the boy and I will be your dog." Shifting roles to prompt a student on what to do and say during the practices will make it easier for him to be successful at each step of the way in learning how to deal with different kinds of safety problems.

7 *Look for progress, not perfection.* If your student has a hard time at first, manage your own anxieties. Give him the time to learn. He is far more likely to keep going if you encourage him than if you get upset or criticize him. Explain what needs to be improved in a positive way. Often someone will need to be walked through a practice several times before being able to do it effectively. Say things like, "You did a great job of looking at me and saying, 'Stop!' Now try doing the same thing standing up as tall as you can and using a bigger voice." Remember that children, just like adults, often integrate new skills over time. Take a break if you need to and practice again a few days later.

8 *Keep in mind that mistakes are part of learning.* Be patient with yourself and with the children you are teaching. If a child feels upset about making a mistake, say something encouraging like, "This is tricky. That's why we practice." If *you* make a mistake, tell yourself the same thing. Especially if you are working on learning new behavior to replace behavior that has become a habit, be patient with the fact that changing habits takes time.

9 *Accept the fact that testing the rules is part of growing up.* Most children will sometimes push boundaries, forget rules, or experiment with negative uses of their power. Trying to scare children into learning does not work well for the long run, because fear-based learning tends to backfire. Avoid the temptation to lecture or scold. If a child gives the wrong answer on purpose or deliberately uses the skills in a silly way, you can say something to build a bridge, like, "I understand that joking about this can seem funny. For my peace of mind, please show me that you understand what to do and can do it well." A very appropriate management technique when a child says or does something in a way that is not safe is to have the child practice doing it again in a way that is safe.

10 *Change details to be relevant for different ages and life situations.* All of the practices in the following chapters have been successful with people of many different ages and abilities. Adapt the details of what you say to be appropriate for each child in terms of where she might be, what activities she might enjoy, what possessions might be hard to walk away from, and who she might go to for help. Find out the kinds of hurting words or insults that these particular children are saying to each other rather than practicing with language they never use.

11 *Adjust your pace and style.* Some students might need you to go very slowly through a practice. Others might be able to see you do something or even read it for you and then just do it. Use a more playful tone with younger children. Be more serious with older children and teens so that they don't feel as if you are talking down to them.

12 *Err on the side of safety.* With children, remember that the information about why we teach what we do is intended for adults. Use discretion about what you decide to say. Even though some children might sound quite cynical, they vary widely in their degree of actual sophistication. Even if a child pushes to know the "whys" behind a safety rule, remember that upsetting details are more likely to cause harm than be

helpful. Even adults are emotionally safer practicing how to protect themselves rather than obsessing over the frightening details of an assault.

13 *Be conscious about differences.* Unless you know for sure, use inclusive language about families. Sometimes a child is living with one mom and no dad, or one dad and no mom, or two moms, or two dads, or a grandpa or grandma and no moms or dads, or foster parents. When in doubt, talk about a child's "adult" or "grown-up" rather than a child's "mom" or "dad". Adapt for different abilities. If a child uses a wheelchair, use the word "moving" instead of "walking". If a child cannot see, use the word "noticing" instead of "looking".

14 *Be persistent.* Insist that children rehearse and use People Safety skills with the same determination that you would insist on other issues important to you, such as learning to ride a bike safely. Do not give up just because a child says that she or he doesn't want to. As adults, we have many resources for motivating or persuading children if we truly decide that something is a "Must".

Motivating Kids and Overcoming Resistance

In order to make an activity interesting to kids, attitude is everything. Once, on a hike with my Girl Scouts, the girls started complaining about being too tired to climb the next hill. If I had believed them, we might still be there. Instead, I pointed to the top of the hill and asked cheerfully, "I know that you are too tired to climb the hill, but who wants to chase those cows?" Shrieking like banshees, the girls charged up the hill! By the time they got there, the cows were long gone but the girls were full of energy and joy.

Attitude Equations

Any activity can be fun, dreary, or scary, depending on the attitude of the person in charge. These are simple equations:

Ask kids anxiously, "Does this scare you?"	=	Scared kids.
Lecture to kids in a monotone, "This is really important so I want you to listen up."	=	Bored kids.
Tell kids sadly, "This is really hard but we have to do it."	=	Resistant kids.
Yell at kids worriedly, "If you don't do this right, you will get hurt!"	=	Scared and resistant kids
Plead with kids tentatively, "Please do this to make me feel better, okay?"	=	Reluctant kids.
Explain to kids firmly and enthusiastically, "We are going to practice being safe, and I'm excited to do this with you!"	=	Willing kids, most of the time

Even when a child is still very reluctant, persisting with enthusiasm is likely to work better than getting frustrated or discouraged. Children usually like doing things with their adults, and they like feeling as if they know how to take care of themselves. At the same time, it is normal for some kids to complain, no matter what they are being told to do. I believe that children have the right to complain in a respectful way, and that adults have the responsibility to insist when necessary, also in a respectful way.

Adults must be clear that the learning of self-protection skills should be treated as a basic health and safety issue, not as a matter of choice for children. Parents who would never dream about giving their children a choice about whether or not to brush their teeth, for instance, are often confused about this. "It's up to her," they will say, when thinking about having a child come to a Kidpower workshop. Or, "I'm waiting until he decides he's ready."

I used to be much more tolerant about adults giving in to children's resistance to learning these skills. Yet, too many times I have spoken with heart-broken parents whose children had been molested or even kidnapped. Sometimes these parents felt horribly guilty because they never made it a priority for their children to learn to protect themselves. Now I tell adults that, even though we do our best to make it fun, learning safety skills is not recreation. Learning to be safe with people is a set of essential life skills and should not be a choice for children.

While of course this decision is up to you, we are talking about knowledge that could prevent a horrible experience or even save a child's life. This is information adults need to have in making decisions; this is not information that adults should dwell on in explaining the reasons for their decisions to children. Instead of scaring children into compliance, you can just tell children that you have decided that learning these skills is something they have to do.

Sometimes children have already developed negative feelings about personal safety. Like many adults, children are often resistant to doing something unfamiliar to them, or to dealing with issues that remind them of unpleasant situations. With some creativity, you can often figure out a win-win solution with a reluctant child. As ten-year-old Kalia's mother explained, "No matter what I said, Kalia absolutely did not want to practice anything. Finally, I asked her what reward would make it worth her while. For years she had been asking me if she could get her ears pierced, but I had told her she was too young. For years I had thought about getting my own ears pierced, but I had told myself I was too busy. Kalia ended up negotiating with me that not only could she get her ears pierced, but, since she didn't want to do it alone, that I would go with her and get my ears pierced too!"

When you are doing something this important with children, you need to be prepared to persist. Your job is to sound matter-of-fact, cheerful, and firm. The bottom line is that your child's safety is too important to be treated as a choice. Here are some common ways that kids have expressed their resistance, and some replies that have worked:

Child: Talking about this stuff is too scary!
Adult: Most kids feel less scared when they practice what to do. I believe that you will like seeing how well you can protect yourself.
Child: I really, really, really don't want to.

Learning to take care of yourself can be enjoyable, even if it's not a choice

The bottom line is that your child's safety is too important to be treated as a choice.

As adults, we need to think about what message we want children to learn when facing problems.

Adult:	The peace of mind I will have from your practicing how to be safe would be the best birthday present you could give me!
Child:	This is boring. I know it all already.
Adult:	Show me that you can do these skills well and I will be less worried. If I am less worried, it will be easier for you to get permission to do more things.
Child:	But I am taking a martial arts class! I already know everything!
Adult:	Martial arts are great. But the top martial artists know that practicing different ways of doing things over and over is the best way to get good at them.
Child:	Not now! I'm too busy. Maybe later.
Adult:	We can do this now, or we can do it after dinner instead of watching your favorite TV show. It's up to you.

Show kids that learning People Safety is a priority for you by ensuring that the time you spend together for discussion and practice is protected from interruptions or distractions. Once you get going, learning to be safe is both easy and fun.

Be a Powerful and Respectful Leader

When I want to begin a class in a noisy room full of children and adults, I step into the middle of the crowd with a lot of energy so that they have to see me. I smile, and say loudly and cheerfully, "I really appreciate how well all of you are paying attention!" This "power of positive thinking" approach works like magic most of the time. My enthusiasm and humor capture the interest of my audience long enough for me to get them involved in what we are going to do next.

Suppose I were to plead tentatively, "Wouldn't you like to pay attention, please, please, please????" We might still be there wringing our hands as the children run wild and the adults chatter to each other. Suppose I were to put my finger to my lips and say, "Shhh!" impatiently or even snarl, "Shut up you little brats or you'll be sorry!" This would probably get people to be quiet. Unfortunately, they might be thinking about how awful I am or worrying about being in trouble instead of listening to what I am saying next. Children benefit hugely from seeing models of adult leadership that are powerful and respectful rather than wimpy or mean.

The problem is that many adults have had childhoods where their parents or teachers were unfair, unkind, and even destructive in their use of authority. Some adults follow this example, reasoning, "After all, I turned out okay. Children need adults to tell them what to do." Do you remember being physically hurt, threatened, or emotionally shamed when you were disciplined as a child? What else do you remember about that experience? Most adults say that they remember being upset with the person who punished them rather than remembering the lesson that was being taught.

As adults, we need to think about what message we want children to learn when facing problems. Children learn much more from how they see adults handling problems than from what adults tell them that they should do. Suppose children see their adults trying to get them to obey by hitting, yelling, or making sarcastic, insulting comments. We should not be surprised when these children do the same things in order to get what they want or when they feel frustrated.

Another problem is that some adults are so fearful of being destructive in their use of authority that they go too far the other way and fail to take leadership at all. As caring adults, of course we want to love children, have them like us, and make them happy. However, children need boundaries to help them express their feelings in ways that are respectful, understand that their actions have consequences, and decide to make safe choices. The problem arises when adults try so hard to avoid telling children what to do that they give their own power away. This sets a terrible example for children and usually makes them very anxious. When children feel as if they are the ones in charge instead of the adults, their lives can feel out of control.

Once, an older friend of our family named Fred came for an evening visit. My daughter Chantal, at age five, had had a long day and was tired. She looked away when Fred tried to talk with her and refused his invitation to play a game. Instead, she wrapped herself in her favorite blanket and curled up on my lap. Fred extended his hand towards Chantal and said in a very friendly voice, "If you're feeling angry, you can hit my hand." Astonished, Chantal glanced up at me.

"No she can't!" I said firmly. "Chantal, it's fine with me if you sit quietly here or go play. You already know that hitting people when you're feeling tired or grumpy is not allowed in our family." Chantal nodded and wandered off to check up on what her little brother was doing.

Fred looked very puzzled. "Irene," he said. "I thought you believed in honoring the free expression of a child! I was just trying to give Chantal an outlet for her negative feelings." I curtailed my own free expression of thoughts about where I wanted to put Fred's version of child psychology. I reminded myself that Fred was probably feeling sad that his normal ways of connecting didn't work with Chantal.

"Fred," I explained patiently, "Just like adults, children need the opportunity for free expression within safe boundaries. I believe that unlimited freedom leads to chaos. Anyway, your naming Chantal's desire to be left alone as being angry was almost certainly inaccurate. Sometimes the best way to honor children is to watch them with appreciation as they are going about their own business instead of feeling the need to interact with them."

In the name of giving children freedom, some adults believe that the only way to empower children is to let them make all the decisions. Since children lack experience and judgment, an environment where adult leadership is abdicated and the children are running the show tends to become extremely unpleasant fairly quickly. Instead of just leading, adults then often end up pleading with children, trying to persuade them to agree to behave more constructively. Unfortunately, this cycle can get so out of balance that adults sometimes get to the end of their rope and explode with frustration, often modeling the destructive behavior that they were trying to escape.

Children are best served by seeing their important adults model how to lead

Children need boundaries to help them express their feelings in ways that are respectful, understand that their actions have consequences, and decide to make safe choices.

Adults need to stay in charge to ensure that their kids stay safe

in balanced ways that are both powerful and respectful. Even if children are unhappy in the moment, they will feel more secure in the long run if they understand what is expected of them. Within the security of having clear boundaries and agreements, children can then be encouraged to develop their own leadership skills in situations where they can be successful.

As Molly put it, "All I wanted was for my children to be happy. I gave them everything they asked for. I did everything for them. One day, I stood back and watched them. I suddenly realized that they were whining and rude and sounded miserable. What they needed from me was not for me to try to make them happy and cater to their every whim, but for me to be in charge of helping them grow."

Have Realistic Expectations

Being realistic means accepting that kids often have different priorities than their adults. Here are some typical comments from frustrated parents:

- "I keep telling her to stay with me, but my two-year-old daughter runs away from me as soon as we get into the store."
- "My four-year-old son knows I want him to ask me before he unbuckles his car seat, but he does it anyway!"
- "My eight-year-old daughter understands that it hurts my feelings but she still will say that she hates me when I won't let her go someplace by herself!"
- "My ten-year-old son ignores me when I tell him that I want to talk about a safety issue."
- "My twelve-year-old daughter is constantly teasing her little brother, to the point of tears. She knows I think it's wrong, but she does it anyway."
- "My kids start a game of roughhousing but then they get hurt or break something. Why can't they just be more careful?"

And then these parents throw their hands in the air and ask, "How can I get my children to do what they know I want?" I am sympathetic because I can remember wondering the same thing when my own kids were younger.

The first step is to have realistic expectations so that we don't waste energy feeling victimized by the fact that children often do not share adult perspectives and priorities. Their intention is not to betray us or disappoint us. The reality is that things that make perfect sense to adults do not necessarily make any sense to their children.

Without letting them dictate what happens, we can accept that children have the right to want different things than we adults do. Children have the right to express anger and sadness about the boundaries that their adults set without having their unhappy feelings devastate their adults. They have the right to figure out where their own boundaries are. They have the right to forget and make mistakes without being seen as bad people. They have the right to be just the way they are without risking a loss of love.

Comparing children to each other is unfair, because they are individuals with different ways of being in the world. Some are naturally cautious. Some are quite reckless. Some will try hard to please adults, and others seem to need to define their own identity by pushing against adult boundaries. Being realistic means being prepared to set tight boundaries for a child who pushes against them.

Adult interventions are often essential in order to ensure that children stay safe. On a practical level, having realistic expectations means that adults need to be ready to:

- Hang onto a young child who keeps running away. The reason can be explained by saying, "Last time you ran away and that is not safe, so this time I am going to hold your hand. When you show me that you understand that you have to stay next to me, then we can try letting you walk next to me without holding hands."
- Stop the car and refuse to move unless the seat belt and car seat stay fastened.
- Set boundaries with a child who uses hurtful words to express anger, "You have the right to be angry and to say that you are angry. But our safety rule here is that people do not use hurtful words or attack relationships to express anger. If you want me to listen, please try again and tell me that you are angry without saying that you hate me."
- Insist that children stop and listen when something is important to you by interrupting all other activities until this happens, including turning off or taking away the mobile communication device, TV, headphones, or computer.
- Interrupt a game of roughhousing and have children make a plan for how they are going to keep their game safe for everyone and for the furniture.
- Interrupt games of mean teasing with the same commitment that we would interrupt a game of throwing stones through windows by saying, "Please stop. Teasing that puts people down is not safe. It is against the rules here to let people be mean to each other."
- Notice when children change their behavior – either by being extra quiet, by giggling, or by yelling – and go check what they are doing.
- Insist that children stay with you until they are old enough to be independent while crossing the street, being in a crowd, being dropped off or picked up from school, going to a public restroom, etc.

And of course, being realistic means being prepared for the possibility that children will often dislike being told what to do and resist it. If possible, take time to problem-solve with children so that they understand the reasons and find mutually acceptable solutions. However, when it comes to safety, adults must be prepared to insist in a calm and firm way, even if a child disagrees, without taking the child's behavior personally.

Helicopters or Protectors? – How to Decide When to Hover and When to Let Go

When my kids were young, we were warned not to be "paranoid, neurotic, overprotective" parents. The popular term now is "helicopter parents" who hover over every aspect of their children's lives. Though the words are different, the phenomena are the same. As parents, we want so much for our children to be happy and safe that we have to be careful not to deprive them of opportunities to make their own mistakes, to face the consequences of unwise behavior, to learn how to overcome failure, and to

When it comes to safety, adults must be prepared to insist in a calm and firm way, even if a child disagrees, without taking the child's behavior personally.

develop the independence they need to become successful adults.

The problem is that fear of negative labels can get in the way of common sense. As parents or other caregivers, we don't want avoidance of being overly protective to cause us to provide too little protection. Instead of worrying about labels, we can:

- Gather information about each specific situation so that we are realistic about potential hazards.
- Trust our own intuition and judgment about when children are ready to do what.
- Help kids develop the skills and confidence they need to stay safe while becoming more independent.
- Encourage children to do things on their own as soon as they are truly ready.

Here are five questions to consider in deciding what is enough and what is too much when you worry about whether to hover and when to let go.

1. Is your decision based on your intuition and knowledge about what is best for your child? Separating your intuition and good judgment from anxieties growing out of your own needs can be difficult. Parents and other caregivers sometimes have their identity become so intertwined with their children that they make decisions based on their own drive to feel safe and important rather than on what is truly best for each child. Life is not risk-free, and children's needs are different than ours. A child who is never given the opportunity to try things out on his or her own can become fearful and dependent, or rebellious and risk-taking.

One mother was terrified to let her ten-year-old daughter go on overnight visits with anyone because a friend's father had abused her as a child. Fortunately, she realized that, instead of refusing to let her daughter have fun with friends, she needed to make a plan in order to feel safe by getting to know the parents so she could trust the supervision being provided and by being sure that her daughter had the skills to set boundaries and to get help if need be.

2. Are you trying to protect your child from temporary discomfort or from lasting harm? Emotional or physical discomfort is temporary, and learning how to cope with discomfort is an essential life skill. Emotional or physical harm is lasting and can lead to injury, trauma, or even death. Your toddler can't learn to walk if you prevent him from ever falling down and being scared and hurt for a few minutes, but he needs your protection to avoid falling onto a sharp rock, out a window, or off a cliff.

Occasionally feeling sad, tired, bored, frustrated, scared, hurt, angry, or upset are all normal emotions that children can learn to overcome through self-control, resilience, persistence, and determination. However, being overwhelmed with these feelings much of the time and struggling alone can lead to depression or other emotional damage. Cheerfully helping children deal with discomfort is necessary in order for them to develop new skills.

A child whose parents cannot tolerate her ever getting a little water up her

Fear of negative labels like "helicopter parents" can get in the way of common sense.

nose while she is learning to swim may, as a result, never learn to swim. This means that she is likely to miss a lot of fun and is at greater risk of drowning. The opposite extreme also creates problems. Suppose this child learns to swim by being thrown into the deep end of the pool where she struggles and chokes. Suppose that she is laughed at or pressured instead of being taught in a way that is safe and builds confidence. Many children taught like this become adults with a life-long fear of being in deep water. Others might love to swim but be fearful of learning other new things.

With the right kind of support, learning to walk or swim is likely to be fun even if there are moments of discomfort. The same is true with learning other skills.

3. Are you giving your child ongoing opportunities to learn to be more self-sufficient or constantly taking over things that your child could do? Babies depend on their adults for everything. As children get older, adjusting to their constantly changing needs and abilities is a tricky balancing act. If we always rush to help children instead of encouraging them to do what they can for themselves as soon as they are able, we are teaching helplessness instead of building competence.

For example, children need protection from people who cross their boundaries in emotionally or physically dangerous ways. They also need opportunities to deal with uncomfortable personal situations successfully, or they will not develop their understanding of how to have successful relationships or the ability to set boundaries for themselves. As ten-year-old Julie's mother said, "I was bullied as a child, and I could not bear the thought of anything like that happening to Julie. I was so worried that I stepped in strongly as soon as another child said a harsh word to her or even bumped into her accidentally. Julie started having trouble making friends. Finally, I realized that the problem was that she would come running to me whining as soon as she felt unhappy about anything instead of learning to work things out by speaking up for herself."

Too often, adults take an "all or nothing" approach to conflict between children either by jumping in too soon and too often or by expecting kids to solve problems themselves, without adequate preparation. Instead, we can give children coaching and support as they learn how to deal with conflict and build healthy relationships.

4. Does your child have adequate supervision and support to address potential problems? Children need a level of supervision that is realistically based on their age, abilities, judgment, and the environment around them. They need opportunities to practice doing things for themselves within boundaries that protect them from harm as much as practically possible.

In one childcare center, three-year-old Mario was giving juicy kisses to all the children. The teachers watched Mario closely to intervene when he did this and worked with him to change this behavior. They also taught the Kidpower program to give the children practice in setting boundaries. One little girl did just what she'd learned. She noticed Mario coming, put her hands up as he approached her and yelled, "STOP!" Mario was so surprised that he completely stopped giving juicy kisses at school. By monitoring and

Too often, adults take an "all or nothing" approach to conflict between children either by jumping in too soon and too often or by expecting kids to solve problems themselves, without adequate preparation.

redirecting Mario's behavior, coaching him to listen, and preparing other kids to set boundaries, Mario's teachers turned his intrusive behavior into an opportunity for everyone to grow.

5. Are you assessing risks realistically rather than either denying or exaggerating them? Gather information and then trust your own intuition and judgment. In one workshop, a mother said, "My brother let our son ride his bike alone down to the creek because he used to do this at the same age. I got horribly upset and said that our son needed to have an adult go with him. My brother told me that I am being totally paranoid. But I am overprotective, and I can't help it. Should I let my son go even though I feel so worried?" All of the mothers and fathers there nodded their heads and said that they were also neurotic, paranoid, and overprotective. Then they all looked at me anxiously, wanting the right answer on how to fix their unreasonable feelings.

"How old is your son?" I asked the mother who had posed the question.

"Eight." she sighed.

Our challenge is to protect children from danger, separate our identities from theirs, and prepare children in positive and effective ways to protect themselves.

"That's not very old," I said, and then asked, "What is it like down at the creek? Is it far? Can your son be safe with cars on the way there? Is it isolated? What kinds of people go down there? Has the area changed since your brother was a little boy?"

This mother's answers gave everyone a clear way to see that the creek was not a very safe place for her son to be without an adult. I then pointed out, "Our common sense tells us that we want to assess the safety of each situation carefully before making decisions about what is or is not okay for our kids. Sometimes we can become so fearful of labels like 'overprotective' or 'paranoid' or 'helicopter' that we put our common sense aside."

Like these parents, I used to worry being a neurotic, paranoid, overprotective mom and wondered if something was wrong with me. But the truth was that I knew my kids better than other people did. I was responsible for gathering information and then trusting my own intuition and judgment about when my children would be ready to do what. As soon as our children showed Ed or me that they were ready to do something on their own, we not only let them but even encouraged them. Eventually, when people called me "paranoid" or "overprotective," I decided to say, "Thank you! I'm just doing my job!"

Our challenge is to protect children from danger, separate our identities from theirs, and prepare children in positive and effective ways to protect themselves.

Ask Leading Questions
Once after a workshop, Timothy Dunphy, the other co-founder of Kidpower, asked me, "Irene, why do children always give you the right answers?"

"Because," I explained, "I ask the right questions, and I give them the answer." Then I added, nodding my head, "Do you see what I mean?" With a grin, Timothy nodded his head.

Questions open windows into people's minds. When you ask a question instead of making a statement, the other person has to think about what you said in order to answer. Right? Imagine me smiling at you and nodding my head, so that of course, you are likely to say, "Yes! That's right!" Much of the Kidpower program uses carefully worded, leading questions to help children build their understanding, manage their behavior, and shape their beliefs. Our goal is to take the guesswork out of learning to be safe.

We also give away the answers. For example, if I want children to acknowledge that something is not safe, I ask seriously, "Does *that* look safe?" I shake my head to show that the answer is, "No!" If I want children to feel successful, then I nod my head as I ask enthusiastically, "Could you hear how loudly you were all yelling?"

Adults can use the Ask Leading Questions technique in daily life. Positive questions that can be answered by saying, "Yes" are usually the most effective. If you want a child to feel stronger, you can use positive questions to highlight behavior that shows strength such as, "Did you notice how well you helped me lift that big box?" If you want a child to develop a self-image of being able to listen, you can ask, "Did you notice how well you listened when I asked you to stay with me?" If you want a child to develop a better sense of boundaries, you can ask, "Did you see how clearly and respectfully you told that kid to wait his turn, all by yourself?"

Be sure to sound as if you believe in what you are saying. Be careful not to add uncertain or conflicting language that changes the message. "Did you notice that you did that well?" is far more likely to get positive results than, "Did you notice that you sort of did that well, even though you usually don't?"

With a little thought and care, adults can figure out how to ask questions that will lead to the "right" answers - answers that will lead children to developing the behavior, understanding, and attitudes that will help them to be safe and successful.

How to Prepare Kids for More Independence

As adults, we are responsible for keeping young people safe while preparing them for more independence, so that they can enjoy their lives on their own. Here are five steps for preparing a child or teen to do an activity without an adult in charge:

Step 1.
Make Realistic Assessments About this Specific Situation and this Particular Child.

Parents often ask us, "How will I know when my child is old enough to do something on his or her own?" Common questions are:
• "When can he play alone in the front yard?"
• "Is she ready to walk to school by herself?"
• "When can he stay overnight with friends?"
• "Are my kids old enough to ride the city bus?"

The answer is, "It depends…" There is no magic age when children are ready for certain activities. It depends on the specific situation and on the skills of this particular child.

For example, suppose your daughter wants to go to a friend's house for an overnight birthday party. Assessment questions about the situation might include: How well do I know this friend's parents? If I don't know them well, can I arrange to meet them and make sure that I feel comfortable letting my daughter go? What activities are planned? What level of supervision will be provided?

Assessment questions about your daughter's skills include: Does my daughter know what our safety rules are and how to follow them? Can she speak up if she feels uncomfortable? Can she say "No" to her friends if they start to do something unsafe even if she feels embarrassed? Does she know how to call me anytime, even in the middle of the night if she needs help?

Suppose that your son wants to walk to school without you. Assessment questions about the situation might include: What is the route to school like? What hazards are along the way? What is the traffic like? Are there crossing guards, cross walks, and stoplights? Are there animals? Are there interesting yet potentially dangerous things that might tempt my son into changing his plan such as ponds, animals, or construction? What kinds of people such as strangers, gangs, or bullies might cause a safety problem for my son? Are there stores, neighbors, or other places he could get help if he needs to?

Assessment questions about your son's skills include: How aware and careful is my son? Does he get lost in daydreaming or can he pay attention to the traffic and people around him? Does my son understand and know how to follow our safety rules? Can my son remember to check with me first before he changes his plan about what he's doing, even if something looks very interesting or his friends start pressuring him? If someone challenges him in a rude way, can my son walk away from trouble and go get help or will he feel the need to prove himself? Can my son interrupt a busy adult and get help if he needs to? Can my son run, yell, and get help if he's scared?

By making realistic assessments, we can determine whether this particular child is ready to handle this specific situation independently and, if not, what this child would need to know and be able to do in order to become ready. We need to remember that children develop skills at different paces and have different personalities. What is going to be safe for one child at a given age in a given situation might take longer or require extra precautions for another child. If you are unsure or concerned that your child might not make the safest choice or if you feel that your child isn't ready to do something independently, take the time to review skills with him or her or make different plans that provide more supervision and support.

Step 2.
Practice together the skills necessary to do the activity safely and successfully.

Most of this book is about knowledge and skills for people being safe with people, but practice is also important for other skills. Kids need to learn how to swim before they go in the water without an adult to hold them up - and even then, we want someone who can save them if need be and who is watching to make sure they don't get into trouble. They need to know how to light matches without getting burned before being given a box of matches and told to start a fire on their own. Before driving on their own, teens need to know the mechanics of using a car, the rules of the road, and how to drive defensively.

Step 3.
Co-Pilot to Field-Test Skills in the Real World.

Co-piloting means that you go with your child on an activity while letting your child lead the way before you let your child do this activity alone. Co-piloting gives your child the opportunity to show you what she or he can do, while giving you the opportunity to notice any unexpected problems and ask questions to check on your child's understanding.

For example, when Chantal was eight, she wanted to be able to walk across the street from her summer school program to her brother's day care without having me come and get her. Even though the school was directly across the street from the day care, there were lots of parents around, and the one street had a crossing guard, I was very nervous about the idea. I followed Chantal as she walked ahead of me on the route she would take from her summer school door to the day care center, so that I could see exactly what she was doing.

As we walked, I peppered her with questions: "If someone stops their car and starts to talk with you, what will you do? If someone has a puppy, what will you do? If someone you know tries to give you a ride, what will you do?" My child's calm awareness as she walked, the level of supervision around, and her answers reassured me that she was ready to take this step to independence. However, we did notice one glitch, which was that the preschool door was sometimes locked. Co-piloting made it possible to see this problem ahead of time and to make a plan for the preschool teachers to watch for Chantal and, if need be, for how she could find someone to let her inside.

Another idea on the use of Co-Piloting came from one of our most experienced instructors, Erika Leonard, when she was teaching a workshop on Internet Safety. Because many children are ahead of their parents when it comes to use of the Internet and other digital technology, parents often feel unsure about how to set boundaries or to keep track of what their children are doing. Erika suggests that parents insist on their child co-piloting with them so that they go together to explore wherever the new forms of technology take them. This makes it possible for parents to discuss with their children how the safety rules apply to each particular situation.

Step Four.
Conduct Trial Runs to Develop Independence in Controlled Doses With Adult Backup.

Rather than giving blanket permission about activities requiring more independence, we can let children develop their skills and understanding by having Trial Runs with our backup. That way, they have the opportunity to do things on their own while having easy access to adult support in case they need help. Once, my friend Maggie's teenagers wanted to camp on their own with their friends. They had had lots of camping experience, but never by themselves. Maggie took a campsite in the next loop from theirs, so that she could be accessible just in case they needed her. Her kids found out that camping on their own was a lot of fun – and a lot of work!

Step Five.
Keep communications open with listening, ongoing check-ins, and review.

Children are safest when they know that the adults in their lives are paying attention to what they are doing and are helpful people to come to with problems. Even after children are used to doing an activity on their own, continuing to check in and review safety plans and skills is important. People can change. Situations can change. Problems can develop that were not there before.

One girl in a workshop told me tearfully about her best friend, whose parents were going through a divorce. The girl's parents assumed that their daughter was happy spending the night at her friend's house, as she had done for many years. Unfortunately, there was much more drinking and fighting than there had been before. This girl felt afraid for herself, and for her friend. In our Kidpower workshop, we made a plan for how the girl could talk with her parents and get their help, perhaps arranging for her friend to only stay at their house, rather than trading back and forth.

Remind children that problems should not be secrets and that you want to know what's happening in their lives. Be a helpful adult to come to by listening without judgment or lecturing. Once in a while, ask your children, "Is there anything you've been wondering or worrying about that you haven't told me?" If you listen with calm appreciation to their answers, you will help your children to develop the habit of telling you how things are going for them, so that you can continue to support them in taking charge of their emotional and physical safety.

Obsessing about what you have done wrong sets a terrible example for your children. Remember, nobody's perfect!

Give Yourself a Break

Too often, when people start to learn more about People Safety, they also start to feel guilty. At times, many of us say things like, "I wish I had known then what I do now." While we sometimes regret choices we have made for ourselves, most adults feel much worse about any of our choices that might have made life harder for our children.

During our workshops, some parents start beating up on themselves and saying, "Oh no! I should have done that differently!" I can remember feeling the same way, so I tell them what I wish someone had told me, "Please stop feeling guilty! This just makes you miserable without making your children safer. In fact, obsessing about what you have done wrong sets a terrible example for your children. Remember, nobody's perfect!"

Parents often ask, "But what should I do to fix things now? I have already scared my daughter by doing exactly what you said not to do and inflicting my own fears on her."

"You could simply start doing things differently," I point out. "Or, you could say that you are learning more about safety from Kidpower just like your child is. If necessary, you can then correct any inaccurate information you might have given."

The good news is that most children are more resilient than most adults. They tend to live more in the moment than adults do. When adults start being positive in dealing with safety issues, their children are likely to start doing the same. Fearful children will often become more confident by being successful in practicing how to handle situations that they are worried about with the help of enthusiastic adults.

Sometimes I meet parents who are grieving because they trusted people who were not safe, and their children ended up being molested or otherwise harmed. I tell them, "It is very sad that this happened to your child and it is normal to grieve. But please also honor yourself for having the courage to change the situation and for getting help for your child now."

So, whatever has happened in the past, please give yourself a break. As Maya Angelou said, "I did then what I knew how to do. Now that I know better, I do better!"[15]

"I did then what I knew how to do. Now that I know better, I do better!"

Maya Angelou

Chapter Three

Building a Foundation of Emotional Safety for Young People

Emotional safety means knowing that:
- *You are loved just the way you are;*
- *You are worth protecting;*
- *You have the right to be safe;*
- *You are important;*
- *You can speak up for yourself and others;*
- *You have the power to make your world a better place; and*
- *You have the ability to defend yourself from harm.*

As adults, we can offer children opportunities to have positive experiences that will help build their foundation of emotional safety. We can do our best to protect children from destructive experiences that might undermine their confidence in themselves and diminish their ability to get the most out of their lives. Even when bad things happen that are outside of our control, we can do a great deal to help children learn from these experiences rather than be damaged by them.

Kidpower's Underlying Principle - Put Safety First!
Kidpower's Underlying Principle is that:

The safety and self-esteem of a child are more important than anyone's embarrassment, inconvenience, or offense!

A simple way of stating this principle is to: Put Safety First. This principle seems easy to agree with, but can be hard to live by in daily life. Right now, you might be thinking, "Well, of course, I agree to Put Safety First!" That's great, but try asking yourself these questions. Do I hate to be embarrassed? Do I try to avoid embarrassing others? Do I hate to be interrupted when I'm busy? Do I dislike bothering most other people? Do I get upset when other people get mad at me? Do I hate the feeling of being angry myself?

When I ask these questions in my parent education workshops, most of the adults will say, "Yes, I do hate those feelings!" Most will agree that their children usually feel the same way. Most of us don't like being

If children can tell the people who love them when they are uncomfortable, and have their boundaries respected, they will be safer from people who might cause them harm.

bothered, embarrassed, or annoyed. And most of us don't like having to embarrass, bother, or upset others. While we believe that safety and self-esteem are more important, these uncomfortable feelings are powerful social forces that can work against our consistently remembering to Put Safety First.

Erika Leonard, one of our most experienced Kidpower instructors, told me this story about a time when she and her young daughter were separated in the library. "I looked all over and couldn't find her anywhere," Erika said. "In spite of all we teach, I was embarrassed to yell for her at first. After all, yelling in a library is against the rules. When I realized that I was stopping myself from the most likely way to find my daughter, I did yell her name from the checkout counter. Everyone in the library turned around and looked at me in what might have been disapproval, but at that moment I didn't care. To my relief, my daughter called back and came running. She said in a shocked voice, 'Mom! You yelled in the library!'"

Noticing times when our actions contradict our Put Safety First values can be uncomfortable. "I used to leave my baby in the car for just a minute, so I could run into the store to pick something up," says one mother. "She would be asleep in her car seat. I was so busy and so tired that I felt better letting her sleep rather than risking waking her up. One day, I got delayed and came back to find a man standing by my car. He told me that he had been afraid for my sleeping baby, so he had waited to make sure that no one would harm her and that she would not get too hot. For a moment, I hated him because I was so embarrassed. But then I realized how much caring he had shown by waiting, and the courage he might have needed to speak up, so I thanked him instead."

Contradictory messages can confuse children. Suppose a kindly neighbor starts to stroke a toddler's curly hair while she's sitting in her stroller? Imagine that this little girl tries to pull away, but her mother lets the lady keep touching her hair, perhaps even telling her daughter to be more polite. What message is the mother giving her child about her right to stop unwanted touch? What message is the well-meaning neighbor giving as she keeps meeting her own needs for connection by touching the child against her will?

If a family member or friend has hurt feelings when told to stop touching or teasing a child who doesn't like it, you can explain that true affection has to be a true choice. If children can tell the people who love them when they are uncomfortable, and have their boundaries respected, they will be safer from people who might cause them harm.

Timothy Dunphy, the other co-founder of Kidpower, has a couple of stories about his daughter Rhiannon when she was a willful toddler long ago. "I was leaving for a two-week trip. When I tried to kiss Rhiannon good-bye, she suddenly decided to say, 'No!'" "I didn't like going away for so long without that kiss, so I was tempted to try to coax her into doing what I wanted. But I realized that my daughter knowing that I respect her boundaries was more important than my being able to kiss her good-bye. My reward came when I got back home, and Rhiannon threw herself into my arms."

A few months later, Timothy's father came for a visit. When her grandfather asked Rhiannon for a hug, she said, "No."

"If you want the present I bought you," Timothy's father said, "you need to give your Grandpa his hug." Timothy worried about how his father would feel, but he knew that he had to speak up for his daughter. "Rhiannon," Timothy said calmly as he inwardly winced and braced for an explosion, "You can tell Grandpa that in our house we do not make people give hugs for presents."

Fortunately, Timothy's father took it well, and he still gave his granddaughter her gift. But suppose Timothy's fear had been true? Even if his father had become really upset, Timothy knew that teaching Rhiannon that giving hugs was her choice was more important than preventing his father from feeling hurt or embarrassed. Children are safest when they know that their adults will back them up about setting appropriate boundaries even when this leads to upset feelings.

Too many children have been harmed because they did not want to do something embarrassing like yell for help, or because they did not want to be rude to someone who was acting nice to them. When we are making hard decisions about where to draw the line with other people, applying Kidpower's underlying principle can help us remember to Put Safety First when making choices about our kids.

Lead With Your Heart Connection

People of all ages are hungry for genuine connection, but empty words of caring can backfire. Many years ago, during my first conflict resolution training, I was astonished to feel extreme irritation towards the sweet, well-meaning helpers who were assisting the lead presenter. I found myself resentfully thinking – I want to slug the next person who says, "Thank you for sharing!" I had to laugh at myself because my increased and uncharacteristic aggression was the exact opposite of what we were there to accomplish. I started to wonder why the written materials seemed to make sense and why the demonstrations with the lead presenter came across as moving, while the helpers words and actions were annoying. Something was profoundly different, but what was it?

Eventually, I figured out that the lead presenter was truly listening to what people were saying. Her responses came from the perspective of paying deep attention to what someone was trying to communicate. Her assistants were trying so hard to copy the techniques that they were going through the motions rather than really connecting with anyone. The way that they were automatically mouthing the words, "Thank you for sharing," seemed insulting because I doubted that what the person had just said actually mattered to them.

The problem was not with the techniques of conflict resolution but with the lack of connection and caring with which those techniques were being used. I believe that the same principle is true in most interactions with children and adults. You can let people know that you care with a few words, a question, a look, a listening silence, or a smile. But if you are just

People of all ages are hungry for a genuine connection

going through the motions, people will notice and your credibility with them will be diminished. I have found that people of all ages are hungry for genuine connection and will respond like thirsty plants in a gentle rain when you offer it to them.

Believing that you are loved is essential to emotional safety. The Search Institute is a nonprofit organization that pioneered the concept of 40 Developmental Assets - building blocks of positive development crucial for advancing academic success, civic engagement, and the reduction of risk behaviors - that children and youth need in order to thrive.[1] For each age, being loved and supported by their families is at the top of the Developmental Assets list. No matter how busy we are or how annoyed they make us, our children need to know that they are important to us just the way they are. No matter what they do, they are not going to become less important to us. Having consistent boundaries is also a Developmental Asset as long as we set boundaries in a way that makes it clear that our love does not depend on what a child does or who the child is.

The problem was not with the techniques of conflict resolution but with the lack of connection and caring with which those techniques were being used.

In his insightful book, *The Seven Habits of Highly Effective People*, management expert Stephen R. Covey explains that loving someone is a decision that does not depend on your feelings of the moment.[2] You might feel tired, irritated, or fed up, but you can still decide what actions you are going to take and what attitude you are going to adopt with the children in your life.

This same theme is part of Logotherapy, which was invented by one of my heroes, Victor Frankl, a psychotherapist who was imprisoned in a concentration camp during World War II. Dr. Frankl realized that he could not control most of what was happening around him but he could choose to control his response to what was happening. In a famous quote from his book *Man's Search for Meaning*, he writes, "The last of human freedoms is the ability to chose one's attitude in a given set of circumstances."[3]

I remind myself that if Dr. Frankl could choose his attitude while surrounded by death and destruction, I can decide to communicate love no matter what my mood is of the moment and regardless of what other people are doing. Making a decision to communicate unconditional love is essential to building a foundation of emotional safety for young people, and this foundation is crucial for the development of effective People Safety concepts and skills.

Give Specific, Genuine Approval Instead of Automatic Praise

Amanda Golert, our Swedish Center Director and Training and Curriculum Consultant, wrote, "When I first saw Kidpower classes in California, all the applause you led and your constant enthusiastic encouragement seemed odd. In Swedish culture, people rarely applaud or show any other kind of appreciation openly and loudly – except at the end of a performance. I was worried about the reactions when trying this at home, but gave it a shot.

"Many adults looked surprised, but our Swedish children loved the clapping and cheering because we were celebrating their success each step of the way! Seeing the look on the children's faces when we were clapping for

Each child is on his or her own path

them convinced me that even though clapping like this wasn't 'typically Swedish,' we were going to do it anyway!"

The key to getting kids to keep on trying is to encourage them for their efforts. The book *Nurture Shock* describes research studies showing that automatic praise can backfire and cause children to avoid trying in order to avoid failing.[4] Children who were constantly told that they were smart didn't do as well as children who understood that they needed to expend effort in order to succeed.

As in the Conflict Resolution training story above, meaningful applause and praise must be genuinely connected with what someone is saying or doing rather than being mechanical or coercive. In Kidpower, our goal is to create a joyful environment where our students are supported in being successful as they learn to keep themselves safe. We cheer each of them on for their effort and specific actions instead of giving them blanket praise about how wonderful they are or approval conditional to their level of performance.

Appreciate Each Child's Unique Path

Leo the Late Bloomer, a children's book written by Robert Kraus and illustrated by Jose Aruego, tells of a little lion who can't seem to do anything well. His father worries, but his mother says, "Just wait." Eventually, Leo triumphs.[5]

Logically, we know that each child needs appreciation as a unique being who is following a unique path. Unfortunately, resisting the temptation to compare children with each other is hard. As Josh told me, "My partner Roger and I kept worrying about our son Mitchell, who was several months older than most of our friends' kids before he started walking and talking. We fretted, even though Mitchell was healthy, cheerful, and bright. We pored over the charts in child development books, wondering if there was something wrong with him. Suddenly, seemingly overnight, Mitchell started making long speeches and climbing flagpoles! Now we're feeling sad because he seems to be growing up so fast!"

Instead of making comparisons, try to be realistic about what each particular child most needs to learn. Different ages, different life situations, different family priorities, and different personalities help determine how best to build an individual child's safety and confidence. Is Isabelle a "super hero" who thinks she's invincible and seems to lack caution? Is Juan so shy he might freeze if someone scares him? Rather than being anxious, focus on a child's strengths – and then work on adding needed skills. The child who knows no fear often has a lot of energy and can be very effective at boundary setting. The shy child is often extremely aware of the environment and able to avoid trouble.

No matter what their personalities are like, children can learn how to take charge in an emergency. "I was amazed," one father told me, "I have always worried that my sensitive eight-year-old daughter Tara would be too shy to speak up if she had a problem. Last summer, Tara went away to a week-long camp. One of the counselors played a game with the kids that got out of hand. The children were jumping on the counselor to the point that she was too injured to stop them. Even though the counselor was silent and the kids were laughing, Tara could see that something was wrong. She yelled, 'STOP!' so loudly that the other children were startled into listening. Then she ran to get help from another counselor. Later, I asked my daughter how she had known what to do. She reminded me that she had learned how to yell and get help in Kidpower!"

Get Kids to Tell You and Show You What They Think They Should Do

Children gain more understanding from what they say and do than from what they see and hear. They tend to be more literal than adults, and they often have different ideas than we do about how the world works. We can learn a lot by asking children to tell us and show us how they would handle different situations.

One day, when he was ten, my son Arend was home sick from school. While a storm raged outside, Arend watched a movie on television. I had to leave to pick up his sister, and wanted to let him stay indoors. Even though I was only going to be gone for a few minutes, I reminded Arend of all the rules about being home alone that I could think of. Suddenly, I thought to ask him, "Suppose that the electricity goes out while I'm gone. What would you do?"

"No problem," my son replied confidently, "I'd just take the batteries out of my flashlight and plug them into the TV to make it work again."

"That's very creative, but not a good plan," I explained. "Playing with the TV could get you electrocuted. Do you have any other ideas?" "I guess I could read," Arend sighed. "But I'd rather watch television."

"Suppose that the storm gets bigger and you get scared?" I asked.

Rather than being anxious, focus on a child's strengths – and then work on adding needed skills.

"Should I go outside to stay with Chris next door?" Arend wondered.

"How about trying to call him first?" I suggested. "Usually phones work even when the electricity goes out. Here's the number. And, remember, I am going to be back in less than 15 minutes!"

Asking questions is important in building understanding, but talking about something is not the same as doing it. When we have children show us what they will do, we have a far better picture of how much they actually understand.

After a big earthquake in Santa Cruz in 1989, I often felt nervous about going out of town. Before leaving, I needed to reassure myself that, even if my children were alone in the house in an earthquake, they'd be okay. I told them, "Show me what you'd do if an earthquake came." At the ages of 14 and 11, both Chantal and Arend were exasperated. "Aw, Mom!" they grumbled, "Not now! We already know all about earthquakes."

"Humor me!" I said. "Nothing else good is going to happen in your life until we have an earthquake drill. No television. No books. No dessert. Nothing!"

"When she gets like this, you might as well save your breath," Chantal advised her younger brother. So we went from room to room in the house.

My children ran to stand under doorways or crouch next to our couch when I yelled 'Earthquake.'" Most of the time, they were right. But, in one room of the house, the doorway was next to our gas furnace. I was able to warn my kids that this was not a good place to be in an earthquake. By the time we were done, they were laughing, and I was ready to go on my trip with more peace of mind.

In real life, people tend to do what they've practiced, especially under stress. Asking children questions and then giving them information helps them to develop the ability to think for themselves. Rehearsing solutions prepares children to be ready to choose their safest options, just in case.

Protect Kids From Denial, Panic, and Being on Automatic Pilot

When people are taken by surprise in an emergency such as a natural disaster, a car accident, or an attack, the first feeling is likely to be one of denial. When faced by any unexpected situation, good or bad, it's normal to think, "I don't believe it! This can't be really happening!"

Disbelief can cause people to try to ignore a problem, making the situation more dangerous. For example, when a friend of mine was a child, she thought the fluid in her humidifier looked like apple juice. She drank it and then kept ignoring the pain in her stomach instead of asking her parents for help. Finally, she ended up in the emergency room.

Although getting stuck in denial is normal, we can train our children and ourselves to get unstuck very quickly. The sooner we can get through our denial and pay attention, the sooner we can start taking appropriate action.

When we have children show us what they will do, we have a far better picture of how much they actually understand.

Disbelief can cause people to try to ignore a problem, making the situation more dangerous.

When people feel threatened by danger, fear triggers a flood of adrenaline. Often, this rush of adrenaline causes us to go on "automatic pilot." Think of a deer that stands frozen in the middle of the road and then suddenly dashes into an oncoming car. Standing still and then zigzagging fast can help a deer escape from a mountain lion, but the same response creates a safety problem when the danger is an automobile.

When people are full of adrenaline, they are more likely to panic. Running in a panic away from a threat can make a situation more dangerous. "My nephew and his friends were waiting for me to pick them up outside a big store in downtown San Francisco," one upset uncle said. "A gang of older teens drove up and threatened them. The boys panicked and ran in all directions. A couple of them were caught and beaten up. A car almost hit one because he ran into the street. If only they had kept their wits about them, they would have realized that the big, self-opening doors leading into the store were directly behind them. They could have stayed together, backed up, and gotten help inside the store."

Children need to know when NOT doing what they're told at that moment is a better choice.

We often do not recognize potential problems or select our safest choices if we are operating on automatic pilot and start acting out of habit. Many children will automatically do what their adults tell them, especially in a group setting where everyone else is doing the same thing. For example, most adults try to teach children to be kind, friendly, polite, and cooperative. But, children also need to know when NOT doing what they're told at a given moment is a better choice.

"My six-year-old son Chad is a pleaser," Chad's mother mourned. "I've always told him to be a good boy, and his teacher has praised him for being so obedient. Yesterday, Chad suddenly had to go to the toilet urgently but he listened quietly when his teacher told all the children to sit down and work. He got so desperate that he couldn't talk at all and ended up wetting his pants. "I feel awful that Chad was embarrassed, but I'm glad that nothing worse happened. We're going to be changing that 'always do what adults tell you' habit to a 'notice what you need and speak up to take care of yourself' habit!"

Rehearsing solutions for different problems prepares children to make better decisions – instead of getting stuck in denial or reacting without thinking.

Protect Children's World View
The two main reasons adults give for being hesitant to discuss personal safety concerns with young children are:
• My son is already so anxious. I don't want to teach him that the world is a bad place.
• My daughter is in love with the world. I don't want to destroy her beautiful trust.

The problem is, sooner or later, children are going to pick up some frightening information from the people around them and from the media. When adults don't help them understand that information, children can tell themselves some very scary stories. Children often worry without saying anything to their adults because they want to protect their adults from being upset. Also, children can have a hard time bringing up their concerns because they don't know the words to say. They can feel very alone because they have no adult to talk with about their worries.

Kids often already have scary pictures in their minds. Before the time when changing people's looks with digital technology was easy, the TV program *Mission Impossible* showed people changing their looks using masks and trick photography. Six-year-old Nir had clearly been thinking about strangers before I came to teach a Kidpower program in his classroom. With big round eyes and a hushed voice, he riveted his fellow first graders with this question: "What if a stranger made his face look exactly like my Mom's?" Nir continued to ask: "What if he got clothes like my Mom and a car like my Mom? What if I got in the car because I thought he was my Mom? And then, when he drove the car away, what if he peeled the face off?!!!"

"You saw that on television!" I said with an inward groan.

"Yes!" Nir gasped, and all his classmates gasped with him. "I saw it with my own eyes on television!"

"The television camera tricked you," I said, and tried to explain about switching people and trick photography. The whole first grade looked doubtful.

Thankfully, the teacher threw the full weight of her authority behind me. "Irene is right!" she said firmly. "And the television is wrong!" Even today's more "techno-savvy" kids need reminders that what they see on their i-phones, television, computers, or in movies, is often not how the real world works.

Part of protecting our children's world view is by supervising their information diet. Children who are overexposed to images and stories of violence and fear are at risk of developing a bleak worldview, feeling as if terrible things might happen to them at any minute. Pay attention to what children overhear as well as what they are exposed to when they see or hear news on television, videos, radio, the Internet, and in newspapers. Vivid images of bad things happening to real people can be overwhelming for many adults, let alone children.

We understand this responsibility in other areas. For example, we know we need to supervise what children eat and drink until they can make safe choices about what food is edible and what is poisonous or spoiled. If they get sick in spite of our best efforts, we recognize the symptoms and give them antidotes or medical care.

Keeping track of what children do, see, hear, and read is harder but just as important. The symptoms of emotional damage leading to potentially destructive beliefs are likely to be more subtle than the symptoms of food poisoning, but this damage might create huge anxiety that can diminish a child's joy in life.

Show children that you are in charge of the media instead of trapped by it. Sit with children and watch or listen with them so you can discuss what

Children often worry without saying anything to their adults because they want to protect their adults from being upset.

they are seeing or hearing. Interrupt and stop a program or movie if you think it is not appropriate. Look at ratings before allowing children to watch something – in the same way you might read ingredients of prepared food before deciding to buy it.

If you do this, children often ask, "But why? Everybody else gets to see it."

You might say, "We don't want to put scary pictures in our minds that don't need to be there!" Or, "That's too violent, and we don't want to support it by watching it."

Children who are overexposed to images and stories of violence and fear are at risk of developing a bleak world view.

Part of having a positive world view is being able to approach life's challenges with optimism. Dr. Martin Seligman, founder and director of the Institute of Positive Psychology, has done extensive research showing that optimism – the ability to see, hope for, and work towards the best – leads to more happiness, better health, more success, and more resilience in getting through tough times.[6] To help children develop an optimistic attitude, you need to model being optimistic yourself.

Being optimistic means:
- Even when you dislike the behavior of others, you will assume that their intentions are positive (rather than evil unless there are compelling reasons to believe otherwise).
- When life brings frustration or disappointment, you will look for the opportunities that are possible.
- You will seek solutions (rather than indulging in blame or despair when things go wrong).
- You will avoid "catastrophizing" problems or concerns by making them bigger than they are.
- You will imagine the best that can happen, and work towards the best outcomes for yourself and others (rather than the worst that might happen).

When you find yourself being pessimistic or cynical, you can acknowledge your feelings without beating up on yourself and say something like, "I am sounding very negative right now. Being negative is not very helpful. I'm going to take a break and figure out a more positive way to think about this situation."

Tell Kids What They *Really* Need to Know

Remember that adult fears do not make children safer. Sometimes adults become so upset about the world's problems that they feel compelled to explain in detail to the children around them just how bad things might get. I feel sad hearing five-year-olds asking questions like: Will someone shoot up my school? Will a bad guy come into my bedroom and kidnap me? Will I get sick if I open the mail?

At a first-grade open house at the beginning of school, a few parents asked what kinds of curriculum about war would be included. I was relieved to hear the teacher say, "These are just little kids. Let's teach them about the brave people who work for peace, but spare them the horrors of war."

The same principle is true when teaching children to be safe with people.

Our job is to help children understand what they need to know to make safe choices and to protect themselves from harm. Beyond that, raising images that were not there before can be damaging to children. Letting children set their own pace about what they are ready to know can help them build knowledge and skill without becoming overwhelmed. Differences in age, personality, and life situations make what is appropriate vary tremendously from child to child.

When children ask difficult questions, we need to decide what information will best serve them. We can choose not to answer by changing the subject. We can find out what is already in their minds by asking them what they think. We can just answer the questions without giving detailed explanations.

When Chantal was eight, we sat together watching a children's show on TV. During the commercial, there was a public service announcement for the local rape crisis center. My daughter turned to me with curious wide eyes and asked, "What's rape, Mommy?"

My first thought was indignation that this announcement was in the middle of a children's show. I hated the idea of shattering her innocence. "Rape," I said, deliberately oversimplifying, "is a way men have of hurting women."

"How do they hurt them?" Chantal demanded.

"By making them have sex when they don't want to," I sighed.

"Isn't sex supposed to be for making babies?" my daughter wondered. "Or for grown-ups who are married or who are in love with each other?"

"Yes," I said, dreading how much more she was going to ask, "but sometimes people who are hurt inside get things all mixed up, and they hurt other people all sorts of ways. Rape is one of those ways."

"Oh," Chantal said, satisfied for the time being. "Thank you! I like knowing the meaning of words. Today in school we learned what photosynthesis means. Do you want me to explain it to you?"

"Sure!" I said, feeling far more ready to talk about how plants work than why people hurt each other.

Giving kids upsetting details does not make them safer; it just makes them more anxious. For example, children have an easier time learning to swim without knowing exactly what happens when people drown. When we are teaching about safety with cars, we strap children into their car seats or seatbelts without discussing vivid details about what happens in a car accident. In the same way, we can teach children how to be safe with people without giving them vivid details about what exactly happens in a violent or abusive assault.

When necessary, you can explain even very horrible events in a calm, matter-of-fact way that focuses on hope rather than despair. Fear is an appropriate

Our job is to help children understand what they need to know to make safe choices and to protect themselves from harm. Beyond that, raising upsetting images can be damaging to children.

We can teach children how to be safe with people without giving them vivid details about what exactly happens in a violent or abusive assault.

The Joy of "Just" Listening!

response to danger. Sadness is an appropriate response to loss. But hopelessness and helplessness can immobilize us and diminish our lives.

As they were getting ready to drive to the store, six-year-old Angela suddenly clung to her aunt and said, "I'm afraid to go. What if a terrorist blows us up with a bomb or poisons us with gas?"

Puzzled, Angela's aunt hugged her and said, "That almost never happens."

"But it does happen!" Angela protested tearfully. "In wars. And on 9/11 bad guys even turned airplanes into bombs by flying them into buildings. When I was playing with my dollhouse, I heard my mom talking to her friend on the phone about how things are getting worse and worse."

Angela's aunt took a deep breath and decided to have a conversation with her sister later. Then, very calmly and firmly, she told her niece, "You and your mom are right. Those things have happened, and that can be very sad and scary to think about. But most of the time, most people can have great lives without ever having to meet a terrorist. Lots of people are working hard to make sure that this doesn't happen. Now, let's go to the store and buy chocolate so we can make cookies!"

What kids really need to know is that we can have joyful, meaningful lives, even though frightening things sometimes happen.

There Is No Such Thing as "JUST" Listening

Being listened to with full attention and without being judged or interrupted is a rare and valuable gift. Our busy, hectic lives can distract us from remembering to take at least a few minutes of every day to check in with our children. Some of our most precious memories will come from the times when we just stopped and listened to a child. And, children are emotionally safer if they believe that their adults really do want to know about everything important to them – the good and the bad. To develop this belief, children need opportunities to answer questions like, "How was your day? What went well for you? What went wrong?"

If we want our kids to keep talking to us, we need to listen. When children start to talk about their problems or act upset, the temptation to jump in right away with solutions can be powerful. Most of us know better. But, if you're like me, watching someone we care about be unhappy or make mistakes can be hard to tolerate. With our greater life experience, we adults can't help having lots of excellent ideas for what children should do and how they should feel. The problem is that giving advice too quickly robs children of the opportunity to be heard, think of their own ideas, and then get our guidance in the context of their actual experience.

Kids might call our good advice "lecturing," feel judged and pushed, or suspect we think they can't figure things out for themselves. Children sometimes try to protect adults from their upset feelings by hiding the fact that they sometimes feel bad. Many kids end up deciding that talking to adults is just too risky and they try to solve problems by themselves. This decision deprives a child of the important resource of adult guidance and perspective, and having hidden feelings can cause a child to feel very alone.

Children will benefit most from being listened to with interest and without judgment, with an acceptance that all of their thoughts and feelings are okay. Most of the time children are unhappy for reasons that require no action or advice on our part. The best way we adults can get children to trust our guidance is to listen attentively, ask supportive questions, and, unless safety requires our intervention, let them figure out what to do.

We adults often forget that discussing problems can make kids feel worse at first, because thinking or talking about upsetting experiences brings up unpleasant feelings. Understandably, many children would prefer to stop thinking or talking about something when doing so makes them feel bad. They may also lack the words to explain what happened. They might feel like the problem is stupid or their fault.

When children have opportunities to work through difficult feelings with adult help, they learn that dealing with problems sooner can prevent them from getting bigger later. They can start to understand that they will feel better in the long run if they learn to deal with unpleasant feelings rather than ignore them. Encouraging children to develop the habit of talking about uncomfortable issues can prevent a host of problems.

One good technique for opening up discussions is to ask children every once in a while, "Is there anything you've been wondering or worrying about that you haven't told me?"

When Pedro's father asked his ten-year-old son this question, Pedro hung his head and mumbled, "Nothing, really."

Pedro's father sat silently looking at his son for a moment. Then he said quietly, "I really want to know."

"Did you ever get scared for dumb reasons when you were my age?" Pedro asked.

"Of course I did," his father said. "I loved to swim, but I was afraid of wading even in shallow water if it was too murky to see what was in there."

"Well, I keep waking up in the middle of the night afraid that the Green Avenger is going to burst through the wall into my room!" Pedro mumbled, "and then I can't get back to sleep."

"Is it possible that the big poster of the Green Avenger on the wall over your bed might have anything to do with that?" his father wondered, resisting the temptation to laugh or to scold.

"Maybe," Pedro grinned a bit sheepishly. "But actually, I think my poster looks cool."

"So what do you want to do?" his father asked very neutrally, reminding himself not to jump in but to wait for Pedro to come up with his own solutions.

Children will benefit most from being listened to with interest and without judgment, with an acceptance that all of their thoughts and feelings are okay.

*Ask, "Is there **anything** you've been wondering or worrying about that you haven't told me?"*

"Well, I guess I can always move it or take it down. But I want to leave the poster where it is for now," Pedro decided. "I think maybe now that I've told you, the problem will go away."

Give Kids the Right to Feel Bad

In her thought-provoking book *The Right to Feel Bad*, author Lesley Hazleton describes how our society has made such a huge priority of the right to feel good that we need to reclaim our right to feel bad. "Feeling good is no longer simply a right but a social and personal duty. We have become convinced that if we do not feel good, we are at fault, weak, ill, dysfunctional, or wrong."[7]

We want so much for our children to be happy that we can have a hard time accepting their feelings of fear, anger, or sadness.

For most of us, accepting children's feelings when they are happy is easy. The problem is that we want so much for our children to be happy that we can have a hard time accepting their feelings of fear, anger, or sadness. In an effort to protect children from unhappiness, well-meaning adults often say things like, "Oh, you don't need to feel like that!" Or, "Come on, cheer up! It's really not that bad." We repeat sayings like, "Laugh and the world laughs with you. Cry and you cry alone."

Unfortunately, statements like these can cause children to believe that their unhappy or upset feelings are unacceptable. This can leave a child feeling terribly alone. Children often try to protect their adults by hiding their problems. Parents have told me stories of children who developed ulcers or depression because they were trying so hard to pretend to be happy. Although we want to teach young people how to manage their feelings, we also want them to accept that it's normal for anyone of any age to get upset and lose control. If only we could accept this truth for ourselves and the people around us, a lot of miserable blame and shame could be prevented, leaving more room in our lives for joy. Feeling unhappy is bad enough. Feeling ashamed and embarrassed about an upsetting experience just makes things worse.

The following stories show how adult reactions can make a huge difference in whether a child will continue to be overwhelmed by upset feelings or will learn to manage them.

The Jumping Dog Story. When a large, overly friendly dog jumped on five-year-old Molly, she fell down sobbing. Molly's mother said matter-of-factly, "You were playing and that big dog jumped on you. Then you fell down and cried."

"I peed a little in my pants," Molly said, sobbing harder.

"It's normal to pee a little when you're startled," Molly's mother said comfortingly. "It happens to me too. But you did a good job of stopping the pee so more didn't come out. And you did a good job of getting up and coming to me for help. I'm proud of you." Molly's mother accepted her daughter's right to cry, normalized what had happened, and pointed out what Molly had done well.

The Fear of the Dark Story. In one workshop, a father said, "I want my daughter to learn how to stop being such a baby."

"What do you mean?" I asked, suppressing my own urge to scold him.

"She is afraid of everything," the father grumbled. "At night, she will never let me turn off the light because the dark makes her fearful. But, with the light on, she has trouble falling asleep."

"Why don't you give her a flashlight?" I suggested. "That way she will have control over whether it is dark or not. Giving your daughter a way to manage her fear of the dark instead of feeling ashamed of it can help her develop a sense of confidence." The father looked startled and then thoughtful. Later I heard from his wife that the flashlight worked perfectly.

The Don't Feel That Way Story. In another workshop, a mother complained that her son was always angry. "I keep telling him not to feel that way," she worried. "But it just seems to make him angrier. He will lash out and hit people or break things."

Again, I resisted the urge to scold the mother, and instead reflected that she had the right to her feelings, too. "Do other people ever tell you that you are supposed to feel or not feel a certain way?" I asked.

The mother laughed. "Yes," she admitted, "and I hate it!"

"Try telling your son that he has the right to feel angry or any way he wants," I suggested. "Give him time to vent without trying to fix anything. Explain that his job is to learn how to stay in charge of his body and his words – even when he is very angry. Help him notice the signals he gets when he first starts to get angry, before he loses control. Instead of pretending that he isn't angry until he explodes, make a safety plan with your son for ways he can get rid of his anger without hitting or breaking things. Maybe you can agree on safe outlets for his feelings like hitting a sofa cushion or throwing a ball outside."

The Lost My Smile Story. Many worried parents have asked, "What if my child is too sensitive? How can I help a child who seems to experience everything as a catastrophe?"

I remember being a child like that. My parents used to sigh, "Why do you have to be so dramatic?" According to my parents, one day when I was about three, I suddenly started wailing in despair. They came running to see me sobbing in front of the mirror in my room. They couldn't figure out what had happened to hurt me so badly.

"What is it?" they begged. "I have lost my smile!" I sobbed. I had been looking at myself in the mirror and then suddenly noticed that my smile was missing. I looked desperately at myself, trying to figure out where my smile had gone. Of course, the more I worried, the more my smile disappeared.

The labels "too sensitive" and "too emotional" framed my self-image for much of my life. For both my parents and me, how I wish that the books of Elaine N. Aron, Ph.D., *The Highly Sensitive Person* and *The Highly Sensitive Child*, had already been written![8] Aron explains that some of us have our

Listen to children's fears and help them to find solutions

emotional volume turned up higher than other people, causing us to feel some things more deeply than others. This quality brings great gifts – and great challenges. The goal is not to have highly sensitive people avoid being out in the real world, but to help us have a better understanding of how to manage our feelings so that we are not so easily overwhelmed.

Although we need to keep our perspective in balance by accepting the right to feel bad, people also have the right to feel good. If children or adults are constantly miserable or can't stop destructive behavior, therapy can make a huge difference in improving the quality of their lives. Our health and well-being are well worth the investment of time and resources to get the professional help we need.

Help Children Be Safe in Their Imaginations

A vivid imagination is both a blessing and a curse. As a child, I would lie awake worrying about monsters coming to eat me up. When I couldn't stand the fear anymore, I used to run to my little sister Elaine's bedroom for protection. Fortunately, the monsters wouldn't get Elaine since she had figured out how not to believe in them.

As a teenager, I once read Fredrick Brown's science fiction book *The Mind Thing* about a creature from outer space that took over people's minds when they fell asleep.[9] Unfortunately, I became too scared to fall asleep and too embarrassed to tell my parents. I suffered through three terrible nights before getting desperate enough to ask for their help.

Learning to be safe in your imagination is a useful skill for people at any age. We can remind children that we want them to talk with us any time they can't stop worrying about something. We can tell kids, "You can make yourself feel more and more scared by imagining horrible dangers where nothing you can do will make you safe. But, it's safer to ask yourself to imagine how to stop the problem before anything bad happens at all. You can imagine how to use what you already know to get out of that situation safely."

The perspective of others can make a big difference. In one class, eight-year-old Ahmed said, "What if I had no safe place I could get to?" His friend asked, "Where would that be?" Ahmed thought a bit and said, "On the moon maybe?" In an indignant voice, Ahmed's friend replied, "And how likely is that?!"

Sometimes children ask for details that are likely to create pictures in their minds that are upsetting rather than helpful. Curious children can be persistent in asking difficult questions like, "What exactly would a bad guy do to hurt you or make you feel bad?"

Suppose you are concerned that a child might already have heard something awful or had a bad experience. Your job is to stay calm and ask supportive questions such as, "What do you think?" Or, "Is there something that you want to tell me?"

If a child is just curious, you can say, "I don't want to talk about the bad things that might happen but probably won't. Doing this just makes us feel scared, and I'd rather talk about how you can keep yourself safe most of the time."

Practicing solutions to upsetting worries about safety can help to reduce anxiety. "After a man walked into a house in our neighborhood and assaulted a little girl in her bedroom, our six-year-old son Ben was so full of fear that he didn't want to sleep in his own room," Ben's father said. "So, we showed him how the locks worked on our doors and windows and let him help us lock up at night. Ben was still worried. We made a game of pretending he was scared so that he could practice yelling from his room and having us come running. That really worked!"

Like adults, children sometimes want guarantees. They will ask worried questions like "What if there are too many bad guys for me to get away?" Or, "What if somebody starts shooting with a big gun?" The underlying question really is, "What if a safety problem is too big for me and I cannot get away?"

You can tell children (and yourself), "The People Safety skills we are learning can work in most situations. Anyone, no matter how careful, no matter how strong, can think of a situation where nothing works. It's just like knowing how to be safe on the street. Even if you do everything right, a drunk driver could drive up onto the sidewalk and hit you. But that almost never happens. You can learn how to keep yourself safe most of the time. Try to use your imagination to think about how you can take charge of your safety instead of imagining yourself being helpless."

Teaching children how to deal with scary dreams can make a huge difference in the quality of their lives. At age eight, Luca woke up crying in the middle of the night. Her stepmother came running to ask what was the matter. "I had a scary dream!" Luca wailed. "I'm afraid to go back to sleep. There were blue boars bursting into my bedroom. They came up the stairs and through the windows. I was afraid they were going to get me."

Her stepmother reassured Luca and explained, "You can learn how to bring your dreams under your control. You can dream whatever you want in your dreams. You can tell yourself to wake up or to turn the dream into something else."

Luca slept peacefully for the rest of the night. In the morning, she said cheerfully, "I dreamed of the boars again. But this time, I put them into blue balloons, and they all floated away!"

Encourage Children to Choose Empowering Beliefs

Empowering beliefs can protect us from harm and help us to make the most out of our lives. In a garden, we know better than to water the plants that we do not want to see grow. And, in the garden of our relationships with people, we have to be careful not to shower the negative beliefs of others with the water of our attention, because our attention can cause these negative beliefs to grow. In both plant gardens and people gardens, we are likely to get the best results if we can water what we do want to see grow - roses, apples, and empowering beliefs.

Try to imagine yourself taking charge of your safety instead of imagining yourself being helpless.

We can "water what we want to see grow" by focusing our attention on how children are making progress in learning much more than on what they might be doing wrong.

Beliefs that help empower people of any age to take charge of their emotional and physical safety are:

• I am powerful.
• I am competent.
• I am valuable.

With children, we can reinforce these empowering beliefs by giving them real-life experiences that help build these beliefs and by protecting them from destructive experiences that diminish them. As much as possible, we want to set situations up so that children can be successful and to focus our attention on how they are making progress in learning much more than on what they might be doing wrong.

Show children how important they are to you by making time to listen to them, even when you are very busy, distracted, or upset. Show children your trust in their competence by giving them opportunities to make choices, to learn from their mistakes, and to persevere in the face of initial failure. Show children your belief in their ability to be powerful by finding many different kinds of activities that they can be good at – and doing them together.

With younger children, you can encourage positive beliefs very directly. Give children activities that are interesting and easy for them to be successful at doing. Point out the positive things that you notice with simple statements and supportive questions. "Did you see how you used your strong legs to get all the way up here? Did you see how hard you worked to figure out that puzzle?" You can make up stories together in which the children are the heroes in solving various predicaments. You can use their stuffed animals to tell them how terrific they are, as an independent, third-party opinion.

As children get older, your opinion is still important, but they need to be part of the thinking process. Tell young people truthfully that they have the right to believe whatever they want, but that you have learned that people are better off if they can choose positive beliefs instead of negative ones. For all of us, knowing how to choose beliefs that help us instead of hurt us is empowering. Brainstorm with kids to get different ideas for what beliefs are helpful or hurtful, and how they can decide what they are going to believe.

Ask supportive questions to highlight the results of kid's actions such as, "Did you see how quickly we could get out the door when you helped me to get ready for the beach?" Or, "Did you see how happy our neighbor was when you brought her the flowers?"

Practicing self-protection skills successfully is another effective way to build empowering beliefs. "I didn't know I could be so strong!" children will often say after a class. Or, "Now I don't have to worry. If something happens, I will know what to do." Or, "I learned that it can take more courage to walk away from a fight than to get into fight."

Belief in themselves based on positive experiences can serve children well for a very long time. Once, I was walking down the street near my home. A young woman I didn't recognize pulled her car up next to me. "You're Irene from Kidpower, right?" she called out.

"Yes." I said, feeling forgetful because I had no idea who she was.

"When I was a little girl," this twenty-year-old woman announced, "you were my teacher. Kidpower has saved me from trouble lots of times. It was an *awesome* class!"

As my former student drove off, I reflected that even though Kidpower workshops last only a few short hours, this young woman had remembered what she had learned for over ten years because learning how to protect herself had helped her to believe in her own power.

When something goes wrong, children's belief in their power, value, and capability can help them to see options that might even save their lives. In one highly publicized case, an eight year little girl who had been abducted escaped when the kidnapper stopped at a gas station. As soon as he left the car, the girl found a key and unlocked the handcuff holding her to the seat. She jumped out of the car and ran to a nearby truck driver to get help. Even though she had been traumatized, this child was able to take advantage of an opportunity to escape because she thought she could. Instead of believing she was helpless, she was able to see her chance and act on it quickly.[10]

Protect Kids From Developing Negative Beliefs

Negative beliefs that can undermine people's ability to act powerfully, believe in themselves, and make safe choices are:

- I am weak because _____ (I'm a girl; I'm small; I hate conflict; I have a disability.)
- I am bad at doing things because_____ (I make mistakes; I have a hard time learning; I have problems.)
- I am worth less than others because _____(My family has problems; my family doesn't care about me; my body doesn't look as nice or work as well as other people's bodies; I come from a poor neighborhood; my race, religion, or sexual orientation or identity is different from most of the people around me.)
- I have to prove I'm tough because _____(I'm a guy; I'm short; someone will hurt me if I don't.)
- People don't like me because _____ (I am different; they are mean; there's something wrong with me.)
- Other people are not worthy of respect because _____ (they are different, they don't think the same way I do, they have problems, someone told me they were.)

Even when kids have to deal with upsetting experiences, we can help them understand the difference between facts and unfair judgments, not just for themselves, but for others as well. For younger children, you might act this out with their toys. For older children, you might discuss examples from movies or books. You might adapt stories from your own childhood to be relevant to children, telling them about times when you realized that you were choosing negative beliefs and how you changed these for yourself.

This young woman had remembered what she had learned for over ten years because learning how to protect herself had helped her to believe in her own power.

Kids often feel bad about themselves or others because of what their adults say. Do your best to avoid attacking children's character by teasing, labeling, or trivializing their interests and relationships. If you lose your temper and say something unfair or unkind, do not blame either your children or yourself. Children identify with their important adults, and you do not want to model acting as if something terrible has happened because you happened to shout or say something insulting. You can simply apologize for what you said, and restate your concern in a calm, respectful way.

Express appreciation to the people around your children who model caring, respectful behavior. Set boundaries with people who do not act caring and respectful, so that children see you making this a priority.

Change Negative Labels to Positive Ones

Labels that allow children to believe that they are weak, helpless, dumb, or useless are destructive to their emotional safety. Changing negative labels to positive ones can be a powerful tool for turning around these negative beliefs. A classic example of this technique comes from the martial arts. Students sometimes get frustrated and say, "I'm a failure!" Their teachers tell them to say instead, "I have not yet succeeded."

Sometimes simply looking at a problem from another point of view can make it better. In one workshop, a teacher of developmentally delayed children asked me, "One of my students says kids call her, 'The ... slowest ... ant ... in ... school.' What positive label can she give herself to take the place of that?" "Well," I suggested, "She might say, 'When ... you ... go ... slow ... , you ... see ... a lot!"

Later, the teacher called me to say that her student beamed and started laughing with this answer. She kept saying over and over, "When ... you ... go ... slow ... , you ... see ... a lot! " Then this girl did some creative thinking of her own, and said, "When ... you ... go ... too ... fast ... , you ... can ... miss ... everything!" (This is a truth that, in our hectic lives, all of us would do well to remember!)

Here are some examples about how to turn negative labels into positive alternatives:

Negative Label:	Timid and shy child
Positive Alternative:	Aware and brave child (Doing what you are afraid of takes courage!)
Negative Label:	Overprotective mom
Positive Alternative:	Protective adult (Just doing my job, thank you!)
Negative Label:	Too sensitive
Positive Alternative:	Sensitive and thoughtful
Negative Label:	Careless
Positive Alternative:	Carefree
Negative Label:	Paranoid
Positive Alternative:	Concerned

Negative Label: Bad
Positive Alternative: Curious and experimenting with boundaries

Negative Label: Lazy
Positive Alternative: Relaxed

Make a game with children of noticing labels that imply negative judgments. You will both find plenty of examples in the media and in daily life. Work together to find ways to describe the behavior or attitude in a positive way instead of a negative one. People sometimes ask, "But what if the negative label is about something that is actually true that I want to change?" A positive answer might be, "Yes I know! And I'm working on it!"

Help Children Understand and Overcome Challenges to Their Confidence

Some lucky people seem to feel confident naturally most of the time, but I am not one of them. When I was growing up, I struggled to learn physical things. I could walk or swim forever, but I could not seem to work out the mechanics of throwing, catching, or hitting a ball, or moving my body to run or swim quickly.

Throughout my childhood, I was always the last person chosen to be on a team during my physical education classes. When a group of kids was stuck with me, they all groaned. On the swim team, I was last in every single race. Instead of being fun, sports were a misery to me.

These experiences left me believing that I was clumsy and terribly slow at learning to do physical things. I wish my teachers and parents had known how to recognize a physically dyslexic child who learned kinesthetically rather than by watching or by being told what to do. I believed I was slow and clumsy for forty-five years. Finally, I discovered that I can learn quickly if someone breaks a skill into very small steps and touches me to move my body through the motions a few times.

Many people have lost confidence in themselves in other ways – such as dealing with social situations, math, or language – and often what they need is to discover techniques for learning that work well for them.

Children also lose their confidence and feel miserable because of shame about how they look, how they talk, how they feel, how they act, who their family is, how they dress, or how they learn. Adults can help children by naming characteristics that cause them to feel bad about themselves, acknowledging their feelings, and finding ways to manage challenges to their confidence.

To a child who gets hurt feelings very easily, you might say, "You care a whole lot about what people think. Because you care so much, you are a kind person. At the same time, you don't want someone else's bad mood to ruin your day. Let's find ways for you to keep feeling good about yourself and having fun even when other people are grumpy."

To a child who explodes easily and has a reputation for being a troublemaker, you might say, "You have a lot of strength in how you express yourself. You have the right to feel any way you want, and you can learn how to show your feelings in ways that are safe for everyone. Let's find ways to help you to stay in charge of what you say and do – even when you feel really upset."

To a child who struggles to learn because of dyslexia or some other learning disability, you might say, "You have your own way of learning. It can be frustrating when people don't teach the way you learn. But everybody has something that is harder for them to do than other people – we just might not see what it is. Let's find ways of learning that will work well for you."

To a child who gets teased or rejected for being different in some way, you might say, "I feel sad when people say unkind things or leave you out because of (your freckles, hair, height, accent, the way you run, the fact that you sometimes cry, your being home-schooled, etc. It is wrong for them to behave this way. I think you are brave to tell me about it. Let's find ways to help you to speak up for yourself and to get help when you need it. People can learn to enjoy differences instead of being bothered by them."

My sister Elaine, who fended off the childhood monsters for me by not believing in them, says that most qualities are gifts when you are in charge of them, and problems when they are in charge of you. Difficulties are challenges that make life harder and are often unfair – but that can lead to treasure as well as to trouble.

Being Tricked, Tested, or Scared Does NOT Make Kids Safer – Practice Does!

A few years ago, I got a call from a TV station that had set up a test for children. "We had an off-duty police officer pretend that he had lost his dog," the reporter told me, "and then we filmed him approaching children in the park. Most of the children went with him all the way to his car. But one little girl grabbed her friends and pulled them with her as she ran to get help from their parents who were across the park. When we asked her parents why their daughter had behaved so differently from the other children, they said that it was because of a program called Kidpower."

Frankly, I was glad that Kidpower had been so helpful but appalled at the messages this approach was giving the children. The TV program even showed the children watching the video of themselves making mistakes while their anxious parents lectured them, demanding to know why they had gone with a stranger.

Well-meaning parents were trying to make themselves feel better, but in the process, they were publicly shaming their children. I believe that it undermines trust for children to be tested in such a sneaky way. Children need to feel that their adults are allies who are helping them to be successful, not setting up tests behind their backs for them to fail.

Success-based practice is a safer way, both emotionally and physically, to learn most skills. When I was growing up, children were usually taught to swim by being dunked into the deep end of the pool, getting water up their noses, and struggling to the surface, gasping for air. Children who cried

"Most qualities are gifts when you are in charge of them, and problems when they are in charge of you."
Elaine Regelson

Children need to feel that their adults are allies who are helping them to be successful, not setting up tests behind their backs for them to fail.

were told not to act like babies. As a result, many children ended up being terrified of the water, even if they learned to swim.

Children are far more likely to enjoy swimming if they can learn in a step-by-step way guided by a supportive adult. Learning to swim can be fun if you start in the shallow end, play by blowing bubbles, be adventurous by dunking your head, sneeze when water gets up your nose, and move your arms and legs with help until you understand how to stay afloat.

The same concept is true with learning how to be safe with people. We have found in our workshops that children learn much more quickly from being successful than they do from failing. This is why we coach children through practices calmly rather than letting them struggle or putting scary ideas in their heads.

Success-based practice is a safer way, both emotionally and physically, to learn most skills.

Children do not become safer when their adults tell them, "If you let a stranger get too close, this person could take you away and we will never see you again." They just get scared. Children also do not become safer by being scolded for every mistake they make. Instead, adults can act as coaches, pausing and guiding a child who forgets what to do. "You did a good job of standing up. Let's practice again. This time, give yourself lots of space and move away quickly!"

Show Kids That We Do NOT Have to Be Perfect to Be GREAT

In her book *The Gifts of Imperfection*, social scientist Dr. Brené Brown, describes how her research on shame and vulnerability led her to identify the attributes of what she calls "whole-heartedness". She tells the story of her personal journey in discovering how to engage with life from a place of worthiness. Accepting imperfection is an important part of letting go of shame.[11]

Children often start to feel shame about themselves when they make mistakes. They think making mistakes or being wrong means that they are bad people. They might start beating up on themselves or become trapped into pretending that nothing went wrong so that they keep making the same mistake over and over again. One of the most important lessons we can teach children is that nobody is perfect and that mistakes mean that we are learning, not that we are failing.

I see parents agonizing when they make mistakes. "Trisha kept ignoring me when it was time to go," Trisha's mother mourned. "And then she rolled a ball down the stairs and it hit her brother in the face. I just lost it and started screaming at her. I feel like a monster."

One of the most important lessons we can teach children is that mistakes mean that we are learning, not that we are failing.

"Not being perfect does not make you a bad mom," I reassured Trisha's mother. "In fact, children need to see that their adults can get upset and then calm down. If you felt like you said or did something disrespectful, this is a great opportunity to model noticing a mistake and then apologizing for it. Be sure you apologize without putting yourself down, because you also want to model being sorry without feeling terrible about yourself."

The shame that comes from hiding mistakes can damage a child's joy in

Nobody's perfect!

Accepting mistakes as normal helps children feel better about themselves and makes them more likely to seek help – especially if they have a safety problem, or know they did something they shouldn't have.

life. In my own childhood, I can remember thinking that I was the only person in the whole world who forgot what she was supposed to do or who accidentally broke things. I started to be afraid that something was horribly wrong with me. I was hugely relieved when I finally figured out that other people sometimes forgot or had accidents.

When adults model being okay with mistakes, their children have an opportunity to learn how to be okay with not being perfect. Point out your own mistakes without sounding upset about them. Show acceptance of your own imperfections by cheerfully saying things like, "I just made a mistake and went the wrong way again! Oh well, I guess we're going to take the scenic route home!"

When a child gets upset about making a mistake in a workshop, I often say, "We all make mistakes. Has anybody noticed any mistakes I have made today?" My students will gleefully point out every one of the times I said something confusing or got something mixed up.

Accepting mistakes as normal helps children feel better about themselves and makes them more likely to seek help – especially if they have a safety problem, or know they did something they shouldn't have.

Teach Children to Persist Instead of Giving Up

Although we can make learning People Safety skills easy for children, actually using these skills out in the real world is often frustrating and difficult. For example, setting a boundary in the face of peer disapproval can be uncomfortable, and persisting in getting help when no one seems to be listening can be very hard work. In order for children to trust in their personal power, they need to know how to keep going even when they feel upset, discouraged, unhappy, embarrassed, or tired.

Adults can support the development of persistence in the following ways:

- Give children opportunities to take on challenges where they can be successful;
- Offer guidance rather than taking over for them when children ask for help;
- Acknowledge unhappy feelings without letting children give up on themselves;
- Break a challenge into smaller steps when children get stuck; and,
- Motivate children to keep going even when they don't feel like it.

Physical activities can help build confidence in the ability to keep going. Some people do this through sports or dance. When my own kids were young, I would do it through hikes and camping trips with our family, our Girl Scout troop, and our Campfire Boy's group. My theory was that, no matter what they said, if the children had energy enough to run around, yell, or splash in streams once we sat down during a hike, they had energy enough to keep on going. I encouraged the children hiking with me not to complain and did my best to reward cheerful perseverance. Their sense of accomplishment at the end of the trail always made whatever struggles we had along the way worth the work.

"But I'm too tired! I can't!" the children often complained. "It's too far!" "I understand," I would say cheerfully. "Just keep putting one foot in front of the other and you'll make it to the top. I promise." Sometimes our hikes took longer and included a bit of moaning and groaning, but we always got there. I offered motivators to help make the hike more interesting and fun. Conversation. Undivided attention. Treats for the trail. Stories. Songs.

When children were really resistant, I did my best to support them in being successful. To one young Girl Scout who was dramatically complaining of exhaustion, I explained, "I love you too much to let you give up!" For two miles, I held this girl's sweaty hand firmly in my own to keep her from falling, since she insisted on staggering to show both of us (and everybody watching) how tired she was. When we got to the part of the trail that involved climbing over rocks with handholds, this girl got interested and excitedly joined her friends.

When children experience the rewards of overcoming discomfort and discouragement, they are more likely to make the effort necessary to keep going in other situations. Learning how to persist is a skill that can serve children well, not only in being safe with people, but in all areas of their lives.

Give Kids Ways to Make a Difference

Children are safer both emotionally and physically when they know that what they say and do matters. We can help build that belief by giving them chances to make a positive difference in their own lives and in the world around them.

Make time to volunteer in a way that works in your life. Take an active part in different communities such as your family, school, youth group, faith, or neighborhood. Give a portion of your earnings to charity. No matter how busy or poor you are, trust that every little bit of your time and money adds up. Tell children why you are giving away your time and money. Encourage children to give to those who have less than they do or to help someone who is going through a hard time.

One Saturday long ago, I took my two young kids and a couple of their friends to an educational presentation at the Santa Cruz City Museum where we learned how dangerous plastic bags are to wildlife.

Next, we visited the bird sanctuary at Neary's Lagoon Park. We were horrified to see an incredible mess of trash, especially plastic bags, that had been left by people who had been bringing stale bread to feed the ducks and geese. We went home and brought back big garbage bags to pick up the trash. These four small children filled about eight large bags of trash, working carefully for hours to untangle them from the bushes by the water. Unfortunately, we had to haul the bags quite a long way to get to a trash can. We decided that having an easier way to dispose of garbage would make people less likely to litter.

The children asked me how to get someone to help the ducks. I explained that the grownups in charge of the city park were the members of the city council, and they would be the right people to tell about the problem. Even

It's hard work to get to the top of a mountain - but the view is worth it!

Children are safer both emotionally and physically when they know that what they say and do matters.

Speak Up Power Safety Sign

though they were tired from their cleanup work, my children and their friends sat around our dining room table with crayons and paper. They each drew pictures of the pond with little stories about birds choking on plastic bags and muttering things like, "Help!"

I sent their colorful, imaginative drawings and their messages to the city council, where we eventually learned they were posted on the wall for several months. The mayor wrote back a nice letter that we posted on our refrigerator for a couple of years.

A few months later, when we visited the park again, two new trash cans had appeared next to the pond, and people had clearly been using them. The kids were amazed and delighted that their cleanup project and their drawings had helped save the ducks. That day, each of those kids knew for sure that they had done something really important!

PART TWO

Kidpower Tools for Teaching "People Safety"

Chapter Four

Five Key Self-Protection Strategies for Preventing Trouble

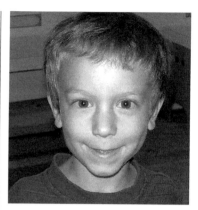

Awareness can prevent many kinds of emergencies

Self-protection means having the tools to prevent most trouble before it starts. Key strategies that can protect children and their adults from many dangers include knowing how to:

1. Use your awareness;
2. Act calm, aware, and confident, no matter how you feel inside;
3. Move out of reach;
4. Pay attention to your intuition; and
5. Be persistent in getting help from busy adults.

Strategy #1: Use Your Awareness

Using your awareness means paying attention to the information provided by all of your senses and noticing changes. Your sight, your hearing, and even your senses of smell, taste, and touch can all help you to keep track of what is happening around you.

Remembering to use your awareness can prevent many kinds of emergencies. Our family often went camping in Sequoia National Park, taking long hikes far into the woods and up into the mountains. On one hike, Chantal, then age nine, pointed to a thin trickle of smoke and asked, "What's that smoke doing there?"

Our family walked off the trail to discover a spot where people had dumped pine needles to bury an illegal campfire. Instead of going out, smoldering embers were eating a large hole in the dry pine needles on the forest floor. With no water nearby, we tried to stamp out the sparks and coals. Unfortunately, the area had gotten so large that just a few gusts of wind could have created a full-blown forest fire.

The four of us raced all the way back to the ranger station to make a report. "Our fire fighting crews have tried to figure out where that smoke was coming from for the last three days," the park ranger marveled. "But it took the sharp eyes of a nine-year-old girl to find it for us."

Noticing what is around you can also prevent accidents. "One of my students, Ellis, was very accident-prone," a teacher told us. "He seemed to walk around in a mental fog. He'd get into all kinds of trouble, tripping over his own feet, bumping into other students, tipping his chair over, and falling off of the climbing structure. Finally, I realized that figuring out how to help Ellis to stay present was going to work better than constantly telling him to be careful. We made a plan to have him describe what he was noticing each time we got ready to move from one place to another."

The teacher smiled and added, "At first it was like pulling teeth, but I kept insisting that Ellis tell me what he saw, heard, smelled, felt, and tasted, and how he thought he could keep himself safe. Soon, he was much more aware of what was going on around him and of what he was doing with his body. He still had accidents sometimes, but far less often."

Looking around to stay aware of your whole environment can help everyone to be safer. Sometimes in a workshop, I tell students to imagine that I am driving a car. I stare forward as I walk forward, my hands clutched to an imaginary steering wheel, looking neither right nor left. Everyone gets the picture that my looking only forward makes me unable to notice what other cars are doing.

Next, I stare to one side as I "drive" forward, telling my students to imagine that I am too interested in what people in another car are doing. Obviously, not looking where I am going would quickly cause a crash.

Both children and adults are safest if we can stay present and alert to the warning signs of potential danger around us.

Questions and Answers to Help Children to Develop More Understanding About Using Their Awareness

Question: How can your eyes help you protect yourself?
Answer: My eyes can help me see if a car is coming so I can get out of the way.

Question: How can your ears help you stay safe?
Answer: My ears can help me hear if someone is shouting to warn me that a ball is about to hit me.

Question: How can your nose protect you?
Answer: My nose can help me smell if something is burning so I get an adult to help me.

Question: How can tasting something protect you?
Answer: My taste can help me tell if food has gone bad and might make me sick.

Question: How can paying attention to your touch help you be safe?
Answer: My touch can warn me if something is too hot or too sharp.

Question: How can your balance help you to keep from getting hurt?
Answer: I can notice if I am about to fall and hold on to something.

Question: Why is the personal space around you important to your safety?
Answer: Knowing how much space I have between myself and other people or things can keep me from bumping into them.

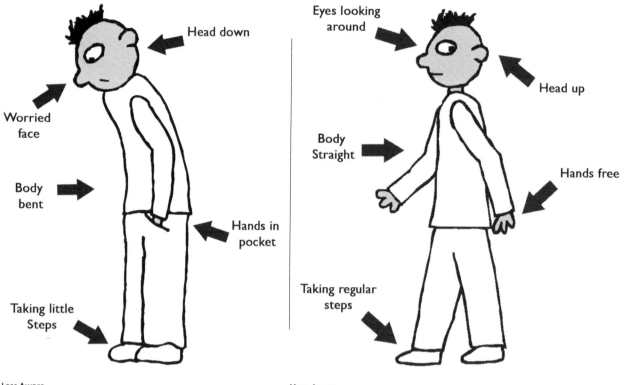

Less Aware

More Aware

Strategy # 2: Act Calm, Aware, and Confident, No Matter How You Feel Inside

One of the most important self-protection lessons is to recognize that we can feel one way and act a different way. When faced with an embarrassing or threatening situation, some people feel like shrinking until they disappear. For others, being uncomfortable or scared makes them feel so angry that they might be tempted to start yelling and acting in a way that increases the likelihood of conflict. Both responses are normal.

Children have the right to their own personalities and the right to all of their feelings, including being timid or mad. They can learn that, no matter how they feel inside, handling possible problems is easier if they pretend to be calm and act as if they believe in themselves. Later, they can talk with an adult they trust about how they really felt.

People who seem calm, aware, and confident are less likely to be picked on by someone who might want to hurt or bother them.

In a Kidpower workshop, our instructor Timothy shows how this works by pointing to a couple of grinning students and saying, "Suppose I'm walking down the street, and I think *you* guys are *trouble*! Suppose that I'm so worried that I try to pretend that you're not there."

Timothy hunches his body and turns his face away dramatically and says, "Suppose that I wish that, if I can't see you, you won't be able to see

One of the most important self-protection lessons is to recognize that we can feel one way and act a different way.

me. Have any of you ever used the Wishing Technique to pretend that a problem wasn't there when someone made you nervous? Let's try this out."

Timothy closes his eyes in front of all the watching students and asks, "Now, I can't see *you*. Can you still see *me*?"

"Yes!" the children and their adults say, usually giggling.

Next, Timothy struts around the room, glaring at the students he's identified as "trouble", and says in a challenging voice, "Suppose I decide to act tough so you trouble-makers won't bother me? When I stare you down, does it look as if I want to fight? Do you think my acting tough might start a fight because someone is afraid that I'm the one who is trouble?"

"Most of the time," Timothy explains, "People will bother you less and listen to you more if you act calm, aware, and confident, no matter HOW you feel inside. Let me try to act calm, aware, and confident. If I get it wrong, you can tell me how to fix it."

Timothy then playfully bends over and staggers across the floor with tiny steps. His face is scrunched up. His hands are in his pockets. His head is facing down.

Students call out directions, developing their own understanding of what awareness looks like from the outside, "Stand up straight! Get your shoulders down. Take bigger steps! No, not that big! Have a regular face! Get your hands out of your pockets. Look around!"

As he responds to the students' suggestions, Timothy ends up walking across the floor with brisk steps, glancing around the room at our students with a friendly expression. "Does this look better?" he asks.

Sometimes adults object, saying, "But I live in the city. I've learned to walk quickly looking neither to the right nor the left. If I pay attention to anybody, I'm giving that person an opening to come after me."
We show the difference between staring at people in a way that is engaging or aggressive and using "soft eyes" by glancing towards others without making eye contact. The message we want to communicate on a public street is, "I know you are there. I am not trying to get involved with you or bother you. I am not afraid of you. I just know you are there."

During one training session for teachers in a school located in a neighborhood with a lot of crime, I had the teachers simply walk across the floor of the auditorium with awareness, calm, and confidence.

They were very doubtful at the time, but a week later, one of the teachers called to tell me this story. "Late yesterday afternoon after everyone else had left, I was walking to my car. A gang of rowdy teenage boys hanging around the parking lot started calling out to me. Suddenly, I realized that my head was down. I picked up my head the way we'd practiced in class and looked in a friendly way right towards them. I realized that I knew a couple of them from a few years ago and said, 'Hello' as I walked past. Not

*People will bother you less and listen to you more if you act calm, aware, and confident, no matter **how** you feel inside.*

The Tiger Story

only did the boys stop harassing me, but lifting my head instead of cringing changed completely how I felt inside."

Having a common language with children when you are in public together can be very useful, as Melia's mother found out. "Early one sunny morning," she said, "my eight-year-old daughter Melia and I were visiting the park. No one seemed to be around, until a homeless man who often sleeps there started to approach us, muttering in an angry tone.

"I turned my face away from him, pulling Melia with me. The man started to follow us. Melia pulled herself up straight. With her head held high, she smiled and waved at the man, who stopped instantly. Holding my hand, my daughter walked briskly away, whispering, 'Awareness, calm, and confidence, Mama! Remember?' I followed her example and the man stood still, watching us go."

Acting aware can work in nature too. While we were developing the Kidpower program, I found a section in the *Smithsonian Atlas of Wild Places* that described a study done with Bengal tigers.[1] We turned this study into our Kidpower Tiger Story. "In a park in India," we tell our students, "there was a forest preserve where Bengal tigers could live and be safe from hunters. This was great for the tigers, but hard on the workers because, about once a week, a tiger would sneak up on a worker and jump on him."

We joke to adults that, "That was creating an employment recruitment problem for the park!" We then continue to everyone, "The rangers studied tiger behavior and recommended that the workers wear masks of people's faces on the backs of their heads. During the study, not one worker wearing a mask was attacked because, in nature, tigers do not normally attack if someone is looking at them! The tigers would try to creep up on the workers and see their faces and then try to sneak behind them and see the masks and then go back into the jungle."

Practicing How to Act Calm, Aware, and Confident

1 Do this yourself as you tell the children, "Everybody, close your body down. Fold your arms. Put your heads down. Pretend to squish yourself into a small ball or to be very cold." Ask these leading questions and wait for the children's answers, "When your bodies are closed down like this, how do you feel? Can you easily see what is behind you? Do you feel very ready to move?"

Next, do this yourself as you tell the children, "Everybody, open your bodies up. Sit tall. Look around." Ask, "When your body is opened up, how do you feel? Do you think you might be more ready to move? If you turn your head, can you see if someone is sneaking up behind you?"

2 Walk across the room while you pretend to be scared, oblivious, or tough. Ask the children to tell you what you need to change in your body language, facial expression, or attitude to look calm, aware, and confident. If they get stuck, ask leading questions to prompt their thinking such as, "Should I keep frowning or make my face calm?" Or, "Should I keep my hands in my pockets or have them free at my sides?"

3 Tell the children to walk across the room and show you that they know how to act calm, aware, and confident. Stand to one side of them or behind them. Tell them to look back at you so they can see what you are doing. If need be, coach them so that they are successful as they go, "Take regular steps. Walk as if you are in a hurry to get somewhere. Make sure your hands are free. Stand up tall. Turn your head so you can look back at me."

Do something silly such as patting your head or tapping your foot. (Please do NOT do something threatening like trying to sneak up on them or acting creepy.) When the children get to the other side of the room, ask them to report what you did. If they didn't see you the first time, tell them that this was a trick question and ask them to do it again.

4 Play the Tiger Game to show the difference from an attacker's perspective between someone who acts aware and someone who doesn't.

Both you and the child (or two children) together will take turns pretending to be the Tiger and the Worker. The first time, pretend to be a Worker. Stand with your back to the child who is pretending to be the Tiger.

Act as if you are busy working so that the Tiger can sneak up behind you and "get you" by growling loudly and touching your shoulders gently with fingers extended to make tiger claws. You might need to kneel down as the Worker for a smaller child. (To prevent children from accidentally playing too rough, coach them before you do the practice on how to be very safe and gentle with their tiger claws.) When the Tiger gets you, give a little screech and put your hands to your face to show that you are scared.

The second time, still as the Worker, keep glancing around so that you can see when the Tiger is starting to creep up behind you. Turn around and put your hands up in front of you like a fence or a wall. Tell the Tiger to pretend to turn into a scared kitten and run away. Then switch roles.

Strategy # 3: Move Out of Reach

We tell children that there is a secret martial arts technique – the best technique of all time – that has been handed down from martial artist to martial artist through the ages. This technique is called "Target Denial." Target Denial means denying yourself as a target to someone who might bother or harm you – or, in other words, "Don't be there!"

Moving yourself out of the reach of a potential safety problem is one of the most effective ways of keeping yourself safe. Moving out of reach can prevent lots of emotional and physical safety problems such as:

• A kid who is always bumping into other kids and knocking them down;
• A friend or family member who is losing her or his temper,
• A wild animal;
• A car that is moving where you are walking or riding your bike;
• A fire in an unsafe place;
• A dog or person you don't know who is approaching you when you're on your own;
• An unfamiliar car driving up to where you are playing; and many more!

Children are safest if they move away immediately from a potential safety problem and go to adults who can help them. A tragic abduction took place in Southern California when a man drove his van up next to a couple of little girls playing on the sidewalk by an empty street in a quiet neighborhood while their grandmother was in the house. A police officer told me that if, as soon as the girls noticed the strange car, they had known to go quickly into the house to tell their grandmother, the man very likely would not have succeeded in kidnapping one of the girls.

At a company picnic with her family, a Kidpower student at age five was startled to see a drunken employee suddenly yelling at her father and threatening him. She pulled her little brother, aged three, out of reach and over to their mother until her father was able to calm the man down. The grateful father said later that having his daughter and son away from the confrontation helped him to manage the problem far more successfully.

Moving out of reach

Target Denial means denying yourself as a target to someone who might bother or harm you – or, in other words, "Don't be there!"

Practicing Moving Out of Reach

1   Tell a child to stand facing you and gently poke her on the shoulder. Say, "**Right now you are in reach because I can poke you. Move back slowly to get out of my reach. Split your awareness by glancing behind you so you don't trip on something and then by looking back at me to watch where my hand is so I won't poke you.**"

2   Very slowly, reach your poking finger towards the child while she backs away from you. If she stops too close, don't poke her. Instead, pause and coach her to keep moving. Keep one foot planted and keep reaching forward until your body is completely extended with your poking arm stretched out. Coach the child to move a couple more steps away from you to get even more space.

3   Tell the child to stand a little closer for the next part of the practice and say, "**I am going to reach towards you quickly, and you are going to step backwards quickly to move out of my reach. So, when I move**

quickly, you move quickly! Ready?" Lunge towards the child in a playful way, not a scary one. If the child does not move quickly back, calmly let her practice again.

4 Next, create a context that puts the moving-out-of-reach skill into a familiar situation. Stand in the middle of the room and tell the child, "Imagine that we are at school (or at the park) and I am a kid who is always pushing other kids. If you walk right next to me, what will happen?"

Gently push the child as she walks next to you and say, "That's right, if you come too close, you'll probably get pushed. Let's do it again. This time, use your awareness to notice me, the Pushy Kid. Instead of coming close to me, move out of reach by walking around me in a big circle. Be sure to look back when you get past me to make sure that I don't follow you."

5 As the child walks past you, reach towards her as if you are going to push her. Help her be successful by pausing if she gets stuck. Coach the child to move further away from you if she comes too close.

How to practice moving out of reach

Strategy # 4: Pay Attention to Your Intuition

In his ground-breaking book, *The Gift of Fear*, best-selling author and violence prediction expert Gavin de Becker describes the importance of using intuition to avoid danger.[2] He describes different "messengers of intuition" such as overwhelming fear, nagging feelings, or thoughts that just won't go away.

Intuition usually happens before you are conscious of a problem and is often ignored. A common belief is that, if a feeling can't be fully explained right away, it's probably not important. We discount intuition by telling ourselves, each other, and our children, "Don't be silly!" "You are such a worrywart!" "It's really nothing!" "You are over-anxious!"

When I was a young mother, I dropped my baby off at the home of the woman who had been taking care of her for several months. I had always felt good about leaving Chantal there, but when I got to work, I could not concentrate. I tried to talk myself out of it, but the feeling that I must go check on my child now would not go away. I tried calling a few times, but the telephone was busy. Scolding myself for being paranoid, I left my office in the middle of the morning.

As I drove up to the house, the babysitter was strapping Chantal into her car seat, even though they were not supposed to go anywhere without telling me. This woman had just gotten a frightening diagnosis from her doctor on the telephone and was going to the office to talk with him. She was so stressed that she hadn't realized that I would much rather stop work than have my baby be driven through the mountains over an hour away to a doctor's office with someone who was too upset to take care of her.

To this day, I don't know what signals let me know that the situation was not okay anymore, but my body registered a concern with my brain that my mind did not.

Children can learn to pay attention to their intuition by describing it in terms that are meaningful for them. With younger children, we say, "Have you ever had an 'uh oh!' feeling that told you that something is not right? You might notice this feeling as butterflies in your tummy, a shiver along your arms, or a big worry in your head. Your 'uh oh!' feelings are a way your body has of telling you to be careful and get help from your adults."

With older children and teens, we explain, "Intuition is a signal that you feel in your body that warns you of possible danger. Suppose that you want to do something or to please someone who wants you to do something, but you get an uncomfortable feeling or even a voice in your head that warns, 'This feels wrong!' Or, 'Bad idea!' Many people say they notice their intuition as a sinking feeling in their guts, their hair standing on end, or a thought in their minds that just will not go away."

We ask our students to tell us how they notice their intuition and then continue, "Instead of ignoring your intuition, pay attention. Ask yourself if you are sure that the situation is safe. Ask yourself what other choices you might have. Remember that your safety and the safety of others are more important than having fun or being cool. As soon as you can, talk these feelings over with adults you trust."

Part of what makes acting on your intuition difficult is that many people confuse intuition with anxiety. Personally, my intuition tends to speak up quietly but relentlessly. In contrast, my anxiety tends to speak up loudly and suddenly.

In my experience, intuition urges people to take a positive action of some kind – stopping and thinking about their safest choices, checking things out directly, leaving a dangerous situation, or asking for help. Intuition is based on subtle cues that our unconscious brain has picked up, direct observations, memory, and experience. It is our unconscious mind giving us information that our rational mind has missed.

Intuition usually happens before you are conscious of a problem and is often ignored.

Your "uh oh!" feelings are a way your body has of telling you to be careful and get help from your adults.

In contrast, anxiety tends to immobilize people and cause them to get stuck. Common causes of anxiety are fear of the unknown, resentment about being told what to do, worry about being disliked, triggers from past bad situations, and shyness. At any age, pushing through anxious feelings in the moment takes courage and determination, but doing so helps people to grow, learn, develop independence, and stay true to their values.

Whether young people are getting a signal from their intuition or struggling with anxiety, they will benefit from having adult help. If they are not sure in the moment, we want them to pay attention to their uncomfortable feelings and make choices that will increase their safety. If this choice stops them from doing something that they want to do or think they should do, they can get adult help in figuring out the best plan for handling that specific situation in the future.

Encouraging Children To Pay Attention to Their Intuition

1 Pay attention to your own intuition. When does it happen? How do you experience it? Are there times in the past when you noticed it? Did you act on it or not? The more you focus on your intuition, the better able you will be to recognize it as well as to describe how it works for you.

2 Talk about intuition in language that is appropriate for a child's age and understanding. Kidpower calls these "uh oh!" feelings for younger children and "Intuition Warnings" for older children and teens. Point out times when people seem to be having these feelings in your daily life, when reading stories, or when watching movies.

3 Ask children to describe how they notice their "uh oh!" feelings or "Intuition Warnings." Does this feel like a lump in your throat? Or, a sinking feeling in the bottom of your stomach? A shiver along your arms? A creepy feeling on the back of your neck? A thought that keeps coming back to bother you?

4 Praise children when they come to you to talk about their feelings. Act interested even if their concern seems silly to you. Remember that your positive response will give children the message that you think that their intuition is important. If children are feeling anxious, you want to know that, too, so that you can help them learn to manage their anxiety instead of being overwhelmed by it.

Strategy # 5: Be Persistent in Getting Help From Busy Adults

Many loving parents and other caring adults have asked us in frustration, "*Why* didn't she say anything?" Or, "*Why* did he wait so long to speak up if he was so upset?"

In order to increase our own understanding, we asked children and teens who had struggled with safety problems alone what had stopped them from getting help. Here are some typical answers:

• *I thought my teacher knew.* A five-year-old girl who was having her dress pulled up by boys during recess said, "It happened right in front of the teacher. I thought she knew."
• *I'm not supposed to interrupt.* A ten-year-old boy, who got hurt because his safety bar wasn't working at an amusement park, told his mother later,

"The ticket lady was very busy, and I know I'm not supposed to interrupt."

- *My teacher told me to fix it myself.* A seven-year-old boy, who eventually got too upset to go to school because kids were making fun of him during recess, explained, "I did tell the teacher, but he told me that I should work things out myself and not be so whiny."

- *Everybody said it was just a joke.* An eight-year-old girl, who was getting hurt by constant unkind jokes from an older cousin at a family gathering, sighed, "I tried to explain how I felt, but no one paid any attention. They said that my cousin was just kidding."

- *I wanted to be able to keep seeing my friend.* A nine-year-old girl, who was scared of the aggressive father of her best friend, said, "My parents were always so busy worrying about their own problems that I didn't want to bother them. Also, I was afraid they wouldn't let me go to my friend's house anymore."

- *I didn't know the words to say.* A group of ten-year-olds, who were scared because the driver of their car on a field trip with their youth group was drunk and driving poorly, explained after they crashed that, "We were too embarrassed to tell anybody. Also, we didn't know what to say or who to say it to."

- *My Dad told me not to complain.* An eleven-year-old boy, who started to hate soccer because his coach kept pushing him to try harder even though he kept getting injured, said, "I tried to tell my Dad, but every time I said anything, he gave me a big lecture about not wimping out just because of a little pain."

- *My Mom got terribly upset.* An eleven-year-old girl, whose teacher was making inappropriate sexual comments to her, eventually explained, "My mom got so upset the first time I told her about a problem at school that she kept worrying all the time and complaining to everybody else about it in a way that embarrassed me. I decided it was easier to try to solve my own problems."

- *I didn't want to get into trouble.* A twelve-year-old boy, who had been followed and threatened by a group of older kids, said, "I promised my friends that I wouldn't say anything because we'd gone downtown instead of staying at the park like we were supposed to. I wanted to be loyal to my friends, and I was afraid that I would get into trouble myself."

- *I was afraid.* A group of sixth graders, who saw a student threatening another student with a knife after school, explained after one got hurt and the other got arrested, "We were afraid that someone would get back at us if we said anything."

To sum it up, the most common reasons that children are reluctant to ask for help is because the adults around them might be too busy, might get upset, might not understand, might tell them they are wrong, might overreact, or might handle the situation in a way that ends up making their lives miserable. They also are often afraid of being embarrassed, of having to deal with retaliation, of letting down their friends, or of having to admit that they did something wrong. From a child's perspective, these reasons make sense. If we want children to believe differently, we need to tell them explicitly that we want them to come to us for help, give them tools for getting help, and be helpful adults for them to come to.

Sometimes, as they get older, children will decide that they want to

The most common reasons that children are reluctant to ask for help is because the adults around them might be too busy, might get upset, might not understand, might tell them they are wrong, might overreact, or might handle the situation in a way that ends up making their lives miserable.

Make sure that older children know that you want them to ask for help from you and other adults even if doing this makes them uncomfortable.

handle problems on their own because they want to feel independent or because getting help does not seem worth the embarrassment. If they sound resistant, make sure that older children know that you want them to ask for help from you and other adults even if doing this makes them uncomfortable.

You can address feelings that might stop older children from getting help by using examples about other kids and by using leading questions. Even if they are irritated, insist that they tell you the answers anyway for your peace of mind. An interaction about this issue, with pauses to allow children to answer the leading questions, might go, "As they get older, kids often feel embarrassed about asking for help in some situations because they don't want to be a bother. Have you ever felt that way? ... But what's more important – not being embarrassed or being safe? ... That's right – being safe! Do you know you deserve to be able to interrupt and insist on getting help, even if adults get angry with you? Great, I thought you knew that!"

Knowledge that Young People Need About Getting Adult Help

Teach kids that, when they feel worried or afraid, or know there is a safety problem, their job is to:

- *Find an adult who will listen and help.* Knowing how to find adults who will help you in different places is part of your safety plan.

- *You might need to interrupt to get the attention of busy adults.* Even if adults are looking right at you, they might not understand that you are having a problem. Remember that "The Wishing Technique" - wishing that something will change rather than doing something about it - does not work, so you have to speak up for yourself. If you have a safety problem, your job is to interrupt adults to get help, even when they are busy.

- *Use a regular voice so that you sound respectful and firm rather than whiny or rude.* Remember to act calm, aware, and confident. You can say, "Excuse me. I need help. I have a safety problem." Explain what the problem is.

- *If the adult doesn't listen at first, be persistent – this means not giving up – and ask again.* Other people cannot read your mind, so you will need to tell the whole story about what happened. Children, especially young children, often think that adults can read their minds. Since the adults around them always seem to know when they are tired, hungry, or upset, this makes sense. Children need to understand that, even if their adults understand them really well, their adults cannot read their minds and know what all of their problems or concerns are. This is why children need to practice telling adults the whole story (what, where, and when the problem happened; why they are worried, upset, or scared, etc.).

- *If one adult will not help you even though you have really tried, then find another adult.* Keep asking for help until somebody understands and gives you the help you need.

Kids also need to know when to wait and when to interrupt and keep asking. Sometimes in solving one problem, you create another. Early in our program development for Kidpower, we learned that children need clear boundaries about using the "being persistent in getting help" skill.

When we became very successful in teaching children how to get the attention of busy adults, their parents and teachers started to complain that these children were interrupting them very effectively all the time. They pointed out that they had been helping children learn how to wait instead of demanding constant, immediate attention, and now we were teaching them how to interrupt!

We now teach children that they often have to wait when they want something, but that their safety rule is to interrupt and keep asking if they need help with a safety problem. We describe what this means using situations relevant to their lives, such as, "In public, you wait at the end of the line when you want to buy something. But, you go to the front of the line and interrupt and keep asking if you need help because you are lost or don't feel safe."

An example for a younger child might be, "Suppose your mom is on the phone. If you want to play a game, do you wait or interrupt? That's right, you wait. But what if the pot is boiling over on the stove? That's a safety problem, and you interrupt."

For an older child, the example could be, "Suppose that your teacher is busy talking to another teacher. If you want to ask questions about your homework, do you wait or interrupt? That's right, you wait. But suppose your friend is throwing up in the bathroom? Yes, that's a safety problem, and you interrupt."

Children will be safer if the adults in their lives tell them clearly, "You can interrupt me or other adults with a safety problem, no matter how busy we are. Even if I tell you to leave me alone so I can get something done, I want you to interrupt me and keep asking if you need help. If a safety problem is really bothering you, you can even wake me up in the middle of the night!" Many families decide that the words, "This is about my safety!" will be a signal that warns adults to stop and listen right away.

If we want young people to seek adult help, they need to feel safe coming to us with their problems. When a young person asks for help, you might feel impatient because the problem seems trivial from your adult perspective. You might feel very upset because any risk or threat to the people you love can cause you to explode with feelings. No matter how you feel, remember that this situation can give this young person an opportunity to develop an understanding about the value of asking you for help.

Here are some reminders about what to do when a young person starts to talk with you about a safety problem:

1. *Before you say anything else, say, "Thank you for telling me!"* No matter how busy you are, no matter what the child might have done wrong, you want to show appreciation to this child for having had the courage to tell you.

2. *Listen and ask open-ended supportive questions to make sure that you understand the whole story.* Nod. Make eye contact. Say, "Hmmm. Please tell me more." Ask, "What else happened?"

Explain to kids that they often have to wait when they want something, but that their safety rule is to interrupt and keep asking if they need help with a safety problem.

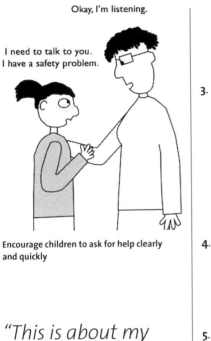

Okay, I'm listening.

I need to talk to you.
I have a safety problem.

Encourage children to ask for help clearly
and quickly

*"This is about my
safety!" can be a
signal that warns
adults to stop and
listen right away.*

Glaring and demanding to know, "Why did you do that?" is not asking a supportive question. Avoid asking leading questions, because children might say what they think you want them to say rather than explaining their true concerns.

3. *Stay calm.* Young people often want to protect their adults from getting upset. They are likely to feel alarmed if you sound hysterical or start making threats. They might even change their story to calm you down or be sorry that they said anything. Take a deep breath if you need to gather yourself. Instead of getting caught up in your feelings of the moment, think through the best ways to handle the situation with the big picture of what you want to accomplish in mind and what behavior you want to model.

4. *Don't lecture or scold, no matter what this young person might have done to cause the problem.* Later, after you have heard the whole story, you might decide that some consequences for misbehavior are necessary. If so, be sure to also offer her or him some benefit for having had the courage to come and tell you.

5. *As much as possible, involve this young person in figuring out what to do and how to do it.* Remember that how you handle this situation will have a lot to do with whether or not you will be seen as a helpful person to come to in the future. In addition, your job is to make sure that young people are in safe environments with safe people. This means that feelings of embarrassment must not stop you from taking action to make the situation better. Offer choices about how problems are solved, not about whether they are solved.

6. *When YOU need it, get help yourself.* The knowledge, skill, and experience of others can provide perspective and alternatives that might not occur to you. Also, you might need to find someone with the authority to take action in solving the problem.

Practicing Being Persistent in Getting Help From a Busy Adult

1 Make up a safety problem that is relevant to the young person you are teaching. For example, you might tell a preschooler, "Imagine that you saw the pot boiling over on the stove!" You might tell an elementary-aged child, "Imagine that some kids locked you in the bathroom at school, and you were scared and want to tell me about it." You might tell a teenager, "Imagine that you saw a kid bring a weapon to school, and you want my help to figure out what to do." Or, you can let your student pick a situation to practice.

2 Ask children and teens if they have ever noticed that sometimes you and other adults are "Too busy!" Ask your student what person he would go to if he had a safety problem. Very likely, he will say, "My mom." Ask him what his mom might be busy doing. Offer choices that you think would be appropriate such as using the computer, washing the dishes, or reading.

Start the practice by pretending to be his mom (or whatever adult he chooses) who is busy doing something. If you are practicing with your own child, think of something that you are often busy doing. Think of an activity that might be hard to interrupt. Pretend to be busy doing this activity.

3 Coach your student to interrupt politely by saying, "Excuse me, Mom. I have a safety problem. Some kids locked me in the bathroom at school today, and I felt scared."

4 Keep looking at what you are pretending to do and say obliviously, "Go ahead, honey! I'm listening. I'm glad you had a nice time at school."

5 With pauses between the leading questions, ask, "Am I listening? No! Have you ever noticed that adults say, 'Ummm hmmmm. That's nice. I'm listening,' when they are not paying attention? What do you need to know that your mom is listening?" Point to your eyes if he is not sure and say, "That's right. You need her to be looking at you."

If you are doing this with your own child, do so in the first person by asking, "What do you need to see from me to know that I am listening?"

6 Coach your student to touch your arm, look you in the eyes, and say, "Mom! Please look at me. I need help!"

7 Pretend to get angry by glaring and snapping, "Can't I have a minute's peace? I told you not to bother me when I'm busy!"

8 Ask leading questions that your student can answer "Yes" to, such as, "Do adults sometimes get grumpy when you bother them while they are busy? Is it important to keep asking for help anyway?" Coach your student to say again, "But this is about my safety. Some kids locked me in the bathroom at school."

9 Get very interested and calm and say, "Oh, why didn't you tell me right away?" (Children enjoy being able to reply, "I did!") Let the child tell you the whole story, and then say, "Thank you for telling me. You did the right thing to interrupt me, and I'm sorry that I was grouchy with you. You deserve to be safe, and we'll figure out what to do." (If you have chosen an immediate safety problem such as a pot boiling over, you can act out turning the stove off first.)

10 For an older child or teen, you could make the practice more challenging by pretending to be so upset that your student needs to calm you down. Act upset, wring your hands and pretend to wail or holler. If you can't think of what to say, just go, "Blah! Blah! Blah!" Coach the teen to stay calm and keep saying, "Mom, Dad, I have a hard time talking with you when you get so upset. Please just listen! This is about my safety!"

Chapter Five

Safety Plans to Prepare Children For the Unexpected

Assuming that young people will "just know" how to keep themselves safe in different situations or where to get help when they have problems is a mistake.

When they know and understand their safety plans, children and teens are better prepared to make wise choices when the unexpected happens. Assuming that young people will "just know" how to keep themselves safe in different situations or where to get help when they have problems is a mistake. Adults forget that children do not understand the world in the same way that we do and that their perspective keeps changing so that they might suddenly handle a situation differently than they have done in the past.

Kids Are Less Safe If They Don't Know How to Get Help

Twelve-year-old Mercedes told me about an upsetting experience when she was walking home from school by herself for the first time. "A man I've seen around the neighborhood but don't know well started to follow me in his car. He said that I was getting to be such a big girl and was so pretty that he couldn't help himself. I cut through the shopping center and went inside a store. But the people were all so busy that I went out again because I didn't want to bother anyone. As I passed through the parking lot, I saw that this man was waiting for me. He followed me as I went into another store. Everybody was busy there too, so I finally hid in the women's dressing room until the man went away. I kept looking over my shoulder for him all the way home. Since no one else was there, I ran inside and locked all the doors quick."

This story is a good example about how not knowing what to do can make a safety problem more traumatic and potentially more dangerous. Also, kids are far less likely to be traumatized or harmed if they are going towards safety rather than just trying to escape from danger.

Remember that a safety plan is only as strong as its weakest link. As one little boy told his mother confidently, "Of course I know, Mommy! If I have an emergency, I just call 9-1-1! The only problem is, I'm not sure what a nine looks like!"

Children need to know how to find trustworthy adults who they can go to and ask for help when they have a safety problem. Younger kids need to understand that getting to safety means communicating with an adult, not hiding in the closet or behind the bushes in the back yard - and that an adult means an adult human, not an adult goldfish or dog, no matter how old and wise. Older kids and teens need to believe that their safety is more important than their being embarrassed or their bothering or annoying someone.

Making a Safety Plan With Kids for Their Daily Lives

Thinking through ahead of time how to get help when you encounter different kinds of safety problems can make a tremendous difference for people of any age. Here is how to make a safety plan with kids:

1 Make a list with children of all the places they might go. Name these places when you are there so that children know exactly what you mean.

2 Brainstorm to think of safety problems that children might encounter. If a child brings up scary ideas, like being captured by a bunch of criminals with laser guns, you can say that you will talk about that problem later but want to deal with more ordinary problems first. For example:

   • A friend does something that is embarrassing or confusing or that you are not sure is okay;
   • Your adult doesn't come to pick you up because of a flat tire;
   • You get separated from your adult in a store;
   • A family member starts telling scary stories on an overnight visit;
   • You are riding your bike and fall down and get hurt, and your grownups are not nearby;
   • You try calling for help on your cell phone, but the cell phone is out of batteries or in a no-service area;
   • Someone you don't know starts talking with you when you are away from your grownups;
   • Someone you know gets so upset that you feel afraid;
   • A person in your neighborhood says or does things that make you feel scared;
   • The person giving you a ride is driving unsafely; or,
   • There is an earthquake, fire, tornado, or snowstorm.

3 As soon as they are able to understand, give children a list of known adults by name who could be part of their safety plan. These can include adult family members, adult friends, teachers, parents of friends, neighbors, etc. Next, come up with a list of people that the children don't know, but who could be resources when these children do not have access to grownups that they do know. These are people who are able to help because of their position, such as cashiers, security guards, police officers, firefighters, rangers, etc. Point these people out in different locations so children can get used to seeing what they look like and where to look for them.

4 Combine the list of places, problems, and people to make a Safety Plan for how to get help. Here's a sample list.

Problem and Place:	Safety Plan:
You see a big snake in your front yard	Go tell an adult in your house.
You get cut and start bleeding at home	Go tell an adult in your house.
Your house catches fire, and no adult is home	Go to your neighbor, and call 911.
A kid keeps tripping you in your classroom	Go tell your teacher or the aide.
Kids keep saying mean things to you at recess	Go tell the yard-duty teacher.
You get lost in a shopping center	Go to a cashier in the nearest store.
Somebody follows you on your way home from school	Run to the lady in the blue house on the corner.
Your parent doesn't pick you up at the park	Go to the secretary in the office across the street, and call. Wait there.
The driver you are supposed to ride with is drunk	Get another ride, even if you have to call a taxi.

5 Make a plan for transitions, as confusion can interfere with making safe choices. Review safety plans whenever the situation is about to change - for example, walking or riding a bike somewhere for the first time, going alone on a bus or airplane, starting at a new school, taking a family trip, moving to a new neighborhood, or sleeping over at summer camp. Remember that children and teens often have a very different perspective on time than their adults. If you are going to a place where you haven't been for a while, ask children to tell you what the safety plan is to refresh their memories, even if you think they already know.

6 Discuss safety plans with all people who are left in charge of children so that you have an agreement about what level of supervision will be provided and how problems will be handled.

Safety is where adults can help you

Make a safety plan for everywhere you go

What to Do if You Are Lost or Bothered in Public

Visiting new places and doing new things can be great fun, but young people need to know how to get help everywhere they go in case they have a safety problem in public. Feeling helpless is a scary experience no matter how old you are. As ten-year-old Sophia told me, "When I was a little girl, I couldn't find my mom in the grocery store. I started to cry, and a lady grabbed my arm and started to take me away. Now I am pretty sure that she was just trying to help me but I was so scared that I still get a sick feeling in my stomach whenever I think about it."

Remember that the world looks different if you are small and don't let young children out of your sight even for a second. More than a few times in stores, I have had a lost toddler grab my leg, thinking that my blue jeans belonged to her or his mother. For little people, whose heads are often below the counter, getting the attention of a busy cashier can be challenging.

At any age, knowing what to do if you get lost or bothered in public can make a huge difference in whether an experience is empowering or traumatic. Children tend to think literally and need very specific directions about how to get help when they are dealing with unfamiliar places and busy people. They need to know how to get help in new places and to be reminded if it has been a long time since they were there.

Without preparation, a child's ideas about the best safety plan will not necessarily agree with an adult's. Once when I was teaching a school workshop for seven-year-olds, the children started talking about Costco, a huge warehouse-type discount store. I asked them, "Where would you go if you got separated from your parents at Costco?"

After much discussion, the kids agreed, "The best place to wait would be by the bathrooms!"

"Why?" their teacher asked, concerned because the bathrooms at their local Costco are in an isolated part of the store.

Several voices said in unison, "Because if you had to go to the bathroom, it would be right there!" This plan is a perfect example of seven-year-old logic!

When kids don't know an adult well, they are likely to find it harder to get that person's attention. Many of us have seen children at a checkout counter wait and wait to buy something, hoping to be noticed, and then walk away sadly or burst into tears. Instead of waiting until a problem comes up, adults can look for opportunities to help shy children get used to interacting with people in public situations. Five-year-old Jacob's mother found out why this was important the hard way and shared this story so that other parents would not make the same mistake. "The first time Jacob ever had to speak to a cashier was when he got lost. Even though he knew what to do, he felt totally overwhelmed. Fortunately, he was safe, but he worried about getting lost for over a year."

One way that children can get used to dealing with people in public settings is by buying things. If a child is shy, start where the child is and go step-by-step. For example, you might give the child something to hand to the cashier, without needing to say anything at all. If you make it fun instead of stressful, you can work up to watching as the child walks away from you and up to the counter to buy something without you.

Older kids who might be out on their own without an adult need to know how to get help if someone's behavior worries them, but they can get irritated about being told what to do. After all, they don't want to be treated like little kids. Instead of telling them, ask for their ideas and agree on a plan together. If that doesn't work, you can just agree with them that of course they know, but for your peace of mind you want to hear them tell you again. As the following stories illustrate, being sure about what to do can make a big difference if someone is acting in an unsafe way in public.

One eleven-year-old girl named Sylvana was walking with a friend in the small town where she lived the week after her Kidpower workshop. A man started to follow the girls in his car, staring at them and making them uncomfortable. Sylvana pulled her friend into her mother's hairdresser's shop. The hairdresser was not there, and her assistant told the girls to leave the store. Sylvana refused and demanded that the assistant call the police. When the police came, they gave the man a warning, took all of his information, let him know that they were keeping an eye on him, and congratulated both girls.

Children tend to think literally and need very specific directions about how to get help when they are dealing with unfamiliar places and busy people.

Instead of waiting until a problem comes up, adults can look for opportunities to help shy children get used to interacting with people in public situations.

After taking a Kidpower workshop, a boy named Evan, aged twelve, was at a skate park with his friend. An older boy on a bike kicked him. Evan immediately thought, "Where is safety?" and went to the recreation kiosk. The recreation worker did not want to help him, saying that this was not her responsibility. Evan dragged her to the doorway just in time to see two boys on bikes starting to rob his friend. When the recreation worker shouted, the boys took off, and Evan's friend was safe.

When children are bothered in public because someone's behavior is rude, threatening, or creepy, they need to know how to move out of reach, not answer back either with their face or body language, leave quickly, get to a safer place where more people are, and get adult help. If this person is physically stopping them from leaving, children need to know how to yell and, as a last resort if they are in danger, how to hit and kick to get away and get to safety.

Because children's perspectives and understandings are constantly changing, review their safety plan about getting lost or bothered each time they go somewhere they haven't been for a while. Remember that even a week can seem like a long time from the point of view of a young child. Older children can be asked to tell *you* their safety plan one more time, just for your peace of mind, including how and where to get help if someone bothers them.

> "Wait! What's our safety plan if we get lost from each other here?"

During our Kidpower Parent-Child workshops, we ask the children to imagine they are going someplace they don't know well. We have them practice interrupting the adult they came with, who pretends to be busy, to ask, "Wait! What's our safety plan if we get lost from each other here?" We ask the adults to imagine that they are in a hurry so they can practice stopping and saying, "Thank you for asking me." Together, the adult and child can then agree on a plan that makes sense for this place, such as meeting at the person in charge of the closest ride in an amusement park.

Most of the time, we want children who are lost to stay where they are to give their adults a chance to find them before they leave to get help. This is especially true in a bigger place such as a shopping mall, a zoo, a park, or a busy sidewalk. We recommend that children go through the following steps before leaving to get help if they are separated from their adults:

1. STOP!

2. Stand tall and strong if it is safe to stay where you are. Otherwise, go to the nearest place that is safe. For example, if you are in the middle of the street, go to the sidewalk and stand tall and strong there. To help them keep upright and calm, we tell younger children to make their bodies strong and still like "the trunk of a tree."

3. Look around for your adults. Most of the time when children think they are lost from their adults, their grownup is actually close by and just taking a minute to stop and look is enough to find them again.

3. If you cannot see the adults you came with, then yell out the names you use to call them. You can yell *anywhere*, even in a library, movie theater, or restaurant.

5. If that doesn't work or if staying where you are is not safe, then follow your safety plan for getting help such as going to the clerk at the checkout counter.

6. If you don't know what else to do, ask a woman with children for help.

7. If there is no woman with children, then look for a grownup that is working there, such as a gardener or salesperson. Ask for help but also be clear that you want to stay in the store or the place where you are. Ask other adults for help if the one you chose first is not listening.

Practicing calling for help!

Children need a backup plan in case they get stuck and cannot figure out what to do. Maybe the store is too crowded to spot a cashier, or the part of the zoo is too far from the ticket seller. Maybe they are lost in a place where there are no people, such as while camping or hiking.

Most of the time, the safest backup plan is for children to ask a woman with children for help in finding the nearest cashier, information center, or ticket seller. Statistically, a woman with children is *least* likely to harm a child. Most people have mobile phones. Tell children that they can ask a woman with children to call your number to help you find each other. Some parents even tape their own mobile number to a younger child's sleeve if they go to a crowded place, just to be sure that they can be easily contacted if the child gets lost. Otherwise, children can get help from a man as long as he stays in the same building or area, rather than taking the child someplace else.

If children are lost in nature, their safety plan is to wait in the closest safe place to where they first noticed they were lost. Sometimes rangers recommend that you teach children to "hug a tree" if they are lost in the woods. Kids need to know that you will look for them and, if they are lost in nature, a ranger or even a search party full of strangers will come looking for them. People will be calling their name. There might be a helicopter. Their job is to call for help so the ranger or search party people can find them. In this case, they would let the ranger or the search party take them to the place where they would meet up with you.

Cell phones are very convenient, but not always reliable. Any safety plan that involves a cell phone should have an alternative in case the cell phone doesn't work.

Children need a backup plan in case they get stuck and cannot figure out what to do.

Part One: Practicing Skills for How to Get Help if Children Get Lost In a Store

Children need to know both what their safety plan is if they get lost and how to act on that plan. Practicing how to get help in public can prepare children to use these skills in real-life situations.

1 Pretend to be someplace where the child is likely to go, such as a big store. Tell the child to imagine that you forgot to talk about this and have her ask you, "What's our safety plan if we get lost?"

2 Make a safety plan to go to a place that is easy to identify, such as "Checkout counter number one." Tell the child to imagine that a spot in the room is "Checkout counter number one." If you are with a group of children, you can have one child act it out with you in front of the group, or you can all practice together.

3 Have the child stand tall and turn her head to look around the room. Make sure she is really seeing what she is looking at by asking about things that are actually in the room. Ask, "Can you see the clock on the wall? The tree through that window?"

4 Coach the child you are practicing with to yell out to the adult she came with, most likely, "MOM! DAD!" If she has a hard time yelling loudly by herself, then yell with her or get others in the room to do so. If you are with a group of children, ask them, "Who are the adults who might be with you in the store?" Have them yell out the actual names such as Mom, Dad, Papa, Mommy, Auntie, Grandpa, Fred, etc. If the children speak different languages or have specific names they use for their adults, you can yell together the names of everybody who is likely to take them to the store.

5 Tell the child, "Now imagine that you have waited, and looked, and yelled, but you are still lost. So, your safety plan is to go to checkout counter number one. Do you go to the front of the line or the end of the line?"

6 Sometimes, children will say "the end of the line." This gives you an opportunity to remind them, "You wait at the end of the line if you want to buy something. But if you have a safety problem, you go to the front of the line, around to the back of the counter if you have to, and interrupt the cashier who might be busy with other customers."

7 Pretend to be the cashier (talking to another "customer" who is either imaginary, a doll, or a real person) and ask your pretend customer, "What is it you wanted to buy, sir?"

8 Coach the child to clasp your arm firmly and interrupt politely, using a strong voice, and saying, "Excuse me, I need your help. I'm lost." If you have a whole group of children acting this out, they can practice it in the air, come to you as a group, or take turns.

9 Pretend to be the cashier and say very impatiently, "You're cutting in line. You need to wait at the end of the line."

10 Coach the child to be persistent and say, "But I'm lost!"

11 In your role as the cashier, pretend to call on the loudspeaker and say, "There is a lost girl. She is wearing a white shirt and green pants." If the child knows, she can be asked the name of the adult she came with for the announcement.

12 Younger children like to see resolution at the end of a practice, especially one about getting lost. Pretend to be the adult who came with the child. Come rushing up, hug the child if this is appropriate, and say, "Oh, *there* you are! Great job following our safety plan."

13 For older children, you can pretend to be a cashier who does not know the safety rules by taking the child's hand and saying, "Oh, you're lost! Well, come with me to the manager's office." Remind the child to follow the safety plan and stay in the public area. Coach her to pull her hand away and say, "My safety plan is to stay at this checkout stand if I'm lost."

14 Here's a different role play that would be useful for younger children if you are going to be in a crowded area and have a cell phone. Tell the child to pretend to be lost and to imagine that you are a mother with children. Coach the child to point to the phone number on her or his arm and say confidently, "This is my mom's number. She's here, but I can't find her. Please call her!"

Part Two: Practicing Skills for Getting Help in Public When Children are Going Out Independently

Discuss with children who are going out in public with no adult what their safety plan is for getting help in different places. To practice, coach children to get someone's attention, to be very clear about what is happening and what they want, and to persist in the face of hostility or impatience. Places could be on a bus, in a store, at the mall, or in a park.

1 To get started, you can say, "Let's imagine that you are at the mall (or another location). Somebody has followed you and said weird stuff to you. We'll pretend that I am working at the store where you are coming to get help."

2 Coach the child to say politely, "Excuse me. I need help. That person is making me nervous."

3 Pretend to be the cashier doing inventory and say impatiently without actually looking, "Him? He's harmless. Don't hang around the store if you're not going to buy something." Or, "I don't want to get involved."

4 Coach the child to persist and say, "I see you're busy, but I feel scared. Please call the security guard."

5 As the cashier, pretend to get annoyed and say rudely, "You kids make things up all the time. Go away!"

6 Coach the child to stay calm and firm and say respectfully, "My parents will be mad at this store and you will get in trouble unless you help me. I am not leaving until I get help."

7 As the cashier, pretend to pick up the phone and say, "Okay! Okay! I'll call!"

Check First Before Changing Your Plan
Safety for young people requires that the adults who care about them know where they are, who is with them, and what they are doing. Knowing what is happening with the children in our lives is also important for our own emotional safety. Teaching kids to develop the "Check First" habit can prevent all kinds of safety problems from the time they are little through their teen years.

Long ago, I was on a panel at a safety fair in a town near my home. The police chief with me on the panel told the audience about a situation that

Remember, we need to CHECK FIRST before we get close to someone we don't know well

Check First before you change your plan

*Safety for children means that the adults who care about them know **where** the children are, **who** is with them, and **what** they are doing.*

has become our Kidpower Pizza Story. We tell our students, "Once there was a boy who was walking home from school. His Dad got off work early and picked him up to go get some pizza. The only problem was that they forgot to call the boy's Mom. When her son didn't come home, what do you think this Mom did? ... That's right, she started worrying. She called her husband, but his cell phone was turned off. Finally, she called the police who did an all-out search of the town and found this boy with his father around the corner eating pizza! When her son and husband came home, of course the Mom was thankful her son was safe - but she was also furious about being so scared!"

We then explain, "Sometimes grownups forget the safety rules. Are there ever times when your adults forget important things? ... When your adults forget the safety rules, you can remind them. Remember that the safety rule is to Check First with your adults before you change your plan."

Teach children to make sure that they really have your attention when they Check First. After asking and seeing her mother nod in an absent-minded way, Luanne's eight-year-old daughter started to play "Hide and Seek" on the playground at the park. Suddenly, Luanne realized that she couldn't see her daughter. Since her daughter was playing Hide and Seek, she didn't answer even though many adults were calling out for her and looking all over. Instead, she crouched down so no one could see that she was at the very top of the play structure. Luanne became so worried that she was getting ready to call 9-1-1, when her daughter finally came down from her hiding place, completely unaware that she had caused such concern.

"Our rule now about Checking First is that you have to be holding hands and seeing each other's eyes," Luanne says. "Just saying something to me is not enough, because I might not be listening that well. I never want to feel that way again!"

A similar story was told by George's father. "George seemed to have disappeared, and I could not find him anywhere," he said. "Finally, I found that George had gone with friends to the park. He had asked me, but I had just said, 'Okay' without really listening. Now our rule is that, before he goes, he has to make me repeat back what the agreement is about changing the plan."

Children need to be clear exactly which people they can go somewhere with without Checking First, as long they let any other adults who might be concerned know that they've gone. At home, a child's adults might be parents, child-care workers, or other adult family members. At school, it will be teachers and other school staff. At other times, it might be the parents of a friend or a youth group leader.

Because so much abuse happens with people who are supposed to be "safe adults," we also want to make sure that children know how to set boundaries with everyone, including people they know, if their behavior becomes unsafe. How to teach boundaries is discussed in Chapter Six, and protecting kids from child abuse is addressed in Chapter Nine. How to teach "stranger safety" and protecting kids from abduction is addressed in Chapter Ten.

Remember that, in order to be able to Check First before changing their plan, children need to know what their plan is going to be for that day. Take a few minutes each morning to start each day with an explanation or an agreement about what the plan is going to be for everyone in the family – adults as well as children. By making this a priority, children experience conversations about daily planning as part of normal, everyday life with people who care about each other.

For example, "Today, you are going to school and I am going to work. After school, you will stay in after-care until Tio José can pick you up. You and Tio José will go shopping for our dinner and then come home." Then, ask the child to repeat his or her understanding of what the plan is. As children get older and more independent, give them choices about what the plan is going to be and permission to make changes within certain boundaries as long as they let you know first.

Most schools, youth programs, and child-care centers now require that parents or guardians sign a card that spells out exactly who has permission to pick up their children. Without written permission, even close family members are not allowed to take a child. Teachers can reinforce the Checking First rule by pointing out that they always get permission before they take children to places away from the school.

Most abuse happens with people kids know, and a potential child molester is likely to avoid children who are in the habit of telling their adults in charge about changes in plans. In a tragic situation in Hawaii, a twelve-year-old girl accepted a ride from her older cousin. She did not realize that he had a lot of problems, and he killed her. We will never know for sure if Checking First with her adults would have prevented what happened, but this girl would have had a better chance of staying safe if she had known to ask her teachers or parents for permission.

Children can also get into unsafe situations with their friends. Unless children follow the Checking First rule, an activity that starts out very innocently can suddenly get out of hand as one thing leads to another. Exploring the backyard can turn into exploring the park or the river. Riding bikes on the sidewalk can turn into riding around the corner and onto a busy street. These are all activities that children will someday be able to do, but we want to make sure that they are prepared to handle problems that might come up before giving them increased independence.

Adults also need to check in with other supervising adults about what the plan is. Make sure that you have agreements with teachers, parents of friends, and youth group leaders about what activities are okay with you and what are not. Be sure that you know who is supervising the care of your children when you are not there.

Many families ask about using secret code words that someone must know before the child can go with this person. For some families, this might work, but in others it might not. Some older children can remember the code word, keep it a secret, and use it appropriately, but many can't. Think of how hard it can be for many people to remember the passwords to

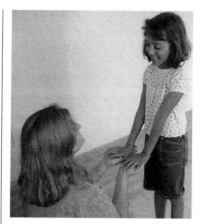

The safety rule is to Check First with your adult before you change your plan

Because so much abuse happens with people who are supposed to be "safe adults," we also want to make sure that children know how to set boundaries with everyone, including people they know, if their behavior becomes unsafe.

their computers. Tricking most children into saying the code word is easy. If someone has bad intentions, this person might try asking something like, "Your code word is "sea anemone," right?"

"No," the child might say. "It's 'octopus.'"

"Oh, that's right! Octopus! Let's go then!"

Instead of trying to figure out whether or not this person has the right code word, we believe children will be safer if they check in directly with the adult in charge, either by going to ask that person or by calling on the phone.

Part One: Practicing Checking First Before Changing The Plan

1 In a family, discuss with children each day what each member of the family's plan is so that you are all on the same page. Agree on how you will check if you want to change the plan.

2 Set the stage for a practice by picking a place where the child might be and pretending to be a person the child knows. For example, "Suppose your plan is to play in your back yard until dinner. Imagine that I am your neighbor and you know me. You've even been to my house before, so it's okay to talk with me and to be close. But you still need to check first before you go with me."

3 Pretend to be the neighbor and say, "Hi, Fiona! (Use the child's name.) How are you doing?"

4 Coach Fiona so that she says, "Fine."

5 As the neighbor, pick something to do that would be tempting to this child – going to the playground, riding bikes, playing a computer game, or seeing new-born puppies. For example, "I've just baked the world's best chocolate chip cookies. Come on over to my house and have some while they're still warm!"

6 Coach Fiona so that she says, "That would be great, but I need to Check First."

7 As the neighbor, say, "Oh, you don't have to check. It will just take five minutes!"

8 Coach Fiona so that she walks away as you are calling after her and says to you and to herself, "I am going to Check First!"

• •

Part Two: Practice for Older Kids on Checking First If Someone They Care About Might Be Having an Emergency

Older children who might be waiting alone to be picked up need to know that their safety plan is to Check First with the adults supervising them, even if someone says that there has been an emergency or that someone is in the hospital. Give children a short list of people who they could go with even without checking first, but make sure everyone is clear on who these people are and when it is okay to go with them. Remind children that they can call to get permission. If someone else is having the emergency and children can check first, their safety plan is to get help rather than to change their plan about going with someone.

1   Pick a place where this child might be waiting. Use the child's name and the name of an adult who would normally pick up this child. For example, "Manny, imagine that you are waiting in front of your school for your Grandpa to pick you up. Pretend I'm your father's friend from the office who has been to your house to visit."

2   As the office friend, pretend to be driving a car up to where Manny is waiting and say, "Manny, I have some really bad news for you! Your Grandpa's been hurt and needs you to come right away to the hospital. Get in the car!"

3   Coach Manny to stand up and move away and say, "I need to have the school office call to get permission first."

4   As Manny's father's friend, get urgent and say, "There's no time! Hurry up and get in the car!"

5   Coach Manny to walk away as he says, "I am going to call first!"

Safety Rules for Answering the Door at Home

Children need to know the rules about answering the door themselves, even when their adults are home. If adults are not able to see what's happening, we might as well not be there. Once, when I was taking a shower, my four-year-old son Arend invited a colleague from my job into our home. She had stopped by unexpectedly to drop off some work papers. My son graciously chatted with her and even gave her a glass of water. As I got out of the shower, wrapped in a towel with dripping wet hair, I was startled to see the two of them at our kitchen table.

One of our instructors works for UPS. He says that his heart stops every time he rings the doorbell and a small child standing alone opens the door. People trust the design of the truck, the uniform, and the clipboard without realizing how vulnerable a child in the doorway might be to all sorts of dangers.

Younger children often do not understand the difference between opening the door to someone who is standing there and opening the door to go outside if they see something interesting through the window. One small boy wandered out the door and down to the highway because he thought he saw his father walking by. Fortunately, a couple saw him and returned him home.

Until children are experienced enough to make these decisions for themselves, they are safest when they Check First with their adults before they open the door either to go outside or to let someone in. For both adults and older children, the safety rule is to Think First about whether or not we are sure the situation is safe before we open the door to anyone, even people we know. As an adult, welcoming anyone into your home should be your choice.

Neighborhoods are very different so the safety rules about when children can open the door are going to vary. Children who are home alone even for a few minutes need to have very explicit directions about exactly which

Children need to know the rules about answering the door themselves, even when their adults are home.

Until children are experienced enough to make these decisions for themselves, they are safest when they Check First with their adults before they open the door either to go outside or to let someone in.

people they can let into the house, and they need to let you know before they change the plan about this.

When kids are at home with no adults in the house, standing silently while someone knocks and waits outside the door can be very scary for a child. Also, someone who is thinking about robbery might ring the doorbell to make sure no one is home. The safest strategy for children is usually to make it clear that people are in the house without admitting to being home alone.

Instead of pretending not to be there, children can pretend that their adults are home and aware of what is going on, which means not taking a shower or being asleep. They can pretend that their adults are not willing to come to the door at this time. Perhaps their adult is on the phone, in a meeting, cleaning, or just "busy." Children can learn to say things such as, "Sorry, my mom is too busy." Or, "Sorry, my dad can't come to the door right now." Or, "My uncle says this is not a convenient time."

Older children, or children who can remember several pieces of information, can move away from the door and shout, "Somebody's at the door." They can pretend to be calling out to their adults. They can pretend to hear an answer and then pretend to convey the message, such as, "My mom says to please leave the package on the porch. She will come get it when she's off the phone." Or, "My Dad is in the middle of something. He says to please come back later."

If the person at the door does not go away or tries to go around the house to a side or back entrance, the safety plan is to call 9-1-1 or another emergency number, such as a neighbor who is normally home.

Part One: Practicing Following the Safety Plan about Answering the Door

Discuss what the rules are in situations relevant to the children you are teaching. A delivery person might drop off a package. A florist might deliver flowers. The mail carrier might bring a special delivery letter. Someone from the office might bring important papers. An electrician might say that she was told to fix a dangerous wire. A police officer might say that he needs to check the house.

Young children should always come to an adult and check first so that an adult is with them when they open the door. As they get older, children can start to open the door to certain people they know without checking. As children develop more understanding, this list can grow. Remind children that the safety rules apply even when people are wearing uniforms or delivering pizza.

1   Pick a situation where a child should not open the door. Pretend to be the person at the door. For example, you might pretend to be a flower delivery person ringing the doorbell or knocking and saying, "Knock! Knock! Hello! I have some flowers to deliver."

2   Coach the child to say something that does not require that the door be opened, such as, "Please leave them on the porch."

3   Pretend to be the flower delivery person and say, "I need someone to sign for them. Please get your mom or dad."

4 Coach the child to move away from the door and call out the name of the adult who is most likely to be there. For example, "MOM! Somebody has flowers!" Coach the child to come back to the real or imaginary door and say, "Sorry, she says to please leave them on the porch."

5 As the person at the door, ask the child, "Are you home alone?"

6 Coach the child to say, "NO. My mom is busy." Point out that following the safety rules is even more important than telling the truth. Children will often need coaching and practice to be able to do this effectively. They need to know that lying in a few specific safety situations is an important safety tool.

7 As the person at the door, say, "Please open the door. I can't leave the flowers without a signature, and I'm running late."

8 Coach the child to say, "Sorry. You'll have to come back later."

9 Pretend to walk away with the flowers saying, "She'll have to come to the store to get them."

• •

Part Two: Practicing Thinking First Before Opening the Door in an Emergency for Older Children

Once you are sure that a child will not open the door inappropriately, you can make the situation more complex for an older child by pretending to be in a uniform and saying, "Imagine that I am dressed like a police officer. Suppose I say that there is a gas leak and the house needs to be evacuated." Coach the child to look out the window and see if everyone is outside his or her houses. If so, the safety plan is to get out of the house and go to where the neighbors are. If not, the safety plan is to call 9-1-1 and say that a police officer is in front of the house telling you that there is a gas leak.

Know Your Telephone Safety Rules
Nine-year-old Les told me an upsetting story that added an important practice to our Kidpower program.

"I answered the phone because I was expecting my friend to call," Les said, "but instead, there was this man breathing hard like he had been running. He asked me my name and started saying embarrassing things. I asked him what he wanted, and he said he was going to hurt me if I didn't tell him where I lived. I started crying and asked him to please not hurt my family. My big sister saw me and took the phone away. She yelled at the man and hung up. Mom asked me why I didn't just hang up on him myself. I told her I didn't want to be rude."

In our Kidpower workshops, we now have children imagine that they have just picked up the telephone and that the other person is sounding weird or scary. The second they feel uncomfortable, their job is to disconnect the phone. We sometimes have a whole room full of children who are pantomiming disconnecting their phone in various ways saying, "Click!" or "Beep!"

The phone is a great tool but children need to practice using the phone to be able to use it safely

Just as with answering the door without opening it, children need safety rules to follow about answering the telephone. Many families simply tell children to let an answering machine or voice mail take the calls. When children do answer the phone, we recommend these rules:

1. Unless you know someone well, do not tell people that you are home alone or give personal information about your address or your family.

2. If someone asks for an adult and you are home alone, say, "They are busy and can't come to the phone right now. Please give me the number and someone will call you back." Tell your adult that someone called.

3. If someone says something weird or scary, or starts asking personal questions, then hang up right way, even in the middle of a sentence, and tell the nearest adult.

Used properly, telephones are also an important tool for getting help. Children need to know how to reach their parents or other adults whenever they have a problem or are not sure that a situation is safe. However, any safety plan that depends on a telephone also needs a backup plan that involves finding people close by to help. What if the mobile phone can't get a signal? What if phone service is out because of a storm?

Part One: Preparing Children to Use the Telephone to Get Help

As soon as they can understand, teach children their full name, address, and phone numbers and the names of their parents or guardians.

1 Practice how to make local and long-distance calls on pay phones, touch-tone phones, mobile phones, and rotary phones. Make sure that children understand that they need to hear a dial tone to know that a telephone is working unless it is a cell phone. Have children memorize and write down important phone numbers. Parents of younger children sometimes write these numbers on the inside of a child's clothing. Tell children about dialing "0" to get an operator.

2 Explain how to call 9-1-1 in an emergency if they cannot get hold of their trusted adults and they are scared or someone is hurt and needs help. It is not okay to call 9-1-1 just because they broke something or are mad at someone in their family.

3 Let children practice getting help on the phone with a not-too-awful problem. "Let's imagine that I hurt my leg and could not stand up to go to the phone. Suppose I tell you to call 9-1-1 to ask for an ambulance." With the phone unplugged, have the child practice dialing 9-1-1.

4 Let children practice making a report. Pretend to be the 9-1-1 operator. Coach the child to give clear information by asking questions, "I need help. My mom hurt her leg and says to call an ambulance. We are at 77 John Street in Los Angeles." Remind children that you are just pretending so they can practice and that it is only okay to call 9-1-1 in a real emergency.

Part Two: Practicing Not Giving Personal Information on the Telephone

1   Pretend to call on the phone or use a real phone, "Ring. Ring."

2   Coach the child to answer, "Hello."

3   Pretend to be a radio announcer and say enthusiastically, "This is your lucky day! You have just won $10,000. All I need is your name and address."

4   Coach the child to say, "Sorry. We don't give personal information on the phone."

5   As the radio announcer, say, "Get your parents."

6   Coach the child to imagine that no one else is home and to say, "They are busy and can't come to the phone right now."

7   As the radio announcer, ask, "Are you home alone?"

8   Coach the child to say, "NO! Good-bye!" while hanging up the phone.

If the child is worried about losing the money, you can explain, "If we had really won, they would probably call back later. You can also call and check with me or another one of your trusted grownups, and we can find out what it was about. Your safety is worth more than any amount of money, so even if it is hard, following your safety rules is more important.

Part Three: Practicing Hanging Up the Telephone

1   Coach children to pretend to answer the phone.

2   Tell them to pretend that you are someone on the phone line saying something weird or scary. Don't actually say anything except nonsense like, "Blah. Blah. Blah."

3   Coach children to act out hanging up the phone, and say, "Click!" Remind them to tell an adult as soon as possible if anyone makes weird phone calls.

Safety Plans for Preparing Children To Do Things That Make Adults Worried

Children's drive to explore and be more independent can give ulcers to their loved ones. Finding the right balance between keeping children safe while letting them visit new places, be with new people, and do more adventurous things can be challenging.

At age four, my son Arend suddenly shimmied up almost to the top of the flagpole in front of his sister's school. I stood looking up, feeling quite helpless, and wringing my hands. "You are up too high!" I said, trying not to sound as nervous as I felt.

"No I'm not!" Arend announced. "Look, Mommy, I can even grip with my legs and let go with my hands." He waved his hands happily to show me, thirty feet above the hard cement. "I bet from here, I could really fly!"

"Please come down right now, Arend!" I said as firmly and calmly as I could, wondering what I was going to do if he didn't. "I see that you are not up too high for you, but you are up way too high for me!"

"Oh all right," my son sighed and slid down.

As scared as I was, telling Arend that he could never climb or even attempt to fly would not have worked. Either he would have been so driven that he would have found ways to try to do this secretly and perhaps more dangerously or he would have become fearful. Instead, we made a plan that Arend had to agree with me ahead of time about where he could climb and where he could not. We looked for places where, if he fell or failed to fly, at least he would have a soft landing. He would leap off the top of a play structure, flapping his arms wildly on his way down to the sand and then announce triumphantly, "See! I stayed up in the air for at least a minute that time!"

One sad day, when he was about six, Arend came to me and said mournfully, "Mommy, I have figured out that I can't fly. I used to stay up for a few seconds, but now I'm heavier and I fall faster. I will never ever be able to fly like a bird."

"Oh, Arend!" I said, hugging him, torn between relief and sorrow. "You will fly in other ways. You have already flown in airplanes. You can go hang-gliding when you're a little older. And you can fly in your dreams."

"None of that is the same!" my son said sadly. And I had to agree that he was right.

Taking small steps towards independence can help to prepare kids and also to reduce the anxiety of their adults. After one of our workshops, nine-year-old Lila's mother pulled our instructor Marylaine aside and asked for help. "I'm a survivor of childhood abuse," Lila's mother said, "and I want to do everything in my power to prevent what happened to me from happening to Lila. She wants to go to a friend's house for an overnight, but I'm afraid to let her go. I have never let her stay overnight with anyone."

"What are you worried about?" Marylaine asked.

"I don't know these parents very well." Lila's mother explained, "and I'm afraid that this family might have different standards for safety than we do. Lila might just go along with whatever this family does instead of saying that something is against her safety rules."

"It's your job to keep Lila safe, " Marylaine said, "but sooner or later, Lila needs to be able to go to a friend's house and stay overnight without you. Instead of taking such a big step right away, I think you could work on smaller steps. Think about what you need to know about this other family to feel comfortable with Lila going there. Think about what you need to see that Lila is able to do in order for you to feel that she is ready to spend the night somewhere without you."

"How do I do that?" Lila's mother worried.

"To start with, I would recommend that you have a visit with this other family in order to get to know them better." Marylaine suggested. "Maybe you can start by inviting Lila's friend over to your house. Discuss with her parents what each of your expectations are about supervision and activities. You can tell Lila that you want to see that she is in the habit of speaking up for herself, checking with you before changing plans, and telling you about problems. Give her specific opportunities to show you that she can do this. Tell her that taking these smaller steps will show you when she is ready to stay overnight somewhere without you."

Marylaine also explained the plan to Lila, who said in a relieved voice, "That could work!"

Adults need to help children find safe ways to get ready to do new things.

Making a Safety Plan for Preparing Children to Do Things That Make Adults Nervous

1   Acknowledge the child's right to want to do something new or adventurous.

2   Ask yourself questions to build your own understanding. What am I worried might happen? What's the best that could happen? What's the worst that could happen? Can I find safer places where I could allow my child to try out this behavior without getting hurt? Can other people offer information or skills to make the activity safer? What in-between steps might help my child develop the skills necessary to be able to handle the situation safely?

3   Make an agreement with the child about safe ways to try out this activity or about what needs to happen in order for you to feel that the child is prepared.

4   Find safe ways to give many outlets for the child's drive for adventure and exploration.

5   Give the child opportunities to practice the skills of assessing the safety of a situation; staying aware, calm, and confident; moving out of reach of danger; and being persistent in getting help.

Chapter Six

Boundaries and Advocacy to Build Better Relationships

Children learn about boundaries and boundary-setting skills from their adults. However, many adults struggle with recognizing and setting boundaries themselves. Healthy personal boundaries, respect for the boundaries of others, negotiation skills, and assertive advocacy skills can prevent a lot of pain and confusion at any age.

In our adult boundary workshops, we tell our students that boundaries are useful in relationships with ourselves, with each other, and with faceless systems, such as the health care industry or the telephone company. We need to know what our own rights are and what the limits are between our rights and the rights of others. In situations where we are interacting with others, many boundaries have to be negotiated. For example, if we are sharing a space with a housemate, we have to negotiate how we clean it, how noisy it is, and where things go.

The Kidpower approach to teaching boundary-setting and advocacy skills to children:

- Uses issues that come up in children's daily lives so they can be safer with words, with touch, and with teasing;
- Prepares children to communicate their boundaries with an assertive attitude;
- Gives children realistic distinctions about where they have choices and where they don't so that they learn to set boundaries appropriately;
- Prepares children to deal with the most common forms of pressure people use to push against boundaries such as emotional coercion, bribes, and misuse of power;
- Gives children permission to lie and break promises to be safe; and
- Makes sure children understand that their problems should not have to be secrets and that they have the right to tell an adult they trust when anything bothers them.

Introducing Personal Boundaries

A boundary is a type of limit or border. In order to make this idea more concrete for young people, we ask in workshops, "What are some examples of boundaries that you can see?"

As our students look around the room and think, they answer, "The wall. The ceiling. The lines in sports. The lines on the floor. My skin."

Healthy personal boundaries, respect for the boundaries of others, negotiation skills, and assertive advocacy skills can prevent a lot of pain and confusion at any age.

Boundaries can protect us from harm and prevent us from crossing into the boundaries of others. With younger children, I sometimes show how boundaries work by having several kids stand in a circle with me. We hold hands and pretend to be a fence. My co-teacher Ryan gets onto his hands and knees and pretends to be a yappy little dog. "Suppose," I say as Ryan acts this out by running around the room, pretending to nip our feet, and then falling over, "Ryan is a yappy little dog that is running loose on the street. He chases people and tries to bite their ankles. He also almost gets hit by a car."

The fence gives the little dog a boundary

We then put Ryan, still on his hands and knees, inside our circle. As the children giggle and move close together to stop him from getting out, Ryan shows how the fence keeps him inside the yard and away from the street. "We want our yappy little dog Ryan to be safe from cars, and we want people to be safe from being bitten," I explain. "He does not know how to stop himself, so our fence stops him. The fence we are making with our bodies is a boundary for this yappy little dog."

Again, a fence is a boundary that you can see. We also have boundaries that we cannot always see, but that we can feel. Our boundaries with people, including ourselves and others, are called personal boundaries. Adults and children alike usually recognize the examples we use to explain this idea. Imagine you are joking with friends, and then suddenly someone says something and you think, "Hey, that's not funny! Ouch! That hurt my feelings!" That ouch feeling you have inside is a sign that your personal boundary just got crossed. To take another example, suppose that you are roughhousing in a playful way, and suddenly you think, "This is too rough! I'm getting hurt!" That feeling of "too rough" is another sign that your personal boundary is being crossed.

Since we usually cannot see our personal boundaries, we often learn where they are through feeling discomfort as they get crossed.

Kidpower's Four Boundary Principles

Personal boundaries are the limits between people. We use personal boundaries to set limits with ourselves and with each other. Kidpower has four main principles or rules about personal boundaries:

1. *We each belong to ourselves.* You belong to you and I belong to me. This means that your body belongs to you – and so do your thoughts, your feelings, your space, and your time – all of you! This means that other people belong to themselves too.
2. *Some things are not a choice.* This is true for adults as well as kids. Especially for kids, touch for health and safety is often not a choice.
3. *Problems should not be secrets.* Anything that bothers you, me, or anybody else should not have to be a secret, even if telling or talking about problems makes someone upset or embarrassed.
4. *Keep telling until you get help.* When you have a problem, find adults you trust and keep telling them about your problem until you get the help you need.

This example from my own life about how the boundary-rules work has

Since we usually cannot see our personal boundaries, we often learn where they are through feeling discomfort as they get crossed.

1. We each belong to ourselves   2. Some things are not a choice   3. Problems should not be secrets   4. Keep telling until you get help

become our Kidpower Bath Story. When he was about eight, Arend used to like to say, "Mom, my body belongs to me, so I do not have to take a bath!"

Of course that wasn't true, so I'd reply cheerfully, "Arend, you belong to yourself, but some things are not a choice. Taking a bath is about your health. You are dirty and you must take a bath!"

Arend would grump, "I'll tell!" and I'd say calmly, "Go ahead. Tell the whole world that your mother made you take a bath!" That was fine. Arend had the right to dislike having to take a bath, to complain to me, and to tell anybody he wanted. I had the responsibility to insist that my son get clean.

But, suppose I had said to Arend, "Oh, please don't tell! That would be too embarrassing!" Even as Arend's mother, my asking Arend not to tell would have been a mistake, because problems should not have to be secrets. Telling my son to keep something that bothered him a secret would have been against the Kidpower safety rules about boundaries.

Helping Children Develop an Understanding of Boundaries

1 Starting as soon as you talk with children about other everyday things like colors, nature, or the weather, point out physical boundaries in everyday life. As soon as they can communicate, encourage children to do the same.

2 Make a game of finding boundaries. For example:

- "We are staying inside the boundary of the crosswalk. This helps drivers know where to stop."
- "We are going to stay outside the flower bed. One side of the boundary is for the flowers and the other is for our feet."
- "This rope makes a boundary to keep us from going through that door."
- "What are the boundaries when you play soccer?"
- "This sign saying 'One Way' is a boundary for cars."

3 Teach kids the four boundary rules, using the Safety Signs shown above to help them remember. Use the word "boundary" in acknowledging feelings and establishing rules:

- "Your boundary is that you do not want to hold my hand. My boundary is that you stay right by my side the whole time we are out."

- "Your boundary tells you that you are not ready to fall asleep yet. My boundary tells me that you must lie quietly on your bed and look at books after eight in the evening."
- "Your boundary is that you do not want to get into your car seat. My boundary is that I am not going to drive the car or go anywhere else until you are safely fastened into your car seat."
- "Your boundary is that you do not want to help me to pick up your building blocks. My boundary is that, if I have to pick them up by myself, I'm going to put them away so you can't play with them for a week."
- "Here at the campsite, the boundary is that you stay inside this line that we are drawing. Check First before you go outside the boundary line."

4 Tell The Bath Story above or another story about a time when someone got to speak up but did not get what he or she wanted. The points are that feelings are okay, setting boundaries that others dislike is sometimes necessary, and that problems should not have to be secrets.

5 Act out stories to show how boundaries work. For example, with younger children, you can use stuffed animals to act out the Yappy Dog story described above, where the fence is the boundary to protect the yappy dog from being hit by cars and to contain the yappy dog from biting people who go by. With older children, you can use objects in their room such as their favorite action figures or dolls, and have them help you create and act out a story about the ways that a boundary might both protect and contain different beings.

Introducing Assertive Advocacy

We use the term "advocacy" to mean "actively speaking up for yourself and others." Kidpower teaches Assertive Advocacy to people of all ages and abilities so that they are effective in:

- Setting boundaries;
- Getting others to listen to them;
- Asking for help; and
- Being included.

How to be assertive can be just as important as what you want to assert. I have heard children as young as five and adults as old as ninety complain that the boundary-setting skills that Kidpower taught them didn't work.

They might mumble passively, "I kind of tried what you told me, sort of anyway, and nobody listened. I don't know why. I guess they just don't like me."

They might yell aggressively, "I did exactly what you said and nobody cared! They just got mad. I think they hate me. They are just creeps, anyway."

How we communicate about what we do and do not want is going to make a huge difference in the results we are most likely to have. Saying all the right words often won't work well unless we communicate our boundaries and wishes with an assertive attitude. The difference between being passive, aggressive, and assertive can be learned at a young age – in fact, as soon as children can speak and understand language fairly well. In Kidpower workshops, we show children the difference with puppets, stories, and role-plays – and then coach them to try out different attitudes themselves.

Here is how to explain the difference between being passive, aggressive, and assertive.

How we communicate about what we do and do not want is going to make a huge difference in the results we are most likely to have.

Passive Communication. When we act passively, the message we communicate to others is, "What I want is not that important, and no one cares anyway, so I might as well give up." Our listeners are likely to agree with us that our message must not be important in the midst of so many other things competing much more persuasively for their attention. People often will fail to notice, will ignore, or will forget our message.

Passive behavior includes:
• A soft, unsure voice;
• A hopeless expression;
• Limp or frozen posture and gestures;
• Eyes that are looking down or to the side so that there is no eye contact;
• An apologetic or whiny tone of voice;
• A closed-down body that doesn't take up too much space;
• Sighs and shrugs;
• Hesitant, unclear language;
• Speaking from too far away to be noticed; and/or
• Waiting and wishing that someone would just know what you want.

Aggressive Communication. When we act aggressively, the message we communicate to others is, "You are not going do what I want anyway, and you are probably out to get me so I am mad at you. You are an awful person." Our listeners are likely to feel attacked and to believe that any message delivered in such a negative way is probably unreasonable. They might avoid us or get angry.

Aggressive behavior includes:
• A glowering face;
• A tense rigid posture;
• An irritated or loud voice;
• Insulting language and loaded words;
• Jabbing or jerky body language and gestures;
• Strutting;
• Leaning forward into someone's face;
• Crowding into the space of others;
• Interrupting others impatiently;
• Ignoring or failing to respond; and/or
• Acting annoyed or angry.

Whining seems passive but is often experienced by the other party as being aggressive. Sometimes we show this by having all the children use a very whiny voice while they say words that would be relevant to their lives, "Teeeeecherrrr! Mooooooom! Daaaaaaaad! Noooooooooooooooooo! Stoooooooop! That's not faaaaaaaair! Coooooome ooooooooon! Pleeeeeeease!"

We then ask some leading questions to reinforce our point, "Does that sound like whining? Is it irritating? I don't even feel like listening to myself! Do you feel like listening to yourself?"

Assertive Communication. Instead of communicating with either a passive or an aggressive attitude, both children and adults can learn how to communicate assertively. Assertive Advocacy means giving others the message, "Of course you are going to care about what I want once you understand what it is. What I have to say is very important to me. I believe that this will be very important to you, too. If not, I am still going to be clear about what I want."

The behaviors that go with communicating an assertive attitude include:
- Using body language that is calm, aware, and confident.
- Making eye contact. When you want people to listen to you, looking into their eyes without glaring rudely and without looking away tends to be most effective.
- Having a facial expression consistent with your message. This means having a neutral face if you are telling someone to stop. Depending on the situation, you might have a concerned or friendly expression if you are asking someone to do something for you.
- Using polite language that is both definite and respectful, such as: "Excuse me!" "Please stop!" "I need your help!" "I'd like to sit here, too." "I'd like to join the game."
- Making your voice loud enough to be easily heard and positive instead of soft, hesitant, whiny, or angry. Sound firm when telling someone to stop. Sound appreciative if you want help. Sound cheerful and friendly if you want someone to do something for you or with you. Sound urgent if you have a safety problem.
- Managing space. Move away from someone bothering you. Move closer to someone who has or can do something you want.
- Using gestures that help to communicate your message.

Walls, Fences, and Bridges
In Kidpower, we teach students how to make fences, walls, and bridges with their bodies. Adding motion to their words helps people to be more clear and effective. Fences, walls, and bridges all work best when you stay aware, calm, and confident and have an upright posture and show an assertive attitude.

wall

fence

bridge

Assertive Advocacy means giving others the message, "Of course you are going to care about what I want once you understand what it is."

A *fence* can be used to show that you are setting a boundary when someone is bothering you. You can make your body like a fence by stepping back and pushing your hands forward with your arms stretched out. Your palms are facing down towards the ground and out towards the other person at about the height of your own waist. Your objective is to be clear that you mean what you are saying.

A *wall* helps to set a stronger boundary if someone is trying to hurt or threaten you and you cannot just leave. You can make a wall with your body by stepping back with your strong leg to help you stay in balance and by bending your arms at the elbows. Your arms are up in front of you with both palms facing towards the other person at a little over chest high. Your objective is to make it clear both that you are not a victim and that you are not attacking the other person.

A *bridge* shows that you want to build a connection with the other person. You might use a bridge when you are asking for help, communicating that you care, or wanting to do something together. Body language for a bridge between people who are close in height could be to have one or both hands in front of you at about waist high with your elbows bent, palms facing up, reaching towards the other person. If you are a child trying to get an adult's attention, you can make a bridge by reaching up and gently but firmly touching the adult's arm. You can move your hands a bit to add emphasis. The objective is to create a connection between you and the other person in order to encourage a positive response.

The Wishing Technique

A major pitfall to avoid is the Wishing Technique. Have you ever wished passively that someone would just know what you want without your having to say anything? Did it work? Did you ever give up and not get what you needed from that person? Did you ever become so frustrated that you blew up at that person aggressively?

Tell children directly that the Wishing Technique almost never works. Children often believe that adults can read their minds. This is logical from a child's perspective because, especially when they are younger, adults do anticipate many of children's needs without them saying anything.

A physical version of the Wishing Technique is the Hinting Technique. This is where you try to show a person that you don't like something with your body language by leaning away, wiggling, or sighing. You are hoping that this person will get the hint. If he or she doesn't understand, you might end up shouting, "Can't you take a hint?!"

Remind children and yourself that it's not fair to give up on people or to get mad at them just because they cannot read your mind. This is why you need to use Assertive Advocacy to speak up for what you do want and what you do not want.

Most of the adults I know, including myself, will admit to using the Wishing Technique at times or to being passive or aggressive. Remember that the children in your life are learning from the examples you set.

Children in your life are learning from the examples you set. Model Assertive Advocacy by being clear, strong, and respectful in your communications – and coach children to do the same.

Model Assertive Advocacy by being clear, strong, and respectful in your communications – and coach children to do the same.

Teaching the Differences Between Acting Passive, Aggressive, and Assertive

1   Show what passive behavior looks like in an exaggerated way. Shrink your body. Put your hands in your pockets or fold your arms. Slump your shoulders. Tilt your head slightly to one side. Shrug. Wiggle. Stand a little too far away so that you are harder to notice. Put a worried look on your face or an apologetic smile. Say something like, "Imagine that you are very busy doing something. I really want something from you so I am going to wish that you will figure out what it is. I am wishing very hard."

Pause to show that nothing happens as you wait and wish. Then continue, "Alas, as usual, wishing is not working. Now, I am going to sigh so that you will notice me." Sigh sadly and slowly several times. "Oh well, that's not working either. So I will ask."

2   Using a hesitant, high-pitched voice with your closed-down body and very unsure language, demonstrate different messages such as, "Don't do that, okay?" Or, "I want to play this game, okay?" Or, "I sort of need a little help maybe, if you're not too busy right now, okay?" Show how raising the tone at the end of the sentence turns a statement into a question.

3   Ask, "Do I sound as if I believe in what I am saying? Do I convince you?"

4   Now coach your students to act out being passive in the same way that you showed them. Have them act out wishing, sighing, and then asking with closed-down bodies, unsure words, etc. Ask them if they believe in their own messages when they communicate passively.

5   Now go through the same process with an aggressive attitude by first demonstrating and then coaching your students to act this out. Clench your fists. Tighten your jaw. Thrust your chin or shoulders forward. Get too close so you are in people's faces. Frown. Glare. Sigh loudly in an irritated way. Put your hands on your hips. Shake your finger towards someone or make jabbing motions in the air.

Using an impatient loud angry voice with some insulting language, try out some aggressive messages such as, "Hey, cut that out!" Or, "Don't you dare do that!" Or, "Let me play!" Or, "Help me right now!" Or, "That's stupid! You have to do what I want!" Remember that children need to see what aggressive behavior looks like without the demonstration getting too scary or overwhelming. This means acting in an aggressive but controlled way, so that children understand that you are pretending.

When you demonstrate, ask your students, "Does my aggressive attitude make you feel more like doing what I want or does it make you feel like staying away from me? Do you feel like snapping at me, 'Don't talk to me like that!'?"

6   Now demonstrate and coach students to practice communicating with an assertive attitude, using the description of assertive behavior above. Make your body language calm, aware, and confident. Use a neutral voice by sounding calm and having a lower pitch rather than a higher one. Stand close enough to be seen and heard easily without crowding anyone. Don't ask questions unless they are really questions. Otherwise, make statements sound definite by lowering the tone at the end of your sentence. Don't use words that might either sound hesitant (like "sort-of" or "okay") or rude.

7   Show how you can vary your expression and tone depending on the message. If you are telling someone to stop some kind of behavior, you want to communicate that you mean what you are saying without being rude. If you smile apologetically, the other person might not believe you. If you act angry, this

person might get upset with you. Giving a clear respectful message works best. Have a neutral face and say, "Please stop."

If you want someone to help you, give you permission, or do something with you, building a connection is a good way to start. Sounding friendly and smiling can help to build a connection. Assertive statements could be, "Excuse me. I need help." Or, "Excuse me, I'd like to join the game." Or, "Hello! I'd like to sit with you!" Or, "I need your attention. Please listen." Or, "May I use that please?"

8 Make a game of having children tell you when characters in books or movies are being passive, aggressive, or assertive – or when they are falling into the pitfalls of using the "proven-to-be-ineffective" Whining or Wishing Technique instead of the "works-most-of-the-time" skills of Assertive Advocacy.

9 Show students how to make fences, walls, and bridges with their bodies and discuss the different situations when these might be useful. Practice the tone of voice, choice of words, posture, and facial expressions that go with these different situations.

Protecting Ourselves From Hurting Words

In the early years of Kidpower, we used to tell our students, "There is an old saying that 'Sticks and stones will break my bones, but words will never hurt me!' But how many of you have ever had your feelings hurt by something mean that someone said to you?" As most of the children, and adults too, would raise their hands, we would add, "Words can hurt a lot. So that saying was a great big lie!" The more modern version of that old saying goes, "Sticks and stones can break your bones, but words can break your heart!"

When children are upset because someone said something hurtful to them, telling them to "just ignore it" doesn't work very well most of the time. On the other hand, overreacting might lead children to believe that they should be devastated any time anyone says something that they don't like.

Long ago, my daughter Chantal and a kindergarten friend of hers who we'll call Marissa were playing at our house. Marissa, who was almost six at the time, came up to me and said in a very upset voice, "Chantal is emotionally abusing me! She said something very awful."

"Oh, dear!" I said calmly, impressed by Marissa's vocabulary. "What did she say?"

Marissa grumbled tearfully, "Chantal said that she is sick of playing ball with me. She wants to play tag!" With a little discussion, Chantal was able to find a kinder way to express her feelings, and Marissa was able to accept that she was not always going to get to decide which game they were going to play.

In workshops, we often show children what happens when they do not protect themselves from hurting words. First, my teaching partner, Timothy, explains that he is going to pretend to be mean so we can practice. He then pushes his hands together with his fingers pointing at me. He walks towards me saying over and over, "Irene, you are so stupid!"

Timothy keeps going until he has walked right into me and his fingers are poking like an arrow into my chest.

As the children watch in intent silence, I act crushed and say, "OOOOOH! Where did the word 'stupid' go?"

"Into your heart!" the children say, sympathetically.

"If you do not protect yourself," I say dramatically, pointing first to my heart and then to my head, "hurting words can get stuck in your heart or your head, and they can stay there for a really long time!" Then, I ask sympathetically, "Has that ever happened to any of you?" All around the room, heads of different ages nod.

"But," I go on, "I do not have to let this happen! Watch what I can do to protect myself!"

Once again, Timothy walks towards me, with his fingers pointing towards my heart, saying, "Irene, you are so stupid!" Instead of waiting there, I step out of the way. Timothy keeps going until he gets to the trash can that is strategically placed behind where I was first standing. He drops the word "stupid" into the trash.

In addition to preventing the words from going inside of me by getting out of the way, I say something nice to myself to take their place; in this case, "I'm smart!"

The children smile and the adults in the room sigh, often saying, "I wish I had known how to do this when I was a child. It would have saved me a lot of misery."

Sometimes we show students a very concrete example of how a trash can works. Kidpower instructor Erika Leonard, who created this demonstration, starts by placing a large trash can in front of a group of students and tossing a dirty piece of paper onto the floor, next to the trash can.

"What is that?" Erika asks.

"Trash!" the children say.

"Does it belong on the floor?" Erika asks dramatically.

"No!" the children shout, matching her enthusiasm.

Erika picks up the crumpled paper, puts it next to her open mouth and asks, "Should I eat it?"

"No!" the children shout again.

"What should I do with it?" Erika asks.

"Throw it in the trash can!" the children giggle.

"This is trash that you can touch!" Erika explains. "Hurting words are like trash that you cannot touch but you can hear them or read them – and you

If you do not protect yourself, hurting words can get stuck in your heart or your head, and they can stay there for a really long time!

Catching Mean Words

can certainly feel them."

We explain to our students that littering the environment with hurting words is harmful in the same way that littering with other kinds of trash is harmful. In addition, we can make ourselves sick by taking in hurting words. This is not safe to do, just like eating rotten food or other garbage is unsafe. The concept of where to throw different things away can be more complicated than we think. Once, when I was teaching in a preschool, I set the classroom trash can in the middle of the circle of children and asked, "What's this?"

"A trash can!" they all exclaimed.

"Yes, and what do you use a trash can for?" I asked the children

"To throw things away!" the children told me.

"You can use this trash can to throw away anything that you don't want!" I explained.

To my surprise, a very little boy jumped up, taking me at my word, and spat into the trash can! His teachers had been trying to get him to stop spitting onto the floor or onto other children, so this was an improvement if not exactly what they wanted him to do.

The Famous Kidpower Trash Can –
An Emotional Safety Technique for All Ages
In over twenty years of self-defense work, the Kidpower Trash Can is the technique I personally use the most. A brilliant educator, Mary D. Geyser, invented this when she realized that her first grade students could use their own bodies to avoid taking in hurting words. At first, we just taught this to little children, but then we found that, as self-defense instructors, we were using the Kidpower Trash Can ourselves, so we started teaching it to everybody.

The concept is quite simple. You catch hurting words, throw them into the trash and put something nice that you say aloud into yourself. Of course, you can do this with your imagination by using your mind, but there is something very powerful about practicing out loud and using your body. Also, practicing in this way helps you remember to protect yourself from hurting words out in the real world.

Sometimes we start by having younger children catch the word "Stupid" by grabbing with their hands to make "Mean Word Catchers."

Next, we all throw the word "Stupid" towards a real trash can. I explain that everybody has perfect catch and perfect aim in Kidpower. Finally, we all pat our chests while we say the nice words that can replace the hurtful ones, in this case, "I'm smart!"

Here's how to use your body to make a Kidpower Trash Can. Put a hand on one of your hips. Imagine that the hole made by your arm is the top of a trash can. When people say mean things to you, you can catch the hurting words with your free hand and throw them into the hole made by your other arm. Finally, you can pat your chest while you say something good to yourself.

One little boy who was just two-and-a-half was getting teased at a birthday party because he had a cast. His mother saw him make his Kidpower Trash Can and shout, "NO! I am not letting your hurting words go inside my body!"

After the Kidpower program has been in a school, teachers tell us they see younger kids on the playground, hands on their hips, throwing away hurtful words, and saying, "I like myself!"

With older kids, we acknowledge that going around in public turning their bodies into trash cans and saying nice things to themselves out loud would not be a good idea. We explain that this practice can help them to use their Imagination Trash Can, by acting as a metaphor or a picture for their minds. In a confrontation, young people are safest if they can protect themselves emotionally, by using an image such as the Trash Can for not taking in the hurting words, so that they can stay calm and then make a conscious choice about whether to set a boundary or to leave quietly.

We have countless stories of how people of all ages have found that using the Kidpower Trash Can either at the time or later, either out loud or in their imaginations, helped them take the power out of upsetting words. As Patrick's mother told us, "At age eleven, Patrick would get outraged when teens on the way home from school would say rude things about his disabled sister. His need to answer them back instead of leaving was causing these teens to pick on both Patrick and his sister even more. We practiced with each insult that had upset Patrick. We said the words aloud sneering and gesturing while Patrick walked away and used his Kidpower Trash Can. Each time, he would say out loud, 'My sister is great.' We had his sister practice too. We told them both that answering people on the street would not be safe, but that taking the power out of these words would help them to stay calm, aware, and confident. Instead of dreading the walk home from school, they started enjoying their independence. When Patrick stopped reacting, the boys left them alone."

Older children sometimes appreciate having an intellectual connection to make the Trash Can Technique seem more relevant to them. Catching the trash helps you react with your brain first, not with your feelings. Throwing it away represents assessing the situation and deciding what to do to make things better. Finally, telling yourself something positive and taking it in is a way of taking care of yourself, just as you might wash your hands after picking up something dirty.

Sometimes people are surprised that children will misuse the Trash Can Technique, either accidentally or because they are testing boundaries. During a teacher training at a preschool, one of the teachers said that she had shown her children the Trash Can Technique. Later that week on the

I Like Myself!

Using the Kidpower Trash Can

In a confrontation, young people are safest if they can protect themselves emotionally, by using an image such as the Trash Can for not taking in the hurting words, so that they can stay calm and then make a conscious choice about whether to set a boundary or to leave quietly.

When children are experimenting with new tools, adults need to be prepared to step in if need be.

playground, when one girl complained that another child had called her a name, the teacher said, "So, do you remember what to do?"

With perfect confidence, this three-year-old said, "Yes I do!" She put her hand on her hip to make a Kidpower Trash Can and then used her other hand to grab the shirt of the girl who was bothering her, with a clear intention of throwing her away.

When children are experimenting with new tools, adults need to be prepared to step in if need be. One way to think about this is to compare it to giving a young child a pair of scissors for the first time. What would happen if you just showed the child how to cut with the scissors and then left the room? A curious child might start cutting the curtains or someone's hair or try flushing the scissors down the toilet to see what happens. Children need supervision when they get new tools of any kind until they show that they know how to use these tools safely.

Comments that might seem silly to adults can humiliate a young person. In one of our classes, a fourteen-year-old boy was mortified because, since he was growing tall so quickly, other kids were calling him "long spaghetti." These words had become so loaded for him that he had to watch the Kidpower teachers practice throwing away the words "long spaghetti" with each other before he could practice for himself. His parents said later that just doing this simple exercise changed his whole attitude about going to school.

Getting kids involved in how best to throw away or dispose of hurting words can change a miserable experience into an interesting one. The ten-year-old daughter of one of our instructors arrived home upset every day. When she rode the school bus, other kids kept calling her "tree stump" because she was short. She felt too old to use the trash can the way she'd practiced, but just using her imagination wasn't enough. So she and her mother invented a mini-trash can that she could use behind her back so the other kids wouldn't see it.

The next day, the girl came flying into the house shouting, "It worked! It worked! When they called me 'tree stump,' I made my little trash can. They asked me what I was doing, and I told them I was putting their words into my mini-trash can. They got so interested that they forgot all about teasing me." To make a Mini-Trash Can, curl up the fingers of

Throwing hurting words away with the Mini-Trash Can

one hand against your palm to make a hole and use your thumb to push words onto the top of the hole.

Often, the words that upset children are "bad words" they are not allowed to say. In some classes with pre-teens or teens, with permission from parents and teachers, we practice having young people throw away these specific words in order to take the power out of them. We explain that these words are just a set of sounds, and their bad meanings came from people, not from the sounds themselves. In different languages, the "bad words" often sound completely different. You do not want a set of sounds to control how you feel or what you decide to do.

Unless we have permission, we never use foul language in Kidpower children's programs. This is partly because families have very different tolerance about "bad words" and also because we do not want to teach children hurtful words that they have not already heard. Instead we tell children, "I want you to think of the worst words you can think of for someone to call you! ... Do Not say these words out loud! ... Suppose that I say, 'You're nothing but a Really Bad Word,' or 'Bleep!' You can imagine that I said the words you were thinking of and throw those words away. Then you can tell yourself, 'I'm proud of who I am!'"

Recycling garbage rather than throwing it into a landfill is better for the earth. Once children really understand the concept of not taking hurting words inside or of littering the world with them, I will say, "Recycling trash like paper or composting trash like orange peels is important. If you think about it, what we are actually doing is recycling the mean words after we throw them away, by breaking them down into their letters and turning them into nice words. In the same way that compost can be used to fertilize plants, the nice words we tell ourselves can help us to grow stronger."

The Mean Words Recycling Machine

Practicing Using the Kidpower Trash Can Technique

1 We are very careful about how we practice using the Trash Can Technique. We do not want children to be harmed by taking in some hurtful words accidentally through the practice. We make this emotionally safe by:

- Saying very clearly, "I am just pretending so we can practice."
  If this is a young child or someone who might get confused, we say this each time we practice.
- Making sure that the child has the answer ready before we say the hurting words.
- Letting the child choose the words to throw away as much as possible. Ask, "Is there anything hurtful that other people say to you or that you say to yourself that you want to practice throwing away?"
- Using words that the child has already heard rather than introducing new insults.
- Picking something the child can change unless the child has asked us to pick something personal. For example, we will not say, "You have an ugly nose!" Instead, we will say, "That's an ugly shirt." Or we might say something generic like, "Shut up!"
- Letting the child decide which kind of trash can to use – a real one nearby, the arm on the hip, the mini-trash can, or some other variation such as the one-handed trash can (just waving the words away with one arm), a dumpster (two mini-trash-cans next to each other), etc. Children sometimes have fun making up their own trash cans. Make sure that the child's trash can of choice is ready for action before you say anything.

2 To practice, agree on the insult, affirmation, and method of trash can to be used. You say the insult out loud. The child physically catches the insult and throws it away. Next, the child uses an affirmation to say something nice to herself or himself and physically takes this in, perhaps by patting her or his chest while saying it. The list below gives you some ideas, but keep the guidelines described above in mind when deciding which to use.

Insult: "You're ugly." Or, "You look nice – Not!"
Affirmation: "I like the way I look." Or, "I have my own way of looking good."

Insult: "Shut up!"
Affirmation: "My words are important."

Insult: "You're lazy."
Affirmation: "I am relaxed, and I enjoy myself."

Insult: "I don't want to sit next to you. You smell!"
Affirmation: "I can find another place to sit. I'm proud of who I am."

Insult: "I don't want to play with you."
Affirmation: "I will find another friend."

Insult: "Duh!" Or, "That sucks!"
Affirmation: "I have the right to my own opinion."

Insult: "Crybaby!"
Affirmation: "Everybody cries. Adults too. It's healthy."

Insult: "Your food looks weird!" Or, "That's a dumb shirt."
Affirmation: " I like my food!" Or, "I like my shirt."

Insult: "How could you make such an awful mistake?"
Affirmation: "Mistakes are part of learning." Or, with a shrug, "Nobody's perfect!" Or, "I don't have to be perfect to be great!"

Insult:	"I hate you!"
Affirmation:	"I love myself!"

Insult:	(to a child wearing glasses) "Four eyes!"
Affirmation:	"I like my glasses. They help me see!"

Insult:	"You're not trying hard enough." Or, "You're not getting enough done."
Affirmation:	"I do the best I can, and I do a lot."

3 If a child is being taunted by foul language, we recommend practicing with the specific words the tormentors are using, even if it makes the adults leading the practice uncomfortable to say these words out loud. If a child is too upset to have the words directed to her or him, then you can start by having adults or stuffed animals practicing with each other to demonstrate. Again, be clear that we are pretending so we can practice!

4 Sometimes older children resist practicing because it seems too childish. Adults can acknowledge their reality by saying, "Of course you won't do this out in the school yard. But practicing with me will help you to remember the Trash Can as a metaphor, or a picture for your mind, when you need it. You can say something positive to yourself silently instead of out loud. If you don't like the Trash Can image, what are some other ideas you have for how to dispose of hurting words instead of taking them inside?"

Setting Boundaries with Yourself Using Your Mouth Closed Power, Hands Down Power, and Walk Away Power

Often, the most important person you need to set boundaries with is yourself. Realizing that you can stay in charge of what you say and do is essential to effective boundary-setting. Our instructor Michelle asks her students, "How many of you sometimes say something rude when you are in a bad mood?" Lots of hands raise. Then Michelle asks, "If someone says something hurtful to you, how many of you feel like saying something hurtful back?" Even more hands raise.

Next, Michelle asks, "Does saying something rude or answering back make your problem bigger or better?"

"Bigger!" her students groan.

"How many of you feel like hitting people sometimes?" Michelle raises her own hand as her students raise theirs and explains, "Feeling like hitting someone who was mean to you is normal. But, is hitting to get even with someone likely to make the situation better or worse?"

"Worse," her students sigh.

Not speaking, not hitting, and leaving are very simple actions that anyone can learn. We need to create better models in our society for honoring the power of *not* getting into conflicts by what we do *not* say, how we do *not* hurt, and how we do *not* confront unless it is truly necessary. Giving these actions names and defining them as *Powers* helps to reframe the definition of power and helps both children and adults to remember to use them in real life.

Often, the most important person you need to set boundaries with is yourself. Realizing that you can stay in charge of what you say and do is essential to effective boundary-setting.

Mouth Closed Power Safety Sign

Hands & Feet Down Power Safety Sign

Walk Away Power Safety Sign

To use **Mouth Closed Power,** squeeze your lips together. Before you speak when you should be quiet, say something rude, or answer an insult, you can use your Mouth Closed Power by stopping and squeezing your lips together instead. You can also use Mouth Closed Power to stop yourself from eating something you shouldn't or being unsafe with your mouth in another way.

To use **Hands Down Power**, imagine that you are very upset and about to hit someone, or that you really want to touch something you shouldn't. Put your hand up or out as if you are about to hit or touch. Now, lower your hand and press your arm next to your side.

Both Mouth Closed Power and Hands Down Power are hard to use for very long, especially if someone's behavior is quite obnoxious. So, remember to use your Walk Away Power.

To use Walk Away Power, peacefully leave the person bothering you while showing awareness, calm, and confidence. Finally, get help by talking the problem over with an adult you trust.

When kids behave unsafely, having them practice staying in charge of what they say and do in order to make more respectful choices can work much better than lecturing. During our adult education workshops, we tell parents, teachers, and other caregivers how useful practicing skills can be as a management tool for addressing hurtful, rude, destructive, or potentially dangerous behavior. The great thing about practicing skills is that it puts the focus on what you want the children to do to prevent a problem like this from happening again; does not take long; does not require that you believe one party or the other; and is not punitive.

For example, a kindergarten teacher told me how she had used this idea in her classroom after a little boy had kicked another in the crotch. The teacher required both him and the boy he had kicked to each practice saying in a big loud voice making a fence, "Stop! I Don't Like This!" She then had both boys practice using their Walk Away Power to leave. They also practiced their Hands Down Power by imagining that they felt like touching someone or something that they shouldn't or hitting someone, and then used their power to pull their arms to their sides and keep them there.

This teacher reported that later she watched an interaction where the boy who had gotten kicked started bothering the boy who had kicked him. This time, instead of kicking, this little boy made his fence and set his boundary and the other little boy, who had meant no harm, immediately stopped!

I congratulated the teacher and said that her story inspired a skill that we now call "Feet Down Power" as a technique to help a child remember Not to kick. To practice Feet Down Power, imagine that you really feel like kicking someone. Instead of kicking, pretend that your feet are glued to the ground and use your power to keep them there or to move them only enough that you can walk away.

Practicing Different Ways of Being Powerful

1 Demonstrate how a conflict grows between two people. One person is unkind, the other person reacts, and then each keeps getting meaner and meaner to the other until a fight starts. Show this with another person or by using puppets or stuffed animals. With younger children, be clear that you are just pretending. You can demonstrate with hurting words that you know the children already hear like "stupid" or "I don't like you!"

Show how the conflict gets bigger by going back and forth while escalating the insults. "You are stupid!" goes to "Well you are stupider!" goes to "Well I don't like you!" goes to "Well I hate you!" goes to the two characters looking ready to hit each other. Pause and ask, "Does this look safe?"

2 Show how the conflict stops if one of the characters takes charge by not being mean back, by not hitting, and by leaving. Remind children that they can throw away hurting words to protect their feelings.

3 Coach a younger child through the practice as you model and explain, "Remember that we are pretending so you can practice. Imagine that I just stuck my tongue out at you. Squeeze your lips together like this (demonstrate) to stop yourself from sticking your tongue out back at me. Good.

"Now suppose I call you a mean word like 'stupid!' Might you feel like telling me that I am much more stupid? That's normal. Or, might that word ever make you feel sad? That's also normal. But you are going to use your Mouth Closed Power by squeezing your lips together like this. (Show and ask the child to do it with you.) Good. Remember that you can throw the word into your Trash Can and leave." Coach the child to throw away the word "Stupid" and to walk away and get help.

4 You can do this same practice with older children without mentioning sticking out their tongues, since this is something that younger children are more likely to do. Let them pick rude words or gestures that they want to practice throwing away, not answering, and leaving with awareness, calm, and confidence. Coach them through the practice, pausing to remind them about what to do if necessary.

5 Now tell children, "Suppose I was hitting or bothering you so much that you felt like hitting me back. Put your hand up as if you are about to hit. Good. Now put your hands down so that I can see you use your Hands Down Power. Good. Now, I am going to gently shove you and say something rude. You can tell me to 'Stop!' without saying anything rude back. Instead, you can use your Trash Can along with your Mouth Closed Power, Hands Down Power, and Walk Away Power."

6 Coach each child through the practice. Gently shove the child and make a rude comment that would be appropriate for this child such as, "You creep!" Coach the child to say, "Stop shoving." Continue the conflict by saying, "Make me!" Coach the child to throw the words away in an imaginary trash can, to not say anything rude back, to not hit back, to leave, and to get help.

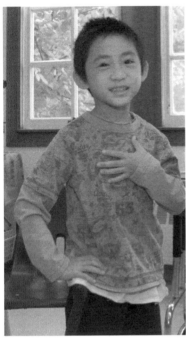

Take compliments into your heart

Throwing compliments into your imaginary trash can makes no more sense than throwing tasty healthy food into the garbage!

Taking in Compliments

If I say one positive thing to you and one negative thing, what are you most likely to remember? Most people will say, "The negative thing!"

Suppose that someone tells you, "You look very nice today!"

Do you ever squirm and come up with a stream of objections such as, "Look at the bags under my eyes. I've put on weight. And I pulled this old thing out of the closet ... and ... !"?

Suppose that someone says, "You did a great job on this project!"

How likely are you to frown and say, "Oh, but here are ten things wrong with it!"?

When you think about it, this behavior is very odd. These are compliments! Throwing compliments into your imaginary trash can makes no more sense than throwing tasty healthy food into the garbage!

We can use the positive things people say to help us build our belief in ourselves. Even if you personally have no trouble taking in compliments, how many people do you know who habitually discount the positive things that others say? Given the examples they see, older children often need to learn how to accept compliments graciously. Most young children have no trouble feeling good about compliments. As they get older, children learn from the behavior of people around them that sounding proud of how you look, what you do, and who you are is somehow wrong.

We practice accepting compliments in classes by saying, "Before I was making up unkind, untrue things for you to practice throwing into the trash. Now, I am going to say some true things for all of you to take into your hearts. I want each of you to catch the compliments, put them into your heart, and say, "Thank you!"

We say things that are true for the whole group such as, "I think you are smart! I think you are powerful! I think you look terrific! I am really enjoying being here with you today." For each compliment, we coach students to catch the words and press them into their hearts, saying with big smiles, "Thank you!"

Using Heart Power to Solve Problems

Heart Power means protecting your heart, taking good things into your heart, and staying connected with your heart so that you can communicate caring to others. Using your Heart Power to set boundaries and give compliments can help to turn a situation around. I have seen a lot of

Heart Power Safety Sign

behavior problems in my work, but I was astonished at how a five-year-old "Sasha" had managed to terrorize the adults and children in her kindergarten. Sasha was healthy and bright and looked like a curly-haired angel. But out of her sweet little mouth came a continual flow of cruel and sophisticated observations that were hard to confront.

When told to stop by her gentle teachers, Sasha said what the adults in her family were most likely saying to each other and to her, "I'm just saying what I think. If it's true, it's true."

During our Kidpower workshop in the classroom, an active little girl named Eve crawled across the circle to sit next to her friend. Sasha pointed and sneered, "Oh, look at Eve! You can see her underwear!"

Eve stopped enjoying the freedom of moving around and immediately became overcome with embarrassment. Indignantly, I told Sasha, "That's a mean thing to say. I do not want people to say mean things in my class!"

Sasha said, "But it's true. Look, a piece is still showing!"

As Eve blushed and tucked her shirt back into her pants, I became more indignant. The children, parents, and teachers in the room turned to look at me to see what I would do. I took a breath and reached deep inside myself to find the part of me that was able to love Sasha even in that moment. With a calm face and a firm voice, I said, "Sasha, I understand that you are just saying what you think is true. The problem is that you can always find critical things to notice about other people, but just noticing things to criticize hides more important truths about someone - and is hurtful. It is against our safety rules for people to say mean things in Kidpower. You can think whatever you want, but I expect you to use your Mouth Closed Power and your Heart Power to stop yourself from making insulting remarks. Instead, you can try to notice nice things about others and give people compliments."

You can always find critical things to notice about other people, but just noticing things to criticize hides more important truths about someone - and is hurtful.

Sasha started to say something but I squeezed my lips together to demonstrate and then said, "Remember, *right now* is a time to use your Mouth Closed Power!" Sasha squeezed her lips together.

As the whole room watched silently, I turned to Eve and with great love in my heart, I said, "Things like the tops of panties showing are actually fashionable in some places and not important when you are having fun. I am going to give you a compliment that is true. Eve, I like seeing how much you enjoy moving around, and you look perfect to me just the way you are."

Eve beamed. She clasped her compliment with her hands, put it into her heart, and said, "Thank you!"

Adults and children around the room sighed with relief.

"Do you have a compliment for me?" Sasha asked wistfully.

I smiled at the circle full of adults and children, who also looked wistful, and decided, "Today, I have a compliment for each person here, including you." With the same loving energy as I had with Eve, I looked into the face of each adult and child there and said something individual and true. Even though it took a while, everyone waited patiently, and each person pressed my words into her or his heart.

I let Sasha have her turn last. Again, I mustered all the love I could find for this troubled little girl and said with great warmth, "Sasha, I really believe that you have the power to be a very kind person."

"Thank you!" she said with a big smile, pressing my words into her heart.

Compliments can be like sunshine in helping people grow.

Compliments can be like sunshine in helping people grow. Remember that the sun shines on all plants, not just the ones that are doing what the sun might want. Be careful not to be manipulative in how you give compliments. The purpose is not to have children trying to get your approval. Instead, you are giving them your support to notice and celebrate the best of themselves.

Practicing Giving and Accepting Compliments

1 Be truthful in giving compliments to children. Remember that you want children to believe what you are saying, so you need to make sure that you believe what you are saying. For example, I often tell people very truthfully that I think that they look wonderful. This is because of their smile and their presence, not necessarily their hairstyle or their clothes.

2 Instead of taking good behavior for granted, give children compliments for any part of their behavior that is going well. See compliments as a form of nourishing children by building their self-esteem. Focus on the part of their behavior that is successful, not unsuccessful.

3 Be careful about backhanded compliments where you are including an insult with your compliment by saying something such as, "I really liked how you stopped whining."

4 When you give compliments, make sure that you sound and look like you mean it. Encourage children to accept their compliments from you graciously by taking them in, looking you in the eye, and saying, "Thank you!"

5 Create opportunities for children to give compliments to themselves. Ask questions such as, "What did you do today that you feel good about?" or "What are some things that you like about yourself?"

6 Encourage children to notice good things about others and to give compliments. You can play an Appreciation Game by taking the time to appreciate each member of your family or group of friends and getting them to do it for each other.

7 If children can write, they might enjoy writing compliments down on Post-It notes and sticking them on each other. If need be, remind older children that sarcastic remarks and putdowns disguised as compliments are NOT compliments and can be very hurtful, even though this is shown to be funny in many TV programs for young people.

Making Conscious Apologies

Part of having healthy boundaries is knowing how and when to apologize. Too often, adults give poor examples by habitually saying "I'm sorry" when there is no reason to or by refusing to apologize for rude or thoughtless behavior. Instead of habitually never apologizing or always apologizing, we can become conscious about when and how to apologize and about what to say and do instead when saying "I'm sorry" is inappropriate. For both adults and kids, conscious apologies can improve our relationships and increase our ability to act as powerful, respectful individuals.

Some people say, "I'm sorry" when there is no logical reason for them to be sorry. Women, especially, are often socialized to please others – and to worry about disapproval. Saying, "I'm sorry" anytime there is potential confusion or discomfort can seem like a way to make everyone feel okay. The problem is that constantly apologizing can make you feel and seem less powerful than you really are. If what happened is truly not harming or upsetting someone else, there is no reason to apologize. For example, suppose you are learning something new. Suppose that, each time the person teaching you gives some feedback about what to do differently, you keep saying, "I'm sorry!" What are you modeling for kids about mistakes being part of learning? Instead you can say, "Thank you for telling me!"

Other people hate to apologize. They deny or ignore rude or thoughtless behavior. They refuse to admit that they are wrong. They act as if being wrong means that they are terrible people. The problem with never apologizing, of course, is that you can cause conflicts to escalate and can severely damage relationships. Kids can learn that, when you say or do something that upsets or harms someone else, the three little words, "I am sorry" can save everyone a lot of time and prevent a lot of heartache.

Sometimes adults think that it will undermine their authority if children or teens see that they are wrong. However, it can be very empowering for young people to see that we as adults are cheerfully willing to acknowledge when we make mistakes instead of inappropriately

Clean apologies means taking full responsibility for your own behavior without attacking the other person.

apologizing for them - and that we can apologize in a caring way instead of denying or ignoring behavior that is upsetting to others. We can show in the moment the truth of the belief that nobody is perfect and that mistakes are part of learning.

Showing Kids How To Apologize

You can show kids how to make apologies in ways that will reduce conflict and move communications in a more positive direction and then encourage them to practice doing this themselves. Here are some reminders to avoid common pitfalls:

1   *Don't get stuck in intentions.* Even if you did not mean to be hurtful, or if what you did was necessary, you can show kids how to apologize for the impact of your behavior. You can be truthful and still be sorry by saying, "I didn't realize that getting this done right away was important to you, and I'm really sorry that my waiting inconvenienced you." Or, "I'm sorry. I didn't mean that the way it came out." Even if you have to set a boundary, you can say, "I'm sorry that my not taking you to your friend's house right now is upsetting for you, and you will still have to wait until tomorrow after you have done your chores."

2   *Stay in charge of what you say and do, no matter how poorly the other person behaves.* Suppose that you say something that insults someone else and that person reacts by getting angry and demanding, "What did you just say?" When someone is being aggressive like that, even if you were wrong in the first place, it's tempting to get mad back and say, "You heard me!" The problem is that, of course, that way of reacting escalates the conflict. In a case like that, try to ignore the other person's bad reaction and take full responsibility for what you have done to contribute to the conflict. Say, "I'm sorry that I said that."

3   *Acknowledge the other person's perspective and offer to make amends.* You can say, "I'm sorry. That was a mean thing to do. What can I do to make it up to you?" Or, "That was thoughtless of me. I would hate it if someone did that to me. I really apologize."

4   *Be specific and genuine.* Overstating an apology can come across as dishonest. For example, "I'm sorry for everything I have ever done that ever bothered you." Or, "I'm such a bad person that you must not want to be with me anymore." Instead, just say, "I'm really sorry that I forgot something that was so important to you. I would have been upset in your shoes. What can I do to help to fix it?"

5   *Make a "clean" apology.* Making a clean apology means taking full responsibility for your own behavior without attacking the other person, even if you feel that the other person contributed to the conflict or you think the person is overreacting. A statement like, "I'm sorry, but you made me mad!" is not a true apology. Neither is an impatient comment like, "I'm sorry - now let's forget about it!" Instead, you can just say, "I'm sorry. I should not have blown up at you."

What Is a Choice and What Is Not?

The second Kidpower Boundary Rule is that: *Some things are not a choice.* This rule grew out of a telephone conversation that I had shortly after we started teaching. The call was from an upset mother who said, "Kidpower has taught my child to be disobedient!"

"Oh, dear!" I said. "Please tell me what happened!"

Indignantly, the mother explained, "My daughter told me that Kidpower says

Not a choice

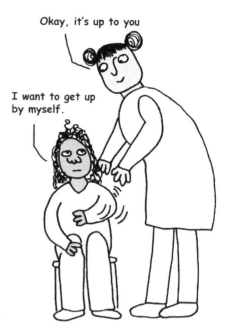

Should be a choice

that her body belongs to her so she does not have to eat her breakfast!"

"Oh, my!" I said. "Please tell your daughter that Kidpower says that, even though her body belongs to her, some things are not a choice. This means that you can tell your daughter that she cannot leave the table to play until she eats her breakfast. But forcing children to eat something when they don't want to can backfire. Instead of making this into a power struggle, you could use this as an opportunity to problem-solve with your daughter to find mutually acceptable choices about what to have for breakfast."

"That's a good idea!" the mother said. Then she asked, "Can I bring my daughter to another class where you explain about some things not being a choice?"

"Sure!" I laughed, and that's what we did.

Adults can acknowledge their children's right to dislike something while informing them that they do not have a choice. Chad at age ten told his father, "The life guard at the pool was abusive to me today."

Chad's father put his instant anxiety about the lifeguard aside, took a big breath and asked calmly, "What happened?"

"Well," Chad complained, "she made me sit down near her chair for a long time instead of letting me swim. And then she gave me a lecture."

"Why did she do that?" Chad's father wondered.

"Well," Chad explained, "she said that I was not looking where I was going

> *Adults can acknowledge their children's right to dislike something while informing them that they do **not** have a choice.*

Learning how to make decisions is essential to being able to set boundaries and to becoming an effective advocate.

just because I sort of accidentally jumped onto a kid in the pool. But, I didn't think it was fair at all."

Chad's father now had to put his indignation at his son aside. He took another deep breath and managed to say matter-of-factly, "I understand that you hate missing any chance to swim. But the lifeguard was doing her job to make sure that everybody at the pool was safe. Is there anything we can do to help you remember to slow down and look before you jump into the pool?"

One reality of life is that none of us are going to like everything that others say or do. We are also not always going to like everything that we have to say or do. This is why we need distinctions between what is and is not a true and appropriate choice. As adults, we know that many kinds of behavior have consequences, both good and bad. If you don't go to work, you will probably lose your job. If you drive recklessly, you will hopefully get a ticket. For young people who are not yet adults, their parents and guardians have the legal right to require them to do many things whether they like it or not. Different countries and cultures put different boundaries on some of these rights

Each family, school, community, and youth group needs to clearly communicate what kinds of choices their children and adults are allowed to make. Parents and guardians are responsible for ensuring that the people supervising their children only offer choices they consider to be acceptable. Our goal is that children will ultimately be able to make wise choices for themselves. If adults make all the choices for them, children will not have the opportunity to develop decision-making skills. Learning how to make decisions is essential to being able to set boundaries and to becoming an effective advocate. In addition, children are happiest when they feel that they have some control over their lives.

As soon as children begin to talk, we recommend that adults look for opportunities to let them make choices. For toddlers and preschoolers, it works best to give two choices that are close-ended. Make sure that these are choices that you feel good about. For example, if you want a child to drink milk, you can ask, "Do you want your milk in the red cup or the blue cup?" Don't ask, "What do you want to drink?" If you want a child to leave the park, you can ask, "Do you want to get ready to go now or after three more pushes on the swing?" Don't ask, "Are you ready to leave?"

As children get a little older, you can offer choices that are more open-ended and varied that still contain a boundary. For example, you can ask, "What kind of vegetables do you want to buy for our dinner?" Don't ask, "Are we going to have vegetables with our dinner or not?" You can ask, "Do you want to get ready for bed and stay up another half an hour or to go to bed right away?" Don't ask, "Are you ready to go to bed?"

With more sophisticated older children and teens, let them brainstorm different possible choices and discuss the pros and cons of these choices. Ask them to tell you which of these choices they think is acceptable to you and to themselves – and to analyze why or why not.

Helping Children to Understand About Making Choices In Different Situations

1   Agree on a definition about what choice means. "When something is your choice, this means that you get to decide."

2   Give children chances to practice making choices within boundaries that are acceptable to you as described above.

3   Point out places where the rules about choices are different. "At our house, you can eat in the living room. At Grandma's house, you can eat only in the kitchen."

4   Discuss when things are a choice and when they are not and why. "At school, it is not a choice to jump on any of the furniture. Here, you can jump on the old mattress in your bedroom, but not on our new couch. Why do you think that is?"

Taking in Useful Information While Keeping Out Hurtful Insults

The purpose of personal boundaries is not to shut ourselves off from others. Instead, effective personal boundaries let us take in important information about what others say and do while we protect ourselves from harmful interactions with other people. We can teach kids how to make a distinction between unpleasant information and hurtful words. After Kidpower had been in her fourth-grade classroom, a teacher called me and laughed, "I told my students that it was time to come in from recess and they all made their trash cans and threw my words away!"

"Oh my goodness!" I said. "What did you do?"

The teacher laughed again, "I told my students that the Kidpower trash cans were for throwing away hurtful words, not unpleasant information. I reminded them that many things are not their choice. I told them that they had the right to dislike being told what to do, but that they still had to come inside when recess was over. Then I gave them the challenge of noticing the difference between hurtful words and unpleasant but necessary information in their daily lives and writing about this in their journals. They came up with great examples." She sounded very pleased with herself as well she should have been.

"Please tell me more!" I asked.

"Well," the teacher explained, "One student wrote that his father said that he was lazy because he had not done his chores. He realized that being reminded of his chores was unpleasant but necessary information. He did his chores, but threw away the hurting word lazy. Another student wrote that her neighbor told her that she was careless because she had broken a vase. She said that she threw away the word careless but accepted the unpleasant but necessary information that her neighbor was upset about the vase. She apologized and offered to pay for it."

Because people are saying hurtful things all the time, it is useful to have images to help filter out what is useful from what is hurtful. For example,

Effective personal boundaries let us take in important information about what others say and do while we protect ourselves from harmful interactions with other people.

You can imagine a screen around your feelings filtering out insults while letting in useful information.

The Screen Technique

screens on windows let in fresh air and sunshine but keep out flies. You can imagine a screen around your feelings filtering out insults while letting in useful information.

Older children often like learning about the semi-permeable membrane. We explain that our bodies are made up of billions of tiny building blocks called cells. Each cell is surrounded by an amazing surface called a semi-permeable membrane that lets in the food and oxygen that our cells need to live. This membrane also keeps out the poison and pushes out the waste. If our cells didn't have that semi-permeable membrane, they would die. We can imagine having the same kind of membrane working like an invisible barrier or shield around our whole bodies helping to keep us physically and emotionally safe and healthy.

Learning How to Filter Useful Information From Hurting Words

1   Point out when people combine hurtful language with necessary information. Notice when you are doing this yourself. Discuss what kinds of statements provide necessary but unpleasant information and what kinds of words are just hurtful. Practice throwing away the hurtful while remembering the necessary.

2   Teach children to use "and" statements to connect affirmations with corrective action. For example, suppose a child is told by a friend, "You don't care about me because you forgot my birthday." Have the child practice throwing away the words "You don't care." Coach the child to say something that is true and realistic such as, "I am a very caring person, AND I will write birthdays down so I can remember next time. Right away, I will send my friend a 'sorry I missed your birthday' card."

3   Discuss how to filter insults away from useful information. Explain that this works like a screen and/or a semi-permeable membrane. Encourage children to come up with filtering ideas of their own.

Setting Boundaries About What We Say to Ourselves

Sometimes children internalize the negative messages that they hear from others and start to put themselves down. Sometimes children just naturally compare themselves to others and find themselves lacking. Part of emotional safety requires learning how to set boundaries on what we say to ourselves.

Most people have an inner chatterbox that is not the same as their inner voice, which is usually used to mean their intuition. An inner chatterbox comments on what is happening all the time. Sometimes this chatterbox says nice things, sometimes hurtful things, and sometimes it just makes observations. When children are not sure what we mean, we tell them, "Your inner chatterbox is the voice that right now inside your head is asking you, 'What is she talking about?'"

When their inner chatterbox says nice things to them, children can listen, in the same way that they accept compliments from other people. When their inner chatterbox says mean things to them, it is important for children to throw those hurtful words away, in the same way that they throw away the hurtful things said by others."

For adults, as well as kids, learning to set boundaries about what we say to ourselves will reduce a lot of unnecessary hurt in our lives. For example, how often do you look at yourself in the mirror in the morning and say to yourself, "I don't like the way I look!" Imagine being able to throw that thought into your trash can while you tell yourself, "I have my own kind of beauty!" Or, "I have my own way of looking good."

Have you ever winced with embarrassment at a memory and said to yourself, "I can't believe I said or did that!" Try throwing those words away and telling yourself, "Mistakes are part of learning!" Or, "You do not have to be perfect to be great!"

When you are learning something new, do you ever feel discouraged and sigh, "This is too hard! Everybody understands this but not me! I'll never get it right! I can't!" You can replace the words "I can't!" with the message, "I just need to give myself more time to learn!"

Timothy tells a story about how his daughter at age nine said sadly on her way to school, "Dad, my inner chatterbox just told me that I'm stupid because I forgot to do my homework."

"How are you going to answer that unkind comment?" Timothy asked.

His daughter was quiet for a moment. Suddenly, she brightened up and said enthusiastically, "My *other* inner chatterbox says that it's okay because I can do my homework at recess!"

Preparing Children to Protect Themselves From Hurtful Self-Talk

1 Try to avoid setting a bad example. If you do put yourself down, tell children, "I just noticed that I was being mean to myself. I am going to throw those words away and give myself a compliment."

2 Notice when children are being mean to themselves and point out that they can have other choices. "When you say that you are no good, I feel sad because I think that you are terrific. I want you to practice throwing away the words 'no good' and find something positive to say about yourself."

3 Explain about the inner chatterbox and give children practice in throwing away common ways that people their age insult themselves and replacing the hurting words with an affirmation. Use the following examples or others that might be relevant:

Self-Insult: "How could I make such a stupid mistake?"
Affirmation: "Mistakes are part of learning."

Self-Insult: "This is too hard. I can't do this as well as everybody else."
Affirmation: "I have the right to take all the time I need to learn."

Self Insult: (more common among older children and teens than younger kids) "I don't like the way I look."
Affirmation: "I have my own kind of beauty." Or, "I have my own way of looking good."

Using Boundaries to Help Build a Healthy Body Image

Suppose I were to ask a group of five-year-olds the question, "Do you ever wish that you looked different?" Most of them would look at me as if I were nuts.

Have you ever seen a young child look into a mirror? The child will be fascinated. Many children will make faces and joyous comments along the lines of, "Why, that's me! Wow! I have a spot on my nose. My tummy is big! Look at me!"

Sometimes I have the chance to ask these same children at age eleven the question, "Do you ever wish that you looked different?" Most of them will raise their hands.

Isn't that sad? Now, who do you suppose these children are learning this from? When I ask teenagers this question, they say, "Society."

"And who is society?" I ask these young people, who often torment themselves about their looks.

"Books? Magazine? Movies? TV?" they guess.

"And who decides whether or not to read, watch, or believe this stuff?" I ask again.

"We do," my students realize.

"So who are these little children learning from when they feel bad about the way that they look?" I ask one last time.

My students usually look stricken and groan, "Oh, no! It's us!"

In nature, it is not the rocks, trees, or mountains that look the same that we see as being the most beautiful. In nature, we see the greatest beauty in the rocks, trees, and mountains that look the most different. We need to learn how to do this with people too.

Teaching Young People to Feel Good About the Way That They Look

1   Set a good example. See beauty in yourself, just the way you are. When children and teens are present, talk about what you see as being great about how you look, even if there are things that you have decided to change. Avoid making negative remarks about others' looks.

2   Tell kids often how wonderful they look to you just the way they are instead of criticizing them. If there are things you want to help young people's change, do this with care and separate those changes from any compliments.

3   Be careful not to make fun of anyone's looks even as a joke and stop them from putting themselves or others down.

4   Since so many of our ideas about beauty are shaped by the media, start educating children from a young age to be aware media consumers. Watch programs with children so that you know what they are seeing. Point out when assumptions are being made about what makes someone look good or not.

5   Ensure that schools provide age-appropriate media education programs for their students. Programs such as the Media Awareness Network[1] have activities that show children and teens how their ideas are shaped about what it means to "be a lady" or "act like a man."

The "That's Not True!" Technique

Sometimes the Trash Can does not work for a negative message that others give to you or that you give to yourself. This is especially likely to be a problem when someone takes something that is true and combines it with a negative judgment that is not true. When I was growing up, I desperately wanted to have the straight flowing hair that was the fashion at the time. Instead, my hair was naturally curly. Suppose that I had tried to throw away the words, "Your hair is curly!" by saying to myself, "My hair's not curly; it's straight!" Anyone seeing me do this would have correctly decided that I was out of touch with reality.

The message I was giving myself was, "Your hair is curly so you're ugly."

I wish that it had not taken until I was forty-five years old before I learned to say, "That's not true!" A true statement combined with a negative judgment is not true! As mentioned above in relationship to body image, our ideas about our self-worth are often shaped by our taking in the negative judgments of the people around us. Teaching children how these beliefs are formed through the media and the

In nature, we see the greatest beauty in the rocks, trees, and mountains that look the most different. We need to learn how to do this with people too.

A true statement combined with a negative judgment is not true!

opinions of others enables them to decide for themselves whether or not to accept these different beliefs.

You can increase the power of a "That's not true" boundary by making a fence or a wall with your body. We sometimes coach large groups of people of different ages and life situations to make fences and shout, "That's not true!" to a variety of negative judgments. Here are some examples.

- "You are awful because you are different from me."
- "You are mean because you won't do what I want."
- "You are a bad friend because I am mad at you."
- "You are ugly because you look different from the models in a fashion magazine."
- "You don't care about me because you want to spend time with other friends."
- "You are weak because you are a girl."
- "You are violent because you are a boy."

Practicing Setting Boundaries About Untrue Negative Judgments Tied to Facts

1 Tell young people the Curly Hair story above or a similar story about a time when an adult felt bad because of making a negative judgment about the way he or she was.

2 Point out times when people tie true statements to false judgments. Ask kids to help you to come up with list of examples and discuss the difference between a fact and a judgment.

3 Make these comments or the examples above as if you mean them. For each one, coach children and teens to make their fences and say strongly, "That's not true!"

Having power over your triggers will keep them from having power over you.

Triggers and Verbal Attack

The terms "triggers" and "hot buttons" are used to describe an apparently small action from one person producing a huge emotional reaction in someone else. We tell older children and teens that triggers are thoughts, words, or gestures that cause people to explode with feelings. When you are exploding with feelings, it's hard to think clearly or to make wise choices for yourself.

The people who trigger us the most are often also the people who are nearest and dearest to us – someone in our family or a friend might just raise an eyebrow or give an irritated sigh and you might suddenly feel furious or like bursting into tears. You can learn how to notice your triggers and take the power out of them. Having power over your triggers will keep them from having power over you.

In a Kidpower workshop, a teacher such as Dylan might help me demonstrate an emotional trigger by saying, "Irene, I don't like you!"

I act as though I am exploding inwards by putting my head down, slumping my shoulders and saying, "Oh, my feelings are so hurt. I feel so bad about myself. My friend Dylan says that he doesn't like me. Something must be wrong with me."

Then, I turn to our students and ask, "Does that look safe?" They shake their heads.

Again, Dylan sneers at me, "Irene, I don't like you!"

This time, I explode outwards in response to being triggered by glaring and pointing at Dylan. "Well, I HATE YOU!" I shout.

Dylan raises a fist and snarls, "Oh, yeah!"

I turn to our students and ask, "Did my getting mad back make the problem bigger or better?"

"Bigger," they agree.

One last time, Dylan growls, "Hey, Irene, I just don't like you."

I turn to our students and explain, "In my imagination, I am taking the power out of this trigger. I am throwing those words away and saying to myself, 'How, interesting. My friend Dylan says that he doesn't like me. Now what can I do about this?'"

Going back into the role-play, I smile at Dylan's mean face. I walk away with awareness, calm, and confidence, saying cheerfully, "I'm sad you feel that way, Dylan, because I like you a lot. I'll talk with you when you're feeling better. Good-bye!" I point out that it's important to do this with great sincerity and without a trace of sarcasm, because sounding mocking or sarcastic would be likely to backfire.

Protecting yourself from an "emotional attack" is a concept that we use with much older children, especially those who are already dealing with difficult experiences, as well as with teens and adults. This idea can be too complicated and potentially scary for younger children. Many times young people are tormented or coerced into feeling bad about themselves, getting into fights, or making what they know are unsafe choices because they get triggered by the words that other people say to them or by their behavior. Can you remember having experiences like that? Do you know others who have?

Although people often accidentally or thoughtlessly trigger each other, an emotional attack happens when someone deliberately uses language or behavior to try to trigger you either into freezing, so that you are easy to pick on, or into reacting, so that the person feels entitled to keep going. By knowing how to identify an emotional attack, young people and adults can protect their feelings and make safer choices in their relationships with others. There are three categories of emotional attack:

1) *"You are worthless!"*
2) *"You are helpless!"*
3) *"Take care of me!"*

> *An emotional attack happens when someone uses language or behavior to try to trigger you either into freezing, so that you are easy to pick on, or into reacting, so that the person feels entitled to keep going.*

"You are worthless" attacks include language and behavior that is intended to insult you, your family, your culture, your religion, your gender, your values, or your looks. Someone might attack your relationship by saying, "I hate you" Someone might use curse or swear words or make racist and homophobic comments. "You are worthless" attacks might be about your character, with remarks like, "You're not trying." Or, "You don't care." Or, "It's all your fault!" Insulting behavior might include rolling eyeballs, a rude gesture, shrugging, looking at someone else and sneering, and sighing in an irritated way.

"You are helpless" attacks include behavior and language intended to threaten you or someone you care about. Comments like, "I'm going to hurt you," "I'm going to beat you," and "I'm going to hurt your family" are all forms of "You are helpless" attacks. Threatening behavior might include shaking a fist at you, pointing at you in an aggressive way, making a slicing motion across the throat, or glaring at you.

Finally, the sneakiest form of emotional attack is called, *"Take care of me!"* because this occurs when someone tries to use your caring or your compassion against you. Someone might act sad and try to pressure you into breaking your safety rules or into doing something that you know is wrong. Someone might try to make you feel guilty. Someone might ask you to lie to keep him or her from getting into trouble or to loan money that never gets paid back. Someone might try to make you feel inappropriately responsible for her or his well being by acting helpless, in despair, or needy. The message is, "Take care of me."

Of course, this kind of language and behavior can be triggering regardless of someone's intention. What makes it an "attack" is when someone does it on purpose as a form of emotional coercion. Depending on the age of the young people we are working with, their actual life situations, and the permission we have from their parents or teachers, we might use very specific language and behavior that these youths are already hearing and seeing. Our goal is to take the power out of the triggers that they already have or are likely to experience soon, without introducing upsetting language or images that are unfamiliar to them and that they are not likely to encounter.

Preparing Young People to Identify Their Triggers And to Take the Power out of Them

Remember that we recommend AGAINST using emotional attack or intense trigger language or behavior with younger kids. Even with preteens and teens, we ONLY do this kind of discussion or practice with permission of parents and teachers who believe that they are ready for it. We do our best only to use language and behavior that these young people have already experienced.

1 Explain about triggers and emotional attack in a fashion appropriate to the ages and life situations of the youths with whom you are working.

2 Have young people identify and write down trigger words and behavior that they might find insulting, threatening, or emotionally pressuring, along with affirmations that they can use to address them.

3 Use the Trash Can Technique for each category with these affirmations that you will be saying out loud for the practice, but in real life, saying to yourself rather than to the other person:

Trigger: "You are worthless!"
Affirmation: "I am valuable." Or, "I am proud of who I am!"

Trigger: "You are helpless!"
Affirmation: "I am powerful!" Or, "I have choices. I can leave and get help."

Trigger: "Take care of me!"
Affirmation: "I am going to keep myself safe." Or, "Taking care of you is not my job."

4 Play a game to take the power out of triggers by asking young people to come up with a list of trigger words and favorite foods. Coach everyone to say a trigger word and then a favorite food. For example: Creep – Pizza, Wimp – Ice Cream, etc.

5 Have each young person choose a word to be called that she or he can practice walking away from. Say the word or phrase as if you mean it and coach your student to walk away with awareness, calm, and confidence. Ask which emotional safety technique your student used to dispose of the trigger words.

6 Have young people write trigger words down on name tags and put the name tags on their sleeves or shirts. Have them practice getting centered while they read the words aloud. Finally, let them pull the name tags with their trigger words off and tear them up and throw them away into a trash can or recycling bin.

Explaining Boundaries on Touch and Games For Play, Fun, and Affection

The Kidpower safety rule is that touch and games for play, fun, and affection should be:

• The choice of each person;
• Safe;
• Allowed by the adults in charge; and
• Not a secret!

The choice of each person means that touch and games are not okay if they are not okay with each person involved in the activity. If one person wants a hug and the other one doesn't, the hug is not okay. If three people want to play tag and one person doesn't, sneaking up and tagging that person is not okay.

Safe means that, even if everyone involved likes the idea, touch and games are not okay if they are dangerous or hurtful to anyone. Hugging or playing tag in the middle of a busy street is not safe, even if each person involved likes the idea.

Allowed by the adults in charge means that, even if everyone in the group wants to get up on the table in a restaurant very safely to hug and play tag, this behavior is probably going to be stopped by the people in charge of the restaurant. If a boy wants to play barber shop with his friend and cut his hair very carefully with the safety scissors, that is probably not going to be okay with either of their parents.

Touch needs to be safe

Instead of not touching or playing with a child, the key is to be clear that affection and play have to be okay both with the child and with the other person.

Not a secret means that children know that they can talk with their adults about any kind of touch, games, or activities that they are doing or that has happened to them. We often emphasize this rule by having our students repeat, "Touch should not be a secret. Presents should not be a secret. Problems should not be a secret."

Well-meaning adults often cross the boundaries of children to meet their own wishes for connection without regard for what is in the best interests of the child. When my daughter was a toddler, I took her to visit my grandmother in a home for elders. Chantal charmed her great grandmother and all the other folks living there with her happy smile. She even chased a ball that her great grandmother threw for her. All was well until the manager suddenly pinched her cheeks.

Chantal burst into tears, and I objected, "She doesn't like that!"

"I know all about babies. She's just overtired. This didn't hurt her!" the manager said, and tried to pinch my child's cheeks again!

Often, people do not realize when a child experiences their behavior as invasive. They mean no harm, but their cheek pinching, tickling, too tight hugs, and too sloppy kisses are not enjoyable and can feel intrusive. Even being stared at with too much interest or talked to in a way that demands a response can feel uncomfortable. The feelings of well-meaning adults might get hurt when you or your children say, "Please stop."

At the same time, children need affection and often love to play physically. I feel sad when grandparents and teachers tell me that they are afraid to be affectionate because they don't want be accused of being abusive. Many adults have difficulty because, from their perspective, the rules about what is and is not acceptable seem to be constantly changing. Instead of not touching or playing with a child, the key is to be clear that affection and play have to be okay both with the child and with the other person. A child should have the chance to say "No" and to have that boundary respected. The adult should also have the right to say "No thank you" to games and touching that are unpleasant instead of enjoyable.

In classes, we show that these kinds of boundary problems are normal by pointing out, "Most of us have been touched in ways we don't like!" As we raise our own hands, we ask, "For example, how many of you have ever been touched in a way that you didn't like? Have you ever not liked it when someone gave you a sloppy kiss or pushed you or grabbed your arm or hugged you too tight or messed up your hair or held your hand when you didn't want to?" As the children raise their hands, we look at the adults in the room and ask, "Has this ever happened to any of you grownups?" The adults raise their hands too.

The reality is that having people cross each other's boundaries is normal. This is why we need to be able to set our own boundaries and to respect the boundaries of others. We continually remind children:

• If they and the other person both like this touch or game, this behavior is okay as long as it is also safe and allowed by their adults in charge, and not a secret;

- Each person gets to decide about touch and games for fun, for play, or for affection; and that
- It is okay to change their minds.

We have to be willing to speak up for our children when they come to us complaining about unwanted touch or attention. This can be extremely difficult with other adult family members. However, we can remind offended family members that, if our children can set boundaries with the people close to them, they will be far more prepared to set boundaries in more dangerous situations. In one evening class with parents of toddlers, Paul's mother asked, "What if the child seems to like it sometimes and hate it other times? My husband plays tickling games with our two-year-old son. Sometimes Paul says 'No!' and then says 'More!'"

I said, "Paul needs to learn that his words have power. He will get the idea if your husband stops when Paul says 'No' and continues when Paul says 'More' or 'Yes'."

Paul's mother said, "But my husband loves this game! He tickles Paul every night as part of getting him ready for bed. It's one of the only ways he knows how to interact with our son. But sometimes Paul really seems to hate being tickled."

I asked, "If Paul can't stop his father from touching him in a way he hates, how is he going to stop someone else?"

With a look of horror dawning on her face, Paul's mother got up and said, "You know, I would never let my husband tickle me the way he's tickling our son. And my husband hated being tickled by his older brothers. It was almost a kind of torture. I'm sorry to walk out on your talk, but I've got to go home right now and tell my husband about this. It's almost time for him to put Paul to bed!"

Sometimes adults worry that, when we give children permission to say no to unwanted touch, they will start saying "NO" to everything. This reaction is possible, but not likely. I am personally a very touchy feely person and would be very sad if Kidpower led to less love in the world. But forced affection is not love. The reassuring news is that, of the many thousands of children we have trained through Kidpower, we have had not one report of a child becoming less affectionate. What we do have are hundreds of reports of children feeling empowered because they know that they have a choice.

I occasionally meet young children who are not the least bit interested in talking with me at first. This is fine with me. Unfortunately, all too often parents want their kids to be nice to the lady who started Kidpower. As these little boys and girls squirm and look away, their parents try to push them with comments like: "This is Irene! Tell her hello. ... Be polite. Say thank you! ... Don't you want to say 'Good-bye' to Irene? ... Don't you want to wave to Irene? Or give her a nice smile? ... Are you being shy right now? You don't need to be shy with *Irene!*"

Having people cross each other's boundaries is normal. This is why we need to be able to set our own boundaries and to respect the boundaries of others.

I find myself intervening and explaining, "In Kidpower, we recommend against forcing younger children to be friendly in social settings. We believe that turning this into a power struggle is a mistake. It's just too hard for younger children to understand the difference between polite friendliness and a forced display of affection. When younger children feel comfortable, their friendliness will come naturally. In the meantime, your child will get the most out of seeing you model the polite behavior that you want him or her to use."

Being the focus of intense adult attention can be overwhelming to a child. If I decide to connect with a young child, I will often do something interesting near that child without paying any apparent attention to him or her at all. I might start playing with toys or objects around me or reading a book out loud to myself. Left to themselves, children almost always get interested in what I'm doing and come to join me.

If our children can set boundaries with the people close to them, they will be far more prepared to set boundaries in more dangerous situations.

Of course, as they are old enough to understand, we want children to act respectfully in social settings with our friends, family, work associates, and neighbors. However, it's another matter entirely to force kids to show affection through kissing or hugging someone when they don't want to. Children have the right not to feel like being affectionate with someone, even if this is a person whom their adults really care about. They may like or love someone, but still not want to show these feelings in a physical way. Forcing children to give or tolerate hugs and kisses gives them a very contradictory message about their right to set boundaries about touch with people they know.

Often older children don't know how to acknowledge others and greet them respectfully or understand the importance of doing this. If so, they can practice greeting people with a handshake and a polite statement such as, "It's nice to meet you." Or, "Hello." They can say good-bye with a handshake and a statement such as, "Thank you for having me here." Or, "Thank you for coming." Children can communicate respect by looking someone in the eyes and speaking in a firm clear voice. They can communicate appreciation with a smile and a simple statement such as, "Thank you for the nice present!"

Margie, whose sister was coming to visit after not seeing her family for a couple of years, got her children to make drawings to give their aunt when she arrived. Ahead of time, Margie told her sister - and the kids - that they could wave at their aunt, shake her hand, or give her a hug. At the beginning of their aunt's visit, the children just waved tentatively, but they all hugged and kissed her when she left.

Introducing Boundaries About Touch, Teasing, and Games

1 Make sure that you are walking your talk about affection and play being a choice. Intervene with adult friends and family who try to force unwanted affection, games, or teasing. Offer adults alternatives to take the pressure to respond off of the child. Some children enjoy having adults watch or be involved in what they are doing. Other children prefer to be ignored at first but can become engaged if the adults seem busy doing something interesting.

2 Describe the safety rule that touch and games for play, fun, and affection should be the choice of each person, safe, allowed by the adults in charge, and not a secret. Give children examples and let them come up with ideas of their own about how this rule works in real life.

3 Intervene with adults who try to force children to be affectionate or play games that they don't want to participate in. Explain about the importance of letting affection and play be true choices instead of forced behavior.

4 Have older children practice acknowledging people respectfully with eye contact and a firm voice. If they seem tentative, give them the chance to practice with you ahead of time so that they will be comfortable with the words to say and how to say it.

Stopping Unwanted Touch: Boundary-Crossing Problems and Solutions

Sometimes I introduce boundary-setting skills in a workshop by having people go around the circle and say, "Yes!" to the person sitting next to them. The job of their neighbor is to say firmly and cheerfully, "No!" Being able to say, "Yes" and accept "No" and to hear "Yes" and to say "No" is the simplest form of accepting and setting boundaries.

When we apply this concept about boundaries to stopping unwanted touch, these skills become very concrete. I put my hand on your arm. You don't like it. You move my hand away, look me in the eye, and say, "Please stop." And, if I am a person who understands about boundaries, I will say, "Okay! Thank you for telling me you didn't like my doing this."

This kind of communication seems pretty easy, doesn't it? But, of course it's not. When boundaries are set, people often react negatively. Maybe they don't like being told what to do. Maybe they feel entitled. Maybe they get their feelings hurt. This is why we work on making boundary-setting concepts relevant to our students and on creating practices to help them set appropriate boundaries.

Setting boundaries works best if you project an assertive attitude the whole time. Don't act whiny or wimpy. Don't act angry or mean. Remember that the Wishing Technique and hinting rather than saying what you want often don't work. To be assertive, make eye contact. Have a firm calm voice. Make clear statements. If someone is too close, back up. Make space for yourself by moving your body away or by removing the other person's hand from your body.

Be sure to act safely when teaching kids about how to be safe with touch.

Sometimes adults act weird, suggestive, or scary when explaining and showing how to stop unwanted touch. This is distracting, potentially upsetting, and totally unnecessary.

If someone doesn't notice, look the person in the eyes, remove her hand, and say, "Please stop!"

Sometimes adults act weird, suggestive, or scary when explaining and showing how to stop unwanted touch. This is distracting, potentially upsetting, and totally unnecessary. In Chapter Nine, we will show how to teach children to use boundary-setting skills to protect themselves from potential sexual abuse.

In introducing and building these skills in our workshops, we use appropriate touch that is not even a little hurtful or scary such as:

• Putting a hand on the child's shoulder;
• Holding hands with the child;
• Leaning on the child's shoulder;
• Giving a gentle hug;
• Pretending to tickle without actually doing it;
• Patting softly on top of the child's head;
• Playing with the child's hair;
• Putting an arm around the child's shoulder;
• Giving the child a back rub;
• Shoving the child gently; or
• Tapping the child's shoe.

We let our students tell us what kind of touch they would like to practice stopping or check with them to make sure that the touch we are choosing is okay.

Five Levels of Boundaries on Touch Problems and Solutions

The following five levels of intrusion are based on the ways that people often cross each other's boundaries. Understanding how to address these kinds of intrusions in daily life can prepare young people to deal with more dangerous situations:

1. Someone doesn't notice.
2. Someone doesn't listen.
3. Someone makes you wrong/uses emotional coercion.
4. Someone breaks the safety rules/crosses the line.
5. Someone makes you promise not to tell.

1.*Someone Doesn't Notice.* People accidentally cross each other's boundaries on touch all the time. We might bump into each other, stand too close, hug too tight, play too rough, and kiss too much. Part of the reason that this happens is that people's boundaries are changing all the time. Touch that we like with one person might not be okay with another. Touch with the same person that was okay yesterday might not be okay today. Touch that is nice for a few seconds might become annoying after a few minutes.

The solution is to tell someone assertively if you don't like something. You can use your eyes, words, and body to set your boundaries.

Suppose that you are a child and I am your teacher. If we both like it when I put my hand on your shoulder, is that okay? Sure it is. But suppose that you change your mind? Do you have the right to change your mind about what you do and don't like? Of course you do! But please don't expect me to read your mind. So if I don't notice that you don't like it when I am touching your shoulder, just tell me. Look at me. Take my hand off of your shoulder and give it back to me. Say, "Please stop touching my shoulder."

Most of the time, just giving someone a clear message with your eyes, words, and body is enough.

2. *Someone Doesn't Listen.* As a playful way to introduce this idea, a Kidpower instructor will cheerfully ask a room full of children, "Have you *ever* noticed that sometimes other people don't *listen* to you?"

Of course, they all shout, "Yes!"

Not listening might include someone agreeing to stop and continuing to bother you. The person might start arguing, "But this is fun!" Or, "But you always let me do this!" Or, "Come on, you know you like this!"

When someone doesn't listen, the solution is to make more space and to use body language and words that communicate the boundary both forcefully and respectfully.

Again, suppose that you are a child and I am your teacher. Suppose that you have told me to stop touching your shoulder. Instead of stopping, suppose that I put my hand back on your shoulder and say, "But I like touching your shoulder." Am I listening to you? No I'm not!

If I don't listen, you can set a stronger boundary by standing up, moving away from me, making a fence with your hands, and saying clearly in a strong calm voice, "I said, 'Please stop.' I don't like it when you keep touching my shoulder."

3. *Someone Makes You Wrong/Uses Emotional Coercion.* Do you like being told what to do? I don't! Getting embarrassed or upset when another person says that he or she didn't like what you did is normal. We explain to children that sometimes people try to make you feel bad for telling them to stop. With teens, we say that this is called "emotional coercion." Emotional coercion means someone using your caring against you to pressure you into changing your boundary and make you feel guilty. Common "Making You Wrong" statements are, "But I thought you cared about me! If you liked me, you'd be friendlier." Or, "Talking to me like that is rude." This person might be sad, have hurt feelings, or act angry because a boundary is being set.

You might feel like saying, "Well, that's just too bad!" when someone gets hurt feelings because you set a boundary. This reaction does not lead to mutually positive relationships and could cause unnecessary trouble.

Instead, a more effective solution is usually to acknowledge the person's importance to you and your good intentions and to restate your boundary. Children often act like they have been given a piece of gold when they find out that they can put what seem to be opposing thoughts together and say something like, "I care about you and I want you to stop." Or, "I don't mean to hurt your feelings and I want you to stop." Or, "I am sorry that this upset

If someone doesn't listen, stand up, make a fence with your hands, and say, "I said, 'Stop!'"

Children often act like they have been given a piece of gold when they find out that they can respond to emotional coercion by saying, "I like you, and I want you to stop."

you and I want you to stop." Or, "I don't mean to be rude. I just want you to stop." Or, "I'm sorry you think this is disrespectful. I do respect you, and I want you to stop." Or just, "Sorry and stop." Some children like being able to add, "Our family's safety rules are that I don't have to be hugged if I don't want to be."

Suppose you are a child and I am your teacher. When you tell me to stop touching your shoulder, I act very sad and say, "But I thought I was your favorite teacher! If you liked me, you'd let me touch your shoulder."

You can move away from me, make a fence with your hands again, and say, "You are my favorite teacher. I do like you – and I want you to stop!"

4. *Someone Breaks the Safety Rules/Crosses the Line.* Sometimes people will try to pressure others into changing their minds and dropping their boundaries in ways that are not safe. With children, we describe this behavior as "Breaking the Safety Rules." With teens, we use the term, "Crossing the Line." For all ages, we describe three different ways that people might "Break the Safety Rules" or "Cross the Line" – unsafe bribes, misuse of power, and dangerous behavior.

Unsafe Bribes. Bribes are like trades, where someone offers you a gift or a favor in exchange for your agreeing to do something. Safe bribes are ways to encourage you to do safe things, and it's okay for everybody to know about them. For example, a teacher might say, "Get the room cleaned up quickly, and we can go out to recess early." An unsafe bribe is when someone tries to use gifts or favors to get you to do something that is wrong, is unsafe, or will get you in trouble. If someone wants you to keep a gift or a favor to you a secret, this is also an unsafe bribe. An unsafe bribe message is, "I'll do something you really want if you'll just do what I want, even though doing this is not in your best interest. And don't tell anybody, okay?"

Let's consider an adult bribe. Suppose that I were to say to you, "I will give you an expense-paid guilt-free trip to Hawaii, for as long as you want, if you just do something a little bit dishonest."

When I use this example in a workshop, a lot of people sigh wistfully and ask, "*How* dishonest?" I then point out that children might find toys, candy, or the chance to do something special to be as temping as that trip to Hawaii. We explain to children, "The problem with accepting an unsafe bribe is that you end up feeling bad inside. And you deserve to feel good inside."

Misuse of Power. Another way that someone might "Break the Safety Rules" or "Cross the Line" is by misusing his or her power. The person might try to force you to drop your boundaries by physical threat, a misuse of authority, or by continuing to bother you no matter what you say. We tell children that sometimes people break the safety rules by using their power in a wrong way. The person crossing your boundaries might say, "I'm bigger than you, and you have to do what I say even though it's against your safety rules." Or, "I'm the adult. You're the kid. You have to obey me even though you know it's wrong." Or, "You can't stop me so I am going to keep doing whatever I want."

If someone breaks the safety rules, leave if you can or say, "Stop or I'll tell!"

Sometimes people misuse the power of a relationship by saying "I won't be your friend anymore." Or, "I'll tell all the other kids what a creep you are."

Dangerous Behavior. The third way that someone might "Break the Safety Rules" or "Cross the Line" is by doing something dangerous such as hurting someone, scaring someone, doing something illegal, or getting someone into trouble. Dangerous behavior includes crossing appropriate boundaries by being intimidating or by using physical force.

Dangerous behavior also includes being inappropriate in a sexually suggestive way. Because this behavior has the potential to be upsetting, we recommend introducing the concept of "Breaking the Safety Rules" to children by concentrating on "Unsafe Bribes" and "Misuse of Power." We will give more information about how to help children deal with potential sexual abuse in Chapter Nine.

The solution for all three of these ways of "Breaking the Safety Rules" is to let the person know that there will be a consequence if this behavior continues. You can do this powerfully and respectfully by making space, using clear words, and having strong body language.

If it is safe and possible to leave, all children are best off if they leave and go get help when someone breaks the safety rules. If leaving is not both safe and possible, we teach younger children to say, "Stop or I'll tell!"

We give older children and teens different choices depending on the situation when someone crosses the line. What they might do is going to depend on who this person is – an adult, someone else with more power and authority, or a peer. It also depends on where they are. The response is, "Stop or else _____!" What the "or else" is will depend on the situation. We tell older children that, if the person crossing the line has more power than you, you can say, "Stop or I'll report you." If the person is a peer and in

People who harm children often take advantage of their wish to be honest, honorable, and kind. This is why children who are old enough to understand this idea need clear permission from their adults to lie and break promises in order to escape from potentially dangerous situations.

your space, you can say, "Stop or you have to leave.' If the person is a peer and you are in that person's space or a neutral space, you can say, 'Stop or I'll leave." Older children can also simply decide to leave as they say, "It's time for me to go now."

Children of all ages need to be told clearly, "Even if the person does stop, it's still important to tell an adult you trust anytime anyone does something that makes you uncomfortable."

Again, imagine that you are a child and I am your teacher. When you ask me to stop touching your shoulder, suppose that I say, "I'm in charge, and you have to do what I say!" Or, "I'm your teacher. If you want to get a good grade in this class, you need to be friendlier." Would that be a safe thing for me to do? Of course not. This is why we call this behavior, "Breaking the Safety Rules." If I am breaking the safety rules, you can step back to move away from me, make a fence with your hands, and say, "Stop or I'll tell!"

5. *Someone Makes You Promise Not to Tell.* Suppose that someone who has crossed your boundaries starts begging you not to tell or threatens to harm you or someone you love if you tell. If someone is making threats or pleading about telling, it might be dangerous to keep saying, "I'm going to tell! I'm going to tell!" If what someone says or does makes you afraid to tell, the safest thing to do is to say whatever the person wants to hear so that you can get out of that situation and then leave and get help. Unfortunately, the most effective solution for handling this problem almost always means that you have to lie and break promises.

Adults often express concern at the thought of teaching children to lie and break promises. After all, we work very hard to teach our children to be honest and keep their commitments. We want them to care about others. People who harm children often take advantage of their wish to be honest, honorable, and kind. They have many ways of coercing children into agreeing not to tell. They will say, "You won't tell on me, will you? You promise, don't you? You aren't lying to me, are you?"

This is why children who are old enough to understand this idea need clear permission from their adults to lie and break promises in order to escape from potentially dangerous situations. You do not want to put upsetting ideas into children's minds as you explain why they might need to do this. You can get the point across by saying in a calm upbeat voice, "Someone might say, 'You'd better promise me not to tell – or you'll be sorry!' Or plead, 'Look, I could lose my job if you tell. Please, please don't say anything. Promise?'"

Notice that these threats are implied and general rather than specific. Please do not say, "Someone might threaten to kill your family if you tell." Remember, our goal is to build skills, not fear.

In Kidpower classes, I have all our students, both children and adults, imagine that I have broken the safety rules. I coach them to stand up, make their fences with their hands, take a step back away from me, and shout at me, "Stop or I'll tell!"

I frown, shake my finger at them, glare and in a playfully rather than realistically mean voice say, "You'd better not tell. Something really bad will happen if you tell!"

Immediately, I very calmly change back into being the teacher and ask the children, "If someone did that, would it be scary? ... Well, this is a time when you can lie and break a promise to someone because you are going to say, 'Okay, I won't tell if you stop!' Everybody say that."

All of the students, still using their strong body language, say, "Okay, I won't tell if you stop."

I then ask, "And what are you going to do as soon as you get away from this person?"

All the students shout, 'Tell!"

I remind the students, "Most of the time we want you to tell the truth and to keep your promises. The reason it's okay to lie and break a promise is because you are doing it to be safe and because you are going to tell an adult you trust as soon as you can."

Suppose that you are a child and I am a teacher. When you say that you are going to tell unless I stop, suppose that I say, "You'd better not tell. If you do, I'll tell everyone that you were bad!"

You can move away, make a fence, and say, "Okay, I won't tell if you stop!"

And then, as soon as you are away from this teacher, what are you going to do? That's right, you are going to tell an adult you trust as quickly as you can.

> *The reason it's okay to lie and break a promise is because you are doing it to be safe and because you are going to tell an adult you trust as soon as you can.*

Teaching Children How to Persist in Stopping Unwanted Touch

1   Show in a light-hearted way what not stopping unwanted touch looks like. Always choose examples that should be a child's choice. With younger children, you can show this by taking two stuffed animals or puppets. Have one pretend to tickle the other while the other turns its back and doesn't do anything. Ask, "Does this look safe?"

For older children, demonstrate by having a person touch you in a way that might look uncomfortable, such as leaning on your shoulder or messing up your hair. Show how the Wishing Technique doesn't work. Roll your eyes and sigh. Wiggle. Ask, "Does this look like I am taking good care of myself?"

2   Either just put your hand on the child's shoulder as in the Child and Teacher Example above or let the child pick a different kind of safe touch to practice with such as roughhousing, tickling, hugging, holding hands, playing with a shoe, etc. Whatever you choose, just go through the motions of starting to be intrusive. Your focus is on giving the child the chance to stop unwanted touch, not on being intrusive. Point out that, "If you like this touch, it is okay. And, it is okay to change your mind."

3   Tell the child to suppose that you are someone who *Doesn't Notice* that this touch is bothering her or him. Coach the child to take charge by moving your hand away and saying, "Please stop touching

my shoulder." If the child doesn't have a lot of words, then just "Stop" is fine. Coach the child to use a respectful voice and an assertive attitude.

4 Put your hand back and say, "But I like touching your shoulder." Coach the child to set boundaries if this person you are pretending to be *Doesn't Listen* by giving you back your hand, standing up, taking a step back and away from you, making a fence with her or his hands and saying, "I asked you to stop. I don't like it." Again this can be shortened to say just, "Stop."

5 Pretend to have hurt feelings. Pretend to cry or act sad and say, "That hurt my feelings. I thought you liked me. If you liked me, you'd let me touch your shoulder. Coach the child to set boundaries if someone *Makes You Wrong* by saying, "I didn't mean to hurt your feelings. I do like you and I want you to stop." This can be shortened to, "Sorry and stop."

6 To go to the next level, think of something that might be tempting to the child. Ice cream. A computer game. Going to the zoo. Be friendly to the child to reestablish the relationship. For example, you could ask, "Do you like chocolate?" When the child says, "Yes," then you can say, "I'll take you to the candy store and let you have all the chocolate you want, if you will just let me touch your shoulder even though you don't want me to." Coach the child to set boundaries when you are pretending to be someone who Breaks the Safety Rules by standing up, moving away from you, looking at you, making a fence with his or her hands and saying, "Stop or I'll tell!"

7 For children who are old enough to understand that lying and breaking promises is wrong, explain that they have your permission to do this *if* they are doing it to stay safe *and* they tell an adult they trust as soon as they can. Then, pretend to be a person who they need to do this with by acting angry and saying, "You'd better not tell. You'll be sorry if you tell. Promise me you won't tell." Be sure that the child knows that you are playacting. Coach the child to tell a lie to help keep the child safe if someone Makes You Promise Not to Tell by saying, "I won't tell if you stop."

8 Ask the child, "What are you going to do as soon as you get away from this difficult person I am pretending to be?" Coach the child to say, "Tell!"

9 If older children or teens think that it sounds too childish to talk about breaking the safety rules, use the term "Crossing the Line" instead. Coach them to practice different "Stop or else I'll _____ (tell, leave, report you, tell you to leave)!" responses depending on the problem.

Applying Boundary Skills to Dealing With Unneeded Help or An Upset Person

Once young people understand the basic concept of how to set different kinds of boundaries, they can adapt these skills to deal with other situations. For example, sometimes unwanted touch comes in the form of unwanted help. If someone wants to give children help they don't need or that makes them uncomfortable, they can say, "Just show me." Or, "I can do it myself."

One little boy came home from the Kidpower class at his preschool and told his mother, "Kidpower says that I can wash myself now instead of having you do it." His mother realized that her son was telling her that he felt embarrassed being washed like a baby because he was a big boy. They agreed that he would do it himself and she would check a couple of times to make sure that he did a good job.

Sometimes unwanted touch and attention comes in the form of someone who is upset grabbing a child's arm, shaking the child, and yelling. We tell children, "When another person loses control, you can make things safer by staying calm and respectful instead of yelling back or whining. If you make a mistake, you can apologize and offer to fix it, while asking the person to stop yelling and grabbing."

In classes, we show how this works with a role play about an angry neighbor, who is furious because the child has broken a favorite vase. The instructor pretending to be the Angry Neighbor starts grabbing the child's arm (pretending to be rough but actually being very gentle) and yelling, "You stupid little klutz. You broke my vase."

Seeing a child staying calm and respectful in the face of a raging adult is very powerful. We coach the child to stay calm and to keep saying politely, over and over, "I'm sorry I broke your vase. I'll clean it up. I'll pay for it. Please don't yell at me. Please don't grab me. Please don't call me names."

For children who play team sports, we show the same problem in the form of the Team Captain, who is yelling, "You made us lose the game, you creep!"

Again, the solution is for the child being attacked to move away and say calmly and respectfully, "I'm sorry I made a mistake. I did my best. And please don't yell at me or call me names."

Finding Adults to Tell

When they hear that anything that bothers them should not have to be a secret, children from wonderful families often tell me about important issues for them that their parents don't know. I listen, assure them that their parents do want to know, and figure out how they can help their parents understand. Sometimes we enlist the help of the teacher or a school counselor in talking to the parents with the child.

One eight-year-old girl wept as she described her terror about a neighbor who had said that he would kill her cat because it kept escaping from her house. When she tried to talk to them, her parents had told her not to say rude things about the neighbors. After talking with our instructor, this girl went home and told her parents in a clear firm way so that they understood she was really worried.

Taking a child's fears seriously can be hard for adults. A boy about nine told me that he was having nightmares every night and felt watched all the time. After a steady diet of the science fiction he loved, he couldn't get out of his mind a deep belief that aliens were watching him and getting ready to steal him. He said that his parents told him he had a really great imagination, and laughed when he tried to explain that he really was afraid. We practiced having him persist in explaining to his parents that he needed their help so he could enjoy science fiction without becoming upset by it.

An older girl said that she had very mixed feelings about spending the night at her best friend's house. She loved seeing her friend, but the situation at her friend's home had become very uncomfortable. The parents were fighting with

Children are safer when they can tell their adults about their problems

Being persistent in asking for help to be a fundamental self-protection skill.

each other so much that her best friend was hanging out with another girl who had gotten into a gang and was using drugs. She was afraid that if she told her parents, they wouldn't let her see her best friend at all anymore. Her teacher agreed to help this girl talk to her parents.

In classes we often ask children, "Who are some adults you could tell if you had a problem?" Common answers are, "My mom ... my dad ... my grandma ... my grandpa ... my aunt ... my uncle ... my teacher ... my principal ... my counselor ... my minister ... my rabbi ... my big brother ... my big sister ... the police ... the fire department ... my dog."

"Your dog?" we ask.

With great sincerity, some children will explain, "My dog is an adult and listens to me all the time!"

"It's great to tell your dog," we remind children, "but please be sure to tell a human adult as well!"

After a child finds someone to tell, the next challenge is to make sure that the adult being told hears and understands. This isn't always easy because adults, no matter how well their ears work, often have what children's songwriter Minnie O'Leary called, "Beans in their ears." Sometimes in class, we ask children, "When you are talking with your adults, do they ever say, 'Mmm ... hmmm ... that's nice, honey' when they are not listening?"

Most of them will laugh and say, "Yes!"

When my sister was seven, she had a long conversation with my father as he was reading the newspaper. My mother asked my father, "Do you know what you agreed to?" My astonished father learned that he had just promised that we could be the lucky home for one of the chicks about to be hatched in her second grade classroom! To their credit, my parents kept their commitment. Silky was a grand addition to our family for many years. A child's failure to get an adult's attention usually doesn't work out that happily. Too many times, the reason children don't tell their adults about something that upset them is because they think that they already did.

Sometimes children think that adults can read their minds. Sometimes they did tell adults and the adults didn't hear them or lectured them instead of listening. Sometimes even though the adults heard them, they didn't understand what the child meant. This is why we consider being persistent in asking for help to be a fundamental self-protection skill.

Prepare Children to Keep Telling Until They Get Help
I know that I have said this before, but there are many social forces working against children being able to tell their adults about their problems. We are busy and distracted. We get impatient or anxious. We don't understand. We minimize. In class, we ask children, "Do your adults ever get grumpy if you interrupt them when they are busy?" As they nod their heads, we remind them, "Even if they are busy, your adults really do need to know if you are having a problem."

Be sure your children know how to get hold of you or someone else they trust, no matter where they are. They need to know how to get out of uncomfortable situations. Be clear that they have the right to call on the telephone – even in the middle of the night – from school or camp or someone's house. If you are a parent, make sure that the people who care for your children know that you expect them to help your children get in touch with you if they want to.

One role-play we do in class has the child at a sleepover summer camp. We pretend that Camp Counselor Terry is making Ruth, the child helping him, uncomfortable. They imagine that he has taken Ruth out alone for a walk. He insists on holding her hand and asks her to promise not to tell.

Ruth then goes to talk with the Camp Director. After Ruth explains what happened, the instructor pretending to be the Camp Director says, "You're making this up and completely overreacting. Counselor Terry is one of our best people. Work it out with him!"

Ruth says, "I want to call home."

The Camp Director refuses by saying, "It's against our rules for campers to call home. I told you to go away and work it out with Counselor Terry."

Ruth persists by saying, "My safety rule is that I can always call home. I want to use the phone right now or my parents will be angry."

The Camp Director gives Ruth an imaginary telephone and watches anxiously while Ruth then calls her mother.

The instructor pretending to be Ruth's Mother listens sympathetically while Ruth tells her the whole story. She then says very lovingly, "Ruth, you did a great job of taking care of yourself. I am going to come up there to sort things out." Then Ruth's Mother adds indignantly, "And right this minute, I want you to put that Camp Director on the phone!"

Ruth grins and hands the Camp Director the imaginary telephone. "She wants to talk with you!" she says.

The Camp Director winces, holds the phone away from his ear, and groans, "I understand, Ma'am!"

The children watching the role-play giggle and take in the lesson – keep telling until you get help!

There are many social forces working against children being able to tell their adults about their problems. We are busy and distracted. We get impatient or anxious. We don't understand. We minimize.

Practicing Talking About Problems With Busy Adults

1 Even if you have already practiced the Getting Help skills, giving children practice in the context of talking about a problem involving unwanted touch is useful. Agree on a signal to let people in your life know that the problem is important, such as, "This is about my safety."

2 To get started, let the child decide what the problem is, what adult he or she is going to tell, and how that person might be busy. Pretend to be that person being very involved in an activity such as talking on the telephone, watching a football game on television as something important is about to happen, working on the computer, meeting a deadline for work, getting the checkbook balanced, reading a murder mystery and being just about to find out who did it, or getting dinner ready when it's terribly late.

3 For example, pretend to be reading. Coach the child to say, "Can I talk to you? I have a safety problem."

4 Keep reading and say, "That's nice, honey." Or, "Go ahead. I'm listening."

5 Coach the child to put a hand on your arm and say, "Please look at me!"

6 Pretend to be cross. Frown, glare at the child and say in an angry voice, "What is it?!!! Can't I have a moment's peace?" Or, "I told you not to interrupt me!" Or, with an exasperated glower, "What now!?"

7 Coach the child to stay calm and say assertively, "But this is about my safety."

8 Act interested and ask, "Oh, about your safety. Why don't you tell me what happened?"

9 Coach the child to tell you part of the problem. For example, the child might say, "Aunt Jane kept tickling me, and I didn't like it."

10 Minimize the problem by sounding annoyed, misunderstanding and complaining, "You interrupted me for that? You and Aunt Jane joke around and tickle each other all the time. I'm too busy right now for this nonsense!" Pause the role-play to ask the child leading questions like, "Did you tell me the whole story? ... Can I read your mind?"

11 Coach the child to repeat what happened and to tell you the whole story. For example, "But this time I told her I didn't like it. She kept on going even after I asked her over and over to stop until I told her that I was going to tell. And then she told me not to tell you."

12 Act understanding and say something like, "Oh, I'm so glad you interrupted me! That does sound upsetting! I'm sorry that I yelled at you. Let's talk this over and figure out what to do."

13 Another situation to practice is one in which the adult doesn't believe the child. You might say, "You are exaggerating. I'm sure that Aunt Jane was just trying to be friendly." Ask the child who else she or he might tell if you really were not able to listen.

14 Think of different places where children might go and people who they might need to ask for help. Make sure that the child has a safety plan for who else to tell and how to keep telling until someone does something about it.

Explaining to Kids About Safe and Unsafe Secrets

Often during our adult education programs, parents approach us and ask about how to explain to their children what kinds of secrets are okay to keep and what are not. As one puzzled father said, "My seven-year-old daughter 'Pricilla' has so much fun whispering about harmless secrets with her friends. If I tell her not to keep any kind of secrets, she'll just keep the fact that she has these secrets a secret from me!" Here are some guidelines that can help.

1. *As soon as children are old enough to understand, teach them about safe secrets and unsafe secrets.*
Common secrets that are safe to keep include:
• Surprise birthday parties that everybody knows about except one person, who is going to find out.
• Gifts that are going to be opened at a special occasion, at which point they won't be secrets anymore.
• Fun games with kids your age that don't break your safety rules, don't leave other kids out, and don't involve saying bad things about others.
• Gossip about family or friends unless this is about something that worries you, in which case you should tell an adult you trust.

Secrets that are NOT safe to keep include:
• Any kind of touch.
• Games that might break your safety rules or that might be hurtful to anyone.
• Presents that other people give you or favors that they do for you.
• Anything that bothers you.

In the situation mentioned above, Pricilla's father can use times when his seven-year-old is whispering secrets to her friends as a teaching opportunity by asking leading questions in a playful lighthearted way. His goal is to show that he is a safe adult to talk to, while helping his daughter develop some assessment tools about secrets.

For example, Pricilla's father might say, "I see you are having fun whispering secrets with your friends. I'll bet you already know what makes secrets safe for everyone and about what kinds of secrets are not safe. Is anyone getting hurt by your secret because you are leaving someone out or saying bad things about someone? ... Good! Because secrets that hurt people are not safe secrets. Is this a secret about a problem that anyone is having? ... Good! Because problems should never be secrets. Is this a secret about breaking the safety rules? ... Good! Because of course breaking the safety rules is not safe! ... Is this a secret about touch or about presents someone is giving you? ... Good! Because touch should not have to be a secret and neither should presents someone gives you! Thank you for telling me!"

2. *Don't allow or expect toddlers and preschoolers to keep any kind of secrets.*
Very young children are best off having a clear "no secrets" rule. They are too literal to understand about some secrets being safe to keep and some secrets being not safe to keep. This means that adults should not say things where young children can hear them that they do not want them to repeat to others. Don't complain about your Aunt Flossie's bad breath to your

Very young children are best off having a clear "no secrets" rule. This means that adults should not say things where young children can hear them that they do not want them to repeat to others.

friend on the phone as your three-year-old plays quietly nearby unless you are okay with your child telling Aunt Flossie, "My Daddy says that you have bad breath!" Expecting a young child to know why personal comments like these are not public information would be confusing and unfair.

3. *When they can understand, teach children about privacy and confidentiality.* As they develop more comprehension, children can understand the concept that their problems should not be secrets, but that there are times to respect the privacy of others by not discussing everything that happens within a family in public.

You can use daily events to help define the rules. For example, "Yes, I know you think it is funny that your little sister peed her pants and made a puddle on the floor because she was so busy playing with her blocks. Is there anything about what happened that worries you? ... Good! Since this is not a problem for you, please don't gossip about it with your friends – and please don't tease your sister about what happened. No one's health or safety is at risk, and your sister has the right to her privacy."

An understanding of confidentiality can help with communication within a family. When my sister, brother, and I were older, my parents wanted to be able to talk freely about the daily interactions on their jobs. This meant that we would hear things about their co-workers that were not appropriate for us to mention to our friends, who were often children of the people my parents were talking about. This information was not confidential in a professional way, but it was private on a personal level. My parents devised a term called "family confidential" that meant that we would not gossip about what was discussed at the dinner table. This was fine, because what was being discussed was not about problems for us and was not about safety for anyone.

Be careful when discussing "family confidential" issues to focus on problem-solving. To set a good example as adults, we want to avoid venting in front of children in ways that use insults to describe the intentions, actions, looks, culture, or character of others. If we want children to learn healthy relationship-building skills, we need to communicate about others in ways that are compassionate and respectful even if we are upset about someone's behavior or disagree with this person's choices.

4. *When privacy about a problem is important for a family, make sure that children have several adults who they can tell about anything that worries them and find ways they can say something to their friends.* Real-life questions about secrets can often be complicated. The mother of a ten-year-old boy that we'll call Louis explained their family's problem, "My husband has multiple sclerosis and would like to have a feeling of privacy about details that are sometimes involved in his care. He would prefer that his personal struggle not be a subject of conversation among people he sees socially through our son's school. How can we teach Louis when he can talk about what happens in our family and when it's not okay with us?"

"I can understand that you want to protect your husband's privacy as much as possible," I said. "My concern is that, when one family member has a serious health problem, this affects everyone else in the family. Louis is almost certainly worried about his father, which means this means these issues are a problem for him. He needs permission to talk with at least one adult who is not in the family about all his feelings about everything that is going on with his father. You can discuss with Louis what kinds of people both of you can trust to respect the confidentiality of your family while giving him a safe space to talk about his feelings. You can get a referral from your doctor or the hospital social worker about professional counseling resources."

"What about his friends?" Louis's mother asked.

"If you are worried about what Louis might say to his friends, you can discuss ways that he can be honest about what is going on in his life without going into details," I explained. "Otherwise, Louis can end up with the burden of being unable to talk with people he sees every day about something that is huge in his life – or feeling guilty because he couldn't keep everything to himself. It might be a great relief to Louis to be given permission at least to say to his friends, 'I'm sad today because my Dad is having a hard time. I don't want to say more right now, but I wish he felt better.'"

5. *Because these issues are complex, look for opportunities to keep discussing secrets, privacy, and confidentiality with the children in your life.* Literature and movies can be great ways to get discussions going as characters in books, on television and in the media often make very unsafe choices. Did any of the characters keep secrets? Was this a good idea or not? Did any of the characters gossip in hurtful ways? What might they have done instead? You can act situations out, using people, puppets, or even daily objects to show different kinds of problems and solutions about keeping secrets, about gossiping, about protecting privacy, and about finding safe adults to talk with.

The "Touch Should Not Be a Secret" Safety Net

A group of physical therapists came to their Kidpower workshop with an interesting problem. "We often have to do things with children that they hate," these dedicated professionals explained. "Some of them will start shouting, 'My body belongs to me! This is child abuse! Stop! You are hurting me!' We want to be respectful to our patients but we know that we cannot stop just because they want us to. What should we tell them?"

This example shows clearly why it is a mistake to make broad statements about touch to children like, "Your body belongs to you and you get to decide whether or not you are touched." This statement is incorrect and confusing because, of course, many kinds of touch and other things that children have to accept having happen to their bodies are not their choice. We practiced with the physical therapists different ideas for coping with their upset patients:

• They could acknowledge children's right to their feelings by saying, "I understand that this hurts and I wish I didn't have to do it with you. You have the right to be as mad at me as you want."
• They could offer choices that were possible such as, "Do you want to do this first and get it over with or in a few minutes?"

Touch of any kind should not be a secret

- They could be clear when something was not a choice by saying, "Stretching like this is to help your body heal and it is not your choice."
- They could let the child know that it was okay to talk about what was happening. "Tell everybody you want. Problems should not be secrets."
- Finally, they could throw the word "abuse" into their own Kidpower Trash Cans.

Instead of making general statements that are untrue, we need to accept the reality that there are lots of times when children have to put up with unwanted touch just because the adults in charge say so. If they run into the street, we'll grab them if we can. We'll hold their bodies to stop them from hitting or throwing. If they won't do it themselves, we'll make them wear their seat belts, put their shoes on, or leave the park when it's time to go - physically if need be.

Children tend to be literal. If we are not careful about accuracy, children might believe that none of the safety rules that we are teaching them about boundaries are true. This is why it is important for adults to be clear that unwanted touch and loss of privacy for health and safety are often not choices for children. A teacher may help a young child go to the bathroom. A nurse or doctor may examine a child's genitals or give a shot.

Having a safety rule that any kind of touch should not have to be a secret provides a safety net, even for touch or other activities that are not a child's choice. During Kidpower workshops, we show children examples of situations when touch is not a choice and explain that anything that bothers them should not have to be a secret.

In schools, we often enlist the help of the classroom teacher. "Suppose," I tell the children, "I am a kid on the school yard and am about to hit another child." I pretend to get ready to hit someone next to me. "If I don't stop myself, what is your teacher going to do?"

The teacher steps forward, takes hold of my arm, and says, "No hitting. You can use your words to say that you are upset, but hitting is not safe."

I pretend to keep trying to hit so that the teacher has to keep hanging onto my arm. As the children watch, I ask them, "If I don't stop myself, is it my choice whether or not the teacher stops me?"

"No," everyone agrees.

"But," I ask the teacher, "What would you do if I said, 'I'm going to tell!'"

The teacher, getting into the role-play, says firmly, "That's a good idea. We're going to talk about this a lot."

"Would you ever, ever tell me to keep the fact that you stopped me from hitting a secret?" I ask the teacher.

The teacher looks very definite and announces to all her students, "I would never ask you or anyone else to keep a problem about touch or anything else a secret."

Teaching the Safety Rules About Touch, Choices, and Secrets

1   Give children examples of situations in their daily lives where touch is not a choice – getting stitches from the doctor if you have a bad cut, opening your mouth at the dentist's office, having your hand held if you try to run in the street, etc.

2   With each example, ask, "Would it be safe if the doctor/dentist/adult holding your hand asked you to keep this touch a secret?" Coach the child to say, "No!"

3   With each example, think of other behavior from the same person that should be their choice as well as the other person's. "Unless you both want to, you don't have to:

• give the doctor a hug even though you do have to let the doctor fix your cut.
• let the dentist pat your head even though you do have to let the dentist look in your mouth.
• give a kiss to your uncle even though you had to let him stop you from running into the street."

4   Have the child pick a kind of touch that would not be a choice and the person who would be doing the touching. Pretend to be that person and tell the child, "Don't tell anybody we did this." Coach the child to say, "I don't keep secrets about touch."

Communication Bridges and "I" Messages

Communication and conflict-resolution programs teach that strategies such as leading with empathy, using "I" messages rather than "You" messages, and describing specific behavior in neutral terms rather than using attacking language are likely to work best when setting boundaries and bringing up concerns.

Imagine that I was upset with you because you were borrowing my books and not returning them. Suppose that I came up to you and said, "You make me so mad because you are so thoughtless!" Most people say that this kind of "You" message leaves them feeling attacked and not interested in figuring out what the problem actually is. Suppose that, instead, I said, "I feel frustrated when you keep borrowing my books and not returning them. Would you please return my books after you borrow them?" Although nothing works all the time, the odds are that you would be less likely to feel attacked and more likely to return my books.

Once children are speaking well enough to communicate most of their thoughts, they can learn to use "I messages" and non-attacking specific language to set boundaries, express concerns, and make requests. Although there are many different ways of doing this, Kidpower has students practice using the following communication formula:

1.   Make a bridge to acknowledge the other person's situation or feelings. For example, "I understand that you didn't like what I did." Or, "I know you are busy (annoyed, tired)."

2.   State your feeling in words that are about your own feelings or concerns rather than attacking the other person's intentions or character. This language might be, "...AND, I feel _____ (e.g. unhappy, uncomfortable, sad). Or, "It is uncomfortable to me." Or,

Strategies such as leading with empathy, using "I" messages rather than "You" messages, and describing specific behavior in neutral terms rather than using attacking language are likely to work best when setting boundaries and bringing up concerns.

        "The rule here is that we _____ (e.g. are on time, clean up after ourselves, don't use curse or swear words to each other.)"

3.   Continue with a factual description of the specific behavior that is a problem to you, such as "... when you _____ (e.g. drop your things on the floor when you come home instead of putting them away, don't call when you are going to be late, scream at me when I make a mistake.)" Try not to use attacking language like, "You never help!" Or, "You always make a mess!" Or, "You act like a jerk."

4.   State what you specifically want the person to do in neutral words by saying, "Would you please _____ (put your things away before you do anything else, tell me what I've done to upset you in a respectful way, call if you are going to be more than 15 minutes later than we agreed to.) Avoid loaded language like, "Would you please stop being such a slob?"

Here are some examples of how this worked in our family. When my son Arend was about ten-years-old, he liked to chew up raw cloves of garlic, breathe into people's faces, and say, "Smell my breath!"

Finally, I said, "Arend, I know you love garlic, and I feel uncomfortable when you breathe garlic into my face on purpose. Would you please breathe in the other direction?"

Arend used to say to me, "Mom, I understand that you love me, and I feel embarrassed when you call me 'sweetie-pie' in front of my friends. Would you please just call me Arend?"

Arend sometimes said to his father, "Dad, I see that you are upset, and I feel scared when you sound so angry. Would you please just tell me what I did wrong in a regular voice?"

And Arend's big sister, Chantal, used to tell him, "Arend, I understand that you wanted to use my art supplies, and I feel annoyed when you go into my room without asking. Would you please get my permission first?"

In workshops, we have students pick someone who is not there and pretend that the person next to them is that person. We tell them that they can make up a situation if they want to. We go around the circle, with one child saying to the next something like, "Doggie, I am glad you are excited to see me, and I feel annoyed when you lick me in the face. Would you please just lick my hands?"

Sometimes they pick situations that are poignant, "Dad, I know you have a lot to do, and I feel sad when you are too busy to play with me. Would you please find a time we can do something together?"

The job of the person they are talking to is to give a positive reply, such as, "Okay." Or, "I'll try." Or, "I'll think about it."

Just as with any other skill, children will sometimes test the boundaries of their adults when they are practicing. Once a twelve-year-old boy in my class picked the name of a TV star from Baywatch and said, "Pamela, I see that you are very beautiful, and I feel disappointed when you start to take off your clothes and then stop. Would you please keep going?"

I interrupted the practice to announce very firmly, "There are limits to everything and you have just crossed mine. Pick a different example!"

In classes with older children and teens, we explain that, "Having someone not agree right away when you ask this person to change is normal. You can be ready to answer the person and re-state your boundary." We then have the group practice responses to typical ways that people will disagree.

Argument: "But this is fun."
Response: " I see that this is fun for you, AND it's not fun for me. I feel _____ when you _____. Would you please _____?"

Argument: "But I want to."
Response: "I understand, but I don't want to. I feel _____ when you _____. Would you please _____?"

Argument: "You are being rude."
Response: "I don't mean to be rude, but I feel _____ when you_____. Would you please _____?"

Argument: "I just want to help."
Response: "I appreciate that, and I want to do it myself. I feel _____ when you _____. Would you please _____?"

Practicing Using Bridges and "I" Messages in Communicating Boundaries

1   Show what it looks like when you use a "You" message with attacking language. Pick an example that the child might see, such as a friend grabbing something that she or he is using. You can show this with real people or with toys. Pretend to be the person who is unhappy and say, "Cut that out! You are always taking my things!" Have the friend react by being insulting back, "You are so selfish!"

2   Show how you can set boundaries in a respectful, caring, clear way by saying, "I understand that you are tired of waiting, and I feel unhappy when you take something I am using. Would you please wait until I am done before you take it?"

3   Have the child repeat the words after you, "I understand _____ AND I feel_____ when you _____. Would you please _____?"

4   Give the child examples from your own life or from those described above.

5   Have the child pretend that you are someone else and pick an example to practice with. Coach the child to find words that are specific and not attacking and to start with "I understand and I feel."

6   Give older children more of a challenge by arguing and letting them practice the responses as described above.

Practicing stopping cheek pinching

Re-Directing Affectionate Cheek Pinching, Sloppy Kisses, and Too-Cozy Hugs

In classes, I scrunch up my face and ask my students, "Do you like having your cheeks pinched? What about getting big sloppy kisses? How do you feel about people who give you such long squishy hugs that you can't breathe?"

Most kids will groan and say, "Eeeuu." A few will say they like it and of course I tell them that this is fine, as long as it is okay with both people. Sometimes I see adults who are reflexively putting their hands to their own faces and wincing, remembering sore or wet cheeks from long ago! At the same time, children often sense when the person who is being overly affectionate is also vulnerable to them. Especially with older family members and friends, children want an alternative to having to start by telling them to stop.

Children sometimes tell us that they would rather "Just suffer though it." "She doesn't mean any harm," they'll explain. "It's because she loves me." We point out that suffering through affection is not the best way to build a caring relationship. In class, I tell children, "Watch what happens when I don't stop my Uncle Timothy from pinching my cheeks."

Timothy swoops down upon me as I sit and look pained. He pinches my cheeks and shows the children my unhappy face. He asks, "Does she like this?"

"No!" the children laugh.

Timothy approached again, saying, "Oh, I can't wait to pinch your cheeks!"

This time, I stop Timothy by standing up and grabbing hold of his cheek-pinching hands, straightening my arms to make more space, and turning him to the side. "Have some cake," I tell him.

This technique for redirecting affection was first created because a school principal told me that the older man who was the president of her school board would pat her on the head each time they met. She felt very embarrassed when he did this, but knew he meant no harm and wanted a gentle way to stop him. I asked all of our instructors at the time for ideas and got this technique from one of our pilot Kidpower team members, Jerilyn Munyon, who is also a fourth degree Black Belt in Aikido.

Whether it is cheek pinching, head patting, or other intrusive behavior, the first thing you do when you see a known "affection offender" coming towards you is to *Stand Up*. You have much more control of a situation if you are standing than if you keep sitting.

The second thing you do is to *Reach Out With Your Hands*. By extending your arms, you create distance.

Third, you *Take Physical Control* by taking hold of the other person's hands or arms and straightening your arms. This could be with both hands or with one hand as a handshake. The purpose is to be connected and to be in charge of what is happening. Make your arms stiff so that the person is kept away from your body as well as being held onto. If someone is already holding you in a hug, move your body so that you can take hold of the person's hands and then extend your arms.

Fourth, you *Redirect* the person by moving together in a direction away from you and motivating her or him with you to do something else. You could guide the person towards a photo album and say, "Look at these great pictures from our vacation!" Or, "How about some coffee?" Or, "There's someone I want you to meet!"

The "Redirecting Affection" technique described above works most of the time, but not always. You can help children prepare respectful answers in case the person asks for affection. We tell children to keep holding onto the person while they answer. Remember, this overly affectionate person is someone children care about and see as vulnerable, even though this person is being intrusive.

Request: "Can't I get my hug today?"
Reply: "Sorry, no. Let's just shake hands."

Request: "Don't you want to kiss me?"
Reply: "No, thank you."

Request: "I can't wait to pinch your cheeks!"
Reply: "No, thank you. I don't really like that anymore."

Request: "But you used to love it when I pinched your cheeks!"
Reply: "I'm older now! That's not something I like anymore." (Even if you've always hated it, there's no point in saying so.)

Practicing Redirecting Affection

1   Show the stopping-cheek-pinching technique: stop the cheek-pincher by standing up, extending your arms, taking physical control by holding onto this person's hands, and redirecting the person to do something else.

2   Pretend to be an overly affectionate aunt or family friend who is the "famous family cheek-pincher." Tell the child to imagine that you are both at a family gathering. Have the child start sitting down while you approach from across the room. Wave your arms exuberantly and gush, "Oh, you have gotten so big! I am so happy to see you. I can't wait to pinch your cheeks!"

3   Do NOT actually pinch the child's cheeks. Instead, pause if need be and coach the child to stand up, move towards you with extended arms, grab hold of your arms, and give you something else to do. For example, the child might say with a big smile, "Hi! I'm glad to see you too. How about looking at these photos!"

4   Once the child is good at deflecting, give the child the opportunity to practice answering requests. You can use the examples above or make up your own.

5   Practice other times when redirecting affection or attention could work, such as shaking hands instead of hugging, blowing kisses in the air instead of kissing on the cheeks, etc.

Chapter Seven

Self-Defense to Stop Most Emergencies

Children and teens are safest if they have the permission from their adults, the skills, and the confidence to forcibly stop someone from harming them if need be.

People of all ages and abilities need to know that they have the right to defend themselves from a violent assault - and the power to do so most of the time. Kidpower's law enforcement advisors say that most attacks can be prevented or stopped through the awareness, avoidance, getting help, and boundary-setting skills that are described in the previous chapters. In addition, children and teens are safest if they have the permission from their adults, the skills, and the confidence to forcibly stop someone from harming them if need be. As soon as children are old enough, age-appropriate information about how to defend themselves from weapons and groups is also important.

Our goal is to ensure that young people know that they have choices for defending themselves if someone tries to harm them. Early adolescent girls who took a Kidpower workshop participated in a doctoral research study on self-protection including physical self-defense. Author Kim Leisey, Ph.D., reports that these girls expressed self-confidence as one of the most important things they took away from the workshop. They described self-confidence as knowing what to do, feeling strong, and having a choice.[1]

One girl, Samantha, described the following, "Having a choice is the realization that there are options and choices that can be used to take care of one's self. It's knowing that you have options. No one likes to be presented with a situation knowing that the only thing they can do is what someone else is telling them to do."

Nicole, another girl in the study reported, "I have choices. Once you know that you can act a certain way during certain situations you will feel confidence. It felt good to know that if something were to happen, I could actually do something about it."

Three Safety Strategies to Interrupt the Pattern of an Attack
Seventh degree Taekwondo Black Belt and Kidpower Great Lakes Center Director Joe Connelly developed Kidpower's Pattern of Attack and Three Safety Strategies after doing extensive research about how criminals choose their victims, and what happens at the beginning of an attack.

Joe explains, "There are relatively few 'random attacks.' Whether the person threatening or assaulting someone else is a schoolyard bully or a serial murderer, most attacks follow a predictable pattern. In a Queen's Bench study, a group of felons convicted of violent crimes were shown videos of ordinary people walking down the street and asked which persons they would choose to assault. Surprisingly, what was most important was attitude and awareness rather than gender, how someone dressed, how old or young a person was, or how big and strong. These criminals were less likely to approach people who were paying attention, projecting an assertive attitude, and walking purposefully as if they knew where they were going. They were more likely to approach people who seemed timid, oblivious, or unsure. An attacker will often 'interview' people to research if they will be easy victims by approaching, talking, and observing their reaction. Unlike when applying to school or for a job, this is an interview we want to fail."

To understand how this works, put yourself into the mind of an attacker for a few minutes. If you were an attacker, here are the steps that you would be likely to follow:

1. **Selection**. If you were thinking like an attacker, your first step would be to select your victim. Your ideal victim is someone who would be easy to overcome rather than someone who would resist.

2. **Position of Advantage.** Your second goal as an attacker would be to create a position of advantage. You would want privacy so that other people would not see what's happening and stop or report it. You would want control so that you would be in charge of what would happen. Usually the way to create a position of advantage is to be close to someone and to be in an isolated place. As an attacker, you might sneak up on someone who is in a more secluded area of a park, street, or building. You might trick someone into lowering her or his guard by asking an innocent question, offering help, or seeming to be in trouble. You might scare someone into going with you by lying and saying, "Shh. Just do what I say and you won't get hurt." Giving an attacker more privacy and control is like giving more fuel and oxygen to a fire – the problem will almost always get bigger.

3. **Domination**. If you were thinking like an attacker, your goal would be to dominate the other person in order to get what you want. You might scare, hurt, abuse, humiliate, or steal from your victim.

4. **Escape**. Your last goal as an attacker would be to escape. You would want to get away and not get caught. You would not want to have to face consequences for having attacked another person. Usually, the only way that police officers can help victims is by trying to catch the attacker, but this is after the attack has already happened.

The sooner that people can stop the Pattern of Attack, the safer they are likely to be. We teach both children and adults these three Safety Strategies for interrupting the Pattern of an Attack:

Strategy #1. Be Aware. If you show that you are alert and assertive, an attacker will probably decide to leave you alone. If you remember your self-protection tool of staying calm, aware, and confident, you are least likely to be chosen as a victim. You will also be more able to notice a person who is trying to approach you so that you can decide what to do to keep yourself safe.

An attacker will often "interview" people to research if they will be easy victims by approaching, talking, and observing their reaction. Unlike when applying to school or for a job, this is an interview we want to fail.

The sooner that people can interrupt the Pattern of Attack, the safer they are likely to be.

Strategy #2. Take Charge. If you take charge of your space and your environment, you can prevent an attacker from creating a Position of Advantage most of the time. You can stop an attacker from gaining privacy by going where more people are or by shouting for help. You can stop an attacker from gaining control by moving away from this person, or if necessary, by defending yourself physically until you can escape. Taking charge means getting away from the attacker and getting yourself to a safe place. Sometimes taking charge means deciding to change your plan if a situation or person that seemed okay at first no longer seems safe to you.

Strategy #3. Get Help. Any time you face possible danger, the problem is not over until you get help. Getting help includes reporting what happened to people who are in a position to do something about the problem – such as the teacher of a classroom, the principal of a school, the manager of a store, or the supervisor of a park. If an assault has taken place, getting help usually means calling the police. For children, getting help means telling their parents and other adults what happened. For people of any age, getting help means telling people who care about you so that you can get support. Getting help might also mean going to a counselor or taking a self-defense class.

Older children who are already concerned about violence are very interested in the Pattern of Attack because this helps them understand why the Kidpower Safety Strategies work. However, the description above contains information that could be frightening to younger children. Our New Zealand Center Director Cornelia Baumgartner came up with an upbeat way to show both the problem and the solutions to younger children.

The children are sitting in a circle as Martin, Cornelia's partner, pretends to be the famous Pencil Pincher – someone who steals kids' pencils. Each child is holding on tightly to an imaginary pencil. As Martin The Pencil Pincher approaches, each child looks right at him and moves her or his pencil away so that he cannot get it. As soon as a child acts aware, Martin tries to go after a different child.

One child, Simon, has agreed to serve as a helper. Simon sits in the circle with his head down and his imaginary pencil on the floor in front of him. As the children watch, Martin The Pencil Pincher chooses Simon because he is not paying attention, sneaks up on him, steals his pencil, and runs away.

Cornelia then thanks Simon for helping and gives his imaginary pencil back. Next, when Martin The Pencil Pincher approaches again, Simon looks right at him and hangs onto his pencil (Safety Strategy #1: Be and Act Aware). When Martin keeps on coming towards him, Simon stands up (Safety Strategy #2: Take Charge), goes to the teacher, and asks for help (Safety Strategy #3: Get Help), protecting both his pencil and himself.

Showing the Pattern of Attack and the Kidpower Safety Strategies

1 Explain to older children and teens how the Pattern of Attack works. The drawings show how to act this demonstration out in a playful way. Pretend to be an attacker and have an adult helper pretend to be your victim so you can show how easy it is to sneak up on someone from behind. Have your helper sit with his back to you and his body closed down. If you don't have another person to be your helper, then use a doll.

Ask children, "Let's pretend that each of you are on your own. Point to which person you think that I, as an attacker, would be most likely to select." As the children point to your helper, ask, "Why?" This is a leading question to get children to notice that your helper is more likely to be selected as a victim because he is not paying attention and because his body is closed down. Sneak up on your helper playfully to create a position of advantage. Then, dominate your helper. Gently touch his shoulders rather than acting scary. Point out that domination can mean hurting, scaring, or embarrassing someone. Finally, escape after the attack by creeping away dramatically.

Showing Selection of someone who is not looking

It's harder to attack someone who is out of reach

Sneaking up to create a Position of Advantage

Showing Domination in a playful way

Escaping in order to get away and not get caught

2 Show how the Kidpower Safety Strategies can interrupt the attack. Your helper this time can be an adult or a child. Again, tell kids to pretend you are an attacker. Role play in these steps:

• Start to sneak up on a helper who is sitting with her back to you. Coach your helper to sit tall, turn, and glance towards you.
• In response to your helper acting aware, turn and walk the other way, explaining that, usually, being aware will be enough to cause an attacker to leave someone alone.
• Approach your helper again. Show how your helper can take charge if you as the attacker try to approach her even though she is being aware. Coach your helper to move away and go to where other people are. Have your helper imagine that she is in a corner and needs more space to get away. Coach her to set a boundary by putting her hands up and saying, "Stop!" Back up when she does.
• Coach your helper to go to a person you have agreed will be Safety and ask, "Please help me. That person is acting scary." Coach the person acting as Safety to respond, "I will help you!"

3 For younger children, act out the Pencil Pincher demonstration as described above to show both how an attack works and how the Safety Strategies can stop the attack.

4 Review the sections on how to "Act Calm, Aware, and Confident", "Move Out of Reach," and "Be Persistent in Getting Help From Busy Adults" in Chapter Four. Show how these practices can help prevent an attack.

"Less Safe" and "More Safe" Attitudes

Just as you try out different kinds of clothes to see what fits, both older children and adults can benefit by trying out "less safe" and "more safe" attitudes so that they can feel the difference in their own bodies. In workshops, I often tell students as I act out what I'm telling them to do, "Stand up and walk around the room. Make your bodies *closed down*. Fold your arms or put your hands in your pockets. Have your head bent so that you are looking at the ground. When you are tired or worried, it is normal to close your body down, but being closed makes you more likely to be selected by someone who wants to pick on you.

"Now," I go on. "I want you to imagine that you are *lost in thought*. Look up in the air. Get a dreamy smile on your face. Pretend that you are listening to music, talking or texting on a cell phone, or daydreaming. Even though you are not closed down, you are still not aware and this makes you more vulnerable." With older children and teens, I point out that using alcohol or drugs is another way of losing your awareness.

Next, I tell my students, "I want you to pretend that you are feeling very *timid*. You know how people act in a scary movie when they are going towards the haunted house where the screams are coming out? This is a really bad idea, when you think about it! Anyway, shiver. Squish your elbows to your sides. Glance nervously in different directions. Even though you are aware, acting timid is likely to make someone think that you would be an easy victim.

"Now act *aggressive*," I direct my students. "Point your finger or shake your fist at other people. Get close, but don't touch anybody. Stick out your jaw. Glare. This can feel more powerful, but it is actually more dangerous. Acting

| Aggressive | Closed Down | Timid | Oblivious | Aware |

aggressive makes it seem that you are looking for trouble, which can lead to a fight, and fights are not safe.

"Finally let's practice *the safest way* to walk by showing awareness and projecting an assertive, respectful attitude," I say. "Everybody, make your bodies calm, alert, and confident. Stand or sit tall. Look around with a 'soft eye' and a respectful, neutral face. You can wave and say, 'Hi,' or just glance around to make sure that the person behind you is not trying to sneak up on you. The message you are sending to anyone who might be thinking of bothering you is that you know that this person is there. You are not afraid and you do not want trouble. You know where you are going, and you are in charge of your safety."

Teaching the Differences Between "Less Safe" And "More Safe" Attitudes

1 **Get young people to stand up and experiment with different attitudes with you while walking around the room. Have everyone:**

- Close their bodies down by putting their heads down, squeezing their elbows to their sides, putting their hands in their pockets, and shuffling across the floor;
- Act as if their head is in the clouds by pretending to daydream, talk or text on a cell phone, or listen to music;
- Act timid by taking little steps while looking nervously around;
- Act tough by glaring, striding close to each other, jutting their chins out towards each other, and waving their fists in the air; and
- Act aware and assertive by walking with their hands free, giving each other space, standing tall, having a neutral or friendly expression, and looking around.

2 **Look for examples from stories, movies, or real life to point out to children when people are using the different attitudes and discuss what these people look like to them.**

For both predatory and competitive attacks, you are safest if you act calm, aware, and confident and if you take charge by leaving and getting to safety as soon as you can.

Predatory and Competitive Attacks

Especially for teenagers and young adults who are more likely to be exploring the world on their own, understanding the difference between predatory and competitive attacks can be helpful in understanding how best to respond to someone who is threatening them. Most attacks on children and most attacks by men on women are predatory. Predatory attackers are likely to choose victims who they see as weaker so they can feel more powerful, steal something, get sexual gratification, or meet other needs. Predatory attacks follow the Pattern of Attack.

The term "competitive attack" means an attack that takes place because one person wants to show that he or she is better, stronger, or more entitled than the other. Most competitive attacks are between men or boys, but this can also happen with women and girls. Competitive attacks happen when people become aggressive over turf, status, or to prove themselves stronger. Although we teach young people to be assertive most of the time, the reality is that acting aggressively might also work to stop a predatory attack. The danger is that acting aggressively is likely to provoke a competitive attack. Attackers who feel challenged or insulted are more likely to continue a competitive confrontation than those who feel that the other person is not competing with them.

In responding to a competitive attack, if you cannot just leave quietly, your safest choice is to de-escalate the conflict. One way to do this is through "false surrender", which means pretending to agree with the attacker or to act is if you are giving up, so that you can escape or, if need be, be in a better position to fight back. We tell young people who might end up in this situation that you don't owe attackers the truth. It is not your job to educate them or to get even with them. It is your job to get out of the situation as safely as you can.

Suppose that someone is threatening you over territory by saying that you are in the "wrong neighborhood." You can say, "I didn't mean to offend you. I'm really sorry. I just want to leave." For both predatory and competitive attacks, you are safest if you act calm, aware, and confident and if you take charge by leaving and getting to safety as soon as you can.

Preparing Teens to Deal With Competitive Attacks

1 If young people are going out into the world independently, explain what a competitive attack is. Remind them that their safest choice is to leave if they can and not to fight over insults or property.

2 Here's how to practice de-escalating a competitive attack with a teen. This practice is NOT appropriate for most children unless they are already dealing with this kind of attack.

• Tell your student to imagine that you are a dangerous person and that he (or she) is cornered or trapped in a place where leaving is not yet an option. Stand out of reach but start making challenging remarks in an aggressive way, such as, "You don't belong here! ... Who are YOU looking at? ... You are such a *jerk*!..." Use verbal attack with insults and threats that are relevant to your student. Ask for suggestions.

• Teach your student to practice false surrender. Start by making sure that his feet are in a stable, well-balanced stance that would make it easy to move quickly. Coach him to put his hands up folded lightly in front on him at about the level of his heart. This stance looks more passive than our regular ready position described below, but his hands and feet are ready to use if need be.

- As you make obnoxious comments and threatening gestures while continuing to stay out of reach, coach your student to use de-escalating language in a respectful voice, saying things like, "I apologize. You are right. I should not have come here. I am a wimp. I just want to leave."

- Show your student how he can expand his mental and visual awareness to keep paying attention to you as the attacker while also looking for possible escape routes.

Yelling and Giving Orders

We know countless stories of people who have stopped attacks by yelling loudly. To take just one example, a few years ago, two girls were walking on the sidewalk after school in a nice neighborhood near my house. A man jumped out of a car and grabbed them. They pulled away and ran. He chased them down the street until one girl started yelling. As soon as she shouted at him, the attacker ran back to his car and drove away.

Once Timothy and I were teaching a class in the basement of a hospital. A man in the elevator heard our students shouting, "I need help!" He came running down the stairs to see what was going on. Being able to use a loud voice effectively in a dangerous situation is an essential self-defense skill. Yelling can get the attention of others and take away the privacy that an attacker wants. Yelling makes it clear that someone is not going to be an easy victim, which helps take away an attacker's sense of control.

Yelling can also be useful in dealing with other emergencies. One morning, I saw my elderly neighbor running frantically back and forth on her lawn and crying. As other people down the street stood in their front yards nervously watching and wondering what to do, I ran over to her. My neighbor fell into my arms weeping and saying that her husband, who had been sick for a long time, had died from a heart attack. Automatically, I yelled, "Call 9-1-1" so loudly that our other neighbors came rushing to help us. I then went into her home to call 9-1-1 myself. People from three blocks away called 9-1-1 and then came driving over to see if there was anything they could do. Even though the man had already died in his sleep, my neighbor got the help she needed to prevent her from getting hurt, and support in coping with the loss of her husband.

When I tell parents that their children need to practice yelling, they sometimes look at me oddly and protest, "But my kids are always so loud and active. In fact, I have been teaching them not to yell inside."

"I think a clearer rule would be to teach your children to use indoor voices unless there is an emergency," I explain. "For example, what if something caught fire in your home? I'm sure you'd want your children to yell for help as loudly as possible. If something scary happens, many children are likely to freeze unless they've practiced doing something different. Especially as they get older and more self-conscious, children can become too embarrassed to make a scene in front of other people even in the face of possible danger."

Being able to use a loud voice effectively in a dangerous situation is an essential self-defense skill.

If you can yell when you're embarrassed, you'll be able to yell when you're scared.

In our classes, sometimes children don't want to practice yelling because it's "silly" or "embarrassing." We acknowledge these feelings and say that it's normal to feel this way sometimes. Then we ask, "What's more important? Not being embarrassed or being safe?"

"Being safe," our students grumble, knowing that we are making a point. "But it's still embarrassing!"

Joe Connelly, whom I mentioned earlier, tells his students, "Yelling gives you a chance to conquer the E-Word – Embarrassment. That's really important, because if you can yell when you're embarrassed, you'll be able to yell when you're scared."

As an adult, in order to set a good example and also for your own personal safety, be sure that you can yell loudly yourself. Showing children that you are capable of yelling in a strong and effective way is really important. My voice used to freeze up when I tried to yell in front of people. I realized that, if I wanted my children to be able to yell for help, I had to set a good example by showing them that I could yell. We practiced yelling in private places like the car and the beach. Now, any of us can yell if we wish anytime, anywhere.

The most powerful yells are deep, short, and loud. Yelling from your diaphragm is more effective than screaming from your throat because a lower pitch sounds and feels stronger. Also, taking deeper breaths instead of shallow ones can help to reduce anxiety. In class, our instructor Carol will tell our students as she does this herself, "Put your hands on your throat and say 'no' from there." Carol exaggerates making a high-pitched "No ... no ... no ..." Then she asks, "Does that sound very powerful?"

Often students grin and squeak, "no ... no... no ..." Next, Carol puts her hands on her diaphragm and says, "Everybody, put your hands on your belly like this. Breathe quietly in and out so that you can feel your belly move. Now, from your belly, give a deep loud short, 'NO!' ... Doesn't that sound stronger?"

Sometimes children like to yell in a long, drawn-out way, "NOOOOOOOOOOOOO!"

The most powerful yells are deep, short, and loud.

We explain why this is not as effective by saying, "When you yell 'NOOOOO' like that, it sounds as if you are playing rather than as if you really mean it. A short strong 'NO!' is like a punch – a yell has power if it is focused rather than drawn-out."

To warm up our student's voices, we lead them in playing "The NO! Game" either with a partner or with one half of a group against the other half as follows:

1. One side starts by saying, "no" in a whisper, short and deep from the belly, but very softly.
2. The other side says, "No" a little louder.
3. They keep going back and forth until the first side gets very loud, the second side gets even louder.

4.   Pretty soon both sides are shouting at the top of their lungs.

5.   We joke that it's easier to start The 'NO!" Game than to stop it.

Yelling or giving orders in a strong voice can deter an attacker and can also help to overcome the Bystander Effect. The messages that you want to communicate to an attacker are, "No! Stop! I want to leave! Go away!" The message that you want to communicate to bystanders is, "I need help!"

Many people have heard stories about times when bystanders ignored cries for help. They wonder if they should teach children to yell "Fire" instead of "Help!" The theory behind this idea is that bystanders might be afraid to get involved in an assault by responding to a call for help and would be more likely to respond to a call to put out a fire. Our advisors say that there is nothing wrong with yelling "fire" if yelling for help doesn't work – but they say that children are best off giving bystanders clear information about what the problem is. Yelling "fire" might cause people to come to help, but it might also cause them to go look for the smoke from the fire.

In an emergency, people might freeze because of the "Bystander Effect" as a result of fear, not knowing what to do, or denial. A video I watched as Part of a Red Cross First Aid training showed a dramatization of a girl who had just been hit by a car. As she lay in the street next to her crumpled bicycle, we saw the faces and heard the voices of what might be going on in the heads of different bystanders who were looking with concern but not moving. "Poor thing!... Someone needs to do something! .... I hope she's not hurt too badly. ... I've got to get to work. ... Someone needs to help her..." Finally, one voice came clearly out of the fog of confusion and shouted, **"Who here knows first aid?** ... **Who can call 9-1-1?"** People rushed in to help, and the little girl started to move and then sat up by herself.

To break through the immobility caused by the Bystander Effect, we have our students practice giving clear loud information and orders to the people who are nearby. We teach children to yell, "I need help!" as their first response to any kind of danger. If the children are old enough to do this practice without being frightened, they can also yell, "This is NOT my father! Call the police!!"

When possible, giving specific orders to specific people is more effective than yelling in general to the world at large. In workshops with older children and teens, we often practice overcoming the bystander effect in the context of an accident, where someone has been hurt. One person sits or lies on the floor as if hurt. Two "bystanders" stand nearby looking confused. The student practicing points at bystanders, waves them to come over or go to get help, and calls out specific commands until the bystanders respond, such as, "You in the red shirt!, Come help me! ... You on the cell phone! Hang up and call 911! ... You with a white hat! Direct traffic away from the accident! Watch out for cars! ... Does anyone know first aid? You do? Great! You come and help me!"

We remind our students that, in a medical emergency, unlike in an attack, they should not move someone who might be severely injured until professional help arrives, unless there is no other choice. An example of "no other choice" might be that a nearby car is catching fire, not that a

We teach children to yell, "I need help!" as a powerful response to most kinds of danger.

well-meaning but ignorant person thinks that the victim would be "more comfortable" on the soft grass rather than on the sidewalk.

Some of our favorite success stories come from people who gained important knowledge from our students about how to protect themselves. One afternoon, Laura, the friend of one of our Teenpower students, was walking back to her apartment. The street was empty and nobody seemed to be at home. A man started following Laura. This was a long residential street so there were no stores to go into. Laura kept walking faster and faster. The man kept following her. Laura crossed the street and so did he.

Finally, Laura remembered what she'd heard from her friend about not using the Wishing Technique and about yelling. She whirled around, put her hands up and yelled, "Stop following me!"

To Laura's astonishment, the man took off running. Showing awareness, yelling, and giving orders made it clear to this man that she was not an easy victim. We now tell the "Stop Following Me!" story in our classes with teens and adults and have turned this into the practice described below.

Practicing Yelling and Giving Orders

1   Show children the difference between yelling from their bellies and yelling from their throats. Play "the NO Game" with each other, starting with a whisper and then getting louder and louder. Make sure that the yells stay short, loud, and deep.

2   Coach children to yell different messages that are appropriate for their age and understanding. "NO!" "STOP!" "I NEED HELP!" "I AM BEING ATTACKED!" "CALL THE POLICE!"

3   With older children and teens, explain about the "Bystander Effect." This is a practice that people can do in pairs, with one being the Bystander and the other being the Advocate.

• Tell your student to imagine that there is a health emergency. Maybe someone fell and got hurt. Pretend to be a Bystander who is frozen into immobility, perhaps because of denial, fear, not knowing what to do, or not wanting to get involved.
• Coach the Advocate to point to you and give you specific orders in a loud clear voice, such as, " You with the blue hat. Come and help me!" Or, "You on the cell phone. Call 911!" Remind your student not to move someone who is having a health emergency unless there is no other choice.
• As the Bystander, instead of listening right away, stand still and look blankly at the Advocate. Coach your student to persist by pointing at you, waving at you to come over, and repeating the order, adding and getting louder, "This is an emergency! I mean YOU! NOW!" Make the practice more challenging by looking away or staring at your watch. Have your student repeat the message with a loud, firm voice and clear body language at least three times before you respond.

4   With older children and teens, you can also tell the Stop Following Me story and then do a practice on giving orders based on this situation. First, let your young person be the Attacker so that she can feel the difference for herself. Put your back to her and walk with your head down. Coach her to grab your shoulders firmly but not violently. Act scared when she does. Next, coach her to follow you again. This time, glance back, turn around, put your hands up and yell, "STOP FOLLOWING ME!" Even though she will be expecting this, she will probably be startled.

Now reverse roles so that your partner can feel what it's like to let herself be grabbed and what it's like to turn around and yell. Be sure to back up to give her a sense of success when she yells at you by backing up and looking surprised.

Running to Safety

When children know their Safety Plan – they know how to leave and how to ask for help – they are far better prepared to handle a potential assault. If someone is acting in a threatening way, children are more likely to be harmed if they go into a blind panic as they run or hide frantically. Most of the time, children will have the best chance of escaping from danger if they go as quickly as they can to Safety, where there are adults to help them.

In one success story, a boy said, "I was riding my bike in the neighborhood. A man jumped out of the bushes and told me, 'Get over here!' Instead I rode my bike all the way home to Safety as quickly as I could. And, I remembered to watch out for cars on the way."

Yelling

Another one of our students told us, "I was rollerblading on my way to school. A man in the park was grabbing himself between his legs and acting weird. He started calling to me, but I rollerbladed fast all the way to Safety in my classroom at my school." Her father told us later that, had his daughter not practiced leaving quickly when she felt afraid, she would most likely have collapsed into tears, making her far more vulnerable to the man.

In order to be ready to run, your body needs to be ready to move. Sometimes in workshops, children start sitting with their legs tucked up on their chairs or inside their sweatshirts just as we are getting ready to do a practice. If we have time, I like to tell my students a true story that happened many years ago when I was hiking through a meadow in Scotland with my family. One of the sheep got startled and started to run, but tripped and fell down. As I walked over to see if she was okay, the sheep seemed to be having a convulsion. She was lying on her back with her feet moving wildly in the air. The closer I came, the more her body writhed.

My teenaged daughter and son started worrying that the poor sheep was in pain. Suddenly, I figured it out. The sheep was trying to run but she was lying on her back so her legs just moved faster and faster through the air. It looked as if she had forgotten to stand up before running away! I knelt down and gently shoved her onto her feet, and the sheep ran away, completely fine.

I tell students that the moral of this story is that it works best, if you want to be ready to move and to be smarter than that sheep, to have your feet under you. Then I look at the kids whose bodies are curled up into various unready positions and smile. Without fail, each of them sheepishly puts his or her feet on the floor, ready to run.

Most of the time, children will have the best chance of escaping from danger if they go as quickly as they can to Safety, where there are adults to help them.

Practicing Running to Safety

1 Review where Safety is in different places and how children can get help if they need it in a scary situation. Remind them to be persistent in asking for help.

2 To practice, be sure that you are in a clear space such as a room or yard with no obstacles to trip over. Put your students on one side of the space so that they have room to run. Ask an adult to stand on the other side of the space to act as Safety so the kids have someone to run to.

- Tell your students to imagine that you are acting scary.
- Coach them to run to the Safety adult yelling, "I NEED HELP!"
- Ask the adult to put her (or his) hands in front of her, palms up, to show where "Safety" is.
- Coach children to be in charge of their bodies so that they stop in front of the adult, touch her or his hands gently and yell, if they haven't already, "I NEED HELP!"
- Coach the adult to take each child's hands gently and say, "I will help you."

Practicing an arm grab escape

Getting Away From a Grab

If someone grabs your body, one simple and fast way to escape can be to turn your body to release the grip and then to pull away. Twist your body forcefully with a sudden jerk and leave quickly. If someone grabs your shoulder, you can raise the arm that was grabbed and turn your body forcefully to break the hold before pulling away and leaving.

If someone grabs your arm, you can escape in a number of ways. You can twist your arm free. You can grab your own arm and pull your arm out of the hold using your whole body. To do this, hold your own hand. Aim towards the weaker spot made by where the fingers of the person grabbing you come together. If pulling away doesn't work in one direction, reverse suddenly and pull the other way. You will have more power if you yell each time you move to break a hold. We recommend yelling, "NO!" because it is easy to remember and gives a clear message.

Practicing Escaping From a Grab

1 Keep what you do very simple rather than grabbing in complicated ways. Remember that people will learn to use their power effectively more quickly by being successful rather than by failing.

2 Show students how they can get someone to let go by twisting, turning, and moving away.

3 Have students grab their own arms so that they can see the weaker spot or "gate" made by where their fingers meet. Have them pull their own arm out of their grip, aiming for the gate.

4 When you practice, let a weaker student build confidence by making your hold very loose at first. Gently grab the student's arm with your hand on the same side. Coach your student to hold her own hand and use her whole body to turn and pull away from you, as she yells, "NO!" If after you have released the grab, your student keeps standing there, remind her to leave with awareness.

5 Gently grab your student's arm with both of your hands on the same side. Coach him to grab his own hand so he has the power of his whole body. Coach him to turn his body as he pulls away and yells, "NO!"

Show him how, if pulling in one direction doesn't work, pulling in the other direction often can.

The Ready Position and the Stop Sign

When we talk to kids about defending themselves from an attack, some of them start making weird motions in the air with their arms and feet like their idea of the Karate Kid or of a Ninja. Sometimes they start punching or kicking into the air. We tell our students that the high-ranking martial artists in our organization never show off like that, especially in a dangerous situation. In the real world, acting aggressive could lead to a fight or let the attacker know that they are ready to fight. We say, "If you are in a situation where you have to fight, you want the fact that you know how to be a surprise to your attacker."

Other kids go limp at the idea of a physical conflict. We teach the Ready Position so that our students will have practiced a strong, non-aggressive stance from which they are ready to move. We explain, "If you are trapped in a dangerous situation and can't leave right away, you are safest if you can stay calm, aware, and confident. The Ready Position helps you get your body ready to set a boundary, to yell, to run away as soon as you can, and to fight if need be. The Ready Position shows someone who is bothering you that you are not a victim without acting as if you are going to fight."

How to say no with your body

The Ready Position shows someone who is bothering you that you are not a victim without acting as if you are going to fight."

To get into the Ready Position:

- Put your arms up in front of your body to make a wall between you and the attacker.
- Have your hands open with the palms facing outwards as if you are pushing against a wall. You are not making fists because this can escalate the situation.
- Bend your elbows so that your arms are close to your body, with your elbows slightly away from your body just above the height of your waist.
- Put the leg that you would probably kick someone with back about one walking step. For most people who are right-handed, this is their right leg. For most people who are left-handed, this is their left leg.
- Make sure that you are in balance. Have your feet about shoulder-width apart.
- Keep your knees a little bent rather than locked.

The Ready Position can stay in your body for a very long time. During a workshop I was leading at a national conference on violence prevention for youth, one of the participants introduced herself to the group as a former Kidpower and Teenpower student. She was in her mid-twenties and had taken her classes with us well over ten years before.

Suddenly, in the middle of the workshop, this talented youth counselor said, "I just remembered something that happened when I was in college. I was babysitting a four-year-old and we were walking on a street near where I lived. A really big man started following us. He was acting crazy. He started taking off some of his clothes and saying stuff to us. I felt really scared but I did not want to scare the child with me. I wasn't sure it would help,

The Shark Game – A fun way to practice the Stop Sign and yelling

but I did what we practiced in class. I put up my hands in Ready Position and said in a very strong voice, 'I want you to go away! This behavior is not appropriate!' To my surprise and relief, the man turned around and left! The child with me was really impressed!" The therapists, educators, social workers, program managers, and counselors in the room joined me in giving her a round of applause.

The Stop Sign is a strong way to say, "No!" with your body along with your voice. To make a Stop Sign, start in Ready Position. Now, push your dominant hand out towards the face of the person bothering you, as you yell "No!" or "Stop!" Next, pull your arm back close to your body so that you are not leaving it out for someone to grab and back to be level with the other hand. Younger children often make their Stop Sign with both hands, which is fine too.

Even very young kids can learn this skill. As one aunt told us, "I taught my three-year-old niece to make a Stop Sign and yell 'No!' if she felt scared. A couple of days later, a goose started to chase her in the park. When she used her Stop Sign, the goose ran away! My niece was so thrilled that she challenged all the geese in the park! A few days later, she was in her car seat in the back of the car. A bee flew into the open window. My niece did her Stop Sign and yelled, 'No!' and the bee flew right out. I am glad that she feels so powerful!"

A police officer had a more serious story about Ella, her three-year-old daughter. One day, Ella was shopping with her mother and grandmother. Suddenly, Ella ran ahead into the next aisle. A man standing there, as a very unsafe scary joke, grabbed her arm and said, 'You are so cute! I'll take you away and you'll never see your mother or father again!'"

Instead of freezing or bursting into tears, Ella did just what she'd practiced in the Kidpower Parent/Child Workshop. She pulled away, made a Stop Sign with her hand, yelled "No!" and ran to her mother and grandmother yelling for help.

This startled the man who came over and complained, "Your little girl scared me!"

Ella's grandmother, who had not been to our workshop, started to tell Ella, "Say that you're sorry to the nice man."

She was interrupted by Ella's mother, who told her daughter, "You did the right thing!" The man realized that he had been out-of-line and apologized. Instead of being terrified by the experience, Ella was proud of herself.

The Stop Sign can work in nature too. Many years ago, when I was watching the Nature Channel on television, I saw a program about a man who was studying great white sharks. This researcher had a theory that if something made a sudden movement towards a shark, the shark would swim away. "Why that's our Stop Sign!" I said.

I watched in fascination as the researcher tested his theory. Researchers from inside the shark cage, a large metal cage designed to protect them from the sharks, directed a small robot on the ocean floor by remote control. As the researchers filmed from inside the shark cage, the sharks came towards the little robot on the ocean floor. When it stayed still, the sharks would chomp on it. When the researcher made the robot move suddenly, the sharks swam away.

As the researchers filmed from inside the shark cage, the sharks came towards the little robot on the ocean floor. When it stayed still, a shark would chomp on it. When the researcher made the robot move suddenly towards a shark, it swam away. Next, the researcher decided to see if a person could work as well as a robot. I can imagine his associate saying, "That's a wonderful theory. Why don't you go into the ocean and try it out and I'll stay inside the shark cage to film you."

In any case, what they showed on the video was this man floating in the ocean in his scuba gear as a shark approached him. Each time the shark came close, he abruptly pushed his camera through the water towards the shark without touching it and the shark swam sway. When two sharks started circling him, the man used a pole to get more distance. Without hitting the sharks, which were so big that the pole looked a bit like a toothpick compared to them, the researcher poked the pole towards them and the sharks swam away. When three sharks started to circle him, the man got back inside his shark cage, and I was very relieved that he did.

In classes, we have children practice by playing the Shark Game. One partner is a Diver, who stands in Ready Position, not because this is a good idea with a shark but to have a chance to practice. The other is a Shark who swims towards the Diver with hands forward in a point to symbolize jaws. The Diver does a Stop Sign with a loud "No!" and the Shark swims away. We tell our students, "Of course, in real life, you would not just stay there if a shark was coming towards you. You would calmly get out of the water by getting into a boat or going to shore as quickly as possible!"

Once children are confident in the skills of yelling and running for safety, we have them practice escaping from a person who is pretending to be scary. Our instructor, Beth, pretends to be a bad guy or a bully who has them cornered. She designates an adult, often the parent of the child, to be Safety across the room.

Beth lunges forward with one foot planted so that she does not actually get too close to the child. If the child gets stuck, she pauses and coaches the child in what to do rather than getting closer and then goes back to pretending. She is careful to keep her remarks general and to adjust her energy to the age and sensitivity of the child. She yells things like, "Come here, kid!" Or, "Do what I say!" Like all Kidpower instructors, Beth is careful not to put terrifying thoughts into a child's mind by saying something specific like, "You'll never see your parents again!"

Beth coaches the child to interrupt her by making a Stop Sign and yelling, "NO!" loudly. She moves back once the child has used the Stop Sign to give

Getting ready to use a Stop Sign

the child room to escape from the corner. The child runs to Safety yelling, "I need help!" The adult acting as Safety has her or his hands out for the child to touch and says, "I will help you!"

Teaching the Ready Position and Stop Sign

1 Show the Ready Position as described above. Coach your student to stand with her hands up like she is pressing against a wall in front of her, to bend her elbows, and to put her "strong leg" back. Make sure that the she is not pretending to fight, has a balanced stance, and her knees a little bent.

2 Show the Stop Sign. Coach your student to push her hand out with the palm towards your face while yelling, "NO!" and then to pull it back again quickly. You can make it rewarding to practice by approaching her and then, as soon as she uses her Stop Sign and yells, stepping back looking very surprised.

3 With children, tell the Shark Story above and play the Shark Game in pairs, with one person being the Shark and the other the Diver. Have the Shark "swim" towards the Diver who is in Ready Position. When the Diver makes a Stop Sign and shouts, "NO!", the Shark swims away. Then they reverse places. You can also play this game with just you as the Shark and the kids as the Divers.

4 For kids who are confident with the skills of yelling, running, and using their Stop Signs, you can say you are going to pretend to be a bad guy. For older kids and teens, you can tell them to imagine that you are someone who is an Attacker. Here's how to practice:

- Designate a spot across the room or the yard, with no major obstacles in between, to be Safety, which is where there are people who can help you. If possible, have another adult stand there to be Safety.
- Have your student standing in Ready Position, imagining that he is in a place where he cannot just leave.
- Lunge towards your student yelling something very general like, "HEY KID! Get over here!" To avoid scaring younger kids, act like a cartoon character with playful energy. For older kids and teens, you can have more aggressive energy. Do not get close enough to grab or to be hit.
- Coach your student to interrupt you with the Stop Sign and loud "NO!" and then run to Safety yelling, "I need help!" Coach the person being Safety to say, "I will help you!"

What Kids Need to Know About Learning Self-Defense

Real fights can be dangerous and destructive. In Kidpower, we believe in using all of your other options first to escape from an assault. However, knowing how to fight can build self-confidence and can prepare you to escape from a person who is acting dangerously, just in case your other choices fail. The purpose of our self-defense training is to give our students the chance to break away and escape from an attacker. Instead of fighting with the intent of harming someone else or of getting even with someone, we teach our students to leave as soon as they can and to get help.

Even when they know how, many young people won't use self-defense skills to protect themselves because they don't want to get in trouble or they think it is wrong. Have a frank discussion with the children and teens in your life about when you believe that they have the right to hurt somebody to stop that person from hurting them. Otherwise, young people might internalize a "fighting is bad and I don't want to be a bad person" message so thoroughly that they will wait too long to protect themselves.

Sometimes both adults and children worry about learning to fight because they want to be kind, loving people and not hurtful, dangerous people. Our Vancouver Center director, Dave Harrison, M.D., who is an emergency physician, likes to use this example with his students. Suppose you have a sweet, warm, loving cat named Cuddles. Imagine what will happen if a big dog comes up and starts barking at Cuddles. Do you think Cuddles will stay calmly purring on your lap? Almost certainly not! Instead, Cuddles will be scared and want to escape! If you try to hold onto her, Cuddles will probably hiss, scratch, or even bite you – or the dog if it comes too close - until she can get away.

Dave explains that Cuddles is not hissing, biting, and scratching because she is cruel and violent. She is doing this because she wants to protect herself. Cuddles is not worrying about what the big barking dog is feeling or about whether the dog will hurt her more if she bites and scratches. She is also not worrying about what you are thinking. Cuddles is fighting until she can escape and run to safety. Once the dog goes away and she calms down, Cuddles will turn back into a sweet little cat again.

Before practicing fighting, kids also need to agree to take personal responsibility about using these skills appropriately. In our workshops with children and teens, we tell our students, "When we were first starting Kidpower, lots of people told us not to teach kids to fight. They said that kids would misuse what they learned and hurt their sisters or brothers or friends if they got mad at them. We said that we believe that kids are smarter than that. We believe that young people will not misuse these skills if they understand that real fights are dangerous and that it is wrong to fight because you are upset with someone or to get back at someone, even if that person has upset or harmed you. We want you to promise us that you will only fight as a last resort if you are in danger of getting hurt and you cannot leave or get help."

Before we continue the workshop, the instructor goes from student to student as everyone else watches silently. Each youth shakes the hand of the instructor, looks her or him in the eyes and says seriously, "I promise." As of the writing of this book, not one of our students has broken this promise as far as we know. We believe that this is because we had kids practice leaving before they practiced fighting and because they did promise.

Another benefit of practicing self-defense skills with kids is that you can gain a little more peace of mind after something frightening has happened. When my own children were growing up, I felt very vulnerable every time I heard another scary story of a child being bullied, molested, or harmed. I would do my best to stay calm, but I still felt frightened. Without going into any details until they were much older, I would rehearse with my children what might have prevented the particular danger mentioned in the news.

Usually, this just involved moving away and asking for help. But, after a man tried to grab a boy on the street near my nine-year-old son's school, I picked up a sofa cushion for him to hit, saying that it had been a while since he'd practiced. Not fooled at all since the story was headline news, Arend whacked the cushion so hard that I staggered backwards. Then, my son grinned. "Feel better, Mom?" he asked.

We want you to promise us that you will only fight as a last resort if you are in danger of getting hurt and you cannot leave or get help.

Preparing Children to Decide When to Fight

1 Discuss the difference between fighting to escape from a dangerous situation and fighting because you are mad at someone. Tell the story of Cuddles the Cat.

2 Make your expectations clear. Be clear that fighting should be a last resort when other choices for getting away safely are not a choice. Be clear that you do not believe in fighting most of the time, even if someone has been terribly insulting or hit you first. However, state that you believe that people have the right to defend themselves physically if that is what is needed in order to be safe. Have your student give you the Kidpower promise or create your own.

3 Do not teach children to fight until they can take responsibility for using these skills safely. This means that they have good impulse control, know the difference between real and pretend, and have shown you that they know how to leave and get help, even if they are very angry with someone. If they lack these skills, give them practice in staying calm even if the other person is upset, in leaving assertively when someone is threatening or rude, in being persistent in getting help, and in managing their personal triggers as described in previous chapters.

Your fighting spirit helps you to keep on trying and never give up until you get to safety.

What Adults Need to Know About Teaching Self-Defense to Young People

I hope that you and your loved ones never have to fight to escape from an assault, but if you do, I want you to win. Your chances are much greater if you have a strong fighting spirit. "Feeling scared and mad in a fight is normal," we tell our students. "Don't waste energy trying to stop those feelings. And don't let those feelings stop you. You can use your anger and fear to feed your fighting spirit – the part of you that says, 'NO! I am not going to give up, and I am not going to stop fighting until I make this person let me go!' Your fighting spirit helps you to keep on trying and never give up until you get to safety."

I remember Ellen Bass explaining this idea to our Brownie troop. "Imagine that you were a Mommy Lion," she said, "and someone was trying to hurt your baby lion. You would feel fierce and not let anything hurt your baby, right?"

"How little is my baby lion?" one of the girls asked.

"Just born, with its eyes still closed, very fuzzy, and totally cute!" Ellen replied. "Can you feel that fierce feeling?"

All of the girls sighed at the thought of their poor helpless very little, very cute baby lions and nodded. Ellen added, "You would protect your baby with all your energy and all your power. You can use that fierce feeling to protect yourself as well as your baby lion." We then all growled like mother lions!

There are literally thousands of possible self-defense moves. In its simplest form, the strategy behind fighting is to think of the other person's body as having targets and your body as having weapons. In Kidpower, we focus on techniques that involve large muscle movements rather than fine motor movements, because these are usually easier to learn, use, and remember.

These techniques are designed to break away from an attacker so that you have a chance to escape.

We teach students to aim for targets that are on the front of the attacker's body. If someone's back is to you, we believe that you should be running to safety rather than continuing to hit or kick that person. Our purpose in teaching fighting is for our students to get away, not to beat someone up. Common targets are someone's face, neck, groin, solar plexus or mid-section, ankles, knees, and the top of their feet. These targets are likely to hurt when struck no matter how big or strong a person is.

We teach students to use the stronger parts of their bodies as weapons or tools against the weaker parts of an attacker's body. Common self-defense tools are the heel of your palm, your fingers raking as claws or squeezed into a point, your thigh, your shin, your elbow, and the bottom of your fist or the heel of your foot.

Having both power and control makes it easier to use physical self-defense techniques effectively. Using their bodies in a strong, coordinated way comes naturally to some people. These people find it easy to hit and kick with a great deal of force if they feel threatened or upset. Anyone who has tried to pick up a struggling toddler who is throwing a tantrum knows how much power even small people can have when they commit themselves fully to resisting. Children with lots of power often need to learn to stay in control so that they can assess situations and make the safest choices, focus their power into effective techniques, and remember to leave as soon as they have the chance.

Other people are more powerful with their thoughts and feelings rather than with their bodies. They might act weak or seem limp because they have not yet learned how to use their physical strength. Many children with lots of control need to learn how to use their power so that they can be forceful in leaving a situation, yelling, and defending themselves if necessary. Of course there are lots of variations. Being comfortable physically in one arena does not necessarily mean that a child will be strong and coordinated physically in another without practicing. A child who has no trouble with gymnastics might find it difficult to hit a target hard at first. A child who is coordinated might have perfect aim and form but no force. A child who is strong might flail instead of using focused techniques.

As children get older, their abilities can change in many different ways. At age ten, Olivia, who was a basketball star, was a powerhouse in our self-defense workshop. When Olivia came back to take a Teenpower workshop at age thirteen, she seemed barely able to hit or yell at first. Olivia was still excellent at basketball but had learned in the meantime that it was not ladylike to show how strong she was outside of sports. By the end of the workshop, Olivia was very effective – but still far from the intense, joyful energy that she had shown at age ten. Fortunately, I had the chance to see Olivia again at age twenty, and she was back to being her fully powerful self.

Parents often ask me if they should put their children into a martial arts program. My answer is, "It depends on your child and on the teacher.

Anyone who has tried to pick up a struggling toddler who is throwing a tantrum knows how much power even small people can have when they commit themselves fully to resisting.

What we teach in Kidpower is like "emergency medicine." We want children to gain the skills to be safe with themselves and other people as quickly as possible.

Children can benefit greatly from physical activities that they enjoy, whether this is martial arts, sports, horseback riding, dancing, or something else. You want a teacher or coach who is respectful, encouraging, in charge, and safe as well as being good at whatever the activity is. Martial arts classes, like other physical training programs, are like long-term health care. What we teach in Kidpower is more like 'emergency medicine.' We want children to gain the skills to be safe with themselves and other people as quickly as possible."

The key word is "enjoy". Children do not benefit by being forced into staying with a long-term recreational activity just because it is "good" for them. Instead, shop around until you find something that the child has fun doing and a teacher who you feel good about. Some children will want to keep doing the same activity for years. Others will like trying out new things for a while and then will want to move on to learn something else.

About half the teachers in our organization are martial artists. Some are high-ranking, especially in Taekwondo, Krav Maga, and Aikido. Several have their own studios. We have learned a great deal from them and vice versa. Many martial artists enjoy being part of Kidpower because our programs give them the opportunity to teach self-defense to people who are not going to make the long-term commitment that training in the martial arts requires for proficiency – and they often bring Kidpower skills back to their studios to share with their students.

Self-defense skills practiced improperly can cause injury to you or to the children practicing with you.

In practicing physical self-defense safety and effectively, hands-on coaching in the moment from an experienced instructor can make a big difference. Self-defense skills practiced improperly can cause injury to you or to the children practicing with you. You can get hit or kicked accidentally if you are not careful in how you hold a kick pad. The child or other person practicing with you can hyper-extend or jam an arm or a leg, or wrench a shoulder or knee if the practice is not done in a controlled way. This is why we recommend that people who have not yet had the chance for physical practice of how to use a kick pad and how to do physical techniques take a class from Kidpower or from another organization.

Techniques can be practiced in the air or against a target. Often, the target is a kick pad. Using a thick sofa cushion can also work but start by practicing low intensity strikes first to make sure the cushion is strong enough for you to be safe holding it. In our full-force programs, the targets are our head-to-toe padded instructors. In a safe and controlled way, our full force instructors pretend to attack the students so that our students can deliver strong self-defense blows to normally vulnerable targets such as the eyes or the groin to get away.

Many people of any age will have trouble learning physical skills by watching or by being given directions because they are primarily kinesthetic learners, which means that they learn more easily by doing a move correctly rather than by watching or being given verbal directions. Being shown or told what to do over and over can become very frustrating for these people and wastes a great deal of time. The solution is to move a kinesthetic learner's body through a technique as you explain it. We call this method of teaching physical skills "molding" our students. We are shaping their learning experience rather than just letting them struggle.

We have seen students who were very clumsy, physically dyslexic, or slow to learn at first become extremely successful very quickly after a few minutes of molding their bodies. It seems as if we are tuning in on a wavelength that they can receive easily instead of a wavelength where the reception is blocked. Molding can be especially helpful for young people with physical or cognitive challenges.

Part One: Preparing Kids to Learn Self-Defense

1   Look for examples in stories, movies, and books that show how a fighting spirit helps someone overcome overwhelming odds – against a disease, to win in a sport, to succeed in a challenge, or to stop an attack. Also look for examples from the animal world. Have children growl and act fierce like lions or other animals protecting their young.

2   Find physical activities that children enjoy so that they can learn to use their bodies with control, coordination, and power. If a child is physically dyslexic or a kinesthetic learner, be sure the instructor gives physical molding in the moment as well as verbal and auditory coaching. Many of our recommendations on how to choose a good self-defense program below are also relevant for how to choose any training activity.

3   Give children chances to practice aiming and striking through a target rather than stopping short. If children are having trouble hitting hard, let them practice what it feels like to hit all the way through, such as getting a volleyball over the net. Show them the difference between stopping when your hand or foot first touches a ball or kick pad and what happens when you strike with the intention of smashing it far beyond where you first made contact. Many children will improve dramatically once they understand the difference.

4   Explain the idea of targets and weapons in a self-defense emergency. You can do this safely by pointing out places where our bodies are bony and strong like the heel of our palm or our elbow, and places where we can get more easily hurt ourselves such as our eyes, face, solar plexus, or groin.

Part Two: Practicing Self-Defense Skills Safely and Effectively

1   If you know the skills you want to teach, try doing the techniques slowly in the air to make sure you understand how they work. A description of the skills we teach and how to pick a good workshop are below. If you know how to hold a kick pad and can practice safely, give children lots of chances to practice. Instead of worrying, pick up the pad and have your child show you how well she or he can hit or kick. Remember to focus on how the child is being effective and not on how the child might seem helpless.

2   When kids are practicing self-defense techniques, here are a few things to keep in mind to help avoid injury:

   • Make sure that everyone's bodies are ready to move by gently warming up joints and muscles that might be used.
   • Practice slowly with low force and careful, clear, deliberate moves before doing the techniques quickly with higher force.
   • Stay in control so that students are calm, aware, and centered before each strike rather than flailing wildly.

- Make sure that the students keep their arms and legs a little bent and relaxed rather than being rigid or straight. Coach them to place their feet in a well-balanced, deliberate, stable stance that allows for dynamic movement.
- Make sure that the students do not twist or jerk their spines in a sudden way.
- Coach students to step so that they move with their whole body in the direction of strikes that involve the shoulder, such as elbow strikes, to avoid wrenching the shoulder.
- Take charge of the space around students so that they do not bump into each other or into furniture or walls that might be near them.
- If someone has a part of her or his body that has already been injured or is easily hurt, proceed with caution. Go through the moves with very low force to avoid re-injury. Practicing self-defense is not supposed to hurt. Re-adjust what you are doing rather than letting someone keep pushing through pain.
- If you are holding a kick pad, make sure that your body is not in a position where you might get hit or kicked. Also, be aware of the trajectory of the move and hold onto the kick pad so that it does not fly into someone else.

3

To make self-defense practices more effective, remember to:
- Aim towards the target. Look where you are striking.
- Hit all the way through the target. Instead of stopping as soon as you touch the spot you are striking, have an intention of going far past the target. Think of smashing the attacker's head into the ceiling or knocking the attacker back into the far wall.
- Yell a short word such as "NO!" with each technique. Your strikes have more power when you yell. Yelling helps you to keep breathing and tightens your midsection, protecting your body.
  Yelling calls attention from bystanders. Yelling "NO" makes it clear that what is happening is not okay with you.
- Be fully committed to each move. You want to use your fighting spirit and be determined that you are not going to let this person harm you.
- Keep fighting until the attacker lets go and you have the opportunity to run away.

Kidpower Physical Self-Defense Techniques

Although there are thousands of potentially effective self-defense techniques, Kidpower deliberately keeps the techniques and targets we teach very simple. For each technique and target, there are usually tradeoffs involved rather than one right or wrong answer. Our approach is to teach students to use what they have available to hit what they can reach, and to empower them to make choices. We have heard stories of most types of physical resistance being successful in stopping a real-life assault – pulling away, throwing sand into the face of the attacker, shoving the attacker off, pulling the attacker's hair, screaming into or head butting the attacker's face. We do not believe that it empowers students to tell them that any strongly used physical technique would be either "ineffective" or "always effective."

The techniques we teach in Kidpower are easy to learn, do not involve a great deal of coordination or strength, are likely to be effective, and are relatively safe to practice. Again, you are using the strong parts of your body against the more vulnerable parts of someone else's body. These techniques are designed to provide the tools needed to break away from the person who is attacking you, giving you the opportunity to escape and get to safety. These are not intended to be offensive techniques.

Kidpower defines fighting skills as including any physical technique that intentionally hurts another person. We define emergency-only self-defense skills as being physical fighting techniques for use in a serious assault because these techniques have more risk of causing injury, which might be necessary in order for the person being attacked to get out of danger. With bully self-defense skills, we teach targets and techniques that are intended to cause pain, but are less likely to injure the attacker. In all cases, we teach that fighting is a last resort.

Although we do not explain it this way to children, emergency-only skills are designed to help someone escape from a situation where the attacker has more power and is more dangerous, and has the intention of injuring, abducting, or sexually assaulting the intended victim. To be clear without giving unnecessary details, we tell children to use emergency-only skills in emergencies where someone is trying to harm them and they cannot get away or get help. We show them the use of emergency-only skills in a context where an adult is trying to grab them.

Kidpower teaches bully self-defense skills to deal with problems that involve an attacker close in age to the intended victim and behavior that will physically harass or cause pain but is not likely to cause injury. We tell children to discuss different situations with their adults to decide when it is okay to use these skills and when not. We show the use of bully self-defense in a context where a person their age has them trapped in a corner or room, won't let them leave, and is threatening them. The bully self-defense skills are covered in Chapter Eight.

Some of the emergency-only fighting techniques we teach if you are attacked from the front are as follows:

• *Eye Strike.* Jab the eyes with a point made by squeezing your fingers together like a "chicken beak" or rake the eyes with the fingers open and curved like a claw. Both techniques work well, but especially for younger children or smaller people, the "chicken beak" is effective because it uses the force of all of the fingers together.

• *Heel Palm.* Hit the face, nose, or throat with the heel of the palm of your hand. We say, "Hit the soft part of someone's face or throat with the hard part of your hand." We do not recommend using your fists because you can easily hurt yourself. In fact, boxers wrap their hands and wear gloves to protect their own hands. Keep your arm a little bent to avoid hyper-extending your arm.

• *Knee to the Groin.* Plant your foot back and lift your knee up so that you strike into the groin of the attacker with your thigh. You are striking up and under the groin between the legs rather than hitting to the front, because this is where the most vulnerable area of the groin is.

• *Snap Kick to the Groin.* If the attacker is hanging onto your hand but too far away for a knee to the groin, a snap kick will let you strike from further away. Plant your foot back, lift your thigh as if you are going to do a knee strike and then swing your lower leg forward to snap kick up into the

The strategy is to use the strong parts of your body against the more vulnerable parts of someone else's body.

Eye Strike

Heel Palm

Snap Kick to the groin

Full-force self-defense gives students the opportunity to practice strong self-defense moves against normally vulnerable body areas on an instructor who is protected by a head-to-toe body armor.

groin with your shin. Your foot will go all the way between the attacker's legs to the other side.

- *Stomp from the ground.* We teach children that if they fall to the ground, their first choice is to jump up and run away if possible. If need be, they can stomp up into someone's groin as that person approaches to give them time to turn, get up, and run.

In practicing dealing with an attack from behind, we coach students to try to turn and look back towards the target before striking. Looking helps to prevent you from missing, and turning even slightly often makes it easier to hit someone who is behind you. Some of the emergency-only fighting techniques we teach if someone assaults you from behind include:

- *Foot Stomp.* Turn your foot so the toes point to the outside, to give you more surface to stomp with. Lift your leg and stomp with your heel onto the instep of the attacker's foot. Keep your knees a little bent to avoid hyper-extending your leg. It is possible to scrape down the leg of the attacker with the side of your foot, but your first priority is to stomp hard and quickly rather than to scrape.

- *Hammer Fist to the Groin.* Curl your fingers together and lock them in with your thumb on the outside to make a fist. Turn your body to move your hips out of the way and use the bottom of your fist (the area near your little finger) like a hammer to hit the attacker's groin. A slap to the groin with an open hand can also be effective.

- *Low Elbow to the Solar Plexus.* Reach forward with your arm and then thrust backwards into the attacker's mid-section with your elbow turning your body at the same time to make room and add power to the strike. You can add more power by imagining that you are grabbing a doorknob and turning it, so that the twist of your arm gives you more momentum.

- *High Elbow to the Neck or Face.* Reach across your body with your arm and lift your elbow up by your ear. Now do this again and use your whole body to pull and strike up into the attacker's neck or head with your elbow.

Knowing the techniques and believing they can work are two different issues. At a Teenpower workshop for middle school boys, one of the quieter smaller boys pulled me aside during the snack break. "Why are you teaching us something that won't work for half the human race? I mean, being hit in the groin won't hurt a girl. Right?" my student murmured in a soft voice, clearly not wanting anyone to overhear. Since our other two instructors were men, I guess that, as the only member of That Half represented in the room at that moment, this boy figured that I was in the best position to know.

"Actually," I said seriously. "Being kneed or kicked in the groin would work on girls too. Ask any girl who has ever gotten hit hard there by falling on something."

Despite his embarrassment, this kid was not convinced. "How could it work?" he protested, "When girls don't have anything there ... well I mean they don't have ... you know what."

Putting aside an interesting combination of indignation and amusement, I stayed very serious and to the point, and said in an absolutely neutral voice, "It is true that getting hit in the groin would hurt boys more. Girls are built differently than boys there, but this is a very sensitive part of the body for girls too. I have women friends in the martial arts who have been kneed in the groin by accident and it hurt them a lot."

"Thanks!" my student said gratefully and scooted off to fetch a bagel. The boy's look of relief left me wondering what girl he was worried about being attacked by and determined to put more time into target denial and bully techniques.

Again, these are only some of the countless self-defense techniques possible. Here are some other choices for how to fight back and for dealing with different types of attacks. These are not options we discuss with children unless they are in a martial arts program, because they are somewhat overwhelming and potentially confusing, but they can be useful for teens to know.

- *Knees as a target.* You can use a backwards donkey kick if the attack is from the back or a high stomp if the attack is from the front. However, knees are small and move quickly. You need to be able to lift your leg high and have speed and good aim to be effective at striking a knee.

- *Fighting from the ground or the air.* Suppose you are lifted up off your feet or pushed down onto the ground. If you are close to someone's face and your hands are free, you can do an eye-strike or heel palm. If your legs are free, you can do a knee strike or a snap kick. If someone is behind you, you can do an elbow strike. If someone is approaching you while you are on the ground or you end up on the ground in a fight, you can pull your leg close to your body and then stomp up into the attacker's groin, knee, middle, or head.

- *Fighting while being carried away.* You can make yourself heavy by dropping your weight and wiggle to the ground. You can kick backwards into someone's legs or groin or do an elbow strike to the attacker's head or middle. You can cup your hands and slap them against an attacker's ear to pop or disrupt an eardrum.

- *Biting.* There is a small risk of infection from potential fluid transmission if you draw blood, but you can bite someone.

- *Eye gouge.* You can reach around and sink your fingers into the person's eye socket as a pro-longed eye jab.

- *Being choked from the front.* If someone is choking you, your first priority is to get air and your second priority is to get away. For a front choke, get air and protect your throat by tucking your chin and lifting your shoulders like a turtle. Break the hold by "swimming" with a crawl stroke with one

There are thousands of potentially effective self-defense techniques. We teach those that are easy to learn, do not require a great deal of strength or coordination, are likely to be effective, and are relatively safe to practice.

Techniques can be adapted for many different needs and abilities

arm on top of and across the attacker's arms as you turn sharply in the direction you are "swimming." The movement of bringing your arm over and across your body while turning to the side with your whole body is remarkably strong and can be a very effective technique to break the grab. You can also knee or kick a person facing you in the groin.

• *Being choked from behind.* If you have room, you can lift one arm like doing a high elbow, turn, and break the hold similar as described above. Suppose that the attacker is close (such as when the attacker is choking with his or her upper arm rather than with his or her hands). You can turn your head to the side and tuck your chin in as close to your chest as possible (which gives you more air), pull down hard on the arms of the attacker and turn your body to the side to get into a position to release the grab and hit. If you cannot move one way, try turning the other way very quickly. You can then do a foot stomp or a hammer fist to the groin.

• *Using weapons of opportunity.* Virtually any hard, pointy, or heavy item can become a weapon to give you more choices in fighting off an assailant. You can sink a pencil into an attacker's leg, arm, or face. You can clomp the attacker's knee with an aluminum lunch box.

Some attackers target people verbally or physically who seem more vulnerable because they are disabled. When we have students who use wheelchairs, we practice Roll Away Power as an alternative to Walk Away Power so that they can leave a threatening situation safely. If people who use mobility aids are attacked, we show how they can use their wheelchairs or walking tools as weapons. They can hit vulnerable targets with their cane. Be sure to protect the balance of people who are unsteady on their feet, so that they don't fall over when they practice. Stay alert because some people can hit pretty hard.

If people are using a wheelchair, they can ram this forward or backward into the shins or knees or over the feet of the person attacking them. If you do this with someone who has an electric wheelchair, be careful about not having it tip over and about not getting crashed into yourself. Someone using a motorized wheelchair will often warn me in a practice to, "Watch out! This is just like a little car!"

Full-force self-defense gives students the opportunity to practice strong self-defense moves against normally vulnerable body areas on an instructor who is protected by a head-to-toe body armor. With the support of a coaching instructor, students have the opportunity to practice techniques and strategies for dealing with front confrontations, being grabbed from the front, and being grabbed from behind by the full force instructor. The hands-on, more realistic nature of full-force practice helps build people's fighting spirit. Within strong boundaries to ensure emotional and physical safety, full-force self-defense training can be immensely empowering. People who have trained in the martial arts for years are startled to see students able to defend themselves effectively within a remarkably short period of time.

I wish I could bottle the excited, fun energy with which most kids approach full-force practice! Adults are sometimes triggered because full-force training makes them think about all the terrible reasons why we have to learn how to fight. Children are more likely to focus on the fact that they get to hit and kick -- and no one gets in trouble and no one gets hurt. I have often demonstrated a full-force fight to children, then turned to my class, and asked enthusiastically, "Do *you* want to learn how to do that?"

"*YES!*" they all yell.

Sometimes adults feel so anxious about their children's safety that they do not give them enough time to learn. "If you do it like that," they'll say, "then you would never get away. You look so weak." Well-meaning adults, especially worried fathers, also sometimes test or play with children in ways that reinforce their sense of helplessness. They will overpower their children in a way that is completely unrealistic and say, "So what are you going to do now?"

My response is, "We are training your child to do everything possible to not get into such a vulnerable position. Also, self-defense usually doesn't work without the child really being committed to hurting you. When you are roughhousing with your child, that's not realistic."

When young people are encouraged in an upbeat way to hit hard on kick pads or full-force padded instructors in workshops, most of them will grow within the space of a few hours from seeming timid and weak to acting far more confident and strong. Instead of telling them what they are doing wrong, we tell children what they are doing right and we reward even small progress with large enthusiasm. "That's great!" we say, "Now do it with a big yell and hit even harder!"

Choosing a Good Self-Defense Program

At Kidpower, we are deeply committed to providing exceptional self-defense training to our students and to preparing others to teach in an empowering, effective way. We also want adults everywhere to know what to look for when selecting a self-defense class, whether this is a one-time workshop or an ongoing program. The quality of the program and approach of the instructor will make a huge difference in the results of any kind of training. Self-defense is no exception.

Done well, self-defense classes can be fun, exciting, empowering, and useful. Done poorly, they can be boring, discouraging, and destructive. If training is about self-defense or any other important life skills, the potential benefits are real and so are the potential problems. Take the time to make a thoughtful decision. If you are considering an ongoing program such as a martial art, take the time to visit and check things out for yourself, no matter how good a reputation the teacher has. Keep staying involved with what your child is doing. Whether a program uses kick pads for practices or a full force instructor, here are some questions to consider:

1   *Is the content positive, accurate, comprehensive, and appropriate for the ages and life situations of the students?*
    The best programs will teach a range of personal safety skills for being aware, taking charge of the space around you, getting help, setting boundaries with people you know, de-escalating conflict, and staying calm and making choices instead of just getting upset when you have a problem. Physical self-defense skills will be taught in a context of having done everything possible to get out of a situation safely without fighting first.

Look for programs that focus on the skills to learn rather than on reasons why we have to learn these skills. Realize that children can become traumatized by scary stories about bad things that happened to other children. Children learn best if their teacher has a calm, matter-of-fact approach which makes it clear that they can keep themselves safe most of the time by learning how to do a few easy things.

Look for programs that are based on research from a wide variety of fields including mental health, education, crime prevention, law enforcement, and martial arts. Look for endorsements from real people and credible organizations. Look for programs that are willing to give credit for what they have learned from others rather than saying that they have invented "the best and only way to learning true self defense." Be wary of programs that give simplistic, absolute answers such as, "If you wear a pony tail, you are very likely to be assaulted" or "If you train with us, you will never have to be afraid again."

2 Is the teacher clear, respectful, in charge, enthusiastic, and able to adapt?

You and the children and teens in your life deserve to have teachers who are helpful rather than discouraging. Good teachers do not make negative remarks about their students or anyone else and do not allow others to do so, even as a joke. Look for teachers who know how to be both firm and respectful when they set boundaries with students who are doing things that detract from the class.

The best teachers will change what they do to meet the needs of their students rather than having a standard, canned approach. Role-plays to demonstrate or practice skills should be described in terms of situations that students are likely to encounter. The way something is presented should be in terms that are meaningful to a student. Instead of telling a blind student to look at a potential attacker, for example, a teacher who knows how to adapt will say something like, "Turn your face towards the person so that he knows you know he's there."

Good teachers will listen to your concerns with appreciation for your having the courage to raise them rather than with defensiveness. When possible, they will change what they do to make the class work better for you. At the very least, they will explain their reasons for what they do and why they cannot accommodate your wishes.

3 Is the approach more action-oriented or talking-oriented?

In general, people remember more about what they have seen than what they have been told. People are more likely to be able to do what they have practiced themselves than what they have been shown to do or told to do. Look for programs that involve showing more than explaining and that provide lots of opportunity for learning by doing.

4 Is the learning success-based?

Feeling like a failure when learning self-defense skills can be destructive to a student's emotional and physical safety. Success-based learning means that students are guided through what they need to learn in a highly positive way. Practices go step by step starting with where each student actually is. Success is defined as progress for each individual student rather than as perfection according to some standard of the teacher. Students are coached as they do the practices so that they can do them correctly as much as possible. They are given feedback about how to improve in a context that communicates, "mistakes are part of learning."

5 Is the approach more focused on traditional martial arts or on practical self-defense?

Martial arts programs, like other activities involving interactive movement such as sports and dance, can be wonderful for building confidence, character, and physical condition. However, for teaching personal safety skills, the approach of most martial arts is like long-term preventative health care. Practical self-defense is more like emergency medicine. Our goal is to teach in a few hours skills that are very focused on preventing abduction, assault, and abuse from strangers, bullies, and people we know. The increased discipline, coordination, and strength that kids get in an ongoing program can be excellent, but we also want them to learn how to protect themselves as quickly as possible.

6 *What is the safety track record?*
You do not want kids to become injured while learning to protect themselves. How careful is the instructor about defining safety rules and insisting that they are followed? Notice how injuries are being prevented, using the safety guidelines identified earlier in this chapter.

7 *What does your intuition tell you?*
The most important skill in choosing a good self-defense program is being able to act on your intuition without being stopped by feelings of confusion or fear. It can be hard to stay clear about what your needs are or what the needs of your children are when you are bombarded by often conflicting advice from experts. If something someone does seems wrong to you, even if you can't justify your feeling logically, walk away rather than staying in a potentially bad situation. Keep looking until you find the type of program that answers to your satisfaction the kinds of questions described above.

Whether you are looking for a self-defense class or any other important training, pay attention to uncomfortable feelings you have about someone's approach, no matter how highly-recommended the person is and no matter how much you like the teacher as a person. Often very well meaning, knowledgeable people try to teach through talking about what can go wrong rather than through helping their students practice how to do things effectively. Remember that what programs actually do is more important than what their literature or representatives say they are going to do.

What About Weapons?

In 1999, two teenaged boys at Columbine High School in Colorado carried out a shooting rampage that killed twelve students and a teacher, as well as injuring twenty-four other people, before committing suicide.[2] The story horrified people all over the United States and was heavily publicized. A few weeks later, a six-year-old girl in a workshop at a private school near my home asked me, "What if someone comes to our school and starts shooting everybody?" Along with all of the other adults in the room, I looked into her little face and felt ill that she even had to wonder about it.

The issue of armed violence in our schools and communities becomes heartbreakingly real and urgently on our minds each time a new tragedy takes place. The threat of weapons looms over all children no matter where they live or what their family situation is. Violence from guns and knives is occurring more frequently and is ever-present in the media. Although nothing works all of the time, there are lots of ways that young people can keep themselves safe most of the time.

If children are really worried about somebody shooting at school or any other kind of emergency, practicing can help them manage that worry. When the little girl I mentioned above asked her question, the anxiety in the room was huge. All of the children, and their teachers and parents, were looking at me, needing an answer. I said, "Television makes it seem as if scary things like this are happening all the time. But this isn't true. Most of us will live long happy lives and never have to worry about somebody starting to shoot people at school. But it is good to know what to do in an emergency. Most of the time, the safest thing you can do is leave quickly

The issue of armed violence in our schools and communities becomes heartbreakingly real and urgently on our minds each time a new tragedy takes place.

Concerns about weapons are real. If we don't give kids at least a little knowledge, they are likely to develop beliefs that will not serve them well.

The presence of weapons does make an attack more dangerous, but by no means hopeless. The biggest danger is believing the myth that there is no hope.

and quietly when someone is acting violent. Just get up and get out. Suppose that I started acting dangerous. Look around and see if you know how to get out of this room. Now, all of you, very quietly, leave the room."

Thirty children found one of the three exits and silently streamed outside to where their teachers were waiting for them. Then, everyone came back and we went on with our workshop.

Concerns about weapons are real. If we don't give kids at least a little knowledge, they are likely to develop beliefs that will not serve them well. We used to avoid mentioning weapons in Kidpower classes. We wanted to respect parents and teachers who said, "Please don't talk with my child about weapons. It is just too upsetting." As parents and teachers ourselves, we had the same feelings. After there had been a series of incidents with weapons in my community, I asked older children who had had Kidpower training what they would do if an attacker had a knife or a gun. These were young people who were out in public without their adults.

"I'd give up," our students said, "because there would be nothing I could do." Of course having them believe this was unacceptable. The mystique in our culture about the power of knives and guns can leave people feeling helpless at even the thought of a weapon. In one community, two girls who were kidnapped and sexually assaulted near their school by a man who told them he had a gun, even though they never saw it.

Unfortunately, the opposite problem is also common. I hear too many stories about young people who end up injured, in jail, and dead because they don't know how to walk away from an insult or how to give up their stuff. In one incident years ago, a boy got shot fighting over Halloween candy by a friend who had stolen his father's gun. Too often, teens who know each other get into an argument and someone gets stabbed.

I realized that, in not talking about weapons when children were old enough to go out on their own, we were doing our students a great disservice. This is knowledge that can save their lives. The presence of weapons does make an attack more dangerous, but by no means hopeless. The biggest danger is believing the myth that there is no hope.

In Kidpower, our goal is to be truthful about weapons in a way that focuses on what you can do rather than to dwell on what you cannot. We also do not add any unnecessary details. As with other potentially upsetting issues, kids learn best if their adults sound calm and matter-of-fact rather than scared. We are careful to be age-appropriate by not talking about weapons until children are old enough to be thinking about weapons. We give them information that is relevant to their different life situations. Children living in more violent neighborhoods need to know more than children who are not. If there has been a violent incident that children have heard about, it is important to be able to answer the questions they might be worrying about.

In this part of our workshop, children and teens become completely silent and listen intently because they really want to know. We explain, "If someone has a weapon – a knife, a gun, or a club – it would be very scary and you might get hurt. But most of the time you can be safe if you remember a few things. First of all, at the beginning of most attacks, someone who has a weapon does not plan to use it. The weapon is being used to scare you into doing what the attacker wants. If the attacker wants to steal something like your money or property, give it away. You are more important than your stuff."

We give children practice in giving up their stuff by telling them to put their hands in front of them and imagine that they have a thing, not a person, precious to them in their hands. Vivid in our minds are the stories about young people who have died fighting over their property but we don't say this to younger kids. We pretend to have a gun and say, "Give me your stuff!"

We coach the children to lift up their hands in a letting go motion and say, "Take it! It's yours!"

"You are more important than your stuff," we remind our students again. And then we go on, "If an attacker tries to do something that would make things more dangerous for you, like take you away or tie you up or hurt you, you are almost always safer if you yell and fight the best you know how in order to get away and run to safety as soon as possible. Probably the attacker is not going to use the weapon. One girl was walking home from school and a man pulled up in a car. He pointed a gun at her and told her to get in the car. Instead, she yelled and ran away and she was safe."

At this point a few hands go up and a chorus of worried voices ask, "But what if the guy shoots the gun?"

Law enforcement officials have told us that going away with an attacker is almost always much more dangerous than risking getting shot or stabbed to escape as soon as possible. But this is very scary information. We tell children what they need to know by saying, "Police officers tell us that what you see on TV shows and in the movies, where somebody shoots and everybody drops down dead is just make believe. Most of the time, even trained police officers, even at close range, miss a target moving away from them. News stories about someone shooting lots of people in the news are upsetting, but this is very rare. Even then, you will be safest if you run away as soon as you can."

We remind our students that, "Gun rhymes with run!" We start practices by having them walk across the room as if they were walking down the street. An instructor pretends to be standing by his car. He makes his hand into a pretend gun, points it at the children, and says, "Get in the car!" We coach children to turn and run away, in a curve or zigzag if possible to make it harder to aim.

"But what if there's no room to run away?" our students ask. "Suppose the bad guy is grabbing me?"

We answer, "If you don't have room at first, try to notice where the hole at the end of the gun is pointing. As soon as the hole at the end of the gun is not pointing at you, do your best to pull away and run."

In Kidpower, our goal is to be truthful about weapons in a way that focuses on what you can do rather than to dwell on what you cannot and that does not go into unnecessary details.

Most of the time, even trained police officers, even at close range, miss a target moving away from them.

Going away with an attacker is almost always much more dangerous than risking getting shot or stabbed to escape as soon as possible.

"What about knives?" our students ask.

"If there is a knife and you have any room at all, you can run away," we say. "You can also throw anything! You would not want to throw something at a gun because it might go off by accident, but with a knife, you can throw your backpack, a book, sand, or anything else around you to startle the person with the knife and to keep the knife away from you."

Sometimes we have students practice throwing a pillow at an instructor who is pretending to threaten them with a knife. As they throw, they yell, "NO!" and then run to safety yelling for help. With this practice, students can see that when a person has something thrown at his face, it is natural for him to catch it or to cover his face. The attacker is likely to focus on the thing that has been thrown, giving the person being attacked more time to run away and get help.

"But what if there's no room? What if the knife is right next to your body?" our older students sometimes ask.

"If there's no room," we say, "then you might not be able to choose whether you get cut, but you can almost always choose where you get cut. Better your hands or outer arms than your face, throat or mid-section." As our students look alarmed, we ask, "Have you ever been cut when you fell down?" When they nod, we ask, "Did you heal?" As our students nod again, we say, "You can get hurt and heal most of the time."

Young people need to know that their adults do not want them to fight over their property or over insults, even to their family, their culture, or their loved ones.

With older youth who are already worried about this, or teens, we sometimes practice by coaching students to, "Imagine that someone is about to stab you with a knife. Put your arms up in front of you. Use the outside bony part of your arms to block the knife so that it does not reach your face or your body. Yell 'NO!' and run to safety." We also show how to use something nearby to block the knife, like a chair or a sweatshirt.

Weapons in the hands of a child or a teen are extremely dangerous. From the time they were small, many young people have seen repeated media images of people being killed with no consequences. It can seem like a game and they may have no real idea of what it means to shoot or stab someone. In one workshop at a middle school, a boy asked, "Wouldn't it be safer for me to have a weapon so I could protect myself?"

Our instructors, Jamiko and Ryan explained, "The problem with having a weapon unless you have had lots of training is that you are more likely to use it, which means that somebody is likely to get hurt and to get into trouble with the law." The two men demonstrated the problem by standing face to face with their hands shaped into "guns" that were pointing at each other. Everyone could see how dangerous a position this was if either of them were to decide to shoot.

Next Ryan and Jamiko acted out getting mad at each other and, instead of pulling out a gun, both of them running away in the opposite direction, so that no one would get shot. Finally, they showed how, if one of them were to pull out a gun, the other one could run quickly away.

We are more important than our stuff

If young people with weapons at school or on the street are a concern in your community, you can tell your children that, "Sometimes kids like to joke or brag about having or using guns or bombs or about hurting animals or people. Most of the time, they are just pretending, but once in a while, they are not. If someone is talking like this, this person might have big problems. I want you to tell me or another adult you trust about it as soon as you can. If kids say they have a weapon at school, go as quickly and quietly as you can to the office and find an adult you trust to make a report. If you don't have someone you trust at the school to pay attention and to protect you, then call me."

Young people need to know how to get away from anyone who makes them uncomfortable without saying what they think. This might mean that they have to lie to stay safe and say, "Of course I won't tell." If someone is bragging about a weapon, it might be important to say something untrue such as, "Yes, I think that's cool." Children need to know that their adults do not want them to fight over insults, even to their family, their culture, or their loved ones. In order to get away from a person who is acting dangerous, they might even have to agree with a big insult, like saying, "Yes, you're right, I am a wimp. My mom is ugly. My friends are dumb."

Just as with other problems, as soon as possible, we want children who have seen other kids with weapons or heard them talk about killing someone to get help by telling a trustworthy adult. One of the reasons kids don't tell is because they are afraid of having someone retaliate. Make sure that your child's school or youth organization has a plan for dealing with armed violence just like any other emergency. Make sure that adults are trained in how to deal with a young person who makes a report about someone else.

If you are worried about retaliation for telling, find someone at school whom you trust to deal with a report about weapons in a way that protects your identity.

Making an effective safety plan for how to handle an armed intruder at school takes thought, needs to be specific to the school and the type of intrusion in order to make sense, and should be clearly understood.

One girl who was in a very exclusive school in a quiet neighborhood heard a boy bragging about his gun. When she told the principal, the gun was found and the boy was suspended. However, the principal handled the situation in a way that caused the girl to be identified and then he put her back into the classroom. The boy's friends threatened to kill her. The trauma she went through could have been prevented if the school officials had understood how important it was to protect the girl's identity.

If someone in their world is acting in a way that could be dangerous, it is urgent that kids know what to do to take action. They need to find and tell an adult they trust something like, "This is about my safety and about the safety of others here at our school. I need you to promise to protect me from other people knowing that I am the one who is telling you this. I want you to call my parents (or another safe adult) right away so they can be with me."

Find out what the school's bullying and violence prevention policies are. Take a few minutes to check in with one of your child's teachers or the office staff to ask how they would respond to a report of a weapon on campus or other types of violence. Explain that you have taught your child to come to get help from them and that you have also told your child that the adults at the school can be trusted to keep reports anonymous.

If children don't feel safe with any adult at school, they need to tell their parents or another safe adult as soon as they can. The school needs to know if there is possible danger. In some situations, it may be necessary to make a telephone call to the school anonymously to someone in charge, such as the principal. You can disable caller ID or call from a pay telephone. Anonymous telephone calls or notes will only be taken seriously if there are as many specifics as possible included in the message.

Making an effective safety plan for how to handle an armed intruder at school takes thought, needs to be specific to the school and the type of intrusion in order to make sense, and should be clearly understood by all of the parents and teachers. Without proper preparation, armed intruder drills can be very upsetting and do more harm than good. I have seen drills where teachers gather their students, put them into their classrooms with doors that cannot be locked, cover the windows, and stay there until told that the alert is over. Most teachers are not given the permission or tools they need to decide the safest choices for their students in dealing with an armed intruder.

Unfortunately, securing a school can be challenging. For fire safety reasons, many classrooms have large windows and doors that swing out and cannot be blocked shut. Some classrooms cannot be locked from the inside. In most places, the doors and windows are not bulletproof. Depending on the situation, the most effective plan might be to get everyone out of the school to a safer place rather than trying to hide inside the school. Schools and communities are different. We recommend getting professional help to assess the risks at a school for many different kinds of disasters, including armed intruders, and to make a safety plan that is realistic and appropriate to that specific school for each type of emergency. Any plan should be one that all school staff know, understand, and are prepared to follow.

Children who have heard upsetting stories want to know what to do if someone is threatening them or their loved ones with a weapon in their school, home, or car. Imagining a plan for what they can do is less upsetting than to keep imagining being helpless. You can tell children, "If someone starts waving a gun or a knife or starts shooting, almost always the safest thing to do is to get away as quickly and quietly as you can. You will almost always be safer if you keep running away, even if the person with the gun tells you to stop."

Kids also need to know where might be safe places to hide and how to get help. In 2010, during an armed home invasion, a seven-year-old boy rescued his family by locking himself and his younger sister in the bathroom and calling 9-1-1. He said that he knew what to do in an emergency because his mother had practiced with him.[3]

Sometimes attackers will use a threat to a loved one to keep a child from leaving. You can say, "Even if an attacker is saying that he will hurt me or someone else if you try to escape, the best chance you have for helping everyone is to get away and get help. Most attackers do not want to get caught. If you have run away, this person is likely to be afraid that the police will come."

As soon as they are old enough to understand, children need to know how to escape from their home, school, or car in case of danger – whether the safety problem comes from a fire or a person. Help children think of escape routes – out of different doors, climbing out of a window, going down the stairs, breaking glass with something hard like a chair, or jumping out of a window. If children cannot get out and the danger is from a fire, they can look for a place near a window, away from the fire and yell for help. If the danger is from a person and they cannot get out, they can look for a place to hide that covers up their whole bodies.

The risk of injury is worth it in order to get away from someone who is shooting. One of the boys at Columbine escaped by throwing himself out the window. He got cut up badly but he survived. Some of the students who stood still in shock or who were hiding under the tables unfortunately became targets for the attackers. You can explain to older youth and teens that, "You might need to get hurt in order to get away. If a gun is shot, it might sound very loud or you might only hear soft popping noises. The great thing about adrenaline is that it can help you run fast, even if you are hurt or start to bleed. If you are hurt by a gun, you can get better most of the time, just like you get better most of the time when you fall down and get hurt and bloody."

If a child has had a terrifying experience, practicing what to do can help reduce fear. In one of our workshops at a school in a neighborhood with a lot of crime, an eight-year-old boy who had seen his neighbor murdered kept asking, "But what if I get shot? What if I'm bleeding?"

Finally, our instructor said very calmly, "Everybody, look at your arms and pretend that you are bleeding. Say, 'I got shot. I am bleeding. I am going to get help." As all of the children looked at their arms and repeated after our instructor, the boy visibly relaxed.

In 2010, during an armed home invasion, a seven-year-old boy rescued his family by locking himself and his younger sister in the bathroom and calling 9-1-1. He said that he knew what to do in an emergency because his mother had practiced with him.

If a child has had a terrifying experience, practicing what to do can help reduce fear.

If an older child is very worried about getting shot, adults can point out that the media does not normally report all the times that a bullet hit a tree or fell harmlessly to the ground. Adults can help a worried young person gain a sense of perspective with factual information and leading questions such as, "Probably you will never get shot at. If you do, probably the bullet will miss. But suppose that you get shot in the arm, will it hurt? Will you bleed? Will you need medical attention? Will you live? Almost certainly you will!"

Be sure to remind children, "No attack is over until you have gotten help. Once you get away from a dangerous person, as soon as you safely can, find an adult you trust to go to for help. Now, let's think about different places you might be and where you could go to get help."

Teaching children about attacks with weapons is very much like teaching them about out-of-control fires. Most likely, your school or house will not burn down, but, whether the issue is with a weapon or a fire, knowing what to do when things go wrong makes everyone safer, just in case. We need to de-mystify weapons rather than treating them as the symbols for all violence. Essentially, cars, knives, and guns are all tools that can be useful in the right hands and that can cause terrible devastation in the wrong hands. If we choose to own a car, a knife, a gun, or another tool that can harm others, our responsibilities are to be fully committed to preventing any misuse that might harm innocent people, to be emotionally healthy and mature, and to be well-trained in how to use this tool safely and effectively.

Developing a Safety Plan if an Attack Involves a Weapon

1   Listen to children and answer their questions rather than trying to make their fear go away by saying, "That would never happen." After listening, help children understand that most very scary things with weapons rarely happen and that, even if someone does have a weapon, they can keep themselves safe most of the time.

2   Brainstorm ideas with children about getting out of their house, car, or school building. If possible, let them show you how they would get out if there were a fire or another reason why staying in the building would be dangerous.

3   Review safety plans with children for getting help if it is not safe to stay at home, in the car, or at school. Also discuss what might be safe places to hide if need be. Make an agreement about where they are going to go and whom they are going to ask for help. Teach children how to call 9-1-1; give their full name, address, and telephone number; and how to use different types of telephones (especially cell phones, which are all different and can be either very easy or very difficult for a child to use).

4   Use the information and practices described above as seems appropriate for the ages and life situations of your children. Have children practice walking away from insults and giving up their property. As soon as they are out on their own, make sure that children know that the safest thing to do if they are threatened with a weapon is to get away and get help.

5   Ask to see the policy at your child's school about protecting children who tell if a student has a weapon or is causing any other safety problem. Find out what your school has done for emergency preparedness to deal with any kind of dangerous situation. Encourage the school to get training if they do not have a clear practical plan that everyone understands and knows how to follow.

202 | The Kidpower Book **Chapter Seven**

What if There's More Than One Attacker?

Depending on where they live or what they've overheard or seen on television, children sometimes ask, "What if there are lots of bad guys?" Or, "What if there's a gang?" In Kidpower, we show older children and teens how these strategies and skills can work most of the time:

- If you see a group of people who look like trouble, the first thing to try to do is to go somewhere safe and get help. Use your awareness so that you notice what's happening around you. Change your plan instead of continuing to walk the same way.
- If you can't go someplace else, try to calm the situation down. Let people know you know they're there, but don't stare at them. Look around with "soft eyes," which means seeing people without making direct eye contact. You can also act as if there's no problem by smiling and waving in a respectful way, as you leave. This can be very disarming to a group that might have a mixed intention.
- Instead of walking in between people in a group, make a circle and go around them.
- Let people steal your stuff.
- Let people say mean things without answering back. To get away, you can lie and agree with everything an attacker says even if it is insulting.
- If you get surrounded and are about to get hurt, look for an opening to run through. Yell into someone's face. Hit and kick to make an opening and escape.
- Get help from adults you trust. If there is a risk of retaliation, make sure that adults do not let others know that you told.

The police definition of a gang is, "A group of individuals, juvenile and/ or adult, who associate on a continuous basis, form an allegiance for a common purpose, and are involved in delinquent or criminal activity." A gang might be a loosely organized group of individuals who hang out together and commit crimes. A gang might be a very tightly organized group with a leader, rituals, a name, and colors.

Young people join gangs to have a place to belong, to earn money, to do something exciting, and to have protection. Often friends and family members pressure youth to join gangs. In areas with lots of gang activity, schools and communities need to organize and create positive alternatives for meeting these needs. Warning signs that someone might be involved in a gang include: spending time with people who are in gangs, wearing gang colors, deteriorating grades, having unexplained money, using drugs, or having weapons. Gangs create fear, danger, and destruction for their members and for the communities where they are active.

Children who are or who have been in gangs are at high risk of suffering from gang violence. They are also at risk of getting in trouble with the law. Being identified as a gang member or trying to leave a gang increases the likelihood of having to face a violent attack.

Preventing gang violence is a large subject that goes beyond the scope of this book. However, young people who have adults who listen to them, access to interesting activities, enough money in the family for necessities, high self-esteem, good boundaries, positive role models, and hope for their future are less likely to get involved in gangs.

Preparing Kids to Avoid Gang Violence

1 Talk with young people about gangs. Let them know that you disapprove. Remind them that problems should not be secrets. Be a safe adult to come to. Spend positive time with children. If you see signs of your child getting involved in a gang, get professional help.

2 Teach children how to use target denial skill to avoid attacks by more than one person and self-defense skills if they need to, as described above.

3 Join with other parents, teachers, and concerned community members to create positive alternatives to gangs and to make plans to stop gang activities.

If somebody says or does something that makes you feel bad, this does not mean that you are bad.

What if Nothing Works?

For most adults, the thought of something bad happening to the children we love is unbearable. The problem is that, if adults act as if something is too terrifying even to mention, this can make children more afraid. They might want to protect their adults by not sharing their fears and this can leave children who are worried feeling really alone.

The strategies and skills we teach in Kidpower work most of the time. Children need to know that once in a great while there are situations where – no matter how big and strong and skilled they are – they could be overwhelmed. Without going into details about what happens in an assault, we have found that talking about the possibility of nothing working actually relieves most children. The right kind of discussion can put boundaries around the topic.

Dealing with a traumatic situation is hard enough without having to feel guilty. Children who have been kidnapped or harmed in other ways often blame themselves, thinking, "I should have known better. I should have gotten away." If they are sexually abused as part of the attack, they might feel especially ashamed.

Adults can help prevent this by telling children, "If you can't get away from an attacker at first, it does not mean that you did anything bad. It just means that you had bad luck. Even if you made a mistake, it does not mean that you are bad. You just made a mistake. If somebody says or does something that makes you feel bad, this does not mean that you are bad. Do not believe what an attacker says to you. No matter what happens, I will always love you and always want you and will keep looking for you, so keep looking for a new chance to get away."

For their emotional safety, children need knowledge about what to do to be safe without feeding their imagination with gory details. Suppose a child asks, "What exactly would happen?"

You can say, "I don't want to talk about that. I want to talk about how you can keep yourself safe." If you think the child has some specific worry, ask, "Is there something you are worrying about?" Address the child's specific concern rather than discussing all of the different concerns someone could possibly have.

If a child asks for a definition of something – like "What is sexual abuse?" – answer the question in a simple and calm way. When appropriate, pair the question with a safety plan. (See Chapter Nine on Protecting Kids From Sexual Abuse.)

There are frightening examples of children who were abducted and who were so traumatized that they did not take advantage of opportunities to escape, sometimes even for years. There are also inspiring examples of children who were very creative about getting away. One little girl was kidnapped as she was walking home from school in a rural area. The kidnapper was holding a gun to her head and forcing her to walk to his car. The little girl said, "I'm so tired. Can I please take off my backpack?" As this man stood over her, pointing his gun in different directions in case anyone came, the little girl sat on the ground. As soon as the man was not looking at her, she left her backpack on the ground and took off screaming at the top of her lungs.

The man was so frightened that he jumped into his car and raced through two stoplights. A police officer stopped him for running the light and saw the gun on the seat. While they were finding out that the man didn't have a permit for his gun, the report came in about the little girl he had attempted to abduct. The man was arrested – and found to have kidnapped two children from another state.

You can tell a child, "If you can't get away at first, keep looking for other chances to get away – like using the telephone or calling out to someone. This situation is such a big emergency that you should run to any stranger for help as soon as you get the chance."

The reality is that children who have been abducted often know their kidnapper at least a little. Even if this person was a total stranger to them, they might start to believe that they know this person better than the other people around them. Also, children are taught to do what adults tell them to and to believe what adults say. In an emergency, they need specific permission to disobey orders, tell lies, talk to strangers, and not give up.

Children like the story about one boy who was taken away to a hotel room. The attacker made the boy promise not to move and went to the bathroom. The boy got on the telephone and dialed 9-1-1. Even though the boy didn't know where he was, the computer systems they have now in emergency centers can track calls and give the police the address. They got there in time to arrest the attacker before he finished in the bathroom!

In an emergency, kids need specific permission to disobey orders, tell lies, talk to strangers, and not give up.

Preparing Children to Keep Looking for Chances To Escape Instead of Giving Up

1 Once a child is old enough to understand, be clear that, if something bad happens and nothing works at first, or they forget their safety rules, this is not their fault. Tell them to keep looking for a new chance to get away or to get help. Use as much of the information above as seems relevant.

2 If children start to tell scary stories about kidnapping, have them imagine ways that they could avoid this happening in the first place or to escape. Look for stories about children being successful in getting away. See Chapter Ten for more information about preventing abduction.

3 Review what children can do to prevent and escape from danger when their lives change. As young people get older, they become more aware of the bad things that might happen and they become more independent. They might go away on a trip or be living and going to school in a new place.

Knowing First Aid is Also An Important Defense Tool in An Emergency

Most health emergencies are not caused by an attack, but by a fall, car or bike accident, natural disaster, drowning, or illness. Invest in a few hours of first aid and CPR training such as that taught by the Red Cross[3] so that you and your children know what to do rather than feeling helpless. Practice with young people how to handle different types of health problems so that, if you have to face an emergency, all of you are ready!

PART THREE

Kidpower Solutions to "People Safety" Problems

Chapter Eight

Protecting Young People From Bullying

If a child doesn't know how to read, *we teach.*
If a child doesn't know how to swim, *we teach.*
If a child doesn't know how to multiply, *we teach.*
If a child doesn't know how to drive, *we teach.*
If a child doesn't know how to behave, *we* .... *?*
Why can't we finish the last sentence as automatically
as we do the others?
Tom Herner, NASDSE President, Counterpoint 1998[1]

People are not born knowing how to read, swim, multiply, drive, or behave. We have to learn. The problem is that behaving well in relationships is often a challenge for adults as well as for kids - and teaching positive behavior and intervening effectively to stop negative behavior is far more complicated than most other skills. Bullying often occurs when people lack the social and emotional skills to ensure positive behavior. Most of the time, teaching skills and providing support gives children the tools they need to be successful and safe in relationships.

Being bullied causes far too much isolation, sadness, fear, rage, and shame in far too many lives. Young people who are allowed to bully without learning safer ways of interacting with their peers are likely to develop poor social skills that do not serve them well in life. Kids who witness bullying often feel guilty and anxious because they don't know what to do.

If we are going to address bullying effectively, adult leadership is essential. Young people need to see their adults setting and upholding standards for taking charge of safety and for treating everyone with caring and respect. No matter how committed schools and youth groups are in establishing bullying prevention policies and programs, policies and programs alone are not enough to protect kids. In addition, the adults in charge must be prepared to intervene to stop bullying and harassment behavior in the moment and to ensure that their children and teens learn age-appropriate skills for building positive peer relationships.

The "People Safety" strategies and skills addressed in previous chapters can help to protect young people from bullying because:

- Kids who have strong, positive relationships with adults are less likely to be vulnerable to becoming bullies or being bullied. They are also more likely to seek adult help if they need it.
- Kids who know how to stay calm, aware, and confident are less likely to be chosen as targets for bullying.

No matter how committed schools and youth groups are in establishing bullying prevention policies and programs, policies and programs alone are not enough to protect kids.

Projecting a positive attitude makes kids less likely to be chosen as targets for bullying.

- Kids who respond to bullying attempts by setting boundaries and speaking up for themselves – or by calmly leaving with awareness, calm and confidence and going to get help if necessary – are less likely to remain targets of the person bullying.
- Kids who know how to be assertive instead of aggressive and how to communicate respectfully are less likely to act like bullies.
- Kids who know how to be persistent in getting help from busy adults are more likely to know what to do if they see bullying behavior.

Unlike their adults, young people often do not get to choose where they go to school, play, or live, so their options for getting away from bullying are more limited. Bullying tends to occur in environments where children and teens spend much of their time and often takes place in the context of relationships that are important to them. The repeated nature of bullying, the desire to be accepted, and hurt feelings can make using People Safety skills challenging. Young people often need extra help to apply and adapt these skills to deal with their specific problems.

What Adults Need to Know About Bullying

Sometimes we ask children during a workshop, "What is bullying?" Hands shoot into the air and the answers pour out of our students. Because adults have more official words for the same behavior, I have put these in parentheses next to the explanations of our Kidpower experts:

- "When another kid tries to hurt or scare you." (Physical bullying; intimidation.)
- "When someone says bad stuff about you behind your back." (Relational bullying.)
- "When someone calls you names or makes fun of you." (Emotional abuse.)
- "When kids leave you out." (Shunning.)
- "When kids gang up on you and try to make you give them your money or your stuff." (Extortion.)
- "When someone copies you in a way that makes you look dumb." (Mimicking.)
- "When other people say or do things to bother you over and over on purpose." (Harassment.)
- "When someone tries to make you do something that will get you into trouble." (Coercion.)
- "When someone tries to use their power to make you feel bad." (Bullying.)

We then ask our students, "Have you ever been bullied or seen someone else being bullied?" Most of them nod their heads. "How did you feel?" we ask. Again, our young and wise Kidpower experts raise their hands and say:

- "Sad."
- "I thought there must be something wrong with me."
- "Scared and wanting to hide."
- "Embarrassed and like I never wanted to go back."
- "Mad and like I wanted to get back at them."
- "As if I was the only person in the world that this was happening to."
- "Guilty because I was glad it wasn't happening to me."
- "Worried because I was afraid it would happen to me."

- "Ashamed because I didn't know what to do to stop it."
- "Frustrated."
- "Lonely."
- "Like I wanted to throw up or disappear."
- "Like it would never end, and I didn't want to live anymore."

Extensive research about bullying has been done by Ken Rigby, Ph.D. Dr. Rigby was employed as a teacher for ten years in elementary and high schools in England and Australia before becoming a psychology professor at the University of South Australia. He has been doing research on bullying since the early 1990s, has published educational materials that are used by schools worldwide, and is considered a leading international expert on the subject of school bullying.

According to Rigby, a generally accepted definition of bullying is a "repeated oppression, psychological or physical, of a less powerful person by a more powerful person or group of persons." He points out that bullying is different from aggression between people of equal power. He also points out that a child having less power than his or her peers have can be the result of many different issues such as being shy, liking poetry instead of sports, having a problem at home, lacking confidence, looking different, having a disability, being of a different culture, or being small. A child having greater power can also result from different causes such as height, quick wits, charisma, appearance, a sharp tongue, or social status.

In 1999, Rigby presented his research in a paper titled, "What Harm Does Bullying Do?"[2] at the Children and Crime: Victims and Offenders Conference convened by the Australian Institute of Criminology. Based upon extensive surveys of more than 38,000 Australian school children, his study found that at least 50 percent of children reported being bullied at school and approximately one child in six reported being bullied at least weekly by another child or group of students. The majority of these children reported that they felt angry or sad and felt worse about themselves afterwards. In some cases, the cycle continued for weeks, months, and even years.

In a related study reported in the same paper, Rigby found a correlation between illness and being bullied and stated that there is likelihood that approximately one of every ten children who have been bullied will suffer long-term mental or physical health problems. He also indicated that the stress of bullying would be likely to affect academic performance. Rigby's findings are confirmed by many other studies around the world. To take just one example, according to the National Education Association, in the United States alone, 160,000 children miss school each day due to fear of being tormented by their classmates.[3]

Any search for "bullying" on the Internet will show extensive research citations with very similar results. Across many countries, income groups, and cultures, researchers have found that:

- Bullying occurs frequently;
- Bullying is likely to be upsetting and potentially damaging both to the person being bullied and to people witnessing the bullying.;

Bullying is a "repeated oppression, psychological or physical, of a less powerful person by a more powerful person or group of persons."

Positive peer relationships can make a huge difference to a young person's health and happiness

- Being allowed to bully, although sometimes rewarding in the short run, is likely to be damaging to the people doing the bullying in the long run;
- Stopping bullying takes a united, sustained, and consistent commitment by a school's parents, teachers, administration, and students.

Bullying is not new. What is new is our awareness of the damage it causes. Just as smoking, which was once thought to be a harmless habit, is now recognized as a major health hazard, bullying is increasingly understood to be a dangerous social hazard. We are learning about the destructive results of behavior that used to be accepted as a normal fact of life.

When I was growing up, children were told that they needed to learn how to deal with bullying on their own. Typical advice included:

- "*Fight back*. Don't let anyone walk all over you. Give as good as you get." The problem with this advice is that teaching children to fight over insults or property can put them in danger. An aggressive response might solve the problem one day, but lead to an increased likelihood of facing retaliation another day. At Kidpower, we believe that there can be a time and a place to fight to stop bullying but that fighting should be taught as the *last* resort.
- "*Don't let it get to you. Just ignore it*." Unfortunately, chronic aggression directed toward you or jokes at your expense are hard to ignore, especially in situations where you cannot just leave, such as in school or among family members.
- "*Go find another friend*." The betrayal that comes with a friend turning into a bully can be devastating.
- "*You'll get over it*." When I ask adults to tell their childhood memories about bullying, the stories and the pain often sound fresh, as if the bullying happened yesterday.
- "*It isn't the end of the world*." When you have to see people every day who are turned against you, the hurt can seem endless.

In addition to the research mentioned above, well-publicized tragedies have

Bullying is not new. What is new is our awareness of the damages it causes.

caused adults to take bullying far more seriously than they did in the past. Children have killed themselves – and others – because of bullying. Most people don't die because of bullying. However, the effect of bullying is like the effect of pollution. Polluting chemicals in the environment don't usually kill people right away unless they get a strong dose, but even low level exposure over time can undermine health. Continued exposure overtime can increase the damaging effects. The same seems to be true with bullying.

Different forms of bullying include:
• *Physical* – threatened or actual physical harm such as making intimidating remarks, pushing, shoving, hitting, tripping, poking, kicking, or acting in a dominating way.
• *Emotional* – actions intended to make someone else feel uncomfortable such as name-calling, put-downs, insulting gestures, exchanging knowing looks, copying/mimicking, or making rude sounds.
• *Relational* – attacking someone's relationships with others through shunning, repeating destructive gossip, slandering, making embarrassing pictures public, back-stabbing, giving someone "the silent treatment," or breaking a trust not to tell private information.

Bullying can be used to attack you personally, to harm your reputation, to extort money or property from you, or to pressure you into acting in a way that is harmful or forbidden. Parents have told us countless stories of their children being bullied in many imaginative and cruel ways that were not always understood by the adults around them. Here are just two examples:

• "Jimmie has a life-threatening peanut allergy and has to be very careful. He's being tormented by kids who think it's funny to chase him with their peanut butter sandwiches, saying, 'You're going to die!'"

• "A girl in Kim's class was drawing cartoons that showed Kim getting into humiliating situations. This girl would get other kids to look and giggle, because the cartoons were very clever. Then, she'd accidentally leave the cartoons for Kim to find. After this had gone on for months, Kim announced that she didn't want to go to school anymore."

Whether the form of delivery is to someone's face, through others, on the phone, in writing, in pictures, through texting, through social media, or through e-mail, everyone needs to understand that bullying is bullying and is ultimately damaging to everyone involved. While the anonymous nature and efficiency of cyber-bullying create special problems, we need to realize that cyber-bullying is still simply bullying with a modern form of delivery thanks to technology.

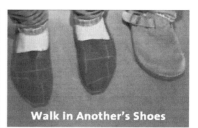

Walk in Another's Shoes

Kidpower Colorado Teen Advisory Board Bullying Prevention Video

Ideas for Discussing Bullying with Young People

1 Ask leading questions such as, "What is bullying? Have you ever been bullied or seen bullying? How did you feel?"

2 Explain the different types of bullying and be clear that you think this is wrong.

3 Point out bullying behavior in stories, movies, or pictures. Ask what different choices each party might make - the one doing the bullying, the one being bullied, and anyone watching the bullying.

4 State very specifically, "You and others have the right to be safe at home, at school, and everywhere you go. Bullying is unsafe. If you are being bullied or see someone being bullied, I want you to tell me. If you make a mistake and do something hurtful to someone, I also want to know so we can figure out how to fix the problem."

5 Have children and teens draw pictures, write stories, or role play about bullying problems and solutions.

6 Watch the free 5-minute video *Walk In Another's Shoes - Teens Speak Out About Bullying* that was created for teens and pre-teens by our Colorado Springs Teen Advisory Board[4]. Use this as a tool for raising awareness about the impact of bullying.

What Makes Bullying Hard to Stop?

Even with all of the media attention on tragic news stories, all of the millions of dollars spent on bullying prevention programs, and the tremendous efforts of countless concerned adults, bullying is not likely to disappear as a social problem anytime in the near future, if ever. Why does bullying continue despite the best efforts of so many people?

Some of the factors that perpetuate bullying and harassment include: natural tendencies and experimentation, conflicting social messages, the "being mean is funny" phenomena, victim behavior, prejudice, bullying adults, resignation that this is just the way things are, and peer attachment.

Natural tendencies and experimentation. Kids are born with the power to think, make noise, and move. Very quickly, they learn how to use this power to affect the world around them. As they grow, most children have the potential to be aggressive and passive, followers and leaders, cruel and kind. At the same time, children come with different tendencies. They might have the tendency to:

• Define themselves by pushing against boundaries until someone or something pushes back;
• Get upset more easily than other children;
• Give in or go along with others;
• Wait and join the side that seems to be winning; or
• Get worried and leave if a situation seems unsafe.

All of this is normal behavior. Part of what makes bullying hard to stop is that "might makes right" behavior is natural. Much of what we require children to do is necessary, but *not* natural. For the sake of functioning in a civilized society, we teach children to contain their natural impulses to grab food, knock others out of their way, look or touch anywhere their curiosity suggests, and use any place they wish as a toilet.

If you watch a group of young children playing, they will often experiment with being bullies, being enthusiastic followers, and being disturbed witnesses – as well as with being unhappy victims. Sometimes they go back and forth between different roles quite quickly. In fact, the minute the power structure changes, bullies often become victims and victims often become bullies.

The way that children learn positive social skills is often by experimenting with negative ones and getting feedback from their adults and other children. Neither catastrophizing this experimentation nor letting it go will help children learn positive ways of interacting. On the one hand, I feel sad when I hear of stories such as the one about the five-year-old boy who was expelled from school for sexual assault because he lifted up the skirt of a little girl. On the other hand, I feel worried when I see adults letting children run wild in the name of not curtailing their natural impulses.

I believe that most of us are good people, but most of us will probably do something that others experience as bullying at some point in our lives. As a child, I occasionally bullied my younger sister and brother. I was supposed to be in charge of them, but I didn't know how. Mostly, I bullied them because I felt frustrated and overwhelmed. Also, I hate to admit this now, but sometimes I thought they were little brats, and they just annoyed me!

When I tell kids this, they giggle. I explain that I feel sorry about it now, but I didn't know better at the time. I then ask them, "Can you think of times when you bullied someone and why you did it?" Given a safe space and permission, young people can be painfully honest in their replies:

- "I was bored and picking on her felt like fun."
- "I was scared some kids would get me so I got them first."
- "I wanted to feel important, and making him cry was a way to get people to look up to me."
- "I wanted something he had, so I took it."
- "She hurt my feelings, so I wanted to get even."
- "My mom and dad were always fighting at home, and I felt so angry and sad all the time. I wanted to hit something or yell at someone just to try to feel better. Something about yelling or hurting someone else made me feel like I was giving some of my pain away."
- "I thought it was just a joke and not that important."
- "I was jealous, and she seemed so stuck up. I wanted to bring her down to size."
- "He was *so* pathetic and seemed to be just asking for it."

If a child is looking for attention, recognition, entertainment, distraction, or release of anger, bullying can be an effective way to get what she or he wants, at least in the short run. Unless adults acknowledge this reality, figuring out how to provide positive alternatives along with the clear message that this destructive behavior is unacceptable will be difficult.

Conflicting social messages. Part of what makes this issue confusing for young people is that behavior that is seen as bullying in one context can be defined as leadership in another. People who are highly successful in fields such as sports, business, and politics are often shown in the popular media as being rewarded for what we would consider to be bullying behavior in a

"Something about yelling or hurting someone else made me feel like I was giving some of my pain away."

Good sportsmanship makes playing more fun!

different situation. The rules for what is and is not acceptable are changing and vary in different societies.

My descriptions in this section reflect what young people are likely to see – and perhaps misunderstand – in the world of politics, business, and sports. These are not social or academic contexts; they are government and business environments. The participants usually make an informed, adult decision to be in these contexts, and they have the power to leave. For example, the players in a professional basketball game are not in the same context as players in a children's school basketball game. The professional players have entered into an agreement with a major money- making business, and they are paid to play. The children may not even have a choice about whether or not to participate in a sport. Talking about these differences with kids can lead to interesting conversations and realizations for everyone.

In competitive sports, athletes often need to push physically and aggressively right up to the boundaries to win. However, if they go over the boundaries in the opinion of the referee, the team is penalized and the offending member might even lose the right to continue to play in the game.

Sometimes the popular media sends a message that business leaders have to be "bullies" in order to be successful. The reality is that success in highly competitive, fast moving markets often requires someone who can lead decisively, hurt the feelings of others sometimes, and take calculated risks. Taken too far, however, a corporate culture that rewards intimidation and bullying behavior can find itself engaging in unethical and even illegal behavior. In extreme cases like that of Enron, a major American energy company that went bankrupt after committing accounting fraud, a bullying culture can also lead to the financial collapse of a major company, the loss of jobs for thousands of workers, and felony convictions for corporate officers.

Behavior in politics can also look like bullying behavior. In the United States, negative campaigning or publicly criticizing an opponent seems to be part of every election cycle for both parties. Stretching the truth or even outright lying also seems to be tolerated up to a point to further a politician's agenda. However, there are checks and balances in terms of how much of this behavior is tolerated. If politicians say or do something that "goes too far" according to the changing court of "public opinion," they can lose elections or be forced to resign from their positions. And, someone who breaks the law is likely to be held accountable.

Discuss with children how the rules are different in different situations and how the rules for grownups are sometimes different than the rules for kids. For everyone, acceptable behavior on a basketball court is just not the same as acceptable behavior in a living room, classroom, or store. Your conversations can help young people to develop an understanding that acceptable behavior in professional basketball may highly unacceptable behavior in their local youth league games.

We need to be aware that our children may see many examples of aggressive or bullying-type behavior through the media and in their everyday lives. We need to be careful of our own behavior, remembering that we are important role models of our children. We can explain to children that though they may see examples of negative ways of handling situations, we have different expectations for their behavior. When children are younger, we can say, "Yes, I know that politicians sometimes say mean things about other people to win an election. Even though I don't like this behavior, these people are grown-ups in politics. In our family, youth program, and school, we expect kids and adults to be respectful to each other."

As children get older, we can teach them about values and how to find ways to be powerful and effective leaders without bullying. Children also need to know that some people who feel pressured by them might use the "bullying" label as a form of fighting back. Certainly, I have been called a "bully" when I have had to set boundaries with others, even though I do my best to be respectful and fair in all my interactions with people.

The Being Mean is Funny Phenomena. If we think about it, the word "fun" is being misused when we talk about "making fun of" someone. Young people are bombarded with images showing someone being rude and unkind as also being cool and funny. Kids identify with characters in books, cartoons, movies, and shows, and these characters are giving them countless examples of saying and doing hurtful things to each other as a joke.

Sometimes kids don't understand the difference between reality and pretend. After watching a movie that showed people pulling off each other's pants as a joke, a little boy got into trouble because he tried to do the same thing at school. He was confused because his parents had laughed at the man in the movie but were upset with him. Even more often, kids – and adults, too – don't know the difference between funny jokes and hurtful teasing. Funny jokes can be about what someone is good at or doesn't mind being bad at. If everyone involved or being joked about agrees that it's funny, then a joke is funny. If they don't all agree, then it's hurtful, not funny.

As child psychologist and entertainer Peter Alsop[5] says, "Before I tell a joke about green Martians with four eyes, I go ask some of my four-eyed green Martian friends what they think of the joke. If they don't think it's funny, then I can learn something about them I need to know. And if they think it's funny, then I feel fine telling it to a whole roomful of four-eyed green Martians!"

Hurtful teasing usually means making fun of the ways someone has trouble doing something or putting someone down for being different. Stopping hurtful teasing is just as important as stopping hurtful hitting. What seems like a joke to one person can be devastating to another. As one successful professional woman told me, "My childhood was a misery because the other kids made fun of me for being fat. Years later, I found myself in therapy dealing with the pain caused by their laughter."

Even if some children are protected from developing the "being-mean-is-funny" belief in their homes, just one child in a group can affect the

Sometimes the popular media sends a message that business leaders have to be "bullies" in order to be successful.

Unfortunately, our society teaches kids that it is cool and funny to be rude and unkind.

dynamic of a group, leading to a behavior epidemic of many of the children saying hurtful things to get their way, to be cool, to be funny, and to try to keep themselves from being targeted.

Finding out what children actually say to each other can be eye opening. A teacher once asked me to come to her third grade classroom because the teasing had gotten completely out of hand. Of course, the teacher stopped the children when she heard them, but she couldn't be everywhere all the time. She wanted her students to stop themselves. I started by asking the children, "Well, what is it that you're saying to each other?" They looked at their teacher to see if answering me was okay. No adult had asked them this question so bluntly before. Then, the words came pouring out. Both the teacher and I were shocked. It was quickly obvious that this was not language that could be said out loud in an adult's presence in any school without parental permission. Instead, we had the children write the words down.

What had started as a game between a few children because of annoyance or boredom had grown into a destructive culture involving the whole classroom.

I still have a file with their misspelled words on smudged torn scraps of paper in childish printing. Curse words. Toilet words. Swear words. Graphic sexual language. Terribly threatening words. Words attacking race, religion, gender, sexual orientation, body size, and body parts. All from bright innocent eight-year-olds! These children were from great homes in an excellent school with a wonderful teacher. What had started as a game between a few children because of annoyance or boredom had grown into a destructive culture involving the whole classroom. By taking the time to address the issue and to help her children understand the consequences of their language, the teacher turned a bad situation into a positive learning experience.

Victim behavior. Caring, confident, respectful children are sometimes selected as targets for bullying for reasons that have nothing to do with their behavior. However, there are behaviors that can make it more likely for a child to be chosen as a target for bullying. Both kids and adults are more likely to pick on someone who is acting helpless, hopeless, or whiny. As adults, we prefer to avoid someone who is constantly complaining and putting others down. Why should we expect kids to be any different?

I have had kids, and adults too, ask me in frustration, "But what if the person *deserves* it?"

I tell them, "No one deserves to be bullied, but some people have trouble with boundaries. Even if someone is very annoying, you can set boundaries without being mean."

Just as some children have learned to get attention by acting like bullies, other children have learned to get attention by acting like victims. Setting boundaries can be difficult if you are dealing with someone who seems to be submissive but whose actions are actually quite negative. This is called passive-aggressive behavior. Kids who do not feel powerful might try to get their way through passive-aggressive behavior, which can be annoying to adults and infuriating to their peers. The feeling about such people can indeed be they are just "asking for it."

The truth of course, is that even though these young people are not "asking for" a negative reaction from others, their behavior might be provoking it. With both children and adults, passive-aggressive behavior includes:

• Sabotaging activities and relationships though delaying, forgetting, not following through, or losing or breaking things by accident;
• Not being clear about what they do or don't want, so that they say, "Yes" and mean "No" or give mixed signals;
• Going along with people in positions of authority or who they perceive to have more power rather than standing up for themselves or their friends;
• Constantly whining and complaining, with never a good word to say about anybody;
• Lying or exaggerating to get others in trouble; and/or
• Acting put-upon and blaming others for everything that goes wrong rather than taking responsibility.

Adults can help children and teens change passive-aggressive or other victim behavior. When children learn how to communicate assertively, they are more likely to get what they want. They can learn how to manage their emotional triggers in order to deal with delayed gratification and occasional disappointment with dignity instead of by acting negatively towards others. They can practice sounding and acting aware, calm, and confident, no matter how they feel inside.

Prejudice. Teasing often gets dismissed as a natural result of differences. According to cross-cultural communications expert Lillian Roybal Rose[6], "Differences by themselves are never the true problem. What causes the problem is that someone feels a need to dominate others in order to feel good about himself or herself. Unless individuals feel worthy and whole within themselves, they are likely to try to dominate others or to accept domination from others in ways that are hurtful."

Discomfort or curiosity are different from bullying. We need to accept that for many people, feeling uncomfortable if something or someone seems different from what they are used to is natural. In fact, being wary of what is unfamiliar is important survival behavior. However, part of successful evolution for any species also includes the ability to adapt to new situations and to learn what differences are dangerous and what differences are interesting or even useful.

Children are not wrong to notice and comment on different ways that people look, speak, act, dress, and eat. The problem comes when their adults encourage or allow them to do this in ways that are unkind or that lump together people who might share one characteristic into a larger category combining many characteristics. Instead, we can teach young people how to be interested and curious without being rude. They can learn about what it means to use a wheelchair without being cruel to someone who needs to.

Shouting at the kindergarten lunch table, "Eeeu. Why's she eating that weird stuff with those little sticks?" might be normal but is also hurtful. And, this reaction can become bullying when it turns into repeated chronic putdowns. Instead, we can teach children to ask respectful questions, such

Kids who do not feel powerful might try to get their way through passive-aggressive behavior, which can be annoying to adults and infuriating to their peers.

Bullying about disabilities can be devastating

Unless individuals feel worthy and whole within themselves, they are likely to try to dominate others or to accept domination from others in ways that are hurtful.

as, "What's that? What does it taste like? Will you tell me about the sticks you are using?"

Adults need to be aware of the impact of their negative assumptions and thoughtless remarks that might be overheard by children, like, "The crime rate is rising because so many of *those* people are moving into our neighborhood." Or, "Poor thing. He can't help it. His parents are getting divorced." Or, "Prejudice grows when adults make or laugh at jokes that are racist, sexist, homophobic, or otherwise negatively stereotype a group of people."

Try to avoid assumptions that people who are different from the majority group or the group with the most perceived power in some way are less worthy than people who are not. Differences might have to do with income, race, culture, marital status, disability, religion, sexual orientation or identity, politics, age, physical health, mental health, family situations, education, etc. Unless someone's behavior is directly destructive to another person, these differences are not reasons to be aggressive, even if people might strongly disagree about some of them.

Adults can create environments in schools, families, and communities that celebrate diversity and that identify and refuse to accept prejudiced remarks or behavior. Many schools are doing a great job of building understanding by teaching children about different cultures, reading books about different kinds of abilities and different kinds of families, and letting children know about the contributions to our society of people from many different backgrounds. As children and teens get older, they can learn how to become informed consumers of the media and about how prejudice is created and perpetuated in ways that lead to violence and abuse.

Bullying adults. Being rude and belligerent to get your way is often directly modeled for children by responsible adults. Shortly after my husband first came to the United States from the Netherlands, we attended a school board meeting where people had strong disagreements with each other. Many parents had brought their children to put pressure on the school board. Ed was appalled at the threatening remarks and rude behavior, especially in front of children, by people on all sides of the conflict – parents, teachers, principals, and school board members. I remember him asking me in an astonished voice, "Are we still in the Wild West here?"

Even though most of the teachers and other adults in my childhood were wonderful people, I remember a few teachers, camp counselors, and youth group leaders who were terrible role models. They put children down, played favorites, spread gossip, and made threatening remarks.

I have often had teachers or principals tell me of their frustration when parents spread gossip about students or families at the school, sometimes in person and sometimes by e-mail. Spreading gossip that undermines someone's reputation is a form of bullying. Far better modeling from those parents would have been to go directly to the adult in charge – the principal or the teacher – to discuss their concerns. Again, having an interest in what is happening to others is normal. People who slow down when they see an accident on the other side of the road are not evil. Some might just want to understand what's going on. Some might want to see if anyone needs help. However, people who block the road to look at an accident or even to take pictures are being destructive.

The same thing is true with gossip. Concern or curiosity about what is happening in one's neighborhood, family, or school is normal. However, repeating gossip that damages someone's reputation without a very good reason is destructive. Desires to retaliate, punish, "give them what they deserve", or "bring someone down a notch" do not count as good reasons. If adults want children to stop bullying, we need to set an example by not acting like bullies or victims ourselves. Children need to see adults modeling being powerful, respectful leaders. If we notice when we are engaging in destructive behavior towards others, we can set a good example by stopping ourselves and apologizing.

Resignation That This Is Just the Way Things Are. On his first day of school after summer vacation, my son Arend at age nine came home and said, "I had a hard day, Mommy. My shell got soft over the summer."

"What shell do you mean?" I asked him.

"The shell that keeps out the mean things that people say and do to each other," Arend explained. "Without my shell, everything bothered me." My son looked at my troubled face and added, "Don't worry, Mommy. My shell will harden soon." Arend was in a wonderful school that he loved. I was sad that, even in this caring place, my child's perception was that he needed to harden his emotional shell in order not to be upset by the behavior of others.

The reality is that, as hard as I try, I have yet to find a place where either kids or adults are always kind and thoughtful to each other. We can enforce a caring, safe environment in the short-term context of a Kidpower class, but in a longer-term relationship, it is normal for people to get on each other's nerves, to say or do things that someone will experience as hurtful, or to cross each other's boundaries. Where there are different perspectives and interests, there are likely to be disagreements and misunderstandings. What kids need is to see their adults making a sustained commitment to keep working problems out in ways that are respectful, instead of becoming apathetic and accepting that "this is just the way things are."

Peer Orientation. In their wise and compelling book, *Hold Onto Your Kids*, authors Gordon Neufeld, Ph.D., and Gabor Mate, M.D., explain how children's attachment to peers over parents leads to a host of social ills, including bullying.[7] They make a strong case for the importance of parents and other adults seeing their relationships with their children as their top priority, even during the teen years when it can seem normal for young people to pull away.

Neufeld and Gabor point out that children need a strong attachment with a primary "source of authority, contact, and warmth" in order to thrive. If they do not have this with their parents or other consistent adult caregivers,

Desires to retaliate, punish, "give them what they deserve", or "bring someone down a notch" do not count as good reasons.

What kids need is to see their adults making a sustained commitment to keep working problems out in ways that are respectful, instead of becoming apathetic and accepting that "this is just the way things are."

Kids need strong connections with their adults

children are likely to end up becoming oriented towards their peers instead. In our society, children are often seduced into peer attachments at the expense of parental and other adult attachments through a lack of parental time, through peer-oriented school cultures, and through technology such as text messages and e-mail.

Peer orientation can lead to children dominating others, to children accepting destructive behavior towards themselves in order to be accepted, and to children participating in hurtful actions – all in order to meet their attachment needs. The authors explain that children are more likely to learn and to accept boundaries from adults in the context of a strong positive relationship, rather than by quick fix parenting strategies. *Hold Onto Your Kids* includes excellent ideas for parents and other adults on how to create, sustain, and regain attachments with their children.

Dealing with Issues That Make Bullying Hard to Stop

1 Make having a positive connected relationship with the children and teens in your life your top priority. If kids seem to be pulling away, keep reaching out to them. If you get stuck in a negative dynamic, don't just accept this as normal. Try to find ways to reconnect. If need be, get professional help.

2 Make bullying against the rules of your family, school, youth group, sports organization, place of worship, and social groups. Remember that raising awareness and building empathy are important in addressing bullying and other violence in schools or other environments – but are not enough without a sustained adult commitment to supervise closely and intervene quickly when problems occur. This takes a united front with commitment to a set of values, policies, and an action plan with skills and consistent fair consequences, as well as good intentions. Use *Kidpower's Tools for Creating a United Front Against Bullying, Harassment, and Violence*[8] on our website as a template to adapt for your needs or as a checklist for reviewing the policies currently in place.

3 Discuss bullying by asking questions and listening to their answers. Useful questions include: What is bullying? Have you ever been bullied? What happened? What can you do to protect yourself? Have you ever seen bullying? What happened? What can you do if you see someone being bullied? Have you ever bullied someone else? What happened? What can you do to stop yourself from acting like a bully?

4 Make sure that adults are setting an excellent example. Don't let people bully you. Make sure that you are not bullying others. Have adults learn and model skills for communicating concerns assertively and setting boundaries effectively and respectfully with each other as well as with children and teens.

5 Teach conflict resolution skills as described below and have a structure that supports getting adult help when this doesn't work. Young people often need help to re-state concerns or discuss issues in ways that are respectful.

6 Notice bullying behavior and address it immediately. Make the consequence of bullying behavior be to rehearse behaving in a respectful way. If a young person is pushing against boundaries, have her practice how to feel one way and act another. When a kid is acting like a victim, have him practice acting assertively instead. When children or teens start being mean to each other, intervene by changing the context or by saying, "That (be specific about the behavior) looks unsafe to me. Please be in charge of your words and body."

7 If you see a young person whose lack of social skills is leading to other kids avoiding or picking on him or her, use this as an opportunity for everyone to grow. Give in-the-moment coaching to all involved about

how to ask for what you want in respectful ways, project a positive attitude most of the time, accept occasional disappointment, and set boundaries about unpleasant behavior while still giving the other person a chance to connect with you.

8 Keep paying attention to ensure that children and teens stay respectful when you are not directly supervising.

9 Try to ensure a media diet that includes positive role models as well as poor ones. Point out poor role models and say, "That looks like bullying, doesn't it? What would be a more respectful and safer way of handling this situation?"

10 Model empathy and respect for differences. Look for programs that teach about cross-cultural communication. Provide stories, examples, and media presentations that show why it is important to value people for their differences as well as the ways that they are the same.

Managing Emotional Triggers

At any age, bullying can create a vicious cycle of people pushing each other's emotional hot buttons or triggers. People who bully often justify their behavior because they believe that they have been bothered or offended by the ones they are bullying. Instead of handling these feelings in a safe fashion and being stopped if they don't, they say and do hurtful things. People who get bullied often respond by getting triggered in such a way that they might seem like ones who are causing the problem, because they act visibly angry or whiny instead of responding with a firm boundary and by seeking help.

Have you ever replayed someone's cruel or thoughtless words or behavior towards you over and over in your mind, feeling miserable every time the picture of what happened pops into your thoughts? Children and youth do that too. Often their hurt and angry feelings will grow over time, instead of becoming less, especially if the bullying behavior becomes chronic so that they are forced to deal with it constantly. Learning to manage your emotional triggers -- thoughts, words, or gestures that cause you to explode with feelings -- can be a huge help in stopping bullying.

The different emotional safety techniques described in Chapter Six on Boundaries and Advocacy can be adapted to help young people learn how to protect their feelings from name-calling and teasing. The first step is to ask children for specifics about exactly what others are saying or doing that is upsetting to them. General language such as "things we're not supposed to say" is not as useful as the specific words. If we give words so much power that children cannot say them even to explain what's bothering them, it is unreasonable to expect them not to be bothered. The most effective way to take the power out of really foul language is to let children say the words aloud, write them down, and practice not getting hurt or triggered when someone says these words to them.

The same thing is true with intimidating or rude gestures, sounds, or facial expressions. Children often speak in generalities because they don't want

Children need a strong attachment with a primary "source of authority, contact, and warmth" in order to thrive. If they do not have this with their parents or other consistent adult caregivers, children are likely to end up becoming oriented towards their peers instead.

Talking to someone you trust can help

Learning to manage ones personal triggers can be a huge help in stopping bullying.

to sound silly or because the idea upsets them. Language like "She keeps bothering me" is not as useful as "She glares every time I walk close by." Or, "She whispers and nudges my other friends as soon as I come over to talk to them." Or, "Every time I am next to her, she acts like she is going to knock me down or hit me." Encourage children to tell you the specifics so that you have a clear picture of what is going on and can help them make a plan for protecting themselves.

Here are some examples showing how using emotional safety techniques to deal with specific triggers has worked in our classes.

Crybaby success story. For a younger child, the word "crybaby" can be as triggering as the worst foul language that you can imagine for teens or adults. In a kindergarten classroom workshop, a five-year-old boy I'll call Craig did not want to try the Trash Can practice. To use the Trash Can Technique, students take words that hurt them and pretend to throw the words into a real or imaginary trash can instead of taking these words to heart. Up until the name-calling part of the workshop, Craig had been enthusiastic. While the other kids were busy practicing with adult volunteers and teachers leading their little groups, I took Craig aside and we sat next to each other on the floor. "Some mean words won't fit into your trash can," I told Craig, and then asked in a very matter-of-fact voice, "Is someone calling you names?"

"My big brothers call me 'crybaby' every single day!" Craig said, with an expressionless look on his little face.

"Oh, my!" I said. "That sounds upsetting. Can you think of a place besides the trash can to throw away the word 'crybaby'?"

"I want to throw it into my brother's mouth and sew his mouth shut!" Craig said firmly.

"Can you think of another place to throw this hurting word that is not attached to a person?"

"Well, I could cut off someone's butt and throw the word in there!" Craig looked as if this idea really appealed to him.

"It sounds to me as if you are really mad at your brothers!" I said sympathetically, reflecting that the teasing in Craig's home must have gotten pretty intense.

"Yes!" Craig muttered, glowering balefully.

"The problem with throwing mean words into someone else is that the meanness grows and gets bigger," I explained. "So can you think of something to do with the word 'crybaby' that will not go into any part of someone else, either attached or unattached?"

Craig thought for a few seconds while I waited quietly. "Maybe," he said. "I could shrink it and melt it away in some very hot sand!"

"This sounds like a very good plan!" I told him.

Later, in the whole group, without focusing on Craig, I explained, "Usually the Trash Can technique works but not always. If one thing doesn't work, you can always try something else. Sometimes people make fun of you for something that is true. Suppose someone makes fun of me because I have curly hair and says in a nasty voice or with a scrunched up face, 'Eeeu! Your hair is curly!'

"Suppose that I answer, 'My hair is straight!' No one will believe me because my hair *is* curly. What I can do is throw away the hurtful way they are talking about my hair into my trash can and say to myself, 'I like my curly hair!' If that doesn't work, I can think about what they are actually saying when they make fun of my hair, which is that there is something wrong with me because my hair is curly. After listening to people make fun of my curly hair, I might even start to say to myself, 'I am ugly because my hair is curly!' But I can decide that that's not true. "

I then told the class, "Let's all make a fence with our hands. Put your arms in front of you like this and push your hands away from you, like a fence. Now say, 'That's not true!'" They did and I explained, "What we are saying 'that's not true' to is not my curly hair, because that IS true, but to the mean way someone talks about it. Let's try out this idea with some other examples. Suppose a friend tells you in an upset voice, 'You are being a bad friend!' but what he or she is actually saying is, 'You are a bad friend because you want to play a different game than I do!' Make your fence and say, 'That's not true!'"

They did and I clarified, "What you are saying 'that's not true' to is that you are a bad friend." Picking another example, I said, "If someone calls you, "dummy," what they actually are saying might be, 'You are dumb because you made a mistake!' And what do you say?"

Everyone stretched out his or her fences and said, "That's not true."

"What about 'You are a bad person because I am mad at you,'" I ask.

Again, everyone, adults and kids said, "That's not true!"

I reminded the class that having somebody mad at you might be true, but that it is not true that you are a bad person just because someone else is mad at you. Having established the idea, I continued, "Sometimes people make fun of us because we cry. Who here has ever been called a 'crybaby'?" As we all, along with Craig, looked around the room, almost everybody, including the adults, raised their hands.

I asked, "Did being called a crybaby hurt your feelings?" We all nodded and I continued, "What it means if someone calls you a crybaby is that you are a baby if you cry and that's not true!"

To give more information, I added a leading question, "What are tears made of?" I paused so the children could call out answers. "Water," they said, "and salt."

Crying can help our bodies be safe by washing away upset feelings.

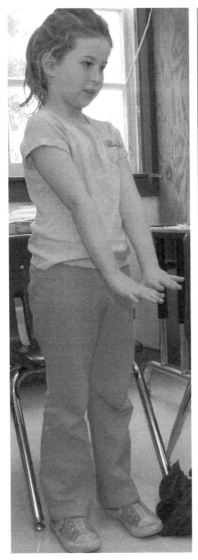

Making a fence to protect your feelings

"Yes," I continued. "And tears also are made of the chemicals that come into our bodies when we have upset feelings. Tears are a way of washing the upset feelings out of our bodies."

The class of five-year-olds was extremely interested and their parents and teachers were riveted, so I kept going, deliberately picking a story that had an older boy in it to reinforce the idea that even big boys cry. "Last year, I had a class with kids older than you and there was a boy we'll call Jim who was having a hard day and crying. Jim was embarrassed about crying and that made him cry harder. Has that ever happened to you?" Most hands, including Craig's, were raised. "Anyway," I continued, "After I explained about tears and how crying can help our bodies be safe by washing away upset feelings, one of Jim's friends asked, 'Does that mean that when Jim cries, he is doing Kidpower?' Of course, Jim's friend was right because Kidpower helps keep you safe and so can crying."

I smiled at my students and said, "If someone says, 'You are a baby because you cry' or calls you 'crybaby' for short, then even if you are crying, what do you say?"

Everyone made a fence with their hands and shouted, "That's not true!"

Because written words have extra power, we then wrote the word "Crybaby" on a big piece of paper and made a drawing of a crying face. I held up the sign and the kids immediately read or at least guessed the word. We passed the sign around and each person tore it part of the way. Finally, we all cheered while Craig crumpled the tattered pieces of the word Crybaby and threw them into the real recycling bin nearby.

Reframing the word "bitch." As kids get a little older, the words might change, but the feelings are the same. I have seen girls torment themselves endlessly over being called a bitch. "Am I a bitch?" they worry. Or they get furious and rage, "How dare she call me a bitch! I'm not going to let her get away with this!"

In researching definitions for the word "bitch," I felt that Wikipedia had the most comprehensive explanation of the different ways this word is used: "A 'bitch' is a female dog or other member of the canidae family. In colloquial use, the word bitch is often employed insultingly to describe a woman as malicious, spiteful, domineering, intrusive, unpleasant, or sexually promiscuous; it may also be used to refer to a male subordinate to another male (especially in prison to show domination over another). A bitch can also refer to somebody, usually a woman, who is mean or inconsiderate."[9]

In one workshop, I was teaching a group of girls who had gotten into trouble with the law to help them learn to control their power. The biggest reason they got into fights was over words and the word that they fought over the most was "bitch." In their group home, they used this saying for reframing the word: "A bitch is a female dog. Dogs bark. Bark grows on trees and trees are part of nature and nature is beautiful so *thank you* for calling me a bitch!"

Even though they understood this idea, these girls still needed to practice staying calm and walking away instead of getting upset in order not to get into fights. We made a plan with the staff in their group home that having to practice how to make safer choices would be a natural consequence of fighting. Instead of giving lectures about fighting, the staff would have the girls re-state their feelings in non-attacking ways and walk away from insults. Later, we heard that the violence in their group home reduced dramatically.

Sometimes girls find words to go with the letters to reframe the word "bitch," such as:

B–beautiful, I–intelligent, T–talented, C–confident, H–happy.

Sometimes, with full permission of teachers and parents, we have whole rooms full of preteen and teen girls all shouting joyously a negative word – BITCH! – and then a positive word, such as their favorite food – PIZZA! The novelty of being given permission to say a swear word – because when else has a teacher asked them to do something like this? – does not take away from the lesson that a set of sounds does not need to make them miserable.

Asshole Success Story. In the early days of Kidpower, Timothy and I were asked to conduct a private lesson with an eleven-year-old boy called Jeremy. Jeremy lived permanently in a group home because he had been abused so badly. He was targeted for relentless bullying by the other kids because he often lost control of his bowels. Jeremy walked into the room so bent over that he looked as if he was in a fetal position. His head was down and he refused to make any eye contact. "So," I asked him, "What hurtful things do kids say to you?"

"I can't tell you," Jeremy whispered. "It's a bad word."

"You have permission from your counselors to tell us the word, even if you aren't supposed to say it." I explained.

With his head completely hidden, Jeremy whispered, "Asshole."

"Well then," I announced loudly. "We are going to take the power out of the word asshole!"

Jeremy looked shocked and sat down. At first, he was too upset to practice with us, so Timothy modeled for him what to do.

"You dumb asshole!" I shouted at Timothy. "You should be ashamed! You are always messing up!"

Timothy took a big breath to get centered and then threw the hurting words away, saying, "I am proud of who I am."

Jeremy looked up at Timothy with big eyes and asked, "Do you really think I can do that?"

"It might be hard at first," Timothy explained. "But you have the right to

Reframing negative words helps increase self esteem

protect your feelings and to feel good about yourself. It gets easier when you practice."

Over and over, Jeremy practiced with Timothy – getting centered, throwing away the hurting words, and saying good things to himself to take inside. He then went on to practice all the self-protection and self-defense skills. He left the room smiling, looking directly at us, and with his head held high. A few weeks later we got a call from the director of the group home saying that Jeremy was doing great and that all of the bullying had stopped completely.

Feeling one way and acting another. The purpose of managing triggers is to be able to manage yourself. Our instructor John tells his students, "All of your feelings are normal, and you should be able to talk with an adult you trust whenever anything bothers you. To stay safe, though, you might feel one way and choose to act in a different way. No matter how you feel, your job is to stay in charge of your body and your words. For example, how many of you sometimes feel like yelling at someone else or hitting someone else and stop yourself?"

John raises his hand and looks at some students raising their hands. "You do this to avoid trouble, right?" As his students' heads nod, John says, "So let's practice feeling one way and acting differently."

With younger children, he uses a silly example, "Right now I want all of you to look at my nose and think about how funny it looks. Pretend that you feel like laughing at my silly nose. Don't say anything. Just think. Great. Right now you are feeling one way and acting another! You can use this technique when you are scared by acting as if you are not scared. You can use it when you are mad by acting as if you are not mad."

With older children, John gets right to the point, acting out what he is saying and coaching his students to copy him. "Everybody raise your hand as if you are so upset that you want to hit someone. Now take a big breath and lower your hands. Everybody flinch as if you are afraid. Now take a big breath and make your bodies strong. Excellent."

Suddenly, one of John's students says, "In real life, this is hard."

"Yes it is," John agrees. "That's why we practice."

> *To stay safe, you might feel one way and choose to act in a different way.*

Practicing Managing Emotional Triggers To Help Prevent Bullying

1 For older children and teens, go over triggers and, as appropriate, how to identify and protect themselves from verbal attack as described in Chapter Six on Boundaries and Advocacy.

2 If a young person is obsessing about things that others have said or done, ask for specifics. Discuss the words or the behavior and why it's so upsetting.

3 Explain that we cannot always control what other people say or do, but we can learn to control our reactions to them. Practice using techniques such as the Trash Can, the Screen, and That's Not True to take the power out of the actual upsetting words or offensive behavior that the child is upset by.

4 If the behavior involves inappropriate, threatening, or abusive touch, practice being about to do the behavior and being stopped before it actually happens with strong boundary-setting skills. In other words, don't actually touch the child in an inappropriate, threatening, or abusive way. If the child gets stuck, pause and coach the child so that she or he can be successful in protecting her/himself.

5 Have the child show you the bullying behavior while you use the boundary-setting techniques and then reverse roles. Remember to coach children so that they are successful each step of the way.

6 Ask children to tell you about times when they have felt upset but stayed in charge of their bodies and words. Demonstrate and practice different ways of doing this.

But What if We Both Like It?

Sometimes when I stop behavior that looks like bullying to me, both children will protest, "But this is fun! I like it." The reality is that sometimes in friendships people do use insults as a way to reinforce their special relationship to each other. In fact, in some cultures, ritualized insults are used as a way of releasing tension and building community. The Dutch and the Belgians both make fun of each other's potato-eating habits without anyone being devastated or going to war.

This kind of playing can truly be a form of endearment rather than bullying if:

• The insults and dominating play are equal in power and go both ways.
• This kind of joking is hurting neither party. In other words, everyone involved understands that the intention of the joking is positive rather than to be hurtful.
• The joking hurts no bystanders and the joking is not directed towards damaging the credibility of other people.

The problem is that, too often, kids will persuade themselves that putdowns or being shoved around is okay with them because they want to be accepted and included. They don't want to lose the relationship and they do want to seem cool. Rude dominating behavior might actually feel okay in the moment because it is familiar and is better than the alternative, which is to be left out. One-sided insults and dominating behavior are actually a way of reinforcing a power imbalance. If one person is doing the insulting and the other is going along with it in order to be accepted, this can be damaging over the long run.

I tell children who want to tease in this way, "This behavior is distracting right now, even if it is okay with both of you." It's important for children to learn that behavior in public settings is often different from acceptable behavior in private settings. If this is an engrained way of interacting, I ask young people to think about it. "Is one person dishing it out and the other person taking it? Does joking in this way cause you to think less of someone else?"

Finally, we always remind adults to remember that, no matter how kids feel

Too often, kids will persuade themselves that bullying behavior is okay because they want to be accepted or included.

Exploring the balance between having fun and being safe

about a game, one of the Kidpower boundary rules is that behaviors and activities need to be allowed by the adults in charge. If a behavior is not acceptable to the adult in charge, the adult can say that the behavior is not allowed, and the kids should be expected to stop for this reason alone.

Target Denial to Prevent Bullying

Knowing when and how to leave a difficult or dangerous situation is one of the most powerful self-protection tools we have. Unfortunately, kids hear a lot of negative labels about someone who chooses to leave a confrontation. They don't want to be seen as weak, wimpy, being a quitter, giving up, or not being tough enough to take it. Sadly, as children get older, the belief that they need to have the last word or fight back to be powerful can lead to their getting injured or killed. Not only can target denial help protect kids from bullying, but it can prepare young people to disengage from potential violence.

We tell our students, "There is a secret martial arts technique handed down from martial artist to martial artist through the ages. It is the best technique of all time. It's called, 'Target Denial', which means denying yourself as a target. You could also call it, 'don't be there!'" Our students practice how to Stay Aware, Calm, and Confident so that they will notice a problem and not be as likely to attract a potential bully. They learn to Move Away from potential trouble and how to use their Walk Away Power to be safe.

Here are some examples of how this can work.

Noticing Potential Trouble. Instructors Liam and Jennifer show students how using their awareness can help them notice when someone's behavior is changing from safe to unsafe. They pretend to be two children who are standing next to each other in line, shoulder to shoulder, watching a game and waiting to play.

Liam asks, "Can we use our awareness and notice each other without staring right at each other?"

"Yes!" the students realize. Jennifer gradually makes a few changes in her posture and facial expression at this point. She glares, clenches her jaw, and furrows her brow. She crosses her arms and makes all the muscles in her upper body tight. She moves her feet a step apart and takes a more aggressive stance.

Liam asks the students, "What can you notice with your awareness that makes you think, 'Hmmm, trouble might be on the way over where Jennifer is standing.....'"

Even Kindergarteners are able to identify these changes easily and confidently. "I notice her eyes," one might say. "The way her arms are pulled in and tight," another will notice. "The way she's standing," says another.

Often, a child will say, "She looks angry." Liam will agree and then add more information: "Yes, it does look like she might be angry. But, is it also possible she has a stomach ache and is looking into the sun?" The students murmur agreement that this could be true.

"We can use our awareness to notice changes in people's behavior. But, that doesn't mean we know for sure what someone is feeling, thinking, or planning to do."

On an everyday basis, adults can help young people build this skill of noticing the difference between observations – "she is crossing her arms and glaring" – and conclusions – "she is angry." Their conclusions might be correct, but the ability to distinguish between the two helps people make decisions more effectively.

Liam says, "Right now, I'm not going to worry about what Jennifer is actually feeling. I can notice the changes in Jennifer's body language and in her expression. I can also notice that these changes make me feel less safe – maybe I've seen Jennifer start to push people in the past soon after she started acting like this. What's my safest choice right now, to stay next to her, or to get some space?.....Yes, I can leave! I can go to another game or another group of kids, or I can go do something on my own."

Don't Be There. In workshops, we tell our students, "A bully wants to cause trouble. Target denial means getting away from trouble both physically with your body and emotionally with your feelings. You don't want a bully to scare you into being a victim or push you into starting a fight. Walking away from a bully is safer than staying put and getting cornered. Walking away is also safer than escalating a situation by shoving someone out of your way or calling names."

We then show how using target denial looks, with two instructors pretending to be kids at school. Marylaine pretends to be a bully. She strides over to Jean and says, "I'm going to get you." The first time, Jean cowers against the wall and lets Marylaine trap her.

As Marylaine pushes her against the wall, Jean goes back into instructor mode and asks the students, "If Marylaine wants trouble and I don't, which one of us is getting what she wants?"

"Marylaine is," the students say.

The second time, as Marylaine swaggers over to Jean in a threatening way, Jean reacts by shoving her out of the way and yelling, "LEAVE ME ALONE!" Marylaine escalates by raising her fist as if she is about to fight.

Jean then goes back into instructor mode and asks, "If I don't want trouble and Marylaine does, and my reaction started a fight, who got what she wanted here, Marylaine or me?"

"She did," the students say.

The third time Marylaine starts to approach Jean, Jean doesn't wait. She immediately leaves the wall moving away with awareness, calm, and

Practicing leaving with confidence

confidence. She cheerfully waves and says, "Have a nice day!"

"Get back here, you wimp!" Marylaine shouts.

"No, thanks," Jean says, as she continues to leave with awareness.

When someone is trying to pick a fight, acting genuinely nice can defuse the conflict.

When someone is trying to pick a fight, acting genuinely nice can defuse the conflict. The key is to stay calm and centered rather than passive or aggressive. Using a mocking tone of voice or making a sarcastic gesture will be provocative. The best approach is to give a bully nothing to react to – neither fear nor anger.

What Most Mothers Prefer. This idea that it can be powerful to leave instead of weak is especially important for teenagers, who sometimes feel that their honor is at stake if they don't have the last word. One of our Kidpower graduates was walking down the street with his friend. Some older boys drove by in a car shouting insults about their mothers. The Kidpower graduate immediately ran into a store to get help. Instead of going with him, the other boy started shouting threats to the boys in the car, who pulled over and beat him up so badly that he ended up in the hospital.

What happened in the above story was that the boy who got beaten up was triggered by the insult about his mother. We ask our students, "What do you think the mother of the boy who was beaten up would have preferred – that her son defend her honor or get to safety?"

I have yet to meet a mother who would rather have her honor defended than risk the safety of her child.

If students say that they are not sure, we encourage them to ask their own mothers. I have yet to meet a mother who would rather have her honor defended than risk the safety of her child.

Walking Past Trouble. Instructor Mike explains to his students, "Imagine that I am a kid at school who is always insulting others and looking for trouble." Mike slouches in the middle of the room with his arms crossed, nodding his head slowly, and glaring. He coaches each student to walk across the floor, veering to get out of his way.

As the student goes by, Mike calls out insults like, "Scared, aren't you?" Or, "Hey stupid get over here!" Or, "I want to talk with you wimp!" Or, "Look at the dumb freak!" Or, with older kids and teens, "Bleep, you bleeping bleep, you!"

If students need it, Mike interrupts the role-play to coach them to be successful, "Keep walking. Walk tall. Use your imaginary Trash Can to throw away what this person is saying. Look back. Go to Safety."

When students get to the other side of the room, they each say out loud the compliment they are giving themselves to take the place of the insults.

The Fallacy of "Giving As Good As You Get". Young people often think that they have to push or threaten back to defend their honor and to protect themselves. This is a dangerous belief, especially for young men in our culture, who are at the highest risk of getting stabbed or shot in their teens and early twenties during confrontations that often started off with threats and pushes and then escalate into dangerous confrontations.

Remember that bullying situations are often chronic and usually involve people who students have to see again. The truth is that "giving as good as you get" by fighting back might stop a confrontation in the moment. The problem is that this response also increases the risk of escalated retaliation on another day. Using Target Denial will stop most situations as effectively if not more so than having an aggressive response, and with less risk of retaliation. This can also be true of an assertive response that sets a boundary but does not directly attack the honor of the other person.

Practicing Using Target Denial to Prevent Bullying

1   Discuss language or behavior that might be upsetting. Ask the young person to stand in a corner of the room. If you are in a setting where the specific word is not okay for you to practice with, agree that the word "Bleep!" means the same thing.

2   Pretend to be a bully. Shout the agreed-upon insults or threats at your student while walking towards him (or her). You can glare and point your finger at him without touching him.

3   Coach your student to walk firmly away from you as soon as you start to approach, throw the words away, look back towards you with a friendly smile, wave a hand, and say something like, "Bye! Have a nice day! See you later!" – and keep on walking. Do the same practice standing in the middle of the room with your student is veering to get around you while staying out of reach.

4   As your student is moving away, wave your fist and shout, "Come back here, you wimp!"

5   Coach your student to look back at you, wave again, and say cheerfully, "No thanks!" If necessary, remind him to be sincere, not silly or sarcastic.

6   Ask your student how he or she was getting rid of the hurting words and what compliments he or she was using inside to replace the insulting language.

Conflict Resolution and Interventions to Solve Problems
At any age, people who understand and can use conflict resolution techniques will be more able to prevent interpersonal disagreements and misunderstandings from growing into bullying problems. Conflict resolution programs for youth and adults have many basic concepts and skills in common. Effective programs will use role plays to rehearse skills and will prepare participants to:

• Understand that conflict is a normal part of life and that knowing how to resolve conflict is a powerful life skill. Common personal conflicts are about our space, what we say to each other, our property, how we do activities together, and our time. Resolving conflicts can be an opportunity to learn about each other and to develop problem-solving skills.

Conflict resolution skills can help friends stay friends

- Use assertive rather than passive or aggressive behavior in working out the conflict.

- Agree to ground rules for the conflict resolution process – no putdowns, no name-calling, making a commitment to solving the problem, and telling the truth.

- Communicate issues through specific respectful "I" messages as shown in Chapter Six. For example, "I understand (acknowledge the other person's perspective). And, I feel (name specific feeling), when you (name specific behavior). Would you please?" (State exactly what you want the other person to do or not do.)

- Listen respectfully when someone speaks to you. Make sure you understand and that the other person knows that you understand through using active listening, empathic listening, apologies when appropriate, and asking helpful questions. Respond with your own "I" message.

- Identify lots of choices that help resolve the conflict in ways that follow the school, family, or youth group rules. Try to find solutions that give each person at least part of what he/she wants.

- Acknowledge pros and cons of each choice and come to a mutual decision that both parties will agree to uphold.

- Thank each other for listening and reaching an agreement.

A mediator is a neutral, impartial third party whose role is to guide people through a conflict resolution process. The goal is to help opposing parties come up with their own solutions to resolving the conflict. A mediator can be a teacher, a parent, another adult, or a child. A mediator's job typically involves the following process:

- Lay the groundwork by meeting with the opposing parties separately to allow them to ventilate, to set objectives, and to prepare them for the mediation. A mediator needs to use active listening and to ask neutral, supportive questions such as: "What do you want to see happen?" "What is the worst that could happen?" "What is the best that could happen?"

- Facilitate positive communication during the mediation session by welcoming the participants, being clear about the ground rules, giving each person a chance to tell his or her story, using active listening and supportive questions to make sure that each person feels that her or his perspective is understood, brainstorming different options, discussing the pros and cons of each possibility, looking for win-win solutions where each side gets at least some benefit, coming to an agreement, making a plan for what to do in case the agreement doesn't work, putting the agreement into writing, and thanking the participants for their commitment to creating a more peaceful world.

- Follow up with each party to see how things are going.

A wealth of resources and tools are available in this field for teaching mediation and conflict resolution skills both to adults and to children. Some schools train children to be mediators. My niece started her training as a "Negotiation Buddy" in the second grade. At age seven, she explained that, "When a kid gets mad at another kid, they put their names on the blackboard. It gets very busy because you get a lot of appointments during recess. You take the kid who was mad and the other kid to a quiet place so nobody will bother us. You help the mad kid fill out a card the teacher gave us to have an 'I' message to say what the mad kid feels and wants. The mad kid gives the card to the other kid who says, 'Yes, I will do what you want.' The mad kid isn't mad anymore and says, 'Thank you for listening.'"

"What happens when that doesn't work?" I wondered.

With utter faith that adults would take care of things, my seven-year-old niece said confidently, "Then we get the teacher!"

Sadly, within a few years, my niece was disillusioned about the effectiveness of conflict resolution training. Too often in her life, kids had not wanted to work things out and adults had not known what to do. Talking it out and making agreements only work if there are clear boundaries defining acceptable behavior and realistic consequences for breaking the agreements made. For children who are bullying to get attention, "talking it out" can become a reward rather than a deterrent.

I have run into many children who have the same feeling – that conflict resolution is a good idea but it doesn't really work. "Sure, some kids who bully talk it out, but when they don't do what they promised, nothing happens," children will explain to me. "Sometimes the teacher is standing right there, but just ignores it. Or lectures them and then walks away. This kind of kid waits until the teacher isn't looking and then does it again."

This perception is unfortunate because conflict resolution skills can often make a great difference in solving problems between people. Children need to see these as tools that work in some situations but not in others. We say that conflict resolution and boundary-setting skills are two sides of the same coin.

As with other dangerous behaviors, adults need to know how and when to intervene when young people are in conflict. Parents need to be clear that bullying is against their family rules. Teachers and school officials need to be clear that bullying is against the school rules. Kids need to see that adults mean what they say by having them stop bullying behavior with the same commitment that they would make to stop someone from throwing all the dishes on the floor and breaking them. As adults, we need to walk our talk by not allowing people to bully us and by exercising the self-control necessary not to bully others.

When young people are extremely upset, they might not be able to "talk it out" at first. They might need time and adult help to calm down and get perspective before they can participate in a conflict resolution process. Rather than ignoring a problem until it explodes, it works better when

No matter how much time, money, and effort you put into your anti-bullying program, nothing is going to work if kids see adults ignoring bullying when it happens in front of them!

Talking it out and making agreements only work if there are clear boundaries defining acceptable behavior and realistic consequences for breaking the agreements made.

adults decide to step in before young people lose control of their tempers.

Stepping in might mean:

- *Creating a temporary distraction by bringing positive energy to a negative situation.* You can buy yourself a little time by saying something very cheerfully like, "Hi! What did you think of the game last night?" Once people are calmer, you can then find out what was going on.

- *Setting a boundary.* "I understand that you are upset. You have the right to your feelings, and we can work on the problem. Please express yourself in a way that is respectful to others."

- *Redirecting young people by getting them to do something with you instead of continuing to bother each other.* "I'd really appreciate having your help in setting up the room."

- *Speaking separately with the aggressor.* Interventions can be done in a compassionate way rather than a punitive one. For example, "Oh my! You sound upset. I really want to understand what's going on. Let's go over here where it's quiet so we can talk about what happened."

Teaching Young People How to Use Conflict Resolution Skills To Address Bullying

1 Learn conflict resolution, negotiation, and mediation skills for yourself. For example, School Mediation Associates[10] (http://www.schoolmediation.com/) offers books, articles, and a free e-newsletter.

2 Research systems of conflict resolution training for all parties to learn. Be sure that any program you select includes role-playing to develop skills and backup plans in case the conflict resolution process isn't working.

3 Teach young people about the conflict resolution process:
- State concerns assertively and respectfully;
- Listen to the other person's perspective and be able to re-state it accurately and compassionately;
- Brainstorm different ways of solving the problem;
- Look at pros and cons of different choices;
- Find win-win solutions where everyone gets at least part of what was wanted;
- Put agreements into writing;
- Appreciate oneself and others for being committed to conflict resolution; and
- Ask for help when agreements don't work.

4 Intervene before young people lose their tempers. Help them calm down before trying to work on problem-solving and conflict resolution solutions.

Self- Protection Skills to Avoid Being Pushed, Tripped, Bumped, Hit, Kicked, or Shoved

Sometimes kids get into fights because they are so afraid that someone might hurt them that they hit or kick as soon as they feel threatened or bothered. Starting a fight can cause them to be the ones to get into trouble, even if they are being constantly harassed by someone bullying them.

Other kids worry a lot about being intimidated and keep hoping that it won't happen again. As the following examples show, young people can benefit greatly from practicing skills to avoid and stop this kind of trouble.

Choosing not to fight. When adults are not able to help, young people need to find the safest way to protect themselves. As thirteen-year-old Richard explained to me about an incident that happened after he had taken one of our workshops, "I knew better. I saw a group of guys from my school in a narrow street near downtown. I knew they were mad at me because I had told on one of them for cheating, but I just didn't feel like going out of my way. When these guys started pushing and hitting me, I knew that if I fought back, there would be more trouble the next day. Instead, I protected myself by shielding my face and body. I practiced false surrender by apologizing even though I didn't do anything wrong. Next time, I will use my awareness and go the other way instead of challenging people who are upset with me by walking right through them."

Richard understood that, although this attack was not his fault, using his awareness could have protected him from these boys who were looking for trouble. Even under the stressful circumstances of being hit and shoved, Richard felt good that, after his initial mistake, he was able to stay centered in order to decide on the safest way to prevent future conflict. He discussed what happened with his parents. They decided that taking further action about these boys in this particular neighborhood was not in his best interest. Fortunately, Richard was able to avoid these boys and soon afterwards changed schools.

This was not a perfect solution from my perspective. I would far rather have had Richard and his parents feel able to tell the police and his school what happened. Realistically, however, their solution might well have been the safest way for Richard to handle the problem.

Getting out of the way. When students are hurrying through the hall or busy playing in a crowded school, there are plenty of opportunities for them to bother each other. After she started going to a new school, eleven-year-old Angela was coming home with bruises caused by a few girls who kept bumping into her "accidentally" and knocking her down.

Angela's father said, "I asked Angela if she knew who these girls were. She did but she did not want me to do anything about it. So, I asked her to show me what the girls looked like before they started to bump into her. When she did, I was able to step out of the way easily. Next, we practiced with my taking on the role of the girls. We made it a game for me to start towards Angela and for her to move calmly out of the way. The problem at school stopped. Once she gave herself permission to pay attention and to act on what she was noticing, Angela had no problem avoiding being bumped without needing to confront anybody."

Regaining Your Balance. Young people can learn how to keep their feet under them and leave rather than shoving back or getting into a fight. Instructors Ron and Janice show their class how leaving in an assertive way rather than becoming aggressive or passive works in this situation. Janice says, "Imagine that we are two people about your age who know each other. Ron is in a bad mood." She and Ron stand close together facing each other. Suddenly, Ron pushes Janice and she staggers backwards, pretending to lose her balance.

Janice moves back to face Ron and he pushes her again. This time, Janice reacts aggressively by making her shoulder rigid, so it seems as if she is shoving back. Janice and Ron then glower and point at each other, snapping, "Hey, cut it out!"

"Look at all the choices I have instead of losing my balance or shoving back," Janice tells her class.

This time when Ron pushes her, Janice lets the force of the shove turn her body away without being rigid or pushing back. She then walks away with awareness. When Ron pushes her again, Janice steps to one side to get out of the way and leaves with awareness. One last time, Janice gets shoved. She goes backwards with the force of the shove in a balanced way by moving her feet so that they stay under her. Once she is out of the way, Janice again leaves with awareness. When they give their students the chance to practice, Ron and Janice push gently so that the students will be successful.

Assessing whether you are trapped or free to leave. Too often, people get stuck in unsafe situations because they don't realize that they are able to leave. Janice shows students the difference between being trapped and being free to leave. She creates an imaginary doorway, using two chairs. Janice then says, "Imagine that this is the doorway to a bathroom. Outside the bathroom is Safety, in the school or the house where other people are. Inside, it is less safe. The doorway is the only way to leave."
Ron stands in the doorway of the "bathroom" waving his fist and making threatening noises. Janice stands outside and shows that she is free to leave. In fact, she has no reason to stay near this guy when he is acting so obnoxiously. She walks away calmly, looking back.

Next, Janice moves inside the bathroom so that Ron is blocking the doorway. Just leaving is not a choice for Janice at this point, because Ron is trapping her. Janice shows how she might still decide to duck under his arm or push past him and leave. However, since Ron is showing a clearly aggressive intent, getting closer to him might make things more dangerous for her.

Ron and Janice give each student the opportunity to practice, so they can experience the difference between being trapped and being free to leave.

Getting Into Ready Position to Show That You are Neither a Victim Nor An Aggressor. Without practice, most people when confronted by someone who is threatening them often act either weak or aggressive, which is likely to make the problem worse. We are safest if we get ready to deal with the problem. The purpose of the Ready Position we teach in Kidpower is to communicate to the other person that we are not a victim, nor a threat, nor a challenge - we are simply ready.

To get into Ready Position, stand with your feet a little apart as if you've just stopped walking, so that you are in balance. Put your two hands in front of you, palms facing out, hands open, elbows bent, as if you were touching a wall several inches away from your body. This is your Ready Position. You are ready to leave, ready to set a boundary, and ready to yell for help. If you need to do this to protect yourself, you are also ready to fight to stop someone from harming you.

Setting Boundaries and Yelling for Help. After teaching her students the Ready Position, Janice then goes back to the demonstration of being trapped inside the bathroom. She explains, "Since awareness and target denial have not worked, I am going to let this person know that I am not an easy victim and let the world know that I have a problem."

As Ron pretends to mock and threaten her from the doorway, Janice steps back out of his reach. She gets into Ready Position and shouts, "Stop! Get out of my way! I need help! Ron is trapping me in the bathroom!" Not wanting to get into trouble, Ron leaves, muttering threats.

Janice and Ron have all the students get into Ready Position and practice setting strong boundaries such as, "*Stop! Don't push me! Go away! Don't follow me!* I need help!"

In the context of a bullying problem, students review the importance of using a clear, strong, assertive tone of voice; choosing words carefully; and keeping their bodies aware, calm, and confident. They all make the same statements, leaning back and sounding whiny or weak. They repeat the exercise, leaning forward and getting into the other person's face, acting as if they want to fight. Finally, they stand or sit upright, repeating the statements with a firm face, a calm definite tone, and a loud voice.

In a school situation, where the bothering is constant, setting boundaries is often effective even if you are not trapped physically. Shirley D. Kassebaum, a counselor at Watson Junior High School, wrote a letter that illustrates this fact. "One of the boys who participated in your workshop used to see me on the average of two or three times a week to complain about someone picking on him. Not long ago, I observed him in the lunch line. The kid in front of him pushed him. He put up his hands up into Ready Position and said, in a loud voice, 'Stop! I don't like to be pushed!'"

The Cower Power Game. In order to build belief in the power of sounding and looking like you mean it, we sometimes demonstrate and then play what we call the "Cower Power Game" in our workshops. We have students stand in two lines facing a partner. Instructor Timothy says, "The first time, those of you in the line on this side are the Bullies and your partners are the Kids."

He directs the Bullies to shake their fingers at their partners and, without touching them, to move aggressively towards them shouting, 'BLAH! BLAH! BLAH!"

Timothy directs the Kids to cower away, with their heads down and their

Getting into Ready Position

Making a Stop Sign

backs turned to the Bullies, whimpering, "Please don't hurt me! Please don't hurt me!"

Timothy then calls the group back into their two lines. This time, when the Bullies advance, the Kids shake their fingers and yell, "BLAH! BLAH! BLAH!" back. Since no one is allowed to touch each other, each pair ends up stuck in shaking, glaring, and yelling.

Timothy asks, "Does this look familiar?" and everyone laughs.

Once again, Timothy has the groups re-form their lines. This time, he tells the Kids to step back into Ready Position, to make a Stop Sign by moving their hand out and back towards the face of their Bully partner without touching anyone, and to shout, "STOP!"

The Bullies move towards their partners aggressively, shouting. Following Timothy's directions, the Kids get into Ready Position, make their Stop Signs, and yell, "STOP!" Most of the "bullies" will act startled, even though they knew what was going to happen.

After the Bullies and the Kids have switched roles, so that everyone gets to try out all parts of the exercise, Timothy calls the group together for discussion. "When you were the Kid and acted like a victim, how did you feel inside?"

Regardless of their culture or age, most students say things like, "Weak." "Scared." "Helpless." "Stupid."

"And," Timothy continues, "When you were the Bully and your partner cowered away, how did you feel?"

"Strong," his students reply, "like I could keep going."

"What about when you and your partner were both shouting and shaking your fingers at each other? " Timothy asks, "How did that feel?"

"Like the other person started it," his students from both groups typically say, "and as if I couldn't figure out how we ended up there."

"How did it feel," Timothy continues, "to be the Kid and to get into Ready Position and to shout 'STOP!'?"

"Strong," his students say. "Like I was in charge." And, "Like I had the space to leave."

Finally, Timothy asks, "And when you were the Bully and your partner used the Stop Sign and shouted at you to stop. How did you feel?"

With a look of realization, most of his students say, "I felt surprised." "I felt like I was the one who was stupid." Or, "I felt stopped, even though I knew it was going to happen."

Practicing self-protection skills to avoid being bullied

1   Find out the specifics of exactly what is being said or done. Have the child or teen show you what the problem behavior of the other person looks like and sounds like.

2   Make a plan for using awareness, staying centered, leaving, and assertive boundary setting to solve the specific problem. Review the difference between being passive, aggressive, and assertive.

3   If pushing or tripping is the problem, let young people practice keeping their balance by stepping out of the way, moving their feet to get them back under their bodies, or letting the force of the push move them away. In each case, add leaving with awareness so that they get used to moving away from someone who is creating problems. When you practice, start with a very gentle shove so that young people can be successful.

4   Play the "Cower Power Game" described above in order to build belief. To ensure safety, remember that no one touches each other in this game. Keep enough space between the lines to allow the Stop Sign to go forward and back while still leaving a few feet of space between the extended hand and the other person's face.

Getting Adults to Help

Our kids are the most important part of our lives. However, as parents, youth group leaders, and educators, we sometimes get so overwhelmed with the sheer magnitude of conflicting demands that we don't notice a problem or have unrealistic expectations of what a young person can do without our help. The result is that older kids and teens often become discouraged and frustrated about the ability of their adults to help them solve problems with other kids.

A 2011 study published by the National School Board Administration[11] reports that only 33.1% of the middle and high school students surveyed agreed or strongly agreed that teachers can stop bullying. This means that

As they get older, young people often become discouraged and frustrated about the ability of their adults to help them solve problems with other kids.

two-thirds of these students were not confident that they could get help from their teachers.

In Kidpower, we tell our students, "Nothing works all the time. Adults might be too distracted and busy to understand that you need their help, but most adults care about their kids a lot and want them to be safe and happy. If you are having a problem, *how* you talk with an adult can make a big difference in how well that adult listens to you." We then practice in how to be effective and persistent in getting adult help even when someone doesn't listen at first.

Kidpower instructor Ashleigh coaches her students to repeat after her, "Everybody say in a whiny voice, 'Teeeeacherrrrr! They're bothering meeeeee.'" She asks her students, "Do you think teachers like to listen to you when you talk like that? Do you like listening to yourselves?"

"No," everyone agrees.

Ashleigh then shows students how to make a report, asking ten-year-old Ruby, who has done this before, to help her. Ashleigh sets the stage by saying, "Imagine that I am a Distracted Teacher talking to another teacher. Another student keeps following Ruby around and bothering her on the school yard."

Distracted Teacher: "Talk. Talk. Talk."

Because she needs help, Ruby interrupts by saying very politely: "Excuse me. I have a problem."

Distracted Teacher: Acts as if she doesn't hear and continues to be busy.

Ruby persists by saying in a louder voice: "Excuse me! I need help!"

Distracted Teacher demands impatiently: "What now?"

Ruby stays calm and says respectfully and firmly: "I have a safety problem, and I need your help. I want to make a report."

Distracted Teacher looks surprised and asks: "A report? About what?"

Ruby gives a full report to describe her problem by saying: "Lisa keeps calling me names. I didn't answer, but she kept interrupting my conversation with my friends. I moved away but she followed me. I asked her to stop, but she didn't. Please help me."

Now that she understands the problem, the Distracted Teacher becomes sympathetic and says: "It sounds like you tried really hard to solve this yourself. I am glad you told me, and I am sorry that I was impatient. With so many people out sick, this has been a hard day. I will help you talk with Lisa."

Ashleigh then has students practice individually or as a group, picking different problems and adult roles. She reminds them that their job is to stay calm and clear when they give their report, tell the whole story, use a regular voice, and have confident body language. She coaches them to not give up even when the adult is very annoyed, impatient, or rude by saying, "That's not so bad. Just ignore it." Or, "What's the big deal? Just stay away from them."

Ashleigh coaches students to tell the whole story, including what they had tried, and to persist in explaining the problem by saying things like, "I don't feel safe here anymore." Or, "This makes me not want to go to school." She finishes the practice by saying, "Thank you for telling me. We will figure out how to help you feel safe at school."

Both kids and adults need to know what to do when someone who is supposed to help acts impatient or rude. Important life-long skills include how to:

- use polite, firm words, assertive body language, and a calm tone of voice even under pressure;
- not give up even if you've tried before and even if you feel discouraged or embarrassed.

Ultimately, adults are responsible for creating a safe environment for the young people in our care. We often also need to use persistence and assertiveness skills in speaking up when something is wrong and not giving up even though people might minimize, ignore, or get upset with their concerns.

Both kids and adults need to know what to do when someone who is supposed to help acts impatient or rude.

Teaching Young People How to Get Adults to Help

1   Ask older children for whom this might be an issue to tell you about times when they asked adults for help and it didn't work out well. If they don't have an example at first, you might start with stories about what happened to you when you were a kid or about someone else. Maybe the adult got mad at them. Maybe the adult ignored them or looked away, or perhaps the adult overreacted and made things worse. Maybe telling the adult ended up giving them more problems with other kids, or maybe the adult was having a bad day.

2   Listen sympathetically to what kids tell you, even if you think their perceptions are wrong or unfair. Reflect back to them what they have said in a way that honors their perspective, so that they feel heard. Sometimes young people have lost trust in adult help. To help them to gain the confidence to try again, they need to be able to tell their stories and to have their feelings acknowledged.

3   Show young people how to use their assertiveness skills to be persistent, powerful, and respectful in making a report to an impatient, distracted adult.

4   Give kids the chance to take on the role of the harassed, impatient adult, while you pretend to be a young person making a report as in the examples above. Then switch roles.

5   Remind kids that, if the adult still does not listen, it is not their fault, but to keep asking until someone does something to fix the problem. Tell them that you always want to know whenever they have a problem with anyone, anywhere, anytime.

Bully Self-Defense Techniques

As was described in Chapter Seven on Self-Defense, Kidpower teaches that fighting should be a last resort – when you are about to get hurt and you cannot leave or get help. Often, bullying situations are not so clear-cut. In an attack or abduction, you are experiencing a very dangerous emergency, in which you might be severely injured or even killed. In such circumstances, techniques such as eye-strikes that are likely to cause injury can be justified.

A bullying attack is often not an immediate emergency. Usually, it is possible to leave and get help. Although this is true, young people often ask the following "What if?" questions:

• "What if the kid follows you?"
• "What if the kid keeps on shoving you?"
• "What if the kid does it only when the teacher is not looking?"
• "What if you cannot get away without getting hurt first?"
• "What if kids push you down and grab your lunch money?"

We explain that we believe that avoidance and getting help is the best policy whenever possible. If young people have permission from their adults, we acknowledge that there are times when the only way to stop a problem might be to fight back. For this reason, we teach "bully self-defense" techniques that are less likely to cause injury than the "emergency-only self-defense" techniques.

Every day, at school or in other youth activities, young people get knocked down, punched, kicked, their hair pulled, their bottoms slapped, their heads smacked, their shoulders tapped hard, their clothes pulled off, and their breasts grabbed in a way that hurts and humiliates them. Schools vary greatly in their ability to handle this kind of problem. Sometimes schools have a no fighting policy that leads to both students getting into trouble if someone fights back, no matter what the circumstances.

Families have very different boundaries about fighting back when you might get hurt, but not seriously injured. This is why we tell kids, "Ask your adults when it is okay to hurt someone to stop that person from hurting, shoving, or grabbing you."

One mother put her thirteen-year-old daughter Jasmine into a workshop because a boy at school was constantly grabbing Jasmine's breasts. After the workshop, Jasmine's mother wrote a letter to the school principal that said, "You have failed to protect my daughter so I have taken her to a program to teach her to protect herself. If she does and you try to give her consequences, I will back her up, all the way to the school board if I have to." Later Jasmine's mother told us that this boy had grabbed her daughter's breast and Jasmine had knocked the wind out of him with a heel palm strike to the mid-section, walked away immediately, and given her teacher a report about what had happened. The school did not punish Jasmine and, after that, the boy left her completely alone.

Techniques that don't involve hurting the other person reduce likelihood of getting into trouble. Especially if you leave respectfully and assertively, using these techniques also make it less likely that the other person will want to

A bullying attack is often not an immediate emergency. Usually, it is possible to leave and get help.

get even. As described in Chapter Seven on self-defense, young people can often escape physically from attacks without counter-attacking by:

- Pulling or twisting away from a grab;
- Dodging or blocking a punch; and
- Lifting their arms and turning their bodies to get out of a choke hold.

The following techniques are designed to give a short amount of pain with a lower risk of injuring someone, so that there is enough time to get away. There are literally hundreds of other physical techniques that could also work, but these are very easy to learn.

Bully "Soccer" Kick to the Shin. Start from Ready Position, with your body upright, both arms in front of you and close to your body, elbows bent, palms open and facing the attacker, and legs a step apart with your strong foot back. Rather than kicking up into someone's groin with your shin, your "weapon" is the inner side of your foot, like in soccer and the target is the shin of the other person. If you have ever bumped your shin on the edge of a coffee table, you will know that this hurts. Kick forward to the shin with a loud "NO!"

"Bully" Heel Palm to the Solar Plexus. Again, start from Ready Position. This is like the Heel Palm to the head described in the self-defense chapter except that now your target is towards the solar plexus or whatever you can hit on the middle of someone's body. If you have ever had the wind knocked out of you, you will know that this can be very effective. Your weapon is the heel or hard spot at the bottom of your palm. Again, we do not recommend using your fists because there is a greater risk of injuring yourself. Keep your arm a little bent to avoid hyper-extending your arm. From Ready Position, hit forward with a loud "NO!" You can add power by taking a small step forward with your front foot and then sliding your back foot forward as you do the technique.

Low Elbow to the Solar Plexus. This is useful if you are being grabbed from behind. Reach forward with your arm, turn your body to make room, and then jab backwards into the attacker's mid-section, hitting her or him with your elbow.

Bully Pinch. Use your fingers to grab a small amount of flesh from the other person's upper arm or inner thigh. Pinch hard and twist. This can be an effective way to make someone who is trapping you in a headlock and rubbing your head to let go. You can pinch and twist any soft fleshy area. (Carefully, you can try this out on your own body if you want to test whether it works.)

After our students have learned these techniques, we give them the chance to practice in a more realistic context. Our instructor pretends to be the Bully by moving close and saying threatening things like, "Do what I say or you'll be sorry!" Or, "Hey punk, I'm going to get you!" Or waving a fist and muttering, "You're getting some of this!"

Each student practices, imagining a situation where leaving does not make

Setting boundaries is safer than fighting

sense, such as being trapped in a corner or room. The steps are:

- Warn the "Bully" by standing in Ready Position, making a Stop Sign, and yelling, "Leave me alone! I mean it!"
- Deliver the Bully Kick to the shin or the Bully Heel Palm with a loud "NO!"
- Leave quickly, going to the adult in charge and make a report.

If we have students practice using the pinch to get out of a headlock, we tell them, "Please just pinch our pants, not us!"

We have had many success stories about children using each of these techniques to put a stop to bullying. As one father told us, "Every day at the swimming pool, my thirteen-year-old daughter was getting dunked under water by an older boy, supposedly in play. When he wouldn't listen to her, she pinched him under the arm. He never dunked her again."

Another father said, "My six-year-old daughter has curly red hair. Other kids can't resist sticking their fingers in it and pulling. She used to cry but, after learning to protect herself, she stopped one very persistent little boy with a bully heel palm. After that, all the kids kept their hands to themselves."

One girl, aged nine, who lives in the inner city, said, "A bully on the playground grabbed my hair and pulled me backwards. I stopped him by elbowing him once in the stomach. The yard duty teacher complimented me on how I took care of myself without being a bully too. She said she wished she knew how to do that."

Learning how to manage their triggers and control their power can help young people have an appropriate response to violence instead of overreacting.

Learning how to manage their triggers and control their power can help young people have an appropriate response to violence instead of overreacting. One mother put her thirteen-year-old son, Todd, into a Kidpower workshop because he kept getting into fights at school. "The principal says that Todd won't be able to go to the graduation if he gets into one more fight," she explained to me. "Todd says that he goes crazy because a group of other boys keeps bullying him and he gets scared. So, I am counting on Kidpower to help my son be in his middle school graduation."

I told her that we would try our best, but I couldn't make any promises. A few weeks after the workshop, Todd's mother called to say, "Thank you for helping my son graduate with his class. One of those boys grabbed Todd from behind and started hitting him. He did one low elbow to the midsection of the bully to make the boy let him go and then went to the teacher and made a report. After that, the boys have left him completely alone."

My own daughter, Chantal, at age twelve, once took away my breath by saying casually at dinner one evening, "By the way, Mom, I used my Kidpower today." She and her friends had been at the park that afternoon. A group of older boys from their school came by and started to bother them. These boys took their ball. The little brother of one of Chantal's friends said, "Give me back my ball!" Instead, a bigger boy started to twist the wrist of this little boy to make him kneel on the ground.

Seeing anyone's little brother hurt in front of her was unacceptable to

Chantal. She got into Ready Position and yelled, "Leave him alone!" When the older boy came towards her, Chantal yelled, "Leave him alone!" He kept coming and she kicked him in the shin. Chantal told me that she had thought, "If two of them come at me, that's an emergency and I am going to kick somebody in the groin."

Instead, the boy she kicked hopped away, yelling "Ow!" The other boys said, "What a powerhouse!" They tossed back the ball and went to the other side of the park.

At that time, Chantal was a small, shy girl and her friends were astounded. "We own the park!" they said. But Chantal thought about the five boys regrouping and made her friends leave the park. She told me later that for the rest of the school year, the boy she had kicked made a big circle around her whenever they passed each other in the halls.

In each of the above situations, one strong move was enough to stop a serious bullying problem. Much more often, though, adults tell us that the physical confidence gained from knowing self-defense has been enough for their children to deal with an aggressive bullying problem without actually having to fight. One mother said, "A couple of years ago, my son was injured so badly by bullies that he had to go to the hospital. After that, his victim behavior made him a continual target. Since taking a Kidpower class, he has used what he learned to stop eleven incidents with bullies without once having to resort to violence."

> *Often adults tell us that the physical confidence gained from knowing self-defense has been enough for their kids to deal with aggressive bullying without actually having to fight.*

Preparing Young People to Use Bully Self-Defense Tactics Appropriately

1   Review all the different ways in which you can get out of a bullying situation without fighting.

2   Explain when to use the Emergency-Only Self-Defense Tactics with targets such as the groin, head, or eyes - and when to use the Bully Self-Defense Tactics. Explain why some targets are less likely to cause injury than others.

3   Be specific with your kids about when you believe that they have the right to hurt someone who is trying to bully them physically.

4   Acknowledge possible consequences at school and say what you will do if this happens. For example, Timothy Dunphy told his daughter that, if she had to hit someone to protect herself from bullying and then got into trouble for it, he would stay home with her and talk to the school officials.

5   Provide opportunities to learn and practice the techniques described above. See Chapter Seven section on *How to Choose a Good Self-Defense Class.*

Coping With Shunning, Exclusion, and Gossip

Being left out in a sustained and public way is a major form of bullying. As described above, this kind of exclusion is different than avoiding someone who constantly puts others down, complains, interrupts what you're doing, or acts aggressively. Like adults, young people should have the right

Relational bullying can hurt a lot

to choose to have closer friendships with some kids than with others. However, there is a difference between inviting friends to a birthday party privately and flaunting who is invited and who is not. Also, kids can learn how to have a private conversation or activity with a friend in a way that does not put anyone else down and to be respectful and kind in explaining this to someone who approaches them.

Relational bullying happens when a group deliberately keeps an individual out and/or attacks this person's reputation, value, and other relationships. Sometimes the group also taunts the excluded person. At other times the group acts as if that person is not there. Usually one person leads the shunning process, but others in the group actively participate or passively let it happen.

Martha was the bane of my childhood. From the time I was seven until I was ten, I'd go to school, dreading recess. All the girls would run to play the wonderful games that Martha would lead and I wished I could be part of them. If I tried to join in, Martha would call the other girls away from me, saying, "You don't want to play with that little brat. You might get her cooties." She and her friends would whisper about my dark ugly hair and skin, point at me, giggle, and turn their backs.

It never occurred to me to ask my parents or teachers for help. Alone, away from the cluster of girls, I'd sit by the locked door of the classroom and read a book, escaping into the world of my imagination and waiting for recess to be over. I suffered this day, after day, after day over three long years.

One day in the fifth grade, Martha and her followers trapped me alone in the bathroom. When I tried to slip past them to get out the door, Martha shoved me backwards, knocking me down. Pushed beyond endurance after years of being left out and made fun of, I got up silently and kicked her hard in the shins. As I left the bathroom, Martha started crying and screamed, "You'll get in trouble for this. I'm telling on you."

Martha and the other girls went running to the teacher, claiming that I had kicked Martha and that she hadn't done anything at all. To her eternal credit, my teacher believed me over the word of the other girls. From my adult perspective, I can imagine that she must have observed the playground situation, even though the policy at that time in my school was to not interfere. Almost fifty years later, I can still remember being a terrified shy ten-year-old who never got into trouble at school, feeling sick to my stomach as the teacher asked to speak with me alone. To this day, I can remember the kindness in her voice. "Speaking unofficially Irene," my teacher said, "Good for you! Officially, please do your best not to let this happen again."

To my astonishment, Martha started trying to get me into her group. It felt wonderful to have her acting so nice to me, until I saw that she was starting to pick on another girl, whose family did not have much money. As this girl stood there alone looking sad, Martha and her followers laughed at her clothes. Martha nudged my arm to get me to join in.

I wanted so badly to be part of their group, but a dawning sense of justice told me that I simply couldn't do to this other girl what had been done to me. It took all the courage I had, but I walked away from the group I had wanted for years to belong to and went to stand next to the girl they were harassing. After that, Martha and I stayed away from each other. Some of the girls in her group eventually ended up becoming my friends.

Much of Martha's behavior was a form of what is now called "relational aggression" or "relational bullying." This term refers to the use of social networks to be hurtful to someone by spreading gossip, encouraging exclusion, and using other covert forms of personal attack. In his profound book, *A Different Drum: Community Making and Peace, author M. Scott Peck, M.D.,* describes how unhealthy groups can create a sense of purpose and value for themselves by choosing another group or an individual to be a common enemy.[12]

In some cultures, both now and in the past, the most devastating punishment anyone can receive is shunning. The experience of being banned from the community can be life threatening and sometimes even deadly. Increasing evidence shows that being shunned can be devastating to people of any age. Children and teens can internalize the message from their peers that they are "losers" and act in self-destructive ways. Some kids have become very depressed or even committed suicide. Some have become bitter and dealt with their hurt in very aggressive ways.

Unfortunately, relational aggression between young people is often hard to recognize and challenging to confront directly. Regular boundary-setting skills usually aren't enough. Following well-meaning suggestions like, "Just ignore them and play with someone else." does not work for most kids.

The best solutions include acknowledging the pain of this experience instead of minimizing it. Direct interventions work best with younger children. Older kids and teens will want to be involved in the solutions rather than having adults take over. Adults can provide support with compassion and, without

Increasing evidence shows that being shunned can be devastating to people of any age.

When others are being unkind, kids and adults can learn to adjust their emotional distance.

lecturing, practice skills that can address the problem.

When others are being unkind, children and adults can learn a variety of ways for protecting their emotional safety. As described in Chapter Six on boundaries, Kidpower teaches our students to throw hurting words away into their personal Trash Cans and recycle them into affirmations. We also teach how to screen out hurtful comments, gestures, and grimaces while taking in useful information. Here are some other practices that can help.

Adjusting your emotional distance. For dealing with important people who go back and forth between being great to being rude, we teach how to Adjust Your Emotional Distance as a useful tool for enjoying the good in the relationship while protecting yourself from what is upsetting. "Libby and I were best friends since we were little kids," ten-year-old Marisa mourned. "But now Libby acts so mean to me. She doesn't want me to spend time with anybody except her, and she says that I am a bad friend when I do. Sometimes, Libby tries to get other girls to stay away from me and play only with her. I don't want to lose Libby's friendship, because sometimes she can be very fun, but I don't know what to do."

"A friend who starts acting like a bully can cause a lot of hurt," I said sympathetically. "People often wonder what they did wrong and feel betrayed."

"This is hard to do at first, but you can learn to change your emotional distance from Libby, instead of keeping your heart completely open to her all the time," I suggested. "That way, when your friend is acting in a way that is emotionally safe, you can be emotionally open. When she is acting in a way that is emotionally unsafe, you can protect your heart by being emotionally further away from her."

I showed Marisa what I meant by using a physical example. First, I pretended to be Libby in a good mood. We stood close and gave each other a hug. Next, I started to be rude, saying, "Why didn't you come over to my house yesterday after school?" I coached Marisa to step away from me each time I was rude, so that her physical distance matched her emotional distance.

Pretending to be Libby, I got progressively ruder, saying, "You are such a bad friend!" "I never liked you anyway. I just hung out with you out of pity." "You are just useless!" Marisa kept moving back, until she realized that she was ready to leave completely.

I acknowledged that Marisa might lose this friendship if Libby's behavior continued, but that this was not something that Marisa could control. It would be sad if this happened, but it would not be her fault.

"I'd like to join the game!" Another way that kids pick on other kids is by not letting them play games. The rule at many schools is that everybody gets a turn or that everybody gets a chance to play. But teachers usually tell kids who are getting left out to try to work it out themselves. In one second grade class, I asked the students what sorts of things kids said to stop other

kids from joining ~~a~~ game. This led to quite a lively discussion with many examples. We then brainstormed answers for these reasons for exclusion.

Reason: "You're not good enough."
Response: "I'll get better if I practice."

Reason: "You're too good and nobody else gets a chance."
Response: "I just want to play. I'll agree to rotate so that everybody will have a turn."

Reason: "Only people wearing yellow can play this game."
Response: "Since green is a mixture of yellow and blue, this green shirt actually has yellow in it."

Reason: "You cheat."
Response: "I didn't mean to. Let's make sure we agree on the rules ahead of time."

Reason: "There are too many here already."
Response: "There's always room for one more."

Reason: "You had to have watched the show on TV last night to play."
Response: "I'll use my imagination. Just tell me what the rules are."

In workshops, we give students the chance to practice being persistent in asking to be included and also in being an advocate for another student. We remind them that being cheerful and assertive works much better than acting whiny or irritated. Our instructor Marc asks Daniel and Roxanne, who are both eight years old and who have done this before, to help him demonstrate. He sets the stage by explaining, "Let's imagine that I am a kid at your school. Roxanne and I are playing catch and Daniel wants to play."

As Marc and Roxanne pretend to toss a ball back and forth, Daniel approaches them. "I'd like to join the game," he says cheerfully and confidently.

Marc pretends to be a bully and says in a nasty voice, "No way! You always spoil everything by dropping the ball."

Daniel stays calm and says firmly, "I'll get better if I practice. I really want to play." (He imagines throwing Marc's words into a trashcan.)

Marc says meanly, "I said that you're not good enough. Go away."

Daniel persists and says, "The rule at school is that everybody gets a turn to play."

Roxanne, who has been watching up until now, speaks up. "Give him a chance," she tells Marc.

"But he drops the ball," Marc complains. "And it takes him so long to get it."

"I'll get better if I practice!"

"I'm sad that you feel that way. I hope you'll change your mind!"

Both Daniel and Roxanne speak up together saying, "The rule at school is that everybody gets a turn to play." (Or, "We don't exclude her for reasons like that." Or, "Leaving people out is unkind.")

Marc pretends to be angry and says, "I won't play if Daniel does."

Roxanne says calmly, "I'm sad that you feel that way. I hope that you'll change your mind." She and Daniel start tossing their imaginary ball.

Marc then gives each student the chance to practice being both the kid who wants to play and the kid who speaks up. Each student chooses which form of exclusion he or she wants to practice dealing with.

The Meet-New-People Personal Safety Tactic. In the sixth grade of a small private elementary school, the students were nervous about having to start at a new much bigger school the following year. Each of these eleven-year-old children said that their biggest fear was of being alone. We decided to turn this problem into a practice by having each student imagine being alone at the new school. The student approached a group of students who acted like they knew each other and said cheerfully and confidently, "Hello, I'm new here. What's your name?"

Sometimes the students in the group pretended to be friendly right away. Sometimes they acted annoyed or ignored the person practicing. We coached each student to find someone who was sitting all alone to approach and introduce her or himself.

The Gossip Game. Talking about what is happening in people's lives is interesting, but passing on unkind gossip is hurtful and can be damaging to people's reputations. The Gossip Game is a fun way to practice changing negative messages to positive ones and to show how each person has the power to change negative gossip.

This is somewhat like the game of Telephone where one person whispers a sentence in the ear of another who whispers it to the next until, after several people have done this, you find that the original sentence has completely changed. In the Gossip Game, you say the sentence out loud and you make it be unkind gossip about someone who is NOT a real person. For example, "I heard that X thinks that Y is really dumb."

A possible reply might be, "Y seems smart to me! X seems nice, too. I'll believe that she says mean things when I hear her myself." You go around the circle taking turns giving negative messages and then finding ways to make them positive.

Compliments Practice. Young people benefit from practice in giving compliments generously and receiving compliments graciously. Have a regular compliments time on a daily, weekly, or monthly basis in your family, day care, youth group, or school. Adults need to lead to ensure that everyone gets complimented an equal amount, that each person says something nice to each other person, and that the receiver responds appreciatively.

Make sure that compliments are genuine and do not contain an insult in the giver's tone of voice, facial expressions, or choice of words. Teach kids to give compliments about something other than what people look like, such as about what they do or how they act. For example, "You know how to listen. You make funny jokes. You are fun to play with. You are a good helper."

Addressing Relational Bullying and Providing Support

1   Listen with compassion to a young person who is upset about being left out. Seek professional counseling if the problem continues.

2   Find opportunities to develop new relationships. Getting involved with social groups away from school and trying out new activities such as doing community service can help to build a sense of self-worth.

3   Get the school to teach about relational aggression. The Internet contains a great deal of excellent information. See relationalaggression.com for a list of resources.

4   Have specific, realistic rules about exclusion and a clear procedure that everyone knows to follow when it happens.

5   Have both kids and adults make written contracts not to gossip, exclude, or badmouth others.

6   Encourage young people to write their experiences and feelings down. Journaling can help relieve pain and increase awareness. Documenting the problem in writing helps to define what is going on and can be a tool to get the attention of the adults in charge.

7   Acknowledge the temptation to gossip because people's lives are interesting and because it is a way of sharing. Follow-up by explaining how gossiping about someone can become damaging when it hurts the reputation of this person.

8   Teach young people how to act confident, be assertive, protect their feelings, adjust their emotional distance, meet new people, be persistent in asking to be included, and be persistent in getting help. Give them the chance to practice staying assertive and confident while being rejected, assessing when it is time to go away, and finding someone else to talk with.

9   Educate young people about the importance of being an advocate instead of a witness. Give young people the chance to practice out loud the words to say in order to speak up respectfully and powerfully, as well as how to leave and get help.

10 Stay aware that there might be more than one side to the story. Jumping in and taking sides is often not as useful as guiding young people to find their own solutions.

Copying you to be mean is **not** funny!

Being Brave to Stop Bullying

Speaking up takes courage. Speaking up takes the skills of knowing the words to say and how to deal with negative reactions. Finally, speaking up takes wisdom, because at times, speaking up is a mistake. What if a dangerous person is insulting you or others at a time when no adult authority figure is around to keep the situation from escalating? In such situations, the best plan is to leave and get help, which is also a form of taking action.

Here are some ways we practice this in our Kidpower and Teenpower workshops.

Setting Boundaries About Mimicking. One form of bullying is to mimic someone else. It is easy to make a caricature of someone's speech, tone, words, posture, and gestures in a way that is very insulting. Even very young children will recognize this. In preschool classes, we use the following demonstration with three-year-olds and a puppet. In the following example, the child is Laurie and the puppet is Duck.

Duck tugs Laurie's hair gently with its wings and looks naughty. Laurie sets a boundary by removing Duck's wings from her hair and saying, "Please stop."

Duck mimics Laurie's words and tone in a way that is clearly intended to make fun of her, "Please stop. Na! Na! Na!" All the preschool children gasp along with Laurie. "What's that called?" I ask.

"Copying," they all say. "That's not nice!"

Laurie looks worried and a bit stuck, so I coach her, "When people are rude, you can be brave and speak up. You can say to Duck, 'That's not funny!'"

Immediately, Laurie pushes Ducks' wings away and says, "Please stop. That's not funny."

Again Duck copies rudely, "Please stop. That's not funny. Spppptttt."

Laurie tries again, "Copying is not funny. I said stop. I don't like it."

To the fascination of my young audience at such amazing badness, Duck copies Laurie again. Duck repeats everything she says over and over, adding obnoxious noises and fluttering around her head.

I ask Laurie, "Do you feel like being mean back to Duck?"

As she nods her head, I add, "You are being very brave to stay in charge of your body.

Now, use your Mouth Closed Power, your Walk Away Power, and your Getting Help Power."

Laurie squeezes her lips shut, walks away with awareness, and tells her teacher, "Duck is copying me. I said stop. Duck's not listening. I need help."

Her proud teacher puts her arm around Laurie and says, "You did a good job. I will talk to Duck!"

Copying becomes cruel when someone mimics people with disabilities in order to ridicule how they move or speak. We can remind kids (and grownups too if need be), "It might seem funny if someone is behaving in a way that seems odd to you, but laughing about the fact that another person has difficulty doing something is very unkind."

Speaking up about putdowns. Whether a putdown is directed toward them or at someone else, young people need to understand that stopping putdowns with their family, friends, and classmates is like stopping pollution or littering. Stopping putdowns might not always be possible, but trying when they can is important, especially with their peers.

Common putdowns include laughing, making rude gestures or sounds, mimicking, and saying insulting things to make someone feel embarrassed, uncomfortable, or ashamed. Putdowns also include making negative remarks about someone behind her or his back for the purpose of getting others to think less of this person. This is different than speaking up about a problem to get help, because the purpose is not to find a solution, but to be hurtful.

Depending on the nature of the putdown and the age of our students, verbal responses that we might have young people practice include:
• That's not funny. Please stop.
• That's a mean thing to say. I don't like it.
• That's not cool.
• What purpose does it serve to say that? It sounds like an insult.
• That's disrespectful. Please stop.
• That's prejudice. That's not acceptable to me.
• That's a mean thing to do. Stop or I'll leave.
• That's bullying. We promised not to do that, and I want to keep our promises.
• That's dishonorable. You are a better person than that.

We also help young people come up with "I" statements such as, "I believe that you mean no harm, and I feel sad when you say unkind things about people. Please stop." Most people don't like being told what to do, which is why we prepare our students to persist when they speak up using the examples described in the practice section below.

Changing the Balance of Power. In workshops with older children and teens, we sometimes demonstrate what happens when people decide not to come to the defense of the victim but stand by and watch as a person bullies someone else. Our instructors Antonie and Ryan recruit some students to help in the demonstration. Ryan has the students stand behind him as he points at Antonie. He tells them, "Imagine that I am your age. My pointing at Antonie like this is not realistic. My pointing represents the many different ways that I might be bullying her by calling her names, giving her the silent treatment, making threats, or making fun of her."

Whether a putdown is directed at themselves or at someone else, young people need to understand that stopping putdowns is like stopping pollution or littering.

Everyone watches as Ryan points at Antonie. He has the group behind him and she is standing alone. "How do you suppose Antonie feels right now?" Ryan asks everyone.

Most students give the same answers: Sad. Alone. Afraid.

"And," Ryan continues, "how do you suppose I feel?"

"Powerful," the students say. "Like you have all the control. Proud."

Finally, Ryan waves towards the young people behind him. "How do they feel?" he asks.

"Part of the group," the students say. "Safe. But not too safe, because your pointing at her could turn towards them. Sorry, but glad that it's not happening to them."

Ryan asks, "Would being the first person to go over and support Antonie be hard to do?"

"Yes," the students say. They watch as the first one of the group and then another goes over to stand next to Antonie.

Next, Ryan helps build understanding by asking leading questions. "Does it get easier when you are not the first? 'Yes.' How does Antonie feel now? 'Better.' How do I feel? 'Less sure of yourself.' How do these kids still behind me feel? 'Like going over, too.'"

The kids behind Ryan continue to walk over to Antonie until he is the one who is standing alone, still pointing at Antonie. "Notice," he explains, "That my behavior hasn't changed at all, but the situation has changed completely. How does Antonie feel now?"

"Good," the students say. "Like she belongs."

Ryan gestures to the group behind Antonie and asks them directly, "How do you feel?"

Almost always, one or more of the group behind Antonie will raise their arms and start pointing back at Ryan.

"This is very interesting," Ryan says. "If you wanted to support Antonie because you thought that my pointing at her was wrong, it is just repeating the same pattern of bullying if you start pointing back. Instead, you want to support Antonie. You could say, 'That was really hard.' Or, 'I'm sorry that happened to you.' You could put a hand on her shoulder. You could ask a teacher or another adult for help. It is safest for everyone if you can support Antonie without acting in an attacking way yourself."

As the students lower their arms and move closer to Antonie, Ryan asks one last question. "How do you think I feel now, with no one behind me?"

The students say, "Alone. Powerless. Left out."

"In fact," Ryan smiles as he walks over to the group with Antonie. "I might get tired of being here by myself pointing and decide to join these kids to do something else instead. It would be fine for me to join this group as long as I didn't do any of the bullying behavior I was doing before."

Antonie then points out that, if someone has been bullying, your plan can be to say, "yes" with a boundary.

In his role as the former bully, Ryan comes up to the group and says, "Can I play?"

"Yes," Antonie says calmly and confidently, "But no pushing!"

In workshops, we then have students practice this in small groups, so that they each can feel what it is like to be the person pointing, the person being pointed at, and the bystanders – and how shifts in the balance of power change your feelings in each role.

Part One: Preparing Young People to be Brave to Stop Bullying

1   Discuss what it feels like to know something is wrong and feel too afraid to speak up. Use stories from your own life when you can. Were there times when you didn't speak up about putdowns or other bullying and felt bad later? Were there times when you did speak up and it didn't work out so well? What did you learn?

2   Discuss times when people show courage by speaking up for themselves and others. This could be from books, movies, or activities like the Balance of Power exercise described above. Again, tell stories from your own life when you can and encourage children to tell their stories. Talk about what courage feels like "from the inside" to each person. How does it feel to do something that you know is right even if you are worried, scared, or uncomfortable about doing it?

3   At the age level that is appropriate, use examples from children's lives to let them practice speaking up about different kinds of putdowns. For younger children, this can be a great time to use a puppet to be the rude person so that you can easily coach.

4   For older children, let them decide ahead of time who the person creating the problem is, what the offensive words or actions are, what words they want to use to speak up, what defensive reaction they want to have to deal with, and what response they want to try. They can even write this up as a little script.

● ●

Part Two. Practicing Positive Responses to Common Negative Reactions

Rehearse with young people how to say out loud in a respectful, positive way, non-attacking responses to these common negative reactions:

1   *The Sense of Humor Reaction*
     Negative Comment: Can't you take a joke?
     Possible Response: That was unkind. Being hurtful to people is not funny to me.

2

The Belittling Reaction
Negative Comment: You're overreacting. You're oversensitive.
Possible Response: Perhaps. All the same, I feel uncomfortable when you make comments like that. Let's talk about something else instead.

3

The Innocent Reaction
Negative Comment: But he/she is not even here. So what does it matter?
Possible Response: It makes people think less of him/her. Being mean behind someone's back does not make it less unkind.

4

The Being Factual Reaction
Negative Comment: I was just stating my honest opinion. It's a free country.
Possible Response: If someone used words like that about you, my honest opinion is that you would feel attacked.

5

The Being Helpful Reaction
Negative Comment: I was just trying to be helpful. Can't you handle the truth?
Possible Response: When you put down something that a person cannot change, it is not helpful. When you use rude words to tell me you don't like something that I might or might not decide to change, that is not helpful.

6

The Blaming Reaction
Negative Comment: It's your fault. I had to say this because you made me mad.
Possible Response: If you say rude things, this is your responsibility. It is not anyone's fault but your own. You can explain why you are unhappy another time.

7

The Changing the Subject Reaction
Negative Comment: You are really wrong because you _____ (a completely unrelated complaint).
Possible Response: You are changing the subject. You can complain about what I did later, but right now I want you to stop saying mean things.

8

The Threatening Reaction
Negative Comment: I'll make you sorry that you said that.
Possible Response: Stop or I'll leave. Stop or I'll tell. (Or just leaving and getting help without saying anything further to this person.)

9

The Denial Reaction
Negative Comment: I never said that. That's not what I meant.
Possible Response:
Option 1 (If there is any possibility you are wrong): If that's true, then I apologize for believing you'd say something so awful.
Option 2 (If this is something that happens repeatedly): I have a different memory about this than you do. So, does this mean that you agree that that would be an awful thing to say?

Walking Our Talk

Like me, you might recognize yourself as well as other people in some of the defensive reactions described above. Respectful communication takes hard work from everyone involved. If we want to stop young people from using putdowns, we must stop making putdowns ourselves. Especially because it is hard, it is important to show children that we can listen respectfully when someone feels insulted by our actions or words. We don't have to agree, but we do need to show that we are willing to understand other points of view.

No matter what our intentions were, if someone was insulted or hurt by something we said or did, we can say, "I am sorry for saying this in a way that was hurtful." If we were wrong, we can say, "I was wrong. That was a dumb thing for me to say. I am sorry." If we were expressing a valid concern, we can say, "I did not mean to hurt your feelings, but I do need to tell you about this problem. Is there a way that I can say it that you will not find insulting?"

Seeing adults do this is tremendously educational for their kids. Adults can tell children as soon as they are old enough to understand, "None of us is perfect, and we all make mistakes. When someone does not like something that you say or do, feeling unhappy about this is normal. Instead of saying something back right away, you can learn to get centered and to listen. Try to ask questions until you can understand why the other person is unhappy with you. Even if you don't agree, you can say that you are sorry for hurting someone's feelings."

Speaking Up About Prejudice

In a perfect world, no one would care if people were different, as long as they weren't being hurtful to anyone. In a perfect world, people would not be bothered or harmed by others because they are of different religions, races, sexual orientations or identities, appearances, incomes, or cultures. Different colors of skin and shapes of faces and bodies would be celebrated rather than judged. Whether children have married parents, divorced parents, two moms, two dads, or foster parents would not matter. If children's families have problems, this would not be a reason for other people to think less of them.

Sadly, I don't have to tell you that this is not a perfect world. Prejudice because of differences can lead to bullying and cruel teasing, which results in misery and even suicide due to young people feeling alone and desperate. One of the ways to make our world safer for everyone is to speak up against prejudice and injustice. Just witnessing or even going along with bullying and putdowns without saying or doing anything means that prejudice and injustice will continue.

Too often, people will tolerate prejudice when it is delivered in the form of a joke. Unfortunately, promoting prejudice through humor also promotes injustice. Most people are clear that some kinds of jokes are destructive, but they will laugh at other jokes that are equally prejudicial. For example, someone might find jokes about race totally out of bounds, but think that jokes about sexual orientation or appearances are really funny.

Choosing when and how to intervene is essential in order to do speak up safely. Sometimes the wisest and most effective choice is to leave and get help. In our workshops with older children and teens, we explain, "Before you speak up, you want to think first. Is this a group of friends being thoughtless,

We can listen respectfully when someone feels insulted by our actions or words. We don't have to agree, but we do need to show that we are willing to understand other points of view.

In a perfect world, people would not be bothered or harmed by others because they are different religions, races, sexual orientations, or identities, appearances, incomes or cultures.

or someone I don't know acting tough on the street? If someone you don't know is making prejudiced remarks, the safest plan is almost always to walk away and get to a place where someone can help you.

But if someone you do know, maybe at work or at school, is making putdown comments and jokes, you can make the choice to speak up. Speaking up against prejudice can be powerful, but takes courage. Be prepared to persist because people are likely to be mad at you at first or go into denial."

Using Role Plays to Practice Speaking Up About Prejudice

In Teenpower and Fullpower workshops where this has been requested, we often use role-plays so students can practice dealing with negative comments relating to size, gender, sexuality, religion, race, ethnicity, ability, and other aspects of personal identity. In each case, the adult leading the practice plays the role of a friend who is making prejudicial remarks. We give students the opportunity to come up with their own examples and coach them if they get stuck on the words to say. We remind them to stay assertive rather than becoming passive or aggressive.

1 *Body Size Role-Play.* First, the adult sets the stage by saying, "Suppose you and I are friends, sitting outside on a bench during school." Next, the adult makes prejudiced remarks in a mean voice like, "Hey look! ... That guy is so fat! ... He needs two seats on the bus!" Or, "Have you seen that girl in sixth grade? She's so skinny you can't see her! ... She's probably stupid too."

The student says assertively, "I feel uncomfortable when you use somebody's size as a put down. Please stop!" Or, "That sounds like prejudice and I don't want to hear it!"

The adult pretends to act upset and says, "Can't you take a joke?"

The student responds assertively, "I don't think prejudice is funny." Or, "That kind of joke isn't funny to me."

2 *Racism Role-Play.* First, the adult sets the stage by saying, "Let's imagine that we are kids the same age having lunch at school." Next the adult starts making racist remarks, perhaps by repeating something, "You know what, my parents were talking about a study that says that black people are just not as intelligent as white people. That's why they have so many problems. And there was another study that shows that those Mexicans are having so many babies that it is hurting the economy."

The student says assertively, "I feel upset when you use a study or quote someone else to make a prejudiced remark."

The adult pretends to be reasonable and says, "But it was a scientific study. You can't argue with science."

The student responds assertively and says, "What we think is scientifically accurate changes all the time and contradicts itself. There are also studies showing that people are equally intelligent regardless of race and that there is great benefit to our society from immigrants. I feel uncomfortable when you repeat negative remarks about groups of people. Please stop."

3 *Homophobia Role-Play.* First, the adult sets the stage by saying, "Let's imagine that we are kids the same age at school and I am talking about someone on the other side of the room and he or she cannot hear us." Next, the adult whispers in a mocking voice, pointing to an imaginary person in an empty spot on the other side of the room, "Yuck, look at that new girl! She looks like a boy. I bet she's a dyke." Or, "You see that guy? I heard he's a fag. Don't you just want to puke?"

The student says assertively, "Lot's of great people are lesbians (or gay)! I feel uncomfortable when you use that as a put down. Please stop!" Or, "That sounds like a prejudiced remark and I don't like that kind of talk!"

The adult sounds irritated and snaps, "Can't you take a joke?" Or, "Are you gay too?"

The student responds calmly, "If I were gay, I'd be proud of it." Or, "My sexual identity is none of your business." She or he then adds, "I don't think prejudice is funny." Or, "This kind of joke isn't funny to me."

4   *Mean Jokes Role-Play.* First, the adult sets the stage by saying, "Suppose that we are with a group of friends and I start making mean jokes." Next, the adult laughs, "Have you heard that joke about the fatso that ate too much?! Or, "Did you hear that great joke about two stupid faggots? Ha! Ha! Ha!!" Or, while pulling the eyes sideways saying, "Look, I can make my eyes like a Chinaman." Or, mimicking someone's accent or behavior.

The student speaks up, "I feel uncomfortable when you joke about somebody's size (or sexual identity, disability, looks, or accent) and use it as a put down. Please stop!" Or, "That sounds like prejudice and it upsets me!"

The adult pretends to be upset and reacts by saying, "But you joke like that all the time!"

The student responds by saying, "I used to joke like that until I realized how cruel it is. I don't want to be acting like a prejudiced person."

5   *Sexism Role-Play.* First the adult sets the stage by saying, "Let's imagine that we are students and we are talking about a girl who is not in class today." Next the adult says in a disgusted voice, "She must be a slut and sleep around to be so popular (get good grades/get ahead)."

The student responds, "Please stop. That sounds like prejudice and I don't want to hear it!"

The adult mimics in an irritating tone, "That sounds like prejudice and I don't want to hear it." With a disgusted face, the adult adds, "Well, I don't want to hear you going on and on about this. You're no fun to be with anymore!"

The student says, "I am sad that you feel that way because I like you a lot. There are lots of other great things we can talk about instead of putting people down. Wasn't the game (or movie) great last night?"

6   *Disability Role-Play.* First the adult sets the stage by saying, "Let's imagine that we are students and we see the special education classroom going out." Next the adult whispers to the student and points, "Look at those freaks. They are just too dumb to live."

The student speaks by saying, "Please don't talk about people with disabilities that way. They have feelings and deserve respect, just like you do."

The adult sighs and says in a sardonic voice, "There you go! Being politically correct again. Can't you lighten up?"

The student says, "If you want to label being respectful to others as being "politically correct", then I guess that's what I am. Let's talk about something else."

Positive peer pressure - let's smile for the camera!

Instead of getting triggered into making a poor decision, you can get centered and think first.

Peer Pressure Tactics

No matter how old or young we are, most of us want to be liked and respected by our peers. Especially as young people move into their pre-teen and teen years, the opinions of their peers often become much more important to them. To make wise decisions, they need to understand the role that peer pressure can play in influencing their choices and develop the skills to stand up to their peers when necessary.

Our Colorado Center Director and Senior Program Leader Jan Isaacs Henry, who added this to our curriculum, defines peer pressure for her students by explaining, "Peers are people your age, and most of us want people our age to like us. Peer pressure happens when someone your age tries to get you to do something. Positive peer pressure helps you do your best, like people cheering at a game. With negative peer pressure, someone tries to persuade you to do something that might hurt someone, be dangerous, or get you into trouble."

Jan describes how managing triggers is a useful tool for managing peer pressure by saying, "Being triggered means that you get so excited or so upset that you stop thinking clearly. When you are not thinking clearly, you are less likely to make wise choices for yourself. Negative triggers make you feel bad. A negative trigger might be wanting so badly not to be left out or thought less of by members of the group that you go along with the crowd. A positive trigger might happen when you get so caught up in doing something exciting that you forget to think about the consequences. Sometimes people do things when they get caught up in peer pressure that they would *never* do otherwise and feel bad about later. Instead of getting triggered into making a poor decision, you can get centered and think first."

Thanks to permission from family counselor Sharon Scott, LPC, LMFT, author of the excellent book on the teen years, *How to Say No and Keep Your Friends*, we have incorporated some ideas from her peer pressure reversal skills program into our Kidpower program. Sharon Scott formerly served as the director of the First Offender Program of the Dallas, Texas, police department, a program for adolescents who commit one to five offenses. She found that the biggest reason that young people broke the law was because of negative peer pressure. She had them practice her Peer Pressure Reversal skills and 79 percent were successful as measured by never being rearrested again. She has a wide range of books and training for all ages about peer pressure and other topics including the parent guide, *Peer Pressure Reversal: An Adult Guide to Developing a Responsible Child.*[13]

Using ideas from Sharon Scott's Peer Pressure Reversal Tactics, Jan directs different students in acting out common problems that young people might face with peers using the role plays described below. She reminds students that they need to be cheerful or matter-of-fact, not sarcastic. Also, if a tactic doesn't work, the safest plan is to leave.

> *The biggest reason that young people broke the law was because of negative peer pressure.*

Part One. Preparing Young People to Deal With Peer Pressure

1   Explain what peer pressure is. Tell stories of times from your own life when your friends supported you in doing your best and times when going along with friends got you into trouble or to do something you were sorry about later. Look for examples from books and movies of this happening.

2   Encourage young people to tell their own stories. Ask for times when their friends have supported them in ways that made their lives better and for times when friends have gotten them to do things that made their lives worse.

3   Explain about how being triggered positively or negatively by peers can cause problems.

4   Read Sharon Scott's books (www.hrdpress.com/SharonScott) for children and for adults. Using her Peer Pressure Reversal tactics, make up role-plays for situations that children and teens might encounter and practice them. [13]

● ●

Part Two. Role Plays to Practice Sharon Scott's Peer Pressure Reversal Tactics

Coach young people to try out these tactics for getting out of the following situations in ways that save face for the other person:

1   *The Cutting Class Role-Play*
Pedro and Bill pretend to be two friends waiting outside before school. Bill says, "Hey Pedro, that substitute is so stupid she'll never notice we're missing. Let's cut class. Come on! Hurry, before they…"

Pedro uses the tactic of Leaving. He interrupts Bill and says, "Gotta go, bye! He walks away cheerfully with a wave.

2   *The Putting Down Another Kid Role-Play*
Carol and Maggie pretend to be two friends sitting in the lunchroom at school. Maggie points and says, "Hey, Carol, look at that new girl. She's really gross. Let's tell everyone to stay away from her."

Carol uses the tactic of Changing the Subject by saying, "Do you want to know what she said about you?" (Asking people if they want to know what someone else said about them is a very effective way of changing the subject.)

Maggie looks surprised and asks eagerly, "Yes! What did she say?"

Carol says cheerfully, "She says that you seem very nice." Maggie looks taken aback.

3

The Showing Off a Gun Role-Play
Billy and Robert pretend to be two friends who are visiting Billie's house. Billy says, "Hey, my Dad just got a gun for protection. See, it's right here in this drawer."

Robert uses the tactic of Making an Excuse and says as he runs out the door, "Oh no! I forgot to feed my dog! Sorry, I gotta go!" (Robert also knows that he needs to get help from an adult because showing off with guns is dangerous.)

4

The Talking in Class Role-Play
Allie and Megan pretend to be two friends sitting next to each other in class. The teacher has warned that the next student who says anything will have to stay after school. Megan pokes Allie and says, "Hey, Allie, guess what I heard at a party yesterday. Psst. Psst."

Allie uses the tactic of Ignoring and pretends to keep doing her schoolwork as Megan nudges and prods her, complaining, "What's with you!?"

5

The Toilet Papering the Neighbor's House Role-Play
Niko and Will pretend to be friends who are standing outside Will's house. Will says, "I'm really mad at my neighbor. He is so mean to me and he's out of town. I know! Let's toilet-paper his house!"

Niko uses the tactic of Acting Shocked. He puts his hands to his face like the little boy in the movie Home Alone and says in a horrified voice, "Are you crazy? We'll be grounded forever if we do that!"

6

The Using Drugs Role-Play
Marjorie and Olivia pretend to be two friends who are really worn out studying for a test. Olivia yawns and says, "I'm tired. I know someone who has some pills that will make us feel really good so we can concentrate. Why don't I call him to see if we can get some?"

Marjorie chooses the tactic of Using Flattery and says, "I like you too much to agree to use drugs with you. It's not worth the risk even if we fail the test. Let's do some stretches and see if that doesn't help."

7

The Sneaking Out of the House Role-Play
Jamie and Tom pretend to be best friends who are staying at Tom's house for an overnight. Tom stretches and says, "I'm bored. Everyone is asleep. Let's sneak out of the house and go into the park. They'll never know."

Jamie uses the tactic of Having a Better Idea and says, "I have a better idea. Let's watch the movie we rented. We already paid for it!"

8

The Stealing Role-Play
Joe and Peter pretend to be two friends in the store. Joe says, "Hey, Peter, you distract the cashier and I'll steal us some magazines."

Peter decides to use the tacking of Using Flattery and says, "I really like you and I don't want to get us into trouble. It could ruin our friendship if we steal." Peter pays for his candy and quickly walks out of the store.

 9 *The Prank Calls Role-Play*
Lila and Latisha are having a sleepover. Lila says, "Hey, Latisha, lets make some prank calls. Let's order a bunch of pizzas for Juan." (Many young people are surprised to find out that prank calls are against the law.)

Latisha uses the strategy of Making a Joke by saying, "We can't. I've got phonophobia today." (Any joke, no matter how dumb, is okay as long as it doesn't put the other person down.)

Understanding and Stopping Sexual Harassment

In 2003, the American Association of University Women[14] (AAUW) commissioned a study by Harris Interactive to survey a nationally representative group of 2,064 students ranging from twelve to eighteen years old about sexual harassment in their schools. This was a follow-up to a similar AAUW study done in 1993.

In the study, sexual harassment was defined as "unwanted and unwelcome sexual behavior that interferes with your life. Sexual harassment is not behaviors that you like or want (for example wanted kissing, touching, or flirting)." "Non-physical harassment" was explained to mean unwanted sexual behavior that does not involve touching such as "taunting, rumors, graffiti, jokes or gestures." The study uses examples such as being spied on while showering or dressing.

The findings, reported in the AAUW publication, *Hostile Hallways: Bullying, Teasing, and Sexual Harassment in School*[15], indicate that:

• Eighty-three percent of girls and 79 percent of boys report having experienced sexual harassment.

• For many students sexual harassment is an ongoing experience: over one in four students experience it "often." These numbers do not differ by whether the school is urban, suburban, or rural.

• Peer-on-peer harassment is most common for both boys and girls, although seven percent of boys and girls experiencing physical or nonphysical harassment report being harassed by a teacher.

• Half of the boys reporting harassment have been non-physically harassed by a girl or woman, and 39 percent by a group of girls or women. In contrast, girls are most likely to report harassment by one boy or man (73 percent in non-physical harassment; 84 percent in physical harassment).

• Thirty-five percent of students who have been harassed report that they first experienced it in elementary school.

• Most harassment occurs under teachers' noses in the classroom (61 percent for physical harassment and 56 percent for non-physical) and in the halls (71 percent for physical harassment and 64 percent for nonphysical).

83% of girls and 79% of boys report having experienced sexual harassment.

- Students acknowledge being perpetrators, too. Slightly more than half of the students (54 percent) say that they have sexually harassed someone else at some time while they were in school.

- Although large groups of both boys and girls report experiencing harassment, girls are more likely to report being negatively affected by it. Girls are far more likely than boys to feel "self-conscious" (44 percent for girls compared to 19 percent for boys), "embarrassed" (53 percent compared to 32 percent), and "less confident" (32 percent to 16 percent) due to an incident of harassment. Girls are more likely than boys to change behavior because of the experience, including not talking as much in class (30 percent to 18 percent) and avoiding the person who harassed them (56 percent to 24 percent).

In response to the above findings, the AAUW developed an excellent resource guide for students, parents, and educators titled, *Harassment-Free Hallways: How to Stop Sexual Harassment in Schools.*[15] This free on-line publication provides surveys for students and staff, educational materials, and policy suggestions to help create a respectful, safe school environment. This guide helps to define the difference between flirting and hurting.

Sexual harassment is fed by sexism and homophobia.

Sexual behavior is against the law in many countries, including the United States. The U.S. Department of Education's Office of Civil Rights publishes an on-line pamphlet titled, *Sexual Harassment: It's Not Academic,* that defines students' rights to a nondiscriminatory, safe learning environment and gives clear definitions of what is and is not considered sexual harassment.[16]

Examples of sexual conduct might include: sexual advances; touching of a sexual nature; graffiti of a sexual nature; displaying or distributing sexually explicit drawings, pictures, or written materials; sexual gestures; sexual or "dirty" jokes; pressure for sexual favors; touching oneself sexually or talking about one's sexual activity in front of others; spreading rumors or rating other students as to sexual activity or performance; etc.

Sexual conduct must be unwelcome to be considered sexual harassment. However, a student might not speak up right away because of embarrassment, confusion, or fear of retaliation. A student might be very upset and uncomfortable, but not have the ability to complain. Invited or not, it is against the law for an adult to sexually approach a person under the age of eighteen. It is against the law for an employer or teacher to put sexual pressure on an employee or student or to create a hostile or uncomfortable environment in work or school settings.

Sexual harassment is fed by sexism and homophobia. According to the Merriam-Webster Online Dictionary, sexism means: "1) prejudice or discrimination based on sex; especially, discrimination against women; 2) behavior, conditions, or attitudes that foster stereotypes of social roles based on sex." Homophobia means, "irrational fear of, aversion to, or discrimination against homosexuality or homosexuals."[17] It is common for young people to use gender stereotypes and homophobia to make each other miserable. Adults need to address these issues in the moment and through education.

The media is one of the most powerful influences on today's youth and the Media Awareness Network in Canada[18] has a wealth of lesson plans for different grade levels on how to teach media awareness skills. In their section, "Gender Stereotypes and Sexual Assault," they have lessons that include asking what it means to "act like a man" and "be a lady," how this affects the students' images of themselves, and how this relates to sexual harassment and violence. They also have lessons on diversity and violence, including homophobia and racism.

Here are some examples of how we've addressed sexual harassment in workshops - and in real life.

"You run like a girl!" To stop sexual harassment, adults must speak up about behavior that happens in front of them. If we don't say anything, it leads young people into believing that this is acceptable to us. Once I was visiting an elementary school and a ten-year-old boy playing tag almost ran into me. His friends all laughed at him, "Hey, you run like a girl!"

I peered at the group of boys over the top of my sunglasses. "I very much hope," I said sternly, "that you intended the statement 'you run like a girl' to be a compliment! Did you?"

The boys squirmed and admitted, "Uh, not exactly."

Without identifying the boys, I repeated the comment to their teacher. She described the running feats of some great women athletes. This class came up with a plan of noticing joking comments that were actually a form of prejudice and finding examples to prove that the stereotype was incorrect.

"But I'M Not Gay!" In another workshop with a youth group where the adult had asked us to address this issue, the pre-teen boys and girls told me that they wanted to throw away the words "faggot" and "gay" and "dyke" because the worst possible insult was for anyone to think that they might be homosexuals.

I said, "It is very sad when people use prejudice as a way of insulting people, so that denying the insult becomes a way of making the prejudice get bigger. People used to do this about race and sometimes still do. They do it about size. They do it about looks. They do it about sexuality. Stopping this kind of behavior is challenging, because it is so much a part of our culture. But, whether you realize it or not, people you know are likely to be hurt by jokes about different sexual orientations and identities, even if they pretend that this doesn't bother them. People you know or someone they care about a lot might be gay, lesbian, bi-sexual, transgendered, or not sure.

"If someone uses a prejudiced remark to try to put you down," I continued, "you could throw away their intention to attack you, and say something that is positive without attacking anybody else, like, 'I'm proud to be who I am.'"

One boy named Dennis said, "But what if I'm not gay and somebody thinks I am if I say that?"

To stop sexual harassment, adults must speak up about behavior that happens in front of them.

The most effective way to prevent getting caught up in someone else's negative reaction is to focus on what you want to see changed.

I smiled at Dennis for having the courage to ask and explained, "You would be in very good company. There are many wonderful people who are gay and lesbian. Anyway, does it really matter what someone else thinks? What matters is what you think. You have to think about what kind of person you want to be. Right?"

Dennis thought for a moment and then smiled back at me. "Call me a faggot," he said.

I pointed at him and sneered, "You faggot!"

Dennis put his hands up like a fence and said, "That's a prejudiced remark and I'm proud to be who I am."

"I was just looking!" Many people do not realize that their behavior is uncomfortable for another person. They may respond defensively at first because being told to stop forces them to change. The most effective way to prevent getting caught up in someone else's negative reaction is to focus on what you want to see changed.

When possible, our goal is to empower young people to speak up for themselves in stopping sexual harassment. Because nonphysical harassment is sometimes harder to confront, we often introduce how to set boundaries with staring. Our instructor Greg explains what he's doing as he stares at Loretta, who keeps moving to different parts of the room, "Imagine that we are two students your age. I have a bit of a crush on Loretta so I keep staring at her. I stare at her in the classroom."

As Greg stares, Loretta glances at him out of the corner of her eye, makes an irritated face, and looks away. Greg continues his explanation. "I stare at her in the lunchroom." Greg stares and Loretta sighs. She glances at him again and he is still staring. "I stare at her when she's reading in the school library," Greg says. "She just can't get away from my staring."

Loretta goes up to Greg and says, "Please stop staring at me. I don't like it."

"I'm not doing anything!" Greg says. "It's just your imagination." Greg pauses in the role-play, turns to the class, and asks, "Well, it's true that I'm not touching Loretta, but am I still bothering her?"

Students' heads nod. Most of them don't like being stared at either. Continuing the role-play, Greg says, "I can look anywhere I want. It's a free country!"

Loretta says, "Yes it is. And I am free to tell you that I expect you, instead of staring at me, to look the other way. Bothering people like this is against the rules here at our school."

"Oh all right!" Greg says in an irritated tone. He looks away.

Greg points out that there is nothing wrong with feeling that someone looks wonderful, but there is something wrong with making that person uncomfortable by staring. If he hadn't stopped, then Loretta would have had the right to ask the teacher for help so that she could feel comfortable at school.

"Your daughter doesn't like me!" Young people are very likely to need adult help when adults are the ones causing the problem. When my daughter Chantal was twelve, she was one of only four girls in her advanced math class. She complained because her math teacher kept looking at her in a leering way and making suggestive remarks. After talking it over with her father and me, Chantal told her math teacher the next time he started this behavior, "I feel uncomfortable when you talk about how I look. Please don't do that."

Instead of respecting her boundary, her math teacher made fun of her. He increased his remarks and started making drawings with women's breasts on the blackboard. Although she didn't like the idea, I persuaded my daughter that it was important for me to tell her teacher that what he was doing was not okay, not only for her sake, but for the three other girls in her class.

I made an appointment to meet the math teacher after school and said very respectfully, "I think you're an excellent teacher. You may not be aware of some things you're doing that make Chantal uncomfortable. I feel that your teasing remarks about how she looks are just not appropriate."

The math teacher, who was a large man, seemed to get bigger and bigger and redder and redder in the face as I was talking, until he exploded, "In my thirty-two years of teaching, no one has ever spoken to me like this!"

"Well," I said cheerfully, feeling thankful for all of my self-defense training, "after thirty-two years, it's probably about time."

"Get real!" he snapped. "Your daughter needs to stop being oversensitive when someone just makes a joke! Anyway, who are you to talk to me like this?"

I'm her mother, I thought, and the co-founder of Kidpower! But what I said in a firm quiet voice was, "There are probably women right now who are sitting in a therapist's office saying that they stopped studying math or other subjects important to them because of that kind of 'just jokes.' And there are probably boys who are making girls' lives miserable by following your poor example. What you're doing is a form of sexual harassment, and I want you to stop. If need be, we can ask the school counselor to help us understand each other."

In the face of this adult version of "Stop or I'll tell," the math teacher deflated like a pricked balloon. "I'll do whatever you want! " he said. This math teacher then added plaintively, "But I feel bad because your daughter doesn't like me!"

I sighed. "She might if you'd stop teasing her! However, it's not her job to like you, and it's not your job to like her. It's your job to teach her math, and it's her job to learn it."

After that, the math teacher's behavior changed, and Chantal did well in the class.

There are probably women right now who are sitting in a therapist's office saying that they stopped studying math or other subjects important to them because of that kind of "just jokes."

Actions to Help Prevent and Stop Sexual Harassment of Young People

1 Check the policy at your children's schools about sexual harassment. Encourage middle and high schools to do the surveys and follow the policy recommendations of the AAUW or another resource.

2 Make sure that pre-teens and teens know what kinds of behavior are considered sexual harassment.

3 Make it clear that you do not consider this behavior to be acceptable and that you want to know if it happens to them or to other kids in their school or youth group. Avoid laughing at sexist or homophobic jokes. Intervene to stop sexual harassment instead of overlooking it. Make sure that young people know that they have the right to be treated with respect and the responsibility to treat others with respect.

4 Ask young people to notice when sexist or homophobic language or images are used in the media, in conversations, in activities, and in books. Help them find people who don't fit these negative stereotypes.

5 Help young people become informed consumers of the media. Ask schools to provide media education or use these resources yourself.

6 As they start to become interested in each other sexually, ask young people to tell you what kinds of attention are welcome and what are unwelcome. Remind them that they have the right to feel any way they want, and that they have the responsibility to act in a way that is respectful to other people.

7 Give young people the opportunity to practice Boundary-Setting and Advocacy skills in the context of sexual harassment.

8 When young people are unable to solve problems for themselves, listen to the whole story, brainstorm solutions, and make a plan of action. If the sexual harassment does not stop, intervene with the adults who are supervising.

Even if we aren't able to find a good solution right away, children and teens are likely to feel much better knowing that their adults are on their side.

If One Solution Doesn't Work, Try Another!

No matter how good a job we do, problems of indifference, unkindness, disrespect, and lack of safety won't go away overnight. Yet, the only way things will change is if we all keep working together to make things better. As caring adults, we want the young people in our lives to tell us when they have problems. We want to empower them to find their own solutions when possible. We want to back them up. Even if we aren't able to find a good solution right away, children and teens are likely to feel much better knowing that their adults are on their side. We want them to know that we are doing our best and not quitting. The bottom line is that, if one solution doesn't work, we'll try another!

Here are some ideas for other solutions to try.

Double-Check for Assertiveness. "People Safety" skills are far more effective if they are used in an assertive way. If our students tell us that they tried these skills and it didn't work, we say, "Please show me exactly what you are doing. Let's act it out. Maybe we forgot to tell you something."

Most of the time, as soon as students show us what they are doing instead of just telling us, we can see immediately what the problem is. Their words aren't clear, even if they think they are. Their manner is either apologetic or rude, without their realizing it. Their body language is hesitant, although they might think they are being firm. Of course, we are as encouraging as possible. "You are doing almost everything right, but this is like an electric circuit. If there is even a small place anywhere along the wire that is not connected, the electricity won't flow." We model what exact changes will increase assertiveness and then give students the chance to practice again.

Change the Deal. One of the habits in the book, *The Seven Habits of Highly Effective People* is, "Win-Win or No Deal." Sometimes a situation is just not going to work, and the best solution is to leave. Perhaps there is not enough adult support in a specific school or youth group to make a commitment to solve problems. Perhaps a social dynamic has become too tough to solve. Changing schools or ending unsafe relationships is a form of target denial.

Often, young people don't like change, even if this means exchanging a bad situation for a potentially much better one. Kids get attached to what is familiar and they often care about unsafe people. They may need support in getting more information about the pros and cons of different choices. They may need permission to grieve about the losses that come from leaving. They may need adults to make the choices for them.

"When she was in the third grade, we decided that Carmen needed to go to a different school mid-year," Carmen's parents said. "She was being bullied constantly and her classroom was completely out of control. At first, Carmen didn't want to go, even though she was miserable. We told Carmen that it was okay to be sad about leaving her old school, and that it would take time to adjust to the new one. Finally, we took her to visit the new school. We asked her to tell us if there was anything we could do to make this change easier. Carmen said that she wanted to have a tee shirt with her new school's name on it, like some of the other kids had. We believe that, hard as it was, changing schools was one of the best decisions we made for our daughter's well-being."

Find Safer Friends. Having safe friends is one of the best protections against bullying. Learning how to judge when a friend is safe or unsafe is a major life skill. The Kidpower office often gets poignant e-mail messages from young people from all over the world who are feeling very alone because of problems with friends. Their perception is that their parents are not available because they are too busy, sick, using drugs or alcohol, or in new romantic relationships and that their teachers don't care. They think that their friends are all they have and their friends are being hurtful.

Below is a typical message and our reply about how to find adult help and how to tell the difference between safe and unsafe friends.

E-Mail Message: I am eleven and live in London. My friends say that I'm ugly and dumb and that I'm lucky they let me hang out with them. They boss me around all the time. If we go to the snack bar, I am always the one who pays for everybody and I don't have much money. My mum works really hard and is always so tired that I don't want to bother her. What should I do?

Kids may need their adults to make the decision for them about changing schools to escape an unsafe situation.

The world is full of wonderful people who can be fun to be with, who will also be respectful and kind, and who would be terrific friends – you just need to find them. And you won't be able to do this if you hang out with people who are not acting like good friends.

Kidpower Reply: This sounds really hard. Even if your mum is busy, she probably really does want to know what is going on with you. Try finding a time to tell her when she is rested up. Make sure that you really have her attention and ask her to please just listen until you can tell her the whole story.

Try thinking of other safe adults you could tell. Maybe there is a teacher at your school who you liked before, even if you are in a different class now. Maybe you have an adult family member who you could call. Think of as many safe adults as possible – neighbors, counselors, youth group leaders, ministers, priests, rabbis, your coach in sports, or the parents of a friend. Finding the right adult to talk to can help you feel less alone and figure out what to do.

Sometimes kids who seem really cool and who do fun things are also mean or disrespectful to you. They might put you down, order you around, try to keep you from being friends with others, borrow money and never pay it back, expect you to pay for everything, want to have things only their way, make up stories about you, tell your secrets to everybody, and try to get you to do things that will get you into trouble.

Safe friends are kind, make plans with you, encourage other friendships, treat you with respect, pay back any money they owe, pay for their share of what things cost, do their share of the work, and encourage you to do things that are good for everyone. Safe friends respect your privacy unless anything unsafe is going on, in which case, they will help you find help.

If your friends say and do things that are hurtful, embarrassing, or disrespectful to you, tell them to stop in a calm, clear, respectful way. If this does not work, tell them again or find an adult you trust to help you work things out.

Remember that you can look for other people to be friends with. The world is full of wonderful people who can be fun to be with, who will also be respectful and kind, and who would be terrific friends – you just need to find them. And you won't be able to do this if you hang out with people who are not acting like good friends.

Brainstorm silly and serious ideas. At age nine, my son Arend came home from school absolutely furious. "Today, that awful girl threw my shoe into the girl's bathroom and you know I can't go into the girl's bathroom," he stormed, clearly feeling outraged. "I had to walk in my socks in the hall until the yard duty teacher got my shoe back for me."

"That sounds embarrassing!" I said, managing not to laugh at his indignation. "Was there anything else?"

"Yes!" Arend exploded. "Every single day, when my best friend and I are building a construction out of sand in our spot in the school yard, that awful girl always comes and messes it up."

"How frustrating!" I exclaimed. Resisting the temptation to make suggestions, I asked, "What have you tried?"

"We've tried letting her help us, but it just doesn't work," Arend grumbled. "That girl takes over and breaks up our tunnel to make a castle. We've tried telling her to stop and leave us alone, but she just laughs at us. She pushes us out of the way and kicks our construction apart on purpose. We've tried telling the yard duty and everybody talks it out, but the same thing happens the next day."

"My goodness!" I said sympathetically. "You've tried everything I know how to do. But I know a lot of people who are experts at protecting themselves. Do you want me to ask them?"

"Go ahead," my son replied gloomily. "But I think it won't do any good. This is hopeless."

I did ask my colleagues and shared their ideas with Arend the following week, starting with Timothy who helped me start Kidpower and who is a martial artist. "Timothy says that your project is like your personal space and at school you should have the right to defend it. He suggested that you stand in front of your construction and tell the girl to leave it alone. If she tries to push you aside after being warned, you could do one bully technique like the shin kick and then go tell the teacher. You'll probably get in trouble with the school, but you won't get in trouble with me."

"What else?" Arend asked, very surprised and interested.

I then told him what Lisa, who is an expert in teaching women's self-defense, had thought. "Lisa says that this would be considered harassment if a boy were doing it to a girl. Harassment means bothering someone on purpose over and over. Lisa suggests that, if this girl is about to attack your project, you can put your arms together in front of you to make a wall. You can then walk towards her, so that you move her away without hitting her. As you do this, you can yell out what is happening so that everybody hears you."

"Go on," Arend said.

I smiled at my son and told him about Kimberly, who is a metaphysical therapist. "Kimberly says that you could imagine a very old, wise man with an extremely long white beard sitting high on top of a mountain who you could tell your troubles to and ask for help."

"You have some very interesting friends, Mom," Arend grinned.

I had saved the funniest for last, which was an idea from Mark, who builds the protective equipment for our head-to-toe padded instructors and whose business is called Nutcase Armor. "Mark says that you could go into the bathroom and fill a toy water pistol with pee. Then, you could squirt that girl with it the next time she bothers you. I'm not suggesting this, mind you!"

With his usual exuberance, Arend roared with laughter. He kept laughing until he toppled over, holding his sides and rolling across the floor.

I heard no more about the problem after that and asked a couple weeks later how things were going.

"Oh," Arend said nonchalantly. "Ever since you told me what your friends suggested, that girl has left us alone. I didn't have to say or do anything at all."

Astonishing, I thought. Maybe something in Arend's attitude changed for this girl to stop so suddenly. Somehow just knowing that he had choices made things better.

Write Things Down. During a workshop for a youth group of twelve-year-old friends, my students wanted to know how to solve a problem with one girl in their class. "We're not supposed to leave anybody out at school, but she is so mean," they complained. "We'll be talking at lunch, and she'll interrupt to say something that hurts someone's feelings. When we tell her to stop, she says that we didn't understand her or that we are making it up."

We practiced some different speaking up tactics. The girls were doubtful about anything working, because their teacher was not willing to help. "Our teacher says that we just have to learn to get along," the girls explained. "We feel bad because we want to include this girl. We are used to having lots of different people as friends. But it's not fair to have to sit at lunch with somebody who is making putdown remarks. We can't ever just relax and have a nice conversation. Isn't there anything else we can do?"

"Well," I said. "This might not work either, but sometimes writing things down has an amazing amount of power. You could each bring little writing pads and keep them next to you at lunch. The minute this girl says something rude, pick up your journals and write it down.

"If the girl asks what you are doing, as is very likely, you can say that you are keeping track of the times she or anyone else makes putdown remarks and of exactly what she says. Tell her that, to be fair, you are also writing down what other people said before and after she made the remark. Explain that you want to document the problem because you want to have a lunchtime that is free of putdowns. Doing this might help this girl pay better attention to what she is saying and it might get your teacher to take your problem more seriously."

I didn't tell my students this, but writing things down would also make them more self-aware of their own behavior, in case that was a part of the problem.

Change the symbol. Sam uses an electric wheelchair at school because the lower half of his body is paralyzed. When I met him at age eleven, Sam had a mischievous grin, tussled sandy hair, earnest eyes, and a dynamite sense of humor. Sam told me about a new boy in the grade above his who was stepping deliberately in his way in the halls between classes. This boy kept trying to hitch a ride on the back of his wheelchair.

Sometimes just knowing you have choices can make things better.

Sam's mother looked at me anxiously and said in a worried voice, "I don't know if there is anything Sam can do. After all, he's pretty helpless."

"Hmm. Sam does not look helpless to me!" I said. "Let's start with the hitching a ride problem first. Suppose I was that boy. ... Try saying loudly, 'Do not touch my chair!'"

Sam repeated, "Do not touch my chair!" and put his hands up to make a boundary.

"Leave one hand on the controls, Sam" I said. "Now suppose that boy climbs onto your chair anyway. Can you make it go backwards suddenly?

Sam's eyes widened as I suggested, "You could say, 'Oops! I can't always control this thing!'" Sam started roaring and doubling over with laughter in the wonderful way boys his age sometimes do. We agreed that he would practice with his mother to make sure that he would just jerk backwards a little – and not run the kid over. This was supposed to be a bully technique, after all, to stop someone from bothering you rather than an emergency self-defense move that might potentially injury an attacker. Sam played soccer in his wheelchair, and I was sure he would be fine with this move.

We discussed the possibility of a sign on the back of his chair saying "Danger! Do not touch!" Sam loved the idea of his wheelchair being dangerous! Changing his wheelchair from being a symbol of "helpless" to "dangerous" changed his feelings about encountering the boy who had been bothering him in the hall from "worried" to "confident."

Figuring out Different Solutions to Bullying Problems

1 Encourage young people to tell you what they have already tried. Act out the problem so that they can show you what they are doing, in case there are ways to increase their assertiveness.

2 Brainstorm to come up with new ideas. Sometimes making up silly plans to be able to laugh at a problem is extremely effective.

3 Help young people think of the differences between safe and unsafe friends. Even if someone is very fun, encourage them to be willing to let go of a friendship if it is not working. Realize that they might need time to grieve over a lost friendship, even if the former friend was very unkind.

4 Encourage young people to document problems by writing down what happened, what they tried, and what they want to see happen. This might solve the problem and it is excellent for their writing skills.

5 Remember that it is the responsibility of adults to ensure that children and youth are in schools and activities that promote their emotional and physical safety. Remind children that, no matter how busy or tired you are, you want them to tell you when they have problems. Supervise what young people are doing, intervene if need be, and if nothing else works, consider the option of changing schools or youth activities.

With cyber-bullying, the ease of being anonymous and of reaching many people all at once can make the target feel a great sense of violation and helplessness.

Addressing Cyber-Bullying

When I first heard about cyber-bullying many years ago, it was before anyone had come up with a name for it, and it happened between adults. A friend of a friend had an anonymous e-mail about her sent out to hundreds of people at her work with false accusations and vivid hurtful personal remarks. Another man I know who is a devout Jew had a message sent to thousands of people at his company from his e-mail address with horrific Jew-bashing remarks. In both cases, the impact was devastating.

The anonymous nature and speed of the Internet, as well as text messages on cell phones have created new opportunities for bullying. Despite increased safeguards and awareness, technology-savvy kids can easily:

• Use instant messaging or text messages to reach hundreds or even thousands of people with cruel language, mean jokes, information given in confidence, or rumors;

• Create Web pages or chat rooms to make direct threats and insults or to attack the reputation and credibility of others;

• Take photos of people with a cell phone or digital camera without someone's knowledge or permission, doctor the photos to make them more embarrassing, and disperse them widely;

• Log onto someone's account, post false information, change existing information, and send out negative messages as if these came from that person; and

• Create upsetting listings about someone with insulting or threatening remarks or start rumors through on-line friend communities such as Myspace, Friendster, and Facebook.

Often young people play with technology because it seems interesting to do something just because they can. When they don't see the immediate result of their actions, they might not realize that what they are doing is destructive. Just as with other forms of bullying behavior, some kids do this to be funny, without thinking through the harm they might be doing to someone else. They tell themselves, "It's just a joke." Or, "It's just an e-mail." Others do it because they are angry or because being able to have this level of impact on someone else gives them a sense of power.

With cyber-bullying, the ease of being anonymous and of reaching many people all at once can make the person it is aimed at feel a great sense of violation and helplessness. Some adults are far less familiar with technology than their kids and become overwhelmed by the many creative ways that technology can be used to hurt, scare, or embarrass people directly and through damaging their reputation.

First of all, we need to recognize cyber-bullying for what it is — a modern version of the ancient problem of people being mean to each other. Bullying is bullying — whether it is done with paper, words, actions, or electrons. Just as with other activities, our job as adults is to know and supervise what young people are doing with technology. Remind young people that the "problems should not have to be secrets" rule applies to the use of technology. Make it very clear that use of technology is a privilege, not a right.

Here are some recommendations for addressing cyber-bullying.

Stay aware of what young people are doing with technology. Sit with children and teens so that you can see what they are doing. Stay up-to-date on what to watch out for. Your Internet provider can help you choose a system that will make it possible to monitor your children's on-line activity if you decide that this is a good idea. My personal recommendation is that adults need to be involved enough that this kind of monitoring is not necessary, but every family is different.

If you are concentrating on something else, you cannot see what kids are doing on a computer, ipod, or cell phone. To help keep this in mind, hold your own hand in front of your face and stare at your palm. Suppose that someone is right next to you doing the same thing. Do you think you can see what might be on her or his palm?

If you give your kids cell phones, make an informed decision about whether or not to allow them to use text messaging or to send and receive photos. Even if these features are included in the cell phone package, you can forbid or limit their use. These features can be fun and they can also be easily misused.

Look up the names of your children in on-line "friend's" communities and search engines to see what is listed about them. Legally, private information about people under eighteen requires parental permission to be made public, but there is no substitute for checking directly. Parents or guardians have the right to insist that their children do not put their names, photos, or other personal information anywhere on the Internet without prior permission.

Give kids the knowledge they need to make responsible choices. The message we want young people to have is that, "You are responsible for any harm done by your actions. When you communicate something either by yourself or with others – whether it is by e-mail, Web site, user group, text messaging, telephone, fax, mail, notes, conversations, drawings, facial expressions, words, gestures, photos, signs, billboards, or pony express – you are responsible for the results. The same thing is true when you throw a stone – no matter what your intentions are, you are responsible for where it lands and what damage it does."

Make sure that young people are aware that, if someone knows their password or has access to their e-mail, this person can send out messages from their e-mail address. If one person has their photo, countless people can have their photo. Anything they post on the Internet can become public information that a parent or future employer might see.

Teachers can build understanding by having students use the Internet

Cyber-bullying is a modern version of the ancient problem of people being mean to each other. Bullying is bullying – whether it is done with paper, words, actions, or electrons.

Clear rules and guidelines can prevent computer safety problems

Parents or guardians have the right to insist that their children do not put their names, photos, or other personal information anywhere on the Internet without prior permission.

to look up cyber-bullying examples and the harmful results. A school assignment could be to write an essay or make posters about what cyber-bullying is, why it is wrong, and how to stop it. Schools can have students sign pledges about not participating in any forms of bullying or harassment, including this one. Families can do the same.

Part of the solution is simply to provide information. We tell young people in our workshops that cyber-bullying is illegal. Police and other adults can usually figure out who sent the messages. Worried students often come up and ask, "It's *really* illegal? Can someone *really* tell?"

Have a plan for dealing with upsetting messages or pictures. When people see an upsetting message on their computer or wireless phone, wanting to get rid of it or to answer it are both normal responses. Instead, document the problem. Warn young people not to reply to any attacking messages, as tempting as it might be to try to defend their reputation by answering, and not to delete cyber-bullying messages, even if they are embarrassing.

Tell young people to save upsetting messages and to let you know when they think they are being cyber-bullied. Make copies of the messages to document what happened. Ask your cell phone company or your Internet provider for help on tracking down the source. Ask what their policy is and insist that they take action. Sometimes the first person you go to in a company is not that helpful so be prepared to insist on going up the chain of command until you find someone who has the authority and the skills to address the problem.

If classmates are the most likely culprits, go to the school principal and classroom teacher to report what happened. Show them the messages and ask what action they are going to take to protect your child. If they don't show concern, say, "My child's privacy and safety have been violated. We need your help." Find out what the school policy is about stopping all forms of bullying, including cyber-bullying.

If there is any kind of threat in any of the messages, report it to police.

Actions to Help Prevent and Stop Cyber-Bullying

1   *Co-Pilot With Your Child.* Many kids have more technological knowledge than their parents, but parents still have more life experience about what is safe and what is not safe. Whether your technical knowledge is a little or a lot, sit with your children and have them show you how they use the Internet and their cell phones. Co-piloting means that you go together so that you can understand how your child is using technology, stay aware of what your child is doing, and agree on safety rules.

2   *Keep technology use public rather than private.* Whether your children are texting on a cell phone, doing social networking even through school-approved activities, exploring the Internet, or using e-mail, stay aware of what they are doing, whom they are doing it with, and where they are going. Know how often and how long your child is spending using technology rather than doing other things such as sleeping, being with people, reading, exercising, etc.

3 *Discuss the issue.* Ask children and youth what they already know about cyber-bullying. You might be amazed at how much they can tell you. Ask if this has ever happened to them or anyone they know. Make sure that the young people in your life know that:

- Cyber-bullying means using computers, wireless phones, social networks, and other technology to hurt, scare, or embarrass other people. It is illegal and unethical.
- Being mean is being mean, no matter how you do it. Don't ask if it's funny. Ask if it will make someone unhappy.
- Even if you think someone was mean to you, being mean back is not a safe way to handle the problem. Instead, get help from an adult you trust.
- Have the courage to *speak up* if you notice anyone cyber-bullying. Say that this is wrong and that you are *not* going to keep it a secret.
- Never post anything on the Internet or send something electronically that you don't want the world to see.
- If you get an upsetting message or see something that is attacking you: *Do not reply. Do not delete. Save* the message, print it if you can and *get help* from an adult you trust. If one adult does not help you, keep asking until you get the help you need.

4 *Be clear about the rules.* The use of computers for anything except schoolwork is a privilege. The use of wireless phones for anything except for emergencies and communication with parents is also a privilege. These privileges will be lost if they are used for unsafe or hurtful purposes. You expect your children to stay in charge of what they say and do, to tell you about problems, and to get your agreement in advance about any changes. Make a clear, written contract using the *Communication Technology Youth Safety Contract*[19] available on the Kidpower website or by creating your own.

5 *Stay involved.* Spend time with young people so that you know what they are doing. Do fun things together that do not involve the use of technology.

6 *Be careful.* Unless this is within a secure system of people who know each other, such as a school, do not allow your children to post personal information or photos in an on-line social network or website.

7 *Give consequences.* If your child bullies, whether through technology or by some other means, have the child apologize and make amends. Give an appropriate related consequence, depending on what happened. Be prepared to pull the plug on all uses of technology for a specific period of time, so that the concept that this use is a privilege, not a right, is reinforced.

8 *Provide help.* If your child is hurt by cyber-bullying, give the child emotional support by saying, "I am so sorry this is happening to you and so proud of you for having the courage to tell me. This is not your fault, and we are going to do what we can to make it stop." Ask for help from school authorities, your Internet provider or cell phone company, and, if necessary, the police.

9 *Practice.* Use ideas from the *Being Brave to Stop Bullying* and *Speaking Up About Prejudice* sections above to define what cyber-bullying might look like, how to speak up, what a negative reaction might be, and what an effective response could be. Let children make up their own story to use for the practice. Switch roles with them.

For example, a friend might say, "I can't stand Roger. Look, I got a photo of him going to the bathroom on the field trip. Let's see how many people we can send this to."

One way to speak up could be: "That's cyber-bullying. It's wrong."

A common negative reaction to this boundary is, "But you have to admit that it would be funny."

An effective response might be, "Even though Roger is not my favorite person, I don't think it is funny to embarrass people. Besides, it is illegal."

Make sure that you tell young people repeatedly that you want to know when they have problems and that you listen compassionately to their answers.

How to Tell if Your Child Is Being Bullied

Sometimes children and teens will tell their adults right away if they have a problem with being bullied. Sometimes they will suffer in silence until they suddenly break down. Make sure that you tell the young people in your life repeatedly that you want to know when they have problems, and that you listen compassionately to their answers.

Symptoms of being bullied might include:
• Having trouble sleeping;
• Having upset stomachs on school mornings;
• Being fearful about going to school or other youth activities;
• Coming home acting sad, gloomy, irritable, or unhappy;
• Coming home with unexplained bruises, cuts, and scratches;
• Being worried, anxious, or depressed;
• Saying mean things about her or himself or sounding hopeless; and/or
• Coming home with torn or damaged clothing, books, or other possessions.

What To Do If Your Child is Being Bullied at School

We hear countless stories from upset parents about kids from toddlers to teenagers being victimized at school.

"My thirteen-year-old son is a good kid who has never been in trouble. Sports are really important to him. A group of boys are always taunting him after games. Recently, he tried to argue with them instead of walking away. After these boys hit him a couple of times, he hit back. Now he is kicked off his team. When I tried to talk with the school administrators, they believed the other boys and not him."

"My eleven-year-old daughter was teased because she has a disability. The teacher stopped the bullying, but never told my daughter that this was not her fault and never informed her father or me. Our daughter came home confused and worried, thinking that she was in trouble for causing a controversy."

"My twelve-year-old son endured months of another boy making up stories that were supposedly just for fun, but that used his name as the anti-hero who was getting blown up or falling into pits or having things fall on him. The intention was clearly to humiliate my son. By the time he finally told me what was happening, he was failing his classes."

"My daughter goes to the first grade and likes to wear dresses. A couple of boys in her class started a game they called humping, where they sandwiched my little girl between them, pulling up her dress, trapping her and acting as if they were having sex with her. When I complained to the school, they talked with the boys, who are now calling my daughter names like 'stupid baby' and 'tattletale.'"

"When my daughter reported that she saw a gun at school, the boy who had the gun was expelled. But this boy's friends have started threatening my daughter in subtle ways that are hard to address. They make gestures like pointing their fingers as if they are shooting at her. They try to walk a little too close to her, almost knocking her down."

"My twelve-year-old son is young emotionally but looks older physically. Girls in his class are constantly making sexual remarks about his body, his clothes and what he says. He comes home feeling embarrassed and is starting to hate going to school."

School is a big part of children's lives. Because decisions about how and where children get an education are the responsibility of adults, the children themselves have no choice about being there. As caring adults, we expect schools to provide an environment that is emotionally and physically safe for our children.

Here are the steps to take if your child or teen has a bullying problem at school:

1. *Stay Calm.* As a parent, it is normal to feel terrified and enraged about any kind of threat to the well-being of your child. You probably want to fix the problem immediately and maybe to punish the people who caused your child to be hurt, embarrassed, or scared.

Instead of acting upset, your job is to act calm. If your child tells you about a problem, take a big breath and say in a quiet, matter-of-fact voice, "I am so glad you are telling me this. I am sorry that this happened to you. Please tell me more about exactly what happened so we can figure out what to do. You deserve to feel safe and comfortable at school." If your child did not tell you but you found out some other way, say calmly, "I saw this happen/ heard about this happening. It looked/sounded like it might be unpleasant for you. Can you tell me more about it?"

Remember, if you act upset, your child is likely to get upset, too. She or he might want to protect you and her/himself from your reaction by not telling you about problems in the future or by denying that anything is wrong. The older a child is, the more important it is that the child is able to feel some control about any follow-up actions you might take with the school.

In addition, if you act upset when you are approaching school officials or the parents of children who are bothering your child, they are likely to become defensive. Nowadays, school administrators are often fearful of lawsuits, both from the parents of the child who was victimized and from the parents of the child who was accused of causing the problem. This is a real fear because a lawsuit can seriously drain the already limited resources of their school. At the same time, most school administrators are deeply committed and truly want to address problems that affect the well-being of their students. They are far more likely to respond positively to parents who are approaching them in an objective and respectful way.

We need to keep in mind that it is a difficult job that teachers and

In my experience, most teachers and administrators are good people who are trying to keep their students as safe, happy, and healthy as possible.

administrators are doing. They are responsible for a large community of students and are often understaffed and have limited resources. Students come to them from many different backgrounds and life situations. Teachers do not get to decide which students they will have in their classrooms and are often dealing with children and families with emotional and physical problems. In my experience most teachers and administrators are good people who are trying to keep their students as safe, happy, and healthy as possible. It is normal to feel very upset, anxious, and angry when you are worried about your child's well-being, but it is important to remember that the professional educators who are responsible for your child during the day are normally caring individuals who deserve to be treated in a respectful way.

No matter how good a job you do, some people will react badly when they are first told about a problem. Don't let that stop you. Stay focused on your purpose, which is to explain what happened and what you want to see changed.

2. *Get the whole story.* It is important not to jump to conclusions or make assumptions. Ask questions of your child in a calm, reassuring way. Ask questions of other people who might be involved, making it clear that your goal is to understand and figure out how to address the problem rather than to get even with anybody.

3. *Look for solutions, not for blame.* Once you understand the situation, your goal is to find ways to repair any harm that was done and to prevent future problems. Try to assume that teachers and school administrators are overwhelmed and doing their best. They deserve support and acknowledgement for what they are doing right as well as to be told in a respectful way what is wrong.

Try to look at the issue from all perspectives. Is the problem caused because the school needs more resources in order to supervise children properly during recess and lunch or before and after school? Does the school need help formulating a clear policy that makes behavior that threatens, hurts, scares, or embarrasses others against the rules? Does your child need help to develop more effective communication skills? Does the child who harmed your child need help too?

4. *Make a plan to prevent future problems.* If the school doesn't have a clear plan in place for handling incidents, help them develop one. A plan should include:

• Stopping the behavior by a direct intervention and by making it clear that this behavior is against school rules;

• Protecting the student who was being bullied from further bullying or retaliation;

• Giving appropriate consequences to the student(s) who did the bullying, depending on the nature of the bullying and the age of the children involved. If nothing else works, kids who cannot stop themselves from being hurtful towards others need to be sent to the principal's office. The principal can involve parents and possibly other resource people in making a plan to change this behavior;

• Giving reassurance to the student who was bullied that what happened was not her or his fault, even though people got in trouble for it;

• If the teacher's perception is that both parties are contributing to the problem, have both parties use a conflict resolution process to work things out and do role-playing of how to use personal safety skills to handle the problem differently in the future;

• Notifying the parents of all parties that the incident occurred and what was done about it; and

• Making the training and availability of resources for their staff, parents, and students a priority.

Young people deserve to be in an environment that is emotionally and physically safe. Concerned parents can help schools find, fund, and implement age-appropriate programs that make a sustained school-wide commitment to creating a culture of safety, respect, and caring rather than of competition, harassment, and disregard.

5. *Protect your child for the long run.* Try to keep the big picture in mind as well as the immediate problem. What protecting your child means will vary depending on the ability of the school to resolve the problem, the nature of the problem, and on your child's needs.

Children and teens can learn to walk away from people who are bothering them, to protect themselves emotionally and physically, and to ask for help sooner rather than later. Make practicing these skills a priority and consider training such as the kind we provide in our Kidpower and Teenpower workshops. In some cases, protecting your child might mean that you work together with the teacher, the school administrator, the parents of the other child, and all children involved to create a realistic plan to stop the problem. In other cases, the best solution for your child might be to change schools.

6. *Get emotional support.* Don't ignore the feelings that come up, even if the problem is solved. Give support to the child in the moment, get support for yourself, and pay attention to whether these feelings persist. A few studies have indicated that some people have post-traumatic stress syndrome because of bullying. Sometimes the harassing and bullying of your child can bring up feelings from bad experiences out of your own past. Parents often have to deal with guilt for not preventing the problem and sometimes struggle with rage. Getting support might mean talking issues over with other caring adults who can listen to you and your child with perspective and compassion. Getting support might mean going to a therapist or talking with counselors provided by the school or by other agencies.

7. *Be realistic.* As parents, it is normal to want to protect our children from all harm. However, if we monitor their lives so closely that they never

Upsetting experiences do not have to lead to long-term damage if kids are listened to respectfully, if the problem is resolved, and if their feelings are supported.

fall, never fail, and never get hurt or sad, then we would be depriving our children of having the room to grow. Upsetting experiences do not have to lead to long-term damage if children are listened to respectfully, if the problem is resolved, and if their feelings are supported. Young people can take charge of their safety by learning skills for preventing and stopping harassment themselves by setting boundaries, avoiding people whose behavior is problematic, and getting help when they need it.

What if My Child Is Bullying Other Kids?

Most parents want their kids to be respectful to others and they worry when they are not. Three typical worries are:

- "Sometimes my son calls other kids names and pushes them around to get what he wants."
- "My daughter encourages her friends to leave another girl out. They even tried making up stories to get her into trouble."
- "My kids are angels at school and mean to each other at home."

Here are some ways that parents can help stop their children from bullying others.

1. *Have a strong, affectionate, and mutually respectful relationship with your children.* There is nothing more important in your life than your children. Have fun together. Give them the gift of your time. It's the only gift that will count in the long run. Model being a positive powerful leader. Make it clear that you are in charge, but involve children in decision-making when you can. Accept their right to have all their feelings, even though they have to learn to manage their behavior. Do the best you can to model the behavior you want them to have and acknowledge when you make mistakes.

A child who is being bullied by a sibling at home might turn around and bully other kids at school. Get help if you aren't sure what to do or feel stuck. Two parenting classics written by Adele Faber and Elaine Mazlish are *How to Talk so Kids Will Listen and Listen so Kids Will Talk*[20] and *Siblings Without Rivalry.*[21]

2. *Make the rules clear.* Show your kids that bullying behavior is not okay with you at home, at school, or anywhere you go. You want to know about it and you want to find ways to stop it. Even if other people let their children behave that way, it is not okay with you for your children to behave that way. Even if other important adults in their lives behave that way, this is not the example you want your child to copy. Especially until children can tell you what happens when they are away from you, make sure that the people supervising your children have the same standards that you do.

3. *Be realistic.* Bullying behavior in a child or teen does not automatically mean that this young person has a permanent character flaw. Remember that grabbing what you want, ganging up on other people, being mean to be funny, and getting back at someone for perceived wrongs is normal behavior and is modeled for children all the time. The solution is to help young people to develop better social skills, more empathy, and better

impulse control. Until they are able to manage themselves, young people need adult supervision.

4. *Pay attention.* Stop bullying behavior sooner rather than later. If you want to give children the chance to handle the problem themselves, monitor the situation and step in to help them to be successful. Reminders of rules and coaching in the moment are far more effective than just letting children flounder on their own.

5. *Try to figure out why.* The purpose of knowing why is neither to blame nor to excuse, but to help you find effective solutions. Is this child still very young and learning? Did she forget? Was he not clear about the rules? Did she lose her temper? Does he lack problem-solving skills? Does she need to learn how to stop herself? Does he need to learn how to see the other person's point of view? Is the child copying someone else?

6. *Have clear consequences.* Consequences should be framed as logical outcomes for the behavior rather than as punishments. For example:

• Apologizing;
• Making amends by doing a chore for the person who was bullied;
• Writing a letter or drawing a picture to show understanding of why this behavior is a problem;
• Role-playing what happened and practicing how to behave more safely in the future;
• Sitting down for a few minutes to think things over instead of playing;
• Coming inside to be with the adult and away from other kids for a little while; and
• Losing some privilege like watching television or playing on the computer for a specific time period.

Do your best not to be angry when you give consequences. Be thoughtful. Avoid repeated threats of consequences that the child will see as negative. Instead, give one warning or reminder and then follow through. You want children to see you as having the integrity of meaning what you say and the fairness of having the consequence fit the behavior. If both children created the problem, both children should have the consequences of at least practicing how they could have handled this situation more safely.

Sometimes bullying grows out of a dynamic between two kids. They might have developed patterns of bothering each other that lead to problems. With help, young people can usually learn how to identify a negative pattern, notice when it starts to happen, and find ways to change their behavior.

One mother told me that after reading and practicing the skills in our *Kidpower Safety Comics*[22] with her two sons, she overheard the older one yell at the younger one, who had intruded in his room, "Use your Walk Away Power right now! I am using my Hands Down Power! I mean RIGHT NOW!" The younger son walked away and a fight was avoided.

7. *Be prepared for resistance.* Kids might deny what happened even if you saw everything – not because they are deliberately lying, but because they

Reminders of rules and coaching in the moment are far more effective than just letting children flounder on their own.

Empathy

With help, children can usually learn how to identify a negative pattern, notice when it starts to happen, and find ways to change their behavior.

don't want to feel like they are bad and selective memory screens things out. Young people might say, "I don't care!" – not because they don't care, but because they don't want to feel bad. They might say, "I hate you!" – not because they don't love you, but because they hate having you tell them what to do. They might blame the other person – not because they really believe this, but because they don't want to have to blame themselves. Your kids might need you to set their boundaries for them because they have not yet learned to set boundaries within themselves.

When kids resist, parents can acknowledge their feelings and re-state the expectation. Sometimes people of any age need a little time to themselves to cool off before they are ready to listen.

8. *Help young people develop "People Safety" and other social-emotional skills.* Give children and teens the chance to practice some of the personal safety skills described in this book in order to stop themselves from bullying. For example, you might have a child practice throwing a mean word in the trash can instead of getting caught up in name-calling. You might have a child practice walking away and getting help instead of getting into a fight. As they become old enough to understand, you can teach children about different kinds of bullying and why this is wrong.

Younger children need to learn how to ask for what they want instead of grabbing. People of all ages need to learn how to negotiate win-win solutions. Disappointments are part of life and learning how to handle them without being destructive includes learning how to calm down and think first when you are upset, learning to wait your turn, and finding other things to do when you cannot get what you want.

Learning to understand other points of view is a major life skill. Most young people can develop empathy for others by hearing stories that inspire them to care, by understanding their feelings, by having shared experiences with people who are different than they are, and by being treated with empathy themselves.

Should I Say Anything to the Parents of a Child Who Is Bullying Mine?

The right answer to this question depends on the individuals involved and how important this relationship is to you or to your child. Some parents definitely want to know and will be very thankful. Others might get upset and start blaming their child, your child, or you. What kind of a relationship do you have? What do you know about this person? Is this something that you are best off doing with the help of a neutral person such as the principal or teacher? Do you think that this parent already knows or not?

When possible, find ways to take charge of the environment your child is in. You can work with your child's youth group, sports team, dance club, or school to ensure that there is a written policy about bullying and educate everyone about what it means, including parents and kids. Keep an eye out on how things are going and step in when you see a problem. Rather than seeing this as disciplining another person's child, take the position that you are ensuring safe behavior of all the children according to the policies the adults have agreed on. Instead of asking children why they have done something hurtful, just set a specific boundary, such as, "Please stop. Leaving people out/saying mean things/pushing is against the rules here."

If you decide to approach the parent, start with appreciation. For example, you might say something like, "I appreciate all you do for our kids and think your daughter is a lovely girl and a natural leader. However, I worry that she is experimenting with negative uses of her power in a way that is often hurtful to my daughter. Sometimes she _____ (leaves people out/etc.). I'd like your help to make a plan where we can intervene when that happens in a way that is supportive to everyone.

Try to avoid labels like "bullying" and stay with the specific facts. For example, "I have something to tell you that is uncomfortable. I am doing this because I would want someone to tell me if the situation were reversed. My daughter says that she doesn't want to come to your house anymore because your son keeps hurting her. Games that start out fun often get too rough, and your son has a hard time listening when my daughter tells him to stop. Also, your son tries to stop my daughter from playing with other kids."

Parents who don't know what to do often minimize their child's bullying behavior. No matter how carefully and kindly you express your concern, don't be surprised if this parent says something attacking about you or your child. Practice what you are going to say out loud ahead of time. Be prepared for negative reactions so you can persist in stating your concern in a positive way.

Don't try to argue. Just say, "Thank you for telling me." This parent might get upset. Stay calm and say something like, "I don't mean to upset you. Again, I am putting myself in your shoes and doing what I would want you to do for me. It is normal for children to have trouble with boundaries sometimes."

Be prepared to offer support. Listen compassionately if this parent expresses frustration or despair in how to help her or his child. Mention

"Your daughter is a natural leader, and I am worried that she is experimenting with negative uses of her power in a way that is hurtful to my daughter."

books, parenting classes, and other resources that have been helpful to you.

What If A Child's Teacher Is Doing the Bullying?

Most teachers are extremely caring individuals, but a few misuse their power. They might be sarcastic, demeaning, or otherwise act in ways that tear down the self-esteem of a child. Parents need to monitor potential problems with adults in the same way that they monitor other types of bullying behavior.

Take the time to observe what is actually happening in your child's classroom and on the schoolyard. Listen when your child complains about the teacher "being mean" and brainstorm solutions. Sometimes all that a child needs is a sympathetic ear.

If you do think that your child's teacher is behaving in a bullying way, don't let it go. It is poor modeling to excuse rude behavior by saying, "That's just the way she or he is." Instead, insist that the professionals caring for your children keep their temper, express their own boundaries firmly and politely, and set a good example of respectful powerful adult leadership.

If you think that there is a problem, remember that acting upset can be counter-productive. Reach out to your child's teacher with your concerns. Use any problems as an opportunity to model speaking up and being clear about boundaries.

How Can We Address Bullying in Sports?

One of my friends told me about her son who had just started high school and was on the football team. With their coach watching during the practices, the older players bullied and harassed the younger players, pushing them around and calling them names, the least offensive of which was "wimp." And, as my friend watched the first game, she saw several parents losing control and screaming insults at the other team and at the coaches.

What do kids learn about character, discipline, and teamwork when they see adults acting this way? What do they learn about commitment to stopping bullying when their coaches don't make rude remarks and threatening behavior on the part of all the players against the rules? – or even participate by shouting insults and making snide remarks themselves?

What would kids learn instead if they saw their coaches modeling powerful, respectful leadership by stopping inappropriate behavior with the same commitment that they would stop someone from breaking the rules of the game? What would they learn if their parents were supportive to them no matter how they played and acted respectfully to everyone? In other words, what if everyone acted like "good sports" instead of "bad sports?"

One excellent resource for reducing bullying in sports is the Positive Coaching Alliance[23], a nonprofit organization that provides training for coaches and parents in how to make character-building the primary goal of participation in sports, along with learning to play well. Clear agreements and understanding about expectations are essential to changing a culture of bullying to one of respect, caring, and safety for everyone. However, adults also need to follow through on setting boundaries to uphold these rules.

During our Kidpower workshop, "Ron", a volunteer coach, asked me for advice on how to deal with bullying parents who were screaming at coaches, including some young teens, even after signing the Parent's Pledge recommended by the Positive Coaching Alliance. With a sigh of exasperation, Ron said, "At the children's soccer games that I coach, we do our best to keep our team members from bullying each other or kids from other teams. But sometimes the kids' parents will start screaming insults and threats at our coaches because they disagree with some decision. Even if they've signed pledges not to, some parents believe that acting this way and booing players is part of sports. What should we do?"

"Why are you coaching children's soccer?" I asked. "This is a volunteer job, right? Is your goal to have children learn to win or for some other reason?"

"I like to coach because team sports build character and discipline," Ron said.

"What are kids learning about discipline and character when they see their adults closing control and behaving abusively?" I asked. "Perhaps the best learning that these young people might gain is by seeing you and the other coaches modeling positive respectful firm leadership."

We role-played the problem. Ron pretended to be an upset parent and yelled at me, "How dare you do that! I'm going to report you."

I calmly replied, "I am following our rules. You are welcome to tell anyone you wish that you disagree! Now please sit down so we can continue the game!"

Ron said that they also have many young teenagers who volunteer to coach. "It's awful," he explained, "when a 35-year-old man starts yelling at a twelve-year-old, 'What gives YOU the right to make this decision?'"

I pointed out that volunteering to be the coach *does* give someone the right to make decisions and that, as unfortunate as it is that a few people act this way, learning how to deal with upset people is an exceptional leadership skill. We discussed how to establish a system to make sure that parents signed pledges about respectful behavior and fair play that included some clearly defined consequences if they refused to honor these pledges. We also explored ways to prepare coaches to protect themselves by:

• Imagining throwing the hurting words away into a trash can and giving themselves a compliment.
• Imagining using an emotional raincoat that would protect them from anger.
• Identifying common attacking comments and practicing calm firm answers.

The emotional raincoat technique can be practiced in partners. Without touching, one person starts screaming, "BLAH! BLAH! BLAH!" while acting

The best learning that young people can gain in sports about character and discipline is seeing their parents and coaches modeling positive, firm, powerful adult leadership.

True friendships make life rich and joyful

very angry. The other person stays calm, keeps facing the angry person in ready position, with hands holding a whistle, and saying in a firm respectful voice, "I am sorry you are upset. We can agree to disagree. I see it differently and it's my call. It's my job to keep everyone safe here. Please sit down so that we can play."

How Can Kids Tell the Difference Between Someone Acting Friendly or Being a True Friend?

We hear many sad stories about young people who were confused by others who pretended to be friendly in order to get their way, but whose actual intent was to get something from them or even to cause them harm. Here are typical examples:

One kindergarten teacher said, *"A few of my students are so charismatic that all the other kids want to be friends with them. Sometimes they will try to control other children by saying that they will only be their friend if they agree not to play with anyone else. I tell my students that real friends don't try to stop you from having other friends."*

One mother said, *"My seven-year-old daughter got into big trouble because a girl she really liked trashed the school bathroom by throwing paper towels into the toilets and sinks. This girl said that, since my daughter was her friend, my daughter had to blame another one of their classmates for making this mess."*

One father said, *"My ten-year-old son keeps getting tricked into doing another kid's homework because he wants so much to be accepted by him."*

One middle school boy said, *"Some girls in our school go along with sex because they want to be popular. I feel bad because some guys tell these girls how much they care about them and then make horrible jokes about what sluts they are behind their backs."*

One teacher of a developmentally delayed teen said, *"Kids in his neighborhood pretended to be his friends and then persuaded him to steal my cell phone because they told him they needed the money."*

No matter how old or young you are, people who deliberately use the trappings of friendship to get you to lower your boundaries and do what they want can break your heart.

Both children and adults need to know that someone who smiles at you, says kind things to you, does nice things for you, and seems funny might be enjoyable to be with, but that this friendly behavior by itself does not make this person a trustworthy friend. At the same time, having misunderstandings and crossing boundaries are normal communication problems in important relationships. Also, sometimes people change, and friendships that worked for a while stop working.

The reality is that some mistakes are probably unavoidable. You have to be willing to take some risks in order to get to know someone well enough to decide whether or not to keep this person as a friend.

So, how do you tell the difference between someone who is behaving in a way that is likable and someone who is going to be a good bet as a friend?

You have to judge by what a person does not just part of the time, but all of the time, and not just with you, but with everyone, in order to figure out whether or not someone is going to be a friend you can count on. Here are six questions that you can ask yourself- and teach kids to ask themselves - to help decide whether or not someone is being a good friend.

1. Does this person do things that are important to both of you? Or, does this person run hot and cold – acting glad to see you when she or he wants something from you, but getting mad and saying you are a bad friend if you want to do something else?

2. Does this person encourage you to do things that are in your best interests? Or, does this person try to use your feelings of friendship to pressure you into wasting your time or money, breaking rules, getting into trouble, doing something dangerous, or hurting someone else?

3. Does this person speak and act respectfully towards you no matter who else is around? Or, does this person sometimes make unkind jokes or ignore you in order to be popular with others?

4. Does this person try to tell the truth, apologize for mistakes, and keep commitments most of the time? Or, does this person blame others for his or her mistakes, lie, and break promises over and over?

5. Does this person treat others with kindness and respect? Or, is this person cruel to some people – or nice to their faces and mean behind their backs? Remember that what someone does to someone else, sooner or later, this person is very likely to do to you.

6. Is this person willing to work problems out? Or, does this person ignore problems and then explode or act ready to give up on the friendship as soon as something goes wrong?

The bottom line is that we all deserve to have healthy relationships in our lives and that healthy relationships take work. No matter how friendly someone acts and no matter how much we might like to be with this person, we need to decide whether this person is behaving in a way that is that is going to make our lives better or worse.

Suppose that you decide that someone you often enjoy is also often not acting like a good friend. Depending on the situation, here are some choices for what you can do:

• *Speak up about the problem in a clear, respectful way.* People often don't see the impact of their behavior on others unless it's pointed out to them. You can't know what will happen unless you let this person know that this behavior is not okay with you.

No matter how friendly someone acts and no matter how much we might like to be with this person, we need to decide whether this person is acting in a way that is that is going to make our lives better or worse.

• *Become unavailable.* You can decide to spend your attention and time with someone else. Many shy people do not act that friendly at first, but, once you get past the surface, can be interesting and fun.

• *Pick and choose.* Many people are great to be with at some times and best to avoid at other times. You can decide when to hang out with someone and when not to.

• *End the friendship.* Sometimes the only way to end a friendship is to tell yourself that the friendship is over. Usually just being unavailable works, especially if you've tried to solve the problem and that didn't work. But once in a while, you might need to say something like, "I really appreciate the fun times we've had, but I've decided that it won't work for me to stay friends with you. I wish you very well and hope for the best for you, but won't be spending time with you any more."

Strong, true friendships make life rich and joyful. They give lasting memories, provide strength and comfort during difficult times, and help both friends to grow and to have fun. They deserve time, attention, and effort. But, that effort should help everyone grow stronger and closer. We can help young people build strong, meaningful friendships by making healthy decisions about who our own friends are and by encouraging them to choose – and to tend – their own friendships kindly and thoughtfully.

Chapter Nine

Protecting Children from Sexual Abuse

Kidpower Founding Board President Ellen Bass has been an author, poet and writing teacher for many years. Her book, *I Never Told Anyone*[1], first published in 1983, was inspired by students in her "Writing About Our Lives" workshops, who, to Ellen's surprise, began to write about the sexual abuse they had experienced as children. Response to this book ultimately led Ellen to co-authoring *The Courage to Heal*. Though we have a long way to go, thanks to the work of Ellen and many others, the issue of child abuse is much more visible than it used to be. Through this increasing awareness, we are far better prepared to recognize potential abuse so we can protect our children from harm.

Over the years, I have heard stories from hundreds of adults about how having their boundaries violated when they were kids diminished their trust and joy in life. Often the abuse would take place right under the noses of their adults.

• "My piano teacher was brilliant, and I loved learning from him. But as I got a little older, he started giving me the creeps in the way he placed my hands, looked at my breasts, and talked to me. I didn't know how to explain to my parents what was wrong. I finally stopped playing the piano, even though I was really good at it, and it took years before I could enjoy it again."

• "At family gatherings, my uncle would pull me playfully onto his lap and have an erection. I thought it was somehow my fault and was too embarrassed to tell anyone."

Abuse is committed by women as well as by men. In E.L. Konigsburg's excellent teen book, "*Silent to the Bone*," an au pair seduces a young teen boy in order to emotionally coerce him to not say anything about her neglect of his baby half-sister.[2]

Kids don't want to upset their parents, and emotional adult reactions when they learn about sexual abuse or even sexual play can also cause children to feel alone, unworthy, and filled with shame.

• "When I told my mom that our neighbor had grabbed my breast and tried to get me to touch his crotch, she went on and on to everyone about how my innocence had been destroyed. I wish I'd never said anything."

• "When we were five, my cousin wrestled with me to the floor and started pretending to have sex. I thought we were just playing, but my mother was so horrified that she wouldn't let us play alone together ever again.

Kids don't want to upset their parents, and emotional adult reactions when they learn about sexual abuse or even sexual play can also cause children to feel alone, unworthy, and filled with shame.

With adult protection and their own skills, kids can enjoy our beautiful world with safety and confidence!

I felt terrible every time the memory came back in my mind - which was often, because my mom kept talking about it."

• "When we were three-years-old, my friend and I started playing doctor by taking off each other's clothes and checking out our differences. My dad discovered us and started shouting that we were bad and were going to go to hell if we did it again. Every time the picture pops into my mind, even forty years later, I feel overwhelmed with humiliation."

As caring adults, our challenge is to protect children from people who might try to molest them, redirect inappropriate play between kids without shaming anyone, give kids skills to stop unsafe touch or attention, and be safe people for kids to talk with about their problems. No matter how busy we are, we must pay attention and stay in charge of the people caring for our kids. No matter how uncomfortable we feel, we must speak up when we see or hear anything that bothers us and take action to address potential concerns.

We can teach children what their safety rules are; how to set boundaries; how to resist emotional coercion, bribes, and threats; and how to get adult help when they need it. When they have these skills, young people are far less likely to be chosen as victims by a molester – and far better prepared to put a stop to abuse if it happens.

What Is Child Abuse?

Professionals often use the word "abuse" to describe behavior that is harmful to another person. In the United States, the Child Abuse Prevention and Treatment Act defines child abuse and neglect as, "at a minimum, any recent act or failure to act on the part of a parent or caretaker, which results in death, serious physical or emotional harm, sexual abuse or exploitation, or an act or failure to act which presents an imminent risk of serious harm."[3] A child is defined for legal purposes in this act as being someone under the age of eighteen. Family members, caregivers, acquaintances, close friends, and strangers all have the potential to cause harm to children and teens who are vulnerable to them.

This harm can take many different forms, including:

• *Physical abuse* – hitting, kicking, pushing, crowding, burning, pinching, or threatening to do any of these things.
• *Sexual abuse* – sexual touching, sexual language, showing or taking sexual photographs or videotapes, or sexualization of a child. Sexualizing a child could include comments or attention focused on the child's sexuality or private body parts, asking about or sharing details of sexual experiences, etc.
• *Emotional abuse* – mean teasing, threatening, mimicking, belittling, name-calling, shunning, or objectifying. Objectifying means treating someone as an object rather than a person with rights.
• *Neglect* – failure by responsible adults to meet a child's basic needs physically, educationally, or emotionally.

Any of these experiences can be damaging to someone of any age, particularly to a child who has less power and rights than an adult and who is dependent on adult care. Just witnessing abusive or violent behavior, especially from family members, is also hurtful to children. Children can be harmed by watching someone else, especially someone they love and care about, being abused or mistreated, even if they are not being abused themselves.

With so much attention being paid to child abuse, people often wonder if things are much worse than they used to be. There is a great deal more to be done, but the reality is children and women have far more rights now than in the past. Behavior that we now call "abusive" used to be accepted as "normal." Sexual abuse of children used to be reported far less because so many people didn't know the words to describe what was happening – or were too ashamed to speak up about the problems they saw and experienced. We have better social mechanisms for identifying, reporting, and addressing sexual abuse today than we did in the past. Research in the US is actually showing a decrease in overall abuse.[4]

What is Sexual Abuse?
Sexual abuse takes place when someone with more power misuses a child for sexual gratification. This includes any sexual activity between an adult and a minor or between one minor with more power and another with less power. Sexual abuse can seem particularly destructive because our society adds the burden of secrecy and shame to this crime. Survivors often feel for years that what happened was somehow their fault. Molesters often persuade children that they "asked for it" or "wanted it."

Sometimes people internalize their abuse and do things that are destructive to themselves. A few externalize their abuse and become perpetrators of abuse to other children. Survivors often say things like, "I felt completely alone ... It was a terrible betrayal ... It was so awful that I made myself forget in order to function ... I couldn't form healthy relationships and didn't know why ... I have eating disorders ... The pain inside was so big that I abused alcohol and drugs ... I am terrified to trust anyone with the safety of my own children."

According to Kidpower Senior Instructor John Luna-Sparks, LCSW and clinician with the Child Protection Center at Children's Hospital and Research Center Oakland[5], "Child sexual abuse is a horrible act AND most children will recover from it. When adults discover a child they love has been abused, they might feel hopeless and worry that their child is damaged and will not be able to recover. However, most children when given appropriate support can work through the harm that has happened to them. Depending on their age at the time, they will likely remember the abuse for life, but the feelings of fear, sadness, anger, and shame can turn into feelings of safety, pride, strength, and confidence.

"Also, not all children require intensive psychotherapy following abuse. For some children, just the belief and support of their caregivers as well as the abuse being put to a stop is enough for them to recover. For other children, the help of a trained therapist or other medical professional is crucial. Adult caregivers may also need to seek emotional help for

"Most children when given appropriate support can work through the harm that has happened to them."

themselves to help them to support their child as well as possible. What is important is to make sure to get the help necessary for you and your child, whatever that help is."

Perceived Misuse Versus Actual Abuse

The word "abuse" has become so loaded that making a distinction between behavior that is experienced as abusive and actual child abuse can be useful for the times when children have to do things that are not their choice. We occasionally provide trainings to physical and occupational therapists who work with kids often in one-on-one sessions and manipulate their bodies in ways that are intrusive, uncomfortable, and painful. Some children will even complain, "You are abusing me!"

We encourage these dedicated professionals to use this interaction as a teaching moment by saying things like, "I'm sorry that this hurts you and understand that you don't like it. You can tell me and tell everybody how you feel. This touch is for your health. It is not a choice, and it is not a secret." If they need to touch a child's bottom or other private areas, we have them practice saying, "Now, I need to clean your bottom. This is for your health, and you can tell everybody."

Most of us have said or done things that other people have felt mistreated by and experienced as abusive. And we have all had other people say or do things that we have felt to be abusive.

When children learn new language and skills, experimentation is normal. As one attorney told us, "My ten-year-old daughter Misha refused to get off the computer so her brother could do his homework. I told Misha that the consequence would be no computer games for a week. She was furious! 'I'm going to report you!' she announced. 'I am going to call the police and tell them that you are guilty of child abuse because you will not let your poor child use the computer!' Thanks to your training, I didn't laugh or put my daughter down. Instead, I told Misha sympathetically that she had a right to her feelings and could tell anyone she wanted – but that she still was not going to be allowed to play on the computer for a week."

In this particular home, the use of the label "abuse" didn't go very far. However, I have seen some adults become utterly horrified by being accused of "abuse" and give in – when what they were actually doing was appropriate care, setting boundaries, or speaking up for themselves.

The reality is that most of us have said or done things that other people have felt mistreated by and experienced as abusive. And we have all had other people say or do things that we have felt to be abusive. Often this happens with the people closest to us.

Any intrusion by someone else into the boundaries of our personal space, time, bodies, feelings, and spirits can seem abusive. We know at the time or realize later that someone did something against our wishes. The process of figuring out when we can or should say "yes" or "no" to others is likely to continue during our whole lives and to keep changing. However, where perceived misuse crosses the line and becomes a crime depends on what the intent was, whether any damage was done, the nature of the behavior, the age of both parties, and the laws of the state or country where it occurs.

Addressing Child Abuse Issues

1   Make a distinction between behavior that children dislike and behavior that is damaging. Accept children's right to have whatever feelings they have about things that bother them rather than making fun of them or getting mad at them for having these feelings. Remind children that, even if something is not their choice, anything that bothers them should never have to be a secret.

2   Be aware of different forms of abuse so that you can recognize potential danger signals.

3   Speak up and get help if you are worried about the safety of a child. Know what the resources are for child protection in your community. If your child has been abused, get professional help for both you and your child. Even if you eventually decide that you or your child don't need it, seeking help sooner rather than later is safer than trying to solve problems like these on your own.

What Adults Need to Know About Child Molesters

There are some unpleasant facts about child molesters that we need to know as adults, but that we do not recommend telling children. Though children can be abused and hurt anywhere, they are most likely to be abused in their own homes or the homes of their abusers – who are often people they know well. This is why we tell children, "Most of the people who bother us are people we know." This truthful statement covers a wide range of situations without putting upsetting images into a child's mind.

People who sexually abuse children can be of almost any age and are from all walks of life. Because young people are most likely to be abused by someone they know well, their abuser will most likely be from the same race, culture, religion, or social class that they are. Statistically, a child molester of both girls and boys is most likely to be a heterosexual man, but women and people of different sexual orientations might also abuse children. Some child molesters are known as pillars of the community before getting caught. Often child molesters will put themselves in situations where they have easy access to young people. That's why we hear in the media about abusers being in day care centers, schools, and youth organizations. That's why abusers are seeking relationships with children through the Internet.

In order to understand how to protect children from sexual abuse, we need to understand how a child molester operates. In her chilling book, *Conversations with a Pedophile: In the Interest of Our Children*, Amy Hammel-Zabin, Ph.D., describes conversations and letters she had over a period of years with a pedophile who is in prison for life for molesting hundreds of young boys.[6] With a rare balance of compassion and outrage, this book gives an inside view of how this man became obsessed in his childhood with molesting young boys; of the systematic way he built relationships of trust with families, churches, and youth organizations; and of how he used kindness and attention to bend children to submit to his will so they participated in their abuse and kept it a secret.

This man was loved by his victims and by their parents. He did many wonderful things with the children he worked with. When asked when

Child molesters sometimes wait as long as two years while they win the love and trust of a family, a school, a youth organization, or a religious institution before they make their first move.

he stopped being kind to children and started abusing them, he said that he was always abusing them because, in his mind, everything he did with them was for that purpose. This man selected children who would keep secrets from their parents by cursing in front of them and then saying something like, "Oops. I accidentally used a word I shouldn't. Don't tell your parents, because then they won't let us be together anymore." If children kept this secret, he knew that they were more likely to keep other secrets.

As is often the case, this man never physically overpowered the children he abused. He abused them by building a relationship and by systematically lowering their boundaries until they were trapped.

The frightening reality is that there are whole organizations of abusers who believe that adults have the "right" to have sex with children and children have the "right" to have sex with adults. Through the Internet and other media, they trade ideas for how to gain access, credibility, and control. Child molesters sometimes wait as long as two years while they win the love and trust of a family, a school, a youth organization, or a religious institution before they make their first move. The language they use for this is "cruising and grooming." They "cruise" to find children to approach. They "groom" a child by building a strong emotional connection while testing a child's boundaries with low level touch or intrusions before making an actual overt sexual move.

Sex offender treatment expert Paul Isenstadt, LCSW, has tested and studied sex offenders for more than 40 years.[7] He says that most abusers persuade themselves that the child wants the sexual contact. They are usually seductive and manipulative rather than physically overpowering in their approach. They look for children who they think have poor boundaries.

Because of the power difference between adults and children, most young people without training such as Kidpower will have trouble resisting the psychological manipulation of a perpetrator. Child molesters might say things to make their victims feel at fault by rewarding their victims with attention and gifts that make them feel that they are part of creating the abuse, and by threatening emotional or physical harm to them, their families, and their other loved ones, if they tell.

Children tend to be literal in their thinking and want to please the important adults in their lives. Molesters deliberately use these qualities to confuse children. Some forms of abuse are disguised as being necessary for medical reasons. One man went to a number of childcare centers with false papers that identified him as a medical doctor coming from the health department. He took children alone into rooms and molested them in the name of "examining" them. After he had done this for several weeks, a couple of children complained to their teachers and parents and he was finally caught.

If children know that anything that bothers them should never have to be kept a secret and how to tell someone, they are better able to get help when they need to. If what is being done to them is necessary for their health, there is only good and no harm done if children are in the habit of openly discussing everything that happens to them.

Other forms of sexual abuse can be disguised as affection. One of our centers was asked to conduct a Kidpower class in an elementary school where a seventy-two-year-old grandfather was a long-time volunteer assistant in a first and second grade combination classroom. He had molested seven little girls in the classroom while there were teachers and other volunteers in the room without the other adults realizing what was going on. He sat with children on his lap in full view of their parents and teachers reading a big book. With a few, he would then put their hands between his legs.

These children had been told not to let anyone touch their private areas except for health or safety but they had *not* been told not to let someone make them touch his private areas, which is what this grandfather was taking their hands and doing. They felt uncomfortable but, especially because this seemed to be happening in front of their adults, didn't know why. This grandfather had been a well-loved member of the school community for years, and the incidents were a shock to everyone.

Good Touch/Bad Touch and Other Confusion

One common way adults have been taught to instruct children about sexual abuse prevention is by explaining about "good touch" and "bad touch." By describing examples of both types of touch, children are taught that "good touch" is okay, but they should not allow "bad touch" or "confusing touch". However well intentioned, we believe this isn't an effective teaching strategy for children because it is too complicated and has a number of pitfalls.

The good touch/bad touch/confusing touch teaching method requires giving children a lot of concrete examples about different kinds of touch. This approach creates a dilemma in providing children with useful safe information. On the one hand, adults don't want to be so explicit about possible problems that they raise images that are inappropriate for children. On the other hand, a too-general definition of what is "good" and what is "bad" or "confusing" leaves children unclear and can make them more vulnerable to abuse.

Child molesters often start with behavior that would not be defined as "bad touch." Instead, they usually start with behavior that children will probably experience as being loving, kind, and playful. After establishing a relationship, most molesters then move into behavior that is inappropriate and intrusive and gradually start doing things that are more explicitly sexual.

Sexual touch or attention might feel good to children at first, and they might not realize when their boundaries are violated until after some abuse has already taken place. While being used for sexual purposes is not safe for children, they do have the right to enjoy their bodies, to be curious, and to have their feelings accepted. Labeling sexual feelings or their own exploration as being "bad" is not a healthy way to introduce children to their own emerging sexuality.

When behavior is not overtly sexual, the difference between the same

If children know that anything that bothers them should never have to be kept a secret and how to tell someone, they are better prepared to get help if they need to.

The problem with "good touch/bad touch/confusing touch" explanations is that many child molesters often start with behavior that children would probably experience as "good."

Kids need healthy physical contact

action being appropriate and loving or being sexual might be hard to define. The difference of course is about intent, and intent is often hard to assess accurately even for adults with lots of life experience. For example, the following safe and caring behaviors might not consistently fit into the "good touch" definition for a younger child:

• being picked up, carried, hugged, held on laps, and wrestled with in a fun way without worrying about what body parts might end up getting touched to do this safely;
• having your grownup pull thorns out of your bottom after you accidentally sit on a blackberry bush; or
• running naked through the sprinklers on a hot day and having your grownup take photos and then dry you off with a towel.

At the same time, the following inappropriate and unsafe behaviors might not fit into the "bad/confusing touch" definition as understood by many children:

• staring at a child with some sexual energy;
• stroking a child's hair in a seductive way;
• manipulating a boy's nipples;
• "accidentally" brushing up against a pre-teen girl's breasts;
• pulling a child onto a lap and having an erection;
• playing an apparently "silly game" to get children with their clothes on to assume seductive poses for pornographic photos; or
• showing children apparently innocent pictures or videos but talking about them in a suggestive way.

When we talk about touching each other's private areas as being unsafe, our real purpose is stop behavior with sexual or other harmful intent towards children. Even adults can get very confused about what "sexual intent" means and explaining this concept to children just doesn't make any sense. Unfortunately, worry about somehow being inappropriate with children can cause loving adults to deprive children of physical play and affection. Grandparents have often told me, "I am afraid to hug my grandchildren, let them sit on my lap, or play wrestling games. I don't see how to do that without having some part of our bodies come into contact with each others' private areas."

I have also had parents complain that grandparents will ask grandchildren to keep something they do with them a secret. This is usually not because they want to abuse the children, but as a joke that they do not expect children to take seriously or because they want to give their grandkids treats that the parents might disapprove of.

I tell grandparents, "Please keep playing with your grandchildren, as long as you both like it and as long as what you do is safe and okay with their parents. Children need healthy physical contact. Pay attention and respect their wishes if they tell you with their bodies or their words that they don't like it – or if they change their minds. Make sure that you are never giving your grandchildren the message that any touch, games, treats, or presents you give them should be a secret."

Context really does matter. A hand cleaning every crevice of a baby's whole body is important care. A hand fondling a toddler's genitals for sexual gratification is sexual abuse. A snowball accidentally landing on someone's crotch during a snowball fight is likely to be seen as extremely funny later to some children. A whole body hug brings the whole front of our bodies including the private areas into contact with each other and, if both people want to be hugged, hugs are great. The same body parts are involved, but the context and intent makes one action safe and the other not.

What is an appropriate and safe touch at one age often becomes intrusive and inappropriate at another. Some babies like to be kissed and tickled all over and there is nothing wrong with that. Others don't and that's fine too. As children get older, we need to be more careful about where we tickle or kiss and about whether or not it is still safe and still okay with them. An affectionate pat on the bottom of a toddler might feel like sexual harassment to a teenager.

One key to making sure that touch is safe is to be clear that touch should never have to be a secret. Once a five-year-old girl whom I'll call Twyla announced cheerfully, "My Daddy touched my bottom and told me not to tell." She didn't seem worried or upset, just interested.

When I talked to Twyla's parents privately, they explained that Twyla's father often gives her back rubs, which she asks for. After getting some safety training from her mother, she pointed out, "Hey, Daddy, you're touching my bottom. That's a private area." Unfortunately, both of Twyla's parents got so worried that they told her that touching her bottom in a back rub wasn't the same as touching a private area and not to make up stories. Of course, from a very literal perspective, Twyla's perception was accurate.

These caring parents knew that they had given Twyla an unsafe message, and they wanted to know what to do to fix it. With my help, they told Twyla, "We made a mistake, and we are glad you said something to Irene. It is true that Daddy touched your bottom when he was giving you a back rub, and you can tell anyone you want that he did that. We are sorry that we told you not to make up stories. We were wrong. Sometimes bottoms might get touched in back rubs. This is okay as long as you like it, if it's done safely, and you know that's it's not a secret. If you don't like it, that's okay too. If you prefer, Daddy can give you a back rub and stop higher up so that your bottom doesn't get touched."

Keeping secrets, misuse of power, and harmful intent are what can make an activity unsafe for a child – not exactly where they might get touched.

What Can Adults Do to Prevent Problems?
As hard as it is to accept, adults need to be aware that anyone could become a danger to the children in our lives. Even pillars of society. Even kind and loving people. We need to realize that even a child who has been a safe person to be with for years might become unsafe as a result of changing and growing, or as a result of something bad happening.

At the same time, we don't want children to have to live in continual fear.

Knowing how to set boundaries about touch makes kids safer

We want children to be able to play happily with their family and friends. We want children to feel safe with many different people in many different places. We don't want them to have to see potential danger in every person they know. Living this way would take away their joy in life – and ours.

We can best protect our children by paying attention. We need to notice and take action when the people around children act in ways that are uncomfortable to us. We should pay particular attention to relationships where there is a strong power imbalance, either emotionally or physically. We can teach children to notice what feels good to them and what doesn't, and to speak up about it. They need to be able to do this with people they love and with people whose approval is important to them. We can be good role models for our children through how we set boundaries to take care of ourselves, and through how we support them in setting their boundaries.

Secrecy is the biggest reason why some abusers can get away with molesting many different children over a long period of time. Children need to know that they should always tell if a person touches or talks to them in a way they don't like, and to keep telling until someone helps them. Not keeping secrets is a powerful line of defense against sexual abuse.

Not keeping touch, presents, games, or problems secret is a powerful line of defense against sexual abuse.

Using Awareness and Boundaries to Protect Kids From Abuse

1   Be aware that anyone might be a child molester, but most people are not.

2   Notice intrusive behaviors including play, affection, or attention that sexualizes children and put a stop to it.

3   Teach children and the adults around them about boundaries rather than about good touch/bad touch. Teach children that for play, teasing, or affection, people should not touch the private parts of their bodies or ask them to touch the private parts of someone else's body. Sometimes people might need to touch their private areas for health or safety, but then that type of touch should never have to be a secret. Remember that keeping secrets, misuse of power, and sexual or other harmful intent are what make an activity unsafe for a child – not where on their body they might get touched.

4   Give children the physical contact and affection that they need while respecting their boundaries. Listen to them when they say, "No," even if you are playing a game (like tickling or roughhousing). Help them see that they have a right to say "No" and expect other people to listen to them.

5   When children set boundaries about unwanted play, teasing, or affection, back them up even if it seems trivial and even if someone you care about is unhappy or embarrassed about this.

6   Be a safe adult to come to. Listen when children talk about their problems and let them know that you care about what is happening in their lives. Create opportunities that encourage children to talk about whatever is bothering, no matter how big or small the problem is. Whenever possible try to make a daily or weekly routine to check in with children and ask in a calm way, "Is there anything that is bothering you or you have been worried about?"

What Kids Do and Do NOT Need to Know

Children will *not* be made safer from sexual abuse by being given this potentially devastating message: "I'm sorry to say that the person most likely to hurt you is someone you love and trust. And this person is likely to trick you into going along with it."

Remember that explicit details are not necessary or safe. We do not want to raise images in children's minds that are not already there. Fortunately, adults can give children valuable and effective skills to stop sexual abuse without telling them the graphic details of what exactly might happen. Instead of using sexual examples, adults can prepare children to protect themselves from sexual abuse by teaching them how to set boundaries to stop other kinds of unwanted affection, games, and play. They will need our support especially in setting boundaries with people they care about the most – with family, teachers, other children, and even with their best friends.

In Kidpower, our goal is to give children tools for staying emotionally and physically safe without overwhelming them with unnecessary upsetting information. Children can learn to protect themselves from most safety problems with people they know if they practice these skills:

- Using their awareness to notice potential problems;
- Setting powerful, respectful, appropriate boundaries with peers and adults they know;
- Protecting themselves emotionally from hurtful words;
- Checking and thinking first;
- Staying in charge of what they say and do no matter how they feel inside;
- Walking away from trouble; and
- Being persistent in getting help.

Instead of mentioning specific abusive or other dangerous situations, we have children practice using their "People Safety" skills to solve common daily problems such as unkind comments, unwanted touch and teasing, disagreements, games that go from fun to scary, and social pressure to make unsafe or inappropriate choices. These skills can be applied to the issue of molestation by giving children information using language that is appropriate for their age and their cultures. Families have very different rules about whether it is okay for children to touch themselves, so we don't address this issue in our explanation. Instead, we stay with the common ground of what the safety rules are.

In Kidpower workshops, after practicing with kids how to set boundaries, we explain the safety rules about private areas by saying, "Your private areas are the parts of your body that can be covered by a bathing suit. The safety rule is that, for play or teasing, other people are not to touch your private areas nor are they to ask you to touch their private areas. It is not safe for people to show you pictures or videos of people and their private areas. Even if someone has to touch your private areas for health or safety reasons, they should *never* ask you to keep this a secret. It is not safe for someone to try to get you to break the safety rules by offering you a gift or to do you a favor. Any kinds of presents or favors to you should not be a secret. Even if the person does stop, then you should still tell. If you don't

"For play or teasing, other people are not to touch your private areas nor are they to ask you to touch their private areas."

*Tell kids, "If someone does something that makes you feel bad, it is **not** your fault and it does **not** mean that you are bad. It just means that you need help."*

tell right away, then tell as soon as you can. It is *never* too late to tell."

As mentioned above about the back rub, if a child asks about a specific situation that involves private areas but is not abusive, we can help them work out a specific exception if this is appropriate, safe, and public.

When bad things happen to children, they often blame themselves, thinking, "It was because I was bad."

This is why adults need to tell children very clearly, "If someone does something that makes you feel bad, it is *not* your fault and it does *not* mean that you are bad. It just means that you need help."

Because children are sometimes led into sexual or other unsafe behavior without realizing it, we practice how to change your mind. "If you like this, is that okay?" a Kidpower instructor will ask, gently stroking a child's hair in a completely appropriate way and nodding her head so that the child nods too. "Is it okay to change your mind?" the instructor asks.

The child nods again and then is coached to move away and say, "Please stop."

If children ask for details about what might happen if someone breaks the safety rules on touching private areas, we recommend asking what they think in private rather than answering their question in front of a group. Their response will give you the opportunity to address any confusion or upset they might already have and to assess if there might be a problem. If they press for details out of curiosity, you can redirect them by saying firmly and cheerfully, "Lots of things might happen, but I'd rather talk about how you can keep yourself safe most of the time. Let's practice sounding both firm and respectful when you ask someone to stop. Let's practice interrupting a busy adult and telling the whole story when you need help."

Most sexual abuse can be stopped if young people know:

• how to speak up about any behavior that makes them uncomfortable,
• how not to keep secrets,
• how to change their minds if something starts to feel wrong or unsafe to them;
• that it is never to late to tell,
• that it is not their fault, and
• how to keep telling until they get help.

Best Friends and Mistakes – A Teaching Story
The following is a true story based on a real-life situation that we tell in Kidpower workshops for elementary school-aged children. We tell this as an interactive story using leading questions to reinforce the lessons we want children to learn. Children get quiet and they listen intently, because this story addresses their concerns in a real way.

In a Kidpower workshop we teach a lot of ways to be safe, but it can be hard to remember these rules in real life. Once a girl who had taken a

Kidpower class went to her best friend's house for an overnight. We do not use the real names of our students, so we will call her Penny, and her friend, Kerry. Penny and Kerry decided to stay awake after Kerry's parents told them to go to sleep.

Leading Questions:
• Have you ever stayed overnight at a friend's house?
• Have you ever stayed up after adults told you to go to sleep?

After everybody else was asleep, Kerry said to Penny, "I'm hungry! Let's go sneak some chips from the kitchen!" So they did. A little later, Kerry said, "I'm bored. Let's go watch a movie. There's a movie for grownups that I know we're not supposed to see. Okay?"

Penny thought this sounded exciting and said, "Okay!" even though it was against the rules. She felt like grownups make too many rules!

Leading Questions:
• Have you ever snuck snacks when you weren't supposed to?
• Do you ever feel like there are too many rules?
• Have you ever broken rules on purpose?

Anyway, while they were snuggled together eating their chips and watching the movie, Penny started to feel uncomfortable about what she was seeing. She thought, "This is gross. But I don't want Kerry to think I'm a baby! And what do adults know anyway?" So she said nothing.

Leading Question:
• Have you ever not wanted your friends to think you were a baby?

Suddenly, Kerry started touching Penny between her legs in her private area. Penny was shocked. She thought, "This is my best friend. I don't want her to get mad at me. But I'm starting to feel real bad! And I already broke a lot of rules. Being up late, eating the chips, watching the movie. I can't stop now. And who can I talk to? I don't know Kerry's parents that well. They might get mad at me." Penny was so confused that she just waited and did nothing.

Leading Questions:
• What other choices did Penny have?
• Could she tell Kerry to stop? Would Kerry be a good friend to get mad at Penny if she said to stop?
• If you make one mistake, should you keep on making mistakes?
• Could Penny call home? Even in the middle of the night? Do you think your adults would want you to wake them up if you had a problem in the middle of the night? (If children aren't sure, tell them to ask their adults.)

Penny felt so upset about what happened that she pushed it out of her mind. It took a lot of work, but every time the memory came up, she made herself forget.

Leading Question:
• Have you ever made yourself forget something you felt bad about?

Have you ever made yourself forget something you felt bad about?

About a week later, Penny had a bad dream. She woke up and said to herself, "Oh, no, that wasn't just a dream. It really happened! I broke all my safety rules. I feel like such a bad person. And I feel so mixed up about Kerry. She did something that makes me feel bad, but she's my best friend. It's been a whole week! I can't tell anybody about it now!"

Leading Questions:
• What other choices does Penny have?
• Is it ever too late to ask for help? (If children aren't sure, say firmly, "No, it is never too late to tell!")

Penny kept feeling bad and making herself forget for a whole year. Then she tried to tell her mother. She said, "Mom, Kerry is acting funny."

Penny's mom asked, "What do you mean by funny?"

Penny said, "Well, she makes me uncomfortable."

Penny's mom said, "That's okay, honey. Things do change with friends, as you get older. Why don't you try talking with Kerry or play with someone else?"

Penny went away feeling really upset, even though she did not show her feelings to her mother. She thought, "Mom does not care about what happened to me! I've felt so awful for so long, and she doesn't even care!"

Leading Questions:
• What do you think? Does Penny's mom care about Penny?
• What else could Penny have done?
• Did she tell her mom the whole story? Can her mom read her mind?

Finally, Penny tried to tell her mom again. She said, "Mom, something really has bothered me for a long time, and I'm scared you'll get mad that I didn't tell you sooner. But one time I was at Kerry's house and we stayed up and watched a movie that we weren't supposed to, and she touched me in a way that I know broke our safety rules about touching private areas. And I feel like a really bad person."

Penny's mom said, "You're not bad, Penny, you just made a mistake. And I'm glad you told me now. We'll talk some more until you feel better. And I'll talk to Kerry's family. I'm sure she needs help too."

Sometimes the People Kids Love Have Problems
With a lot of thought and advice from experts, we have figured out what adults can say to children about people who break the safety rules about private areas that will be truthful, useful, and not overwhelming. Our goal is to focus on getting help rather than on blame – and to avoid any upsetting details.

Here's the message that we give kids in our workshops and recommend that all adults tell their children as soon as they are old enough to understand. Using a very matter-of-fact manner, say "Sometimes the people kids love have problems. Sometimes their problems are so big that they do things to hurt kids or make them uncomfortable. If this happens to you or to someone you know, it does not mean that anybody is bad. But it does mean that everyone needs help. The way to get help is to tell an adult you trust. If the first adult you tell does not understand, try again. If this adult does not help, find another adult to tell. If an adult tells you not to talk about it, tell a different adult. Keep telling until somebody does something about the problem and you get the help you need. And remember that if something like this happens, it was not your fault, and it is never to late to tell."

We then encourage children to think of many different adults they could go to with safety problems, such as their parents, teachers, grandparents, aunts and uncles, friends of parents, school counselors, etc. etc. If we are in a classroom, we might turn to the teacher and ask, "Can your students tell *you* if they have a safety problem?"

And, of course, these loving teachers look into the sweet faces of their students and say, "*Yes*! I will help you if you have a safety problem!"

Getting help is so important for kids that sometimes I will say to my students, "I want you to *promise* me that, even if you have to tell 500 people, you will keep telling until you get help! Do you *promise*!"

Kids nod their heads and say, "I *promise*!"

In one of our most compelling success stories showing the importance of giving kids this knowledge, a mother and her two daughters were driving home after a Kidpower workshop. When they arrived home, the older daughter, aged ten asked, "Can I talk to you, Mom?"

Using the language of the workshop, the mother said, "Does it have to do with your safety?"

Her daughter said, "Yes."

When they got home, the mother went into the bedroom with her daughter, who said that their neighbor had molested her about a year earlier. "I know I should have told you sooner, Mom," she said.

"Kidpower says that it is never too late to tell," her mother replied.

It turned out that this neighbor was still molesting the younger daughter, who was able to tell after her big sister did. The neighbor was the father in a family where these two girls often went over to play. It is suspected that this man's children were also being abused.

Thanks to a great deal of excellent support from their wonderful family and community, the girls are doing well. The man who molested them is now sentenced to a long period of time in a community corrections facility that will require him to participate in programs designed for sex offenders. He will not be allowed unsupervised access to anyone under the age of eighteen.

Sometimes the people kids love have problems. Sometimes their problems are so big that they do things to hurt kids or make them uncomfortable.

Practicing setting boundaries using non-intrusive touch

The mother and father believe that, if their children had not taken the Kidpower workshop, the abuse would have continued and that their daughters would not have known how to tell their parents what happened to them. These courageous girls asked to have their story told so that it might help other children learn that it is never too late to tell.

Preparing Children to Stop Sexual Touch Without Touching Them Sexually

People often wonder how to help children practice setting boundaries on sexual touch without being sexual with them. Fortunately, we have found that if children can stop any kind of unwanted intrusive touch, they will be able to stop most forms of sexual abuse.

It can be tempting to add a sexual context for the sake of realism when practicing these boundary-setting skills in order to protect children from sexual abuse. Be sure to avoid this temptation, because there is no need, and doing this could make the practice emotionally unsafe for the child. The kinds of touch you can use to practice can be normally positive touch such as a gentle pat to the arm, stroking hair, a gentle shove, holding hands, roughhousing, or hugging. You simply tell children to imagine that now, for whatever reason, they don't like this touch or that they have changed their minds. The purpose is to give kids practice in setting boundaries, not to actually intrude on their boundaries.

In Kidpower workshops after children know how to set boundaries on unwanted touch and understand what the safety rules are about touching private areas, we add the context applicable to stopping sexual abuse, still without being explicit. We say, "If you ever get the 'uh oh' feeling that someone might be about to break the safety rule about touching private areas, right away your safety plan is to interrupt and say, 'Stop or I'll tell!'"

We then say things that are intrusive but not explicit such as, "This touch is about being a grown-up." Or, "Keep this touch a secret." We coach children to stand up, make a fence with their hands and shout, "Stop or I'll tell!" Kidpower instructors never use sexually explicit language or gestures while practicing with children unless parents have specifically asked for this practice because of special circumstances. Even then, we are very careful. We want children to be successful in stopping abuse, not to experience what we do as abusive.

For older children, we add another level to the practice by saying, "You'd better not tell. Promise you won't tell!" We then coach children to say, "Okay I won't tell if you stop." We remind them that it is okay to lie and break promises *if* they are doing it to be safe *and* they are going to tell an adult they trust what happened as soon as they can. We remind them to tell, even if the person does stop.

Preparing Children to Protect Themselves From Sexual Abuse

1   Have children practice the skills for setting boundaries, checking first, and getting help described in Chapters Four, Five, and Six.

2 Tell children *The Best Friends and Mistakes Story* above and other age-appropriate teaching stories. Reinforce the lessons in different ways about: the importance of setting boundaries, not believing you are a bad person when things go wrong, knowing that it is never too late to tell, being able to change your mind, and keeping telling until you get help.

3 As soon as they can understand, explain to children what the safety rules are about touching private areas as described above. Then practice:
- Set the stage by saying, "Pretend that I am acting in a way that gives you the "uh oh" feeling that I might be about to break the safety rules."
- Without actually touching the kids, reach your hand towards them and say, "This touch is about being a grownup." Or, "Let's keep this touch our secret." Or, "You don't need to say anything to anyone about this."
- Coach the kids to stand up, take a step away from you, make their fences, and say, "Stop or I'll tell!"
- Ask, "As soon as you get away from this difficult person I'm pretending to be, what should you do?"
- Coach them to shout, "TELL!" Remind them that, even if the person stops, they still need to tell.

Do Kids Abuse Other Kids?

Sexual abuse can happen between minors when one child or teen has more power than the other. Some studies have documented that children as young as four years old have deliberately molested other children. The three-year-old son of the head of a company told the four-year-old daughter of an employee at a company picnic, "You have to let me look in your panties, or my dad will fire your dad!" This girl's parents learned what happened after noticing that their daughter had taken a photo of herself with this little boy and torn it into pieces.

Children molest other children because of power struggles, curiosity, or boredom. They may be acting out sexual behavior that they have seen or experienced directly or copying something they saw in a movie or TV program. Sometimes they do this because they have found that doing something sexual is a powerful way to get attention. Sometimes they are curious and have not yet learned to see and respect other people's boundaries.

A few children who have been or are being abused and who have not received help so thoroughly integrate the abuse that they take on the role of perpetrators. They may be very charming, fun to be with, and attractive. They may manipulate other children in the same way that they were manipulated. They may repeat as best they can the actual abuse that was done to them. However, the vast majority of children who are abused do *not* go on to abuse other children or become child molesters themselves as adults.

The same boundary-setting and getting help skills that we teach kids for dealing with bullying or with adults who behave inappropriately can also protect them in this situation. One Kidpower student, Martin, went on an overnight camping trip with his church group. When the other boy in his tent tried to approach Martin sexually, he shouted, "Get your clothes back on, get in your sleeping bag, and go to sleep!" The boy did what Martin had ordered him to do.

Some studies have documented that children as young as four years old have deliberately molested other children.

" I learned to remind kids about the safety rules right before an activity like changing clothes or taking photos, just as they need to be reminded about the safety rules before going to the beach."

The next day, Martin told his mother what happened. She told the church group leader, who suggested calling a meeting of all the parents. Instead, the mother decided to call the mother of the other boy directly. It turned out that this boy was being abused. Through his actions, Martin was able to protect himself and to help another boy get the professional counseling he needed.

Teens also might abuse or sexually assault other teens. As young people become more independent, defining and setting boundaries about sexual behavior often becomes more complicated as is discussed in the section *Boundaries on Suggestive and Sexual Behavior for Teens*.

What About Nudity?

Most of the time, children's interest in and enjoyment of their bodies is healthy and important to their development. To the great entertainment of our neighbors, my son at age three used to remove every stitch of his clothing on our front porch every time I rushed back in to get the car keys I'd forgotten. Often late getting out the door, I would end up kneeling on the porch, pulling his clothes back on quickly, and wondering what people thought and whether or not my child was an exhibitionist.

Our neighbor across the street, the father of five, laughed and said, "Irene, his clothes annoy him!"

You want to make sure that people who are supervising children agree to the same standards about nudity. These rules might change dramatically based on your child's age and how well you know the people you are sharing time with. One family might be fine with having the children run around in the backyard naked under a sprinkler. Another family might be more comfortable with everyone having a bathing suit or at least underwear on. You might have one set of friends or close family your child spends time with where it is okay for the younger children to take a bath together. With other friends or family, the agreement may be to have no nudity at all.

This topic can be potentially hard to discuss with others, but remember that the safety of children is more important than embarrassment, inconvenience or offense. It is better to have talked about things, and to model to your children discussing these issues in a calm, clear way, than to expect that someone else might have the same standards about nudity as you do.

Not having a clear agreement with both adults and kids about the rules are about taking your clothes off can cause problems. As one mother told me, "We had a play date at our home with my eight-year-old son, his friend, and his younger brother. All three boys joyfully used my son's new digital camera to take photos of all kinds of things. They then rushed into the bedroom to change into swimsuits for a water game. While they were there, they started taking photos of each other with their clothes off in all sorts of silly poses, not mentioning anything about this to me."

She sighed and continued, "When my son's friend went home and told his mom, she was horrified. I felt embarrassed and worried about how things had gone from so fun to so upsetting. We eventually worked it out, but I think this difficult experience could have been prevented if I had agreed with my son's friend's mom about the boundaries on nudity. I could have also told the boys to change clothes in different rooms or the bathroom - and not to take photos of private areas, even as a silly game. I learned to remind kids about the safety rules right before an activity like changing clothes or taking photos, just as they need to be reminded about the safety rules before going to the beach."

Curiosity is a big part of children wanting to look at other's bodies, especially the parts that are covered up. My daughter as a toddler had an intense fascination with the male anatomy. Since she was too little to go to a public bathroom by herself, my husband once had to take her with him into the men's restroom. Her loud, cheerful comments about exactly what she saw and heard made this an experience that her father decided not to repeat. Once our daughter had a baby brother, all of the mystery was gone and the behavior stopped.

Age changes standards and so does culture. Some parents are comfortable with their younger children seeing them without any clothes on. As their children get older, adults often prefer to be more modest. What is important is to do what is comfortable for your family and your children. Adults need to remember that, even if they are still comfortable being nude around their older children, they may need to change their behavior if a child gets uncomfortable.

Because we don't live in isolation, we need to teach more free-spirited kids to respect cultural norms about nudity any time they are not in the privacy of our homes. As my daughter explained to her younger brother before he started school, "You may pee outside when we are hiking with our family in the woods but not on the trees during recess!"

What About Sexual Play Between Children?
Often, young children are curious about their bodies, interested in the ways that bodies are the same or different, and wanting to touch everything they see. Kids trying to copy what they think their adults might be doing in bed together or the examination given to them at the doctor's office does not mean that there is anything wrong with them.

As a result, children often engage in normal play that seems sexual to adults. Without getting upset about this, adults do need to create boundaries for them. Children do lots of unsafe things out of interest – such as climb high in trees, put objects up their noses, or try to do things on their own that they are not ready to do without adult help. We set boundaries on these activities not because they mean that the child will necessarily be instantly hurt by the activity, but because there is the potential for this behavior to be harmful for them. In all areas of life, we want to help children learn safety rules that will keep them safe most of the time.

Sexual play between children might be very innocent and seem harmless. The problem is that, if it goes too far, there is a risk that one or both children

As one big sister explained to her little brother, "You may pee outside when we are hiking with our family in the woods but not on the trees during recess at school!"

Some children just don't know where their boundaries are until they are forced to stop.

might end up feeling ashamed, embarrassed, or even abused. Even if both children seem to be okay with what's happening at the moment, there is a possibility that one child is doing this not solely out of free choice, but at least partly to please the other child. Afterwards, a child who went along with a friend might start to feel upset about what happened. Even adults often have a hard time figuring out when showing sexual interest is really okay with each other!

Another problem is that families have very different boundaries. One family might think nothing of having young girls or boys take a bath together, briefly check out each other's genitals, or sleep in the same bed. Other families would consider this wrong. In addition, our society has such a large concern about anything to do with sex that feelings on this subject can become very inflamed very quickly.

This is why it is important for adults to err on the side of safety in monitoring play between children and to set limits in ways that are not attacking. Some children just don't know where their boundaries are until they are forced to stop. They seem driven to cross the boundaries of others, and the big reaction they often get in response to sexual behavior can actually motivate them to continue. They need clear calm rules with logical consequences, such as having to practice using their Hands Down Power instead of touching inappropriately and using their Mouth Closed Power to stop themselves from making sexual comments.

In one kindergarten, a little boy kept coercing other little boys into pulling down their pants and touching each other when they went to the bathroom. This five-year-old child was so persistent and persuasive that he had to be prevented from going to the bathroom at the same time as any other child without adult supervision until he was able to stop pushing boundaries.

Suppose we see a couple of children taking off their clothes and starting to examine each other's genitals. Most likely, children playing games like this are just curious. Intense negative adult reactions can be deeply upsetting to kids. Remember, children are easily affected by the intensity of the reactions of the adults they care about. Many adults remember with deep shame and embarrassment getting in trouble for exploring their bodies or the bodies of a playmate. We want to stop children from engaging in behavior that could be hurtful but we also want to be careful to do so in a way that doesn't cause children to feel they are bad.

We can stop risky behavior in a clear and calm way by saying something like, "I can see you're curious about each other's bodies. It's good to be curious, but playing games where you touch each other's private areas is against our safety rules. If you want to know more about people's bodies, let's talk about it or look at a book. "

One mother described how her four-year-old son was playing house with his friend in a nice private space behind the door. She was pretending to be the Baby and he was pretending to be the Daddy. When the "Daddy" was changing the "Baby's" diaper, he pulled off her underpants. The mother said, "You can pretend to change diapers, but the rule is that you keep your underpants on and stay where we can see you."

Between parents who understandably do not want their children to get involved in sexual play and parents who understandably do not want their children shamed for testing the rules, schools face a large challenge when problems come up. Again, the key is for adults to supervise the play of children and intervene calmly if a child does something inappropriate. Unless children have an ongoing pattern of pushing against these boundaries, it can make them feel shamed if they are threatened with consequences. Instead, it makes more sense to just tell them what the rules are and to let their parents know what happened.

One little girl raised her hand during circle time at her preschool and announced, "I didn't like it when Mabel showed me her wee-wee today."

The teacher said matter-of-factly, "Thank you for telling me." Later, she discussed what happened with both girls, reminded them of the rules at school, and told both of their parents.

At home, Mabel's mother said to her daughter, "I want to talk about what happened at school today.

Mabel said, "I already know and I don't want to talk about it. Just *think* it at me."

Mabel and her mother sat together for a while in silence, just thinking. Her mother then said, "And it won't happen again, *right*?"

"Right!" Mabel sighed.

Teaching About Privacy

Babies have no sense of privacy. Everything they do and every part of their bodies is public. As children get older, they start to develop an understanding of what privacy means and the difference between public behavior and private behavior. Behavior that is okay in their bedroom might be against the rules in the living room or at school. They might laugh about farts with their friends but not mention farting to their grandma.

Children often feel that having increased privacy is part of their not being treated like babies anymore. One five-year-old boy told his mother after a Kidpower workshop, "Kidpower says that I can take baths by myself now." Of course, that's not exactly what Kidpower says, but it turned out that this little boy really wanted to use the washcloth on himself instead of having his mother do it.

Sometimes children who act sexually are copying what they see adults doing at home, on TV, on the computer, or in a magazine. Adults should be aware of the impact that seeing overt sexual behavior can have on children and do their best to prevent exposure and to explain about what is safe for kids to copy and what is not.

Many parents ask what they should do when their children are the ones

Children often feel that having increased privacy is part of their not being treated like babies anymore.

who are acting sexually. Sexual exploration by children is very normal. They need clear guidance about what the rules are. You can say something like, "People's vaginas, penises, bottoms, and breasts are private. For play or teasing, other people are not to touch your private areas nor are they to ask you to touch their private areas."

Sometimes children will explore what the boundaries are by touching adults inappropriately or by asking inappropriate questions such as, "Do you have sex?" Adults can move children's hands or bodies gently away and redirect their behavior to doing something that does not involve private areas. Adults can refuse to discuss a topic by saying matter-of-factly, "That's private."

We don't want children to feel that there is something shameful about their bodies. At the same time, families have very different standards about what is and is not okay regarding children touching their own private areas when they are by themselves and we want to respect that. Parents are the ones who should be able to decide on the boundaries for their families in a way that fits their values *as long as this is safe for their children*.

Sexual exploration by children is very normal. They need clear guidance about what the rules are.

As six-year-old Paco's mother said, "Paco is just fascinated with his penis. Whenever I read to him, Paco forgets and starts playing with himself! I keep having to remind him, 'If you want to play with your penis, you need to be by yourself in your room. Doing that is private. If you want me to keep reading, you need to stop!'" She laughed and added, "Paco takes his hand out of his pants, leans against me and sighs, 'Oh, all right! Now please don't stop the story!'"

Sometimes children need a change of structure in order to control their behavior in public. One little girl in a kindergarten loved to wear dresses to school, but kept on pulling up her skirt and examining her most private areas in fascination. After many attempts to re-direct her behavior, the mother and the teacher decided to have this child stop wearing dresses to school for a while.

What If a Child Keeps Asking, "But WHY?"

Anyone who spends much time with young children knows that the question "why" comes up all of the time – whether it is why rabbits can't fly, or why do mom and dad yell at each other so much, or why someone won't be my friend, or why can't I show my friend my wee-wee in class?

Some questions are easy to answer. Rabbits can't fly because they don't have wings. Some questions don't have a good answer and are best responded to with caring words and listening. Answering every question and fixing every problem is not always possible or advisable. For example, when a child is sad about something that cannot be changed, the best response is usually to listen compassionately and say gently, "That sounds hard. I am sorry that this is happening to you."

Wee-wee type questions are best answered just by saying, "Because that's the rule." Kids know that adults and families have rules. For example, the adult gets to say when kids get to have cookies and when they don't or that kids have to go to bed at 8 p.m. rather than 9 p.m. The reason that adults get to decide what the rules are is because adults have the job of taking care of children and of keeping them safe.

Kids often question why sexual play or nudity in public settings is against the rules in the same way that they question other rules. As adults, we know that the reason for the safety rules about the private parts of the body is because there is the potential for someone to get hurt physically and emotionally. Between children, this is not necessarily because of the act itself, but because of the potential for misuse for power and because some kids are more vulnerable than others.

Fearful answers like "doing this will hurt you" are too scary and confusing. Children know that showing or touching their private areas is not inherently painful and might be pleasurable. A clearer answer might be, "Because doing this with other people is against our safety rules." Children do not always need to understand the reasons why we have rules, but they do need to know that the rules are there to help keep them safe.

If a child asks why something is against the safety rules, adults can say, "The safety rules are to help keep you safe and it can be unsafe to let someone touch the private parts of your body." If a child asks why again, adults can say, "Because that is our rule."

Kids grow up very, very quickly. Our job as adults is to let them be kids as long as they can while giving them the tools they need to grow up as safely and happily as possible.

Mixed Messages About Sex

As they get older, kids are bombarded with innuendo, language, and images that are sexual, violent, and mean. They watch this behavior on television, share extensive information with each other, and notice much more of what adults say and do than we can possibly imagine. They may well be puzzled about why we want to put a stop to their copying what they see and hear all around them. Older kids often have an acute sense of justice and pay close attention to gaps in perceived fairness.

For behavior that is acceptable neither for adults or kids, parents and other adults can say, "Yes, I know some friends talk like that in their families. And I know that's how your favorite TV character talks. But in our house, the rule is that we speak to each other with respect."

Modeling being responsible for our actions if we break our own rules about safe behavior helps young people learn to take responsibility as well. We can teach children a great deal about being honest if we are willing to say things like, "I'm really sorry for losing my temper and screaming. I don't want members of our family to scream at each other or at me. This means that, even when I am tired from working all day and annoyed because you glued newspapers all over the table, I am going to do my best not to scream at you. Now, let's clean up that table!"

For sexual behavior, all we really need to explain to children is, "Using this kind of language or playing games that copy this kind of grownup behavior

Children do not always need to understand the reasons why we have rules, but they do need to know that the rules are there to help keep them safe.

It is no surprise to children that grown-ups get to do lots of things they can't.

is not safe for kids to do. It is something that grown-ups can do, but not kids." It is no surprise to children that grown-ups get to do lots of things they can't.

Supervising Children to Prevent Potentially Abusive Behavior

1 Figure out for yourself what your boundaries are about children of the same age with no power imbalance being curious, being nude, looking at, and touching each other. Be sure that the adults supervising your children will agree to uphold the same boundaries. Also, be sure that the parents or other caregivers of any children who you are supervising are in agreement with your boundaries. If you choose to have your kids spend time with someone who has different standards than you do, you need to work out these issues ahead of time.

2 Remind children each time they are with a person who they have not seen recently or go to a place where they have not been recently of what the safety rules are for where they go, what they do, and who they are with. When it is relevant to the activities planned or if something has been an issue, remind them about the safety rules for taking their clothes off, taking photos, touching private areas, not keeping secrets, giving or accepting favors or gifts, etc.

3 Supervise play, especially in corners, under blankets, in playhouses, behind doors, and in bathrooms. Check out any long silences. Stop inappropriate or unsafe behavior in a calm firm way.

4 Make sure that the people who are caring for your children have the same standards and ground rules that you do.

5 Be aware of sexual behavior that children might see and copy. Try to monitor what they see and explain anything that might be against your safety rules.

No matter how okay adults make it for children to talk about problems, children may face an experience that shocks them so much that they find themselves unable to tell.

What Are the Warning Signs That A Child Might Be Being Abused?

Every time another story hits the news about abuse that has gone on for years undetected, parents and other concerned adults are likely to worry and wonder, "How will I know if this is happening to my child?" We can stay aware of the possibility of child abuse without jumping to conclusions. Many of the symptoms for what might be caused by abuse could also be symptoms of other problems.

No matter how okay adults make it for children to talk about problems, children may face an experience that shocks them so much that they find themselves unable to tell. They may show stress in subtle ways, such as becoming extra clingy or trying extra hard to please. They may express their unhappiness in ways that upset us, such as suddenly doing poorly in school, being destructive, or starting to lie. These behaviors might reflect underlying stress for many reasons other than sexual abuse, but are still symptoms that a young person needs help.

Ask questions when your child seems uncomfortable. Pay attention to comments like, "I don't want to go visit anymore." Or, "I keep having embarrassing dreams. I can't get them out of my head." Ask in a matter-of-fact voice, "Can you tell me more about that?"

Notice unexplained changes in behavior. Look for reasons any time your child starts:

• Having trouble sleeping or concentrating in school;
• Acting extremely unhappy about a specific person or place;
• Behaving like a much younger child;
• Becoming very withdrawn, overly aggressive, extremely secretive, or irrationally fearful;
• Playing adult-sounding sexual games with toys or people;
• Having unexplained gifts or money; or
• Having any unexplained physical symptoms such as bruises or inflammation, especially around the genitals, bottom, or mouth.

Teaching children to tell their trusted adults about problems will help most of the time, but not always. Sometimes children go into denial and block the memory of what happened. They might literally make themselves forget. Sometimes children think that, because they didn't follow their rules, what happened was their fault. They might feel so ashamed that they can't bear to think or talk about it. Secrecy is one of the biggest reasons that child abuse continues. Children need to know that their adults always want to know, even if it's much later, and that they are not bad, even if they made a big mistake.

What If You Fear That a Child Has Been Abused?

If a child in your care says or does something that leads you to fear abuse, your first challenge is to stay very calm. Some studies show that it takes an average of two years before children report being abused. If the adult they talk to reacts in an upset way, children are very likely to withdraw their story. Children want to protect their adults from the pain that knowing might bring. They do not want to get into trouble. They might care about and want to protect the person who abused them. This is why adults need to listen and children need to persist.

Kids often live in the here and now more than adults do, and the present moment can seem much more important than any past abuse. Once while leading a group camping trip, I learned that an eight-year-old girl had been molested several weeks earlier. She told another child that she was willing to talk with me, but not with her parents, even though they were along.

I took the girl, who we'll call Dina, to sit on a log under the trees away from the group. As the sunlight filtered through the branches above us, and the wind played with our hair, Dina explained how it happened. "We played 'truth or dare' and I took the dare. So I felt like I had to do what he said. Or I would be breaking my promise."

Then Dina added, "Please don't tell my parents."

"Why not?" I asked, knowing that she had a great relationship with them.

"They'll be unhappy, and I don't want to spoil the camping trip." Dina sighed.

Secrecy is one of the biggest reasons that child abuse continues. Children need to know that caring adults always want to know, even if it is much later, and that they are not bad, even if they made a big mistake.

The first thing that children who have disclosed abuse need to hear from their adults is, "I'm very proud of you for telling me."

"I understand how you feel. But that won't work." I said sympathetically. "I have to tell them now. But I'll do my best to explain that you still want to have a fun camping trip."

If you find out that your child might have been molested, expect to feel a flood of outrage, grief, and fear. Your job is to accept your feelings without inflicting them on your child. This is not going to be easy. In a performance worthy of an Academy Award, take a breath, put all your upset feelings aside, and ask your child very calmly, "Please tell me what happened."

The first thing that children who have disclosed abuse need to hear from their adults is, "I'm very proud of you for telling me. That took courage. I know it was hard for you. You didn't do anything wrong. When somebody does something that makes you feel bad, it's not your fault. You are really, really important to me, and we are going to get help."

Next, you need to decide how best to protect your child from further harm. As adults, our job is to take action to make sure that children are physically and emotionally safe. It's important to act immediately. Seek medical and legal help if necessary. If you are not sure how serious the problem is or if you have questions or concerns on what to do, call a child abuse prevention hotline, a social service organization, or a law enforcement agency. It's best to keep the child away from any contact with the person who harmed her or him, even if this is a family member, until you have some answers and have made a plan on what to do.

A great deal of intrusive, inappropriate behavior falls short of what is legally considered abuse. Examples might include a family member who continues to hug or kiss a child even after the child says stop, a family friend who thinks it is funny to slap kids on the bottom, or a neighbor who stands too close and makes embarrassing comments. In order to protect kids from this kind of behavior, their adults need to take action and to monitor these relationships.

Remember that even apparently "minor" incidents of sexually inappropriate behavior can have a major impact in a child's life if they are not dealt with. Talk to the people involved. See what their reaction is. Are they concerned about the child or defensive? Are they open to changing their behavior, or are they denying that there's even the slightest possibility that they've done something potentially harmful even if they didn't have a harmful intention? Protect your child from any repercussions from the person whose behavior he or she reported. In addition, be aware that what seems like unintentionally inappropriate behavior might be really "the tip of the iceberg" of a much larger problem.

Even if the intrusion was minor and the person responds by agreeing to immediately change the behavior, do not leave the child alone with the person who was bothering the child until you are sure that both you and the child feel safe in doing so. Make sure to keep a very open communication with the child so that you know how things are going.

If you find out that your child has been seriously abused, either sexually or otherwise, you will probably be flooded with feelings like guilt, shame, betrayal, and fear. You might go through a time of being consumed with hate for the person who harmed your child. Painful experiences from your own childhood, which you may have long since dealt with and put aside, are likely to resurface. Seek out the help and support that you need and deserve. As lonely as you may feel, you are not alone.

I have yet to meet a parent anywhere who does not feel guilty about having failed her or his child in some way. The parents, teachers, and other caring adults that I know all do the best that they can for their children. It's hard to accept that even our best is not always enough to prevent assault, abuse, or other harm from happening to our children. We can give children the skills to avoid and get out of most bad situations, but not all of them.

It's hard to accept that even our best is not always enough to prevent assault and abuse from happening to our children

Give yourself some relief and hope by putting your energy and time into nurturing and supporting the child who has been abused. The actions of caregivers, even more than the degree of trauma caused by the abuse, is what will have the biggest impact on the long-term outcome for the child. So, even if your child has had a terrible experience, your love, nurturing, and support along with high quality professional help can make all the difference in how quickly and well she or he recovers and moves on from the abuse.

What if Your Child Has Been Abused by Another Child?

First, follow the same guidelines that are described in the section above. Overt sexual behavior and serious physical violence between children should be reported to the appropriate authorities like any other crime. However, much of what we would consider to be harmful behavior is not actually illegal, especially if the children are close in age to each other. For example, a child who keeps turning games with Legos into sexual playacting between the characters might just need some clear boundaries and extra supervision or might have a deeper problem. Seek professional advice to help you to assess whether or not a behavior is illegal or potentially harmful. Any time you are concerned about another child's behavior, make a plan to ensure your child's physical and emotional safety in the future.

Part of the solution is to build your child's boundary setting and safety skills. Without re-traumatizing your child by being too explicit, making up role-plays using skills that might have helped address the specific problem can be very helpful in becoming prepared to handle future problems. Work on providing new options for any behavior that makes victimization more likely. Consider enrolling the child in programs such as Kidpower that give the child the opportunity to practice with other adults and to watch other children using these skills.

Make sure that the authority figures at schools and other settings your child is in take action to stop abusive behavior. One mother told me, "I want my little girl to stand up for herself more. The little boys pull up her skirt. It's a game they play in the second grade with all the girls all the time. Instead of yelling at them, my daughter just cries."

"It's asking a lot of a seven-year-old to stand up to unacceptable behavior that is being tolerated by the people in charge!" I pointed out. "The teacher, the yard duty supervisor, and any watching parents should be putting a stop to games like this one."

You may want to set up a meeting to talk with the people involved in a problem your child is having. This meeting might include the teacher, the other child, the parent of the other child, and/or your child. Be sure to let your child know that you believe what he or she tells you, even if the other child is more articulate. The purpose of the meeting can be to point out the inappropriate behavior and to work out agreements about how to prevent future problems.

Depending on the age of the children, the severity of the problem, and the attitude of the other adults, a meeting might need to be with adults only. If you are unsure how to approach the people involved with the problem your child is having, get professional advice. Though many teachers and principals are extremely skilled at handing behavior and relationship issues, others can find the topic worrisome or triggering. Remember your job is to advocate for your child even if it takes a while to figure out the best way to do so.

It's asking a lot of a seven-year-old to stand up to unacceptable behavior that is being tolerated instead of stopped by the adults in charge!

Sometimes the best answer is to leave. After her Kidpower workshop, one six-year-old girl told her parents that a group of boys had been "humping" her during recess. For several months, they had been playing a game that involved catching her and sandwiching her between them in a very sexual manner. When her parents told the school principal, the playtime was supervised more closely and the boys apologized. However, the mother of one of the boys, who was a volunteer at the school, became very angry. She confronted the little girl and started questioning her about whether she had made the story up. The little girl's parents ended up removing their daughter from the school in order to protect her from further trauma.

If a child in your care has had a traumatic experience caused by another child, make sure that the child who was harmed gets the emotional support to heal. Counseling can be immensely helpful. It is safest if the child who was harmed can be protected from further contact with the child who acted as the perpetrator. If separation is not a choice, be aware that it is risky to leave your child unsupervised with the other child.

Take action to make sure that the child who acted as a perpetrator also gets help. Be aware that other children in that child's environment might have been abused. The goal is to protect everyone involved from further harm. Depending on what exactly happened, taking action may range from a meeting with the child's parents to reporting the abuse to authorities.

What About Reporting Abuse to Authorities?

Laws vary in different states and countries. In most cases, medical, mental health, and educational professionals are required to report suspected child abuse to a government agency such as Social Services or Child Protective Services. Reporting child abuse is important even if a case can't be acted upon. Documentation of a prior report can be helpful if another complaint is filed. Remember that other children might also be at risk. Check your local laws and agencies so that you have complete information about what the definition of "suspicion" is and what the definition of "child abuse" is where you live.[8]

Getting help for a child can be frustrating. Most agencies are overloaded to the point that they are unable to respond to complaints that are vague and uncertain. Some children live in situations where some neglect, emotional attacks, and physical punishment are a daily reality. Although these experiences are damaging, most of them might be difficult to prosecute legally.

Even so, we encourage adults who are worried about the safety of children to do exactly what we tell children to do when they have a problem – keep asking until you find someone who can do something about it. Go up the chain of command in an agency, staying polite and persistent. Seek help from therapists, attorneys, and other community resources.

What About Abuse in Families?

Children who have been abused by a family member need a language and a safe place for telling their story. In addition to the legal, medical, and mental health support that anyone who has been abused needs, incest survivors often need extra help with overcoming the huge betrayal of trust by their families. Because children have no basis for comparison, what is happening to them often seems normal to them at the time. Unless and until they are able to leave or someone takes action to stop it, the abuse is likely to continue.

Remember that children who are being abused by the people they live with usually feel love and loyalty for their abuser. They are very likely to believe that the problem is their own fault, instead of the fault of the abusers.

Many people who have survived incest or physical abuse from their immediate families have told me that they wish they had had Kidpower when they were young. I have wondered how our training would have made a difference. After all, these incest survivors were children in overwhelming destructive homes. They have told me, "Kidpower would have put it into my body that what was happening to me was wrong. I think I would have found someone to help me much, much sooner."

What if a Child Asks About Being Spanked by a Parent?

People from different families and cultures have widely different views about using spanking – the deliberate infliction of pain – to discipline a child. In some countries, spanking is illegal. In others, it is considered a normal form of discipline.

In the United States, it is illegal to hit a child hard enough to leave a mark the next day or to cause injury. It is not illegal for parents to spank a child, but it is illegal in most places for school staff to do so.

Children who have been given permission to talk about their feelings might tell a teacher or another trusted adult, "My Daddy hit my bottom. It made me embarrassed and scared and it hurt."

This puts an adult who disagrees with spanking in the tough position

We encourage adults who are worried about the safety of children to do exactly what we tell children to do when they have a problem – keep asking until you find someone who can do something about it.

Adult incest survivors have told me, "Kidpower would have put it into my body that what was happening to me was wrong. I think I would have found someone to help me much, much sooner."

of not wanting to contradict the parent but also wanting to support the safety of the child. An answer many therapists suggest is, "Thank you for telling me. That sounds hard. This might not work, but you can try to tell your Daddy that it hurts and scares you when he spanks you and to please just tell you what you did wrong."

As with other forms of child abuse, if an adult suspects that a child is being hit in a way that breaks the law, this should be reported to authorities.

What if a Teenager and a Younger Child Seem to Be Inappropriately Affectionate?

Occasionally, adult family members raise a concern on the following lines, "My teenaged son has a very sweet relationship with his three-year-old cousin. She adores him and initiates a great deal of physical contact, following him like a puppy and wrapping herself around his body any chance she gets. She climbs on his lap, throws herself naked into his arms just after she has taken a bath, and kisses him on the lips. He encourages her, carries her like a baby, and calls her pet names. I am starting to feel uncomfortable because it seems as if they are getting close to crossing the line into sexual behavior."

As they are figuring out their own sexuality, many teens, both boys and girls in different ways, sometimes test boundaries and can be somewhat inappropriate sexually. Unfortunately, especially because they have so many models of little girls being sexualized, acting sexually in words or behavior towards little girls can seem like a funny or cool thing to do. Behavior like this does not mean that a teenager who acts this way is a bad person or has harmful intent, but just that he or she has problems with boundaries.

Rather than making any assumptions about this teenaged boy's character or intention, focus on the specific behavior that is a problem. A parent or other adult might tell him, "It is wonderful that you have such a loving relationship with your cousin. But we have been learning a lot about child safety and there are a couple of things that you are doing that have the potential to be risky for her. I know you love her and want her to be safe and to grow into a strong independent woman someday. You can support this by encouraging her to be powerful and helping her get a sense of her own boundaries."

Describe the exact behavior and words that are a concern and make suggestions for other ways of being physically close and affectionate without the risk of it being sexual. The bottom line is that it is unsafe to sexualize little girls or boys, even if they appear to be soliciting this kind of attention.

Raising this subject is likely to be embarrassing for an older child. It also might be a relief because many teen boys don't know how to redirect an overly affectionate three-year-old. Because it is normal for people to hate being told what to do, adults should be prepared to deal with an initially negative reaction without taking this personally and to persist in setting the boundary.

Of course, if there is a concern that something more serious might be happening, then it is crucial to provide close supervision and get professional help.

The bottom line is that it is unsafe to sexualize little girls or boys, even if they appear to be soliciting this kind of attention.

What if a Teacher at Your School Is Accused of Child Abuse?

Whether this happens in a school, a place of worship, or a neighborhood, an accusation of child abuse against a person who is in a position of trust and power is traumatic for everyone involved. Feelings of disbelief, shock, anger, and sadness are all normal. Because no one wants to believe that this could be true, educational and religious communities are often slow to react to potential wrongdoing, which tends to make the problem worse and can lead to a "blame-the-victim" mentality.

Most of the time, children don't make up stories like this. Occasionally, abused children get confused about who did the abuse exactly. In a very few instances, young people have deliberately made false accusations for revenge or attention that have led to great injustice towards those accused.

Keep in mind that anyone can be a child molester *and* that people are innocent until proven guilty. Also, sometimes people who have poor awareness of boundaries accidentally cross the boundaries of others in ways that are experienced as abusive. If someone's behavior makes you uncomfortable, no matter who this person is, it is important to speak up. Even people with no bad intentions might react defensively as first, but you can learn a great deal about someone's intentions by setting a boundary.

If there is a complaint about someone's behavior being improper, make sure that the school, religious organization, or other institution takes a balanced approach. This means:

1. Erring on the side of safety by keeping the person away from children while the matter is investigated.
2. Investigating thoroughly and promptly in a balanced rather than a panic-stricken way.
3. Getting outside professional help as needed.
4. Taking appropriate action to correct the situation and, if need be, to make amends.

Be careful about what your kids might overhear when their grownups are dealing with their own thoughts and feelings. Children who worry about what is going on can be told only as much as they really need to know such as, "Someone says that Mr. Blue did something wrong. The school is figuring out what happened. Problems should not be secrets, and people sometimes make mistakes. If there is a problem, then the school will make sure that everyone gets help."

How Can Your Child Be Safe From Abuse on an Overnight?

A number of parents have expressed the following concern: "I was abused as a child, and I am afraid to let my child go on an overnight visit to a friend's house. How can I make sure that my child will be safe if someone in that family were to approach her in the middle of the night?"

Especially if something bad has happened to you as a child, having extra fears as your own child takes steps towards independence is normal. As with any other new activity, the way to prepare your child to be safe on an overnight is to:

If someone's behavior makes you uncomfortable, no matter who this person is, it is important to speak up.

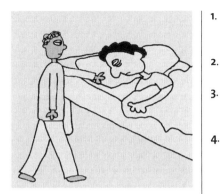

Children need to know they can get help whenever they need it, even in the middle of the night

Give kids practice in walking away from a nice person trying to talk them into coming close to look at something interesting "for just a minute".

1. Take the time to get to know the adults who will be supervising your child. Make sure that you are in agreement on how safety issues and supervision will be handled.
2. Make sure that your child knows how to call you or another adult she trusts, even in the middle of the night, if she has a problem.
3. Agree with your child as well as the parents of her friend about what will be happening and make sure that everyone understands that you want to know if the plan changes.
4. Teach your child to shout loudly for help if she is startled. Make sure that she knows that you want her to yell loudly for help if something scares her, even if everyone is sleeping and this will wake them up.

What if A Sex Offender Is Living in Your Neighborhood?

Many parents are frightened when they discover that registered sex offenders live in their community or their neighborhood, and they want to know how they can keep their children safe. No one wants to learn that someone who is known to be dangerous is living nearby. If this happens, your job is to protect and empower your children without terrifying them.

Worries about what someone might do to their children can lead adults to try irrational solutions that serve the sole purpose of helping them feel safer, but these attempts can make kids more vulnerable by confusing them. Telling children, "Never walk on that side of the street!" or, "Never sit on anyone's lap!" can cause anxiety and questions without making the kids safer.

Instead, simply telling children what you want them to do in any situation in your neighborhood – and giving them the chance to practice – is far more effective. Until kids have the skills and understanding to follow their safety rules, make sure that the people who are supervising them stay with them at all times.

Tell children who are old enough to go out on their own, "Our safety rule is that you will check with me first before you change your plan about whom you are with, where you go, and what you are doing. Do not go into someone's house or yard until I agree that it is okay. I also want you to check with me first about when it is okay to open our door to someone."

Role-play so children can practice walking away and checking first in a variety of situations. Include the opportunity to practice walking away from a nice person trying to talk them into coming close to look at something interesting "for just a minute".

While feeling upset about what someone has done is normal, demonizing this individual will serve no purpose and will not help your children be safer. It is important to be realistic. Legally, this man (or woman) has served his time and can live anywhere he wants. The truth is that most of the people who harm children are not registered on lists. As one of the locally registered sex offenders, this man is likely to be the first person suspected by authorities if a crime is committed.

Unfortunately, though, people who have harmed others sometimes repeat their behavior. This means that you want to make sure that your children are never alone with this person, do not go to his house or into his yard, and do not let him into your home.

If children living in the house where this man is staying are friends of yours, having them come over is fine, but you want to be aware of the possibility that they might have been abused. Children who have been abused who have not had help are more likely to harm themselves, but they might do something abusive to others.

The best way for your children to protect themselves from abuse is to be able to set boundaries and to get help if they need it. Supervise your children's play with all children, including these, until you are sure that they have these skills.

Both you and your children need to be able to say "No" to invitations that would break your safety rules without letting embarrassment or guilt stop you from setting clear boundaries.

Sex offenders may live in your community, but you and your children still have the power to learn skills that can help keep them safe most of the time. Positive, practical personal safety workshops for adults and children, such as those offered by Kidpower, can be very helpful in reducing worry and increasing competence.

Stay in Charge of Who is Caring For Your Children

Most abuse happens with people kids know - and this means that we must stay in charge of the people who we entrust with our children. I used to be appalled at how sometimes the parents of friends of my kids would let me take their children without spending any time with me at all. They were surprised when I insisted that we meet. Accept feeling awkward about checking out safety for your kids, especially with adults you know. For example, parents often feel a little self-conscious asking about guns in the house, hanging around with their kids in a new place, and watching others to make sure they are safe. Remember that safety comes first and check each situation out, regardless of what others might think of you. To do this:

1   *Know what your child is doing.* **Safety for children means that their adults know at all times whom they are with, what they are doing, and where they are going. The younger the child, the more exact this information needs to be. We need to remember that children can be vulnerable in all sorts of ways -- because of cars, cliffs, construction, water, and/or potentially dangerous animals as well as because of people.**

2   *Avoid the Illusion of Safety.* **Your own mobile home park, cul-de-sac, or neighborhood can seem so contained and safe, and neighbors you meet and see coming and going can seem like people you know. But you don't really know someone unless you have spent some time getting to know each other well. Even then, sometimes people who have been trustworthy and safe can make unsafe choices. Often, if we and our children know how to use our awareness, we can notice possible signs of problems. Being honest with ourselves about seemingly small doubts or uncertainties or discomfort we are feeling, and encouraging children to talk to trusted adults, can help prevent problems.**

3   *Take the time to get to know anyone that you are going to trust with your child.* **Go to where your child will be - someone's home, a day care center, or a school. Be very direct about what our expectations are in terms of supervision and safety. Pay attention not just to what the person says, but to how this person**

interacts with any children around and to what the environment is like. If a neighbor or classmate's parent is going to be caring for your child at home, invite this person to your home for a visit. If this person has children, see how secure and well behaved the children seem to you. Ask yourself how stable this person seems and if there are any signs of inconsistencies in temper or character.

4 *Keep Paying Attention.* Have conversations with anyone caring for your child before and after each visit. Ask how things are going. Insist on knowing each time your child goes to visit and ask what the plans are for the activities to make sure that you approve. Drop by unexpectedly while your child is there by coming back early or returning right after leaving to ask one more thing. If your child is going to walk over to a neighbor, call to make sure that the family is there and that this is a good time.

5 *Be prepared to change your plan if things don't seem right to you.* If you feel even a little uncomfortable about someone, then don't leave your child or let your child go. Trust your intuition if things don't feel right, for whatever reason. It may be embarrassing, inconvenient, and offensive to someone if you go to drop your child off at a friend's house and then have a feeling that something just isn't right, and end up taking your child home with you again. You may have a lot of people, including your child, upset with you. But safety is more important.

6 *Make sure your child knows how to get help.* Even very well intentioned and kind people can have moments where they are not safe for children to be with especially if they have something stressful happening. As soon as they are old enough to understand, practice with your children how to notice when a situation is changing (i.e. the adults in the house are having an argument, someone starts drinking and acting unusual, there are lots of people over and the house is very crowded, etc.) and make a safety plan on how they can contact you if needed.

7 *Teach your child boundary-setting and self-defense skills.* Teach children how to tell someone who is bothering them to stop in a clear firm voice if someone is bothering them and to get away and yell loudly if they need help. Teach children to hit, kick, and run to safety in an emergency.

Boundaries on Suggestive and Sexual Behavior for Teens

As young people enter adolescence and become more independent, their choices increase, their own sexual feelings often increase in intensity, and they face new risks. Wanting to be seen as sexually attractive to each other is normal. Acting in a sexual manner is often shown in the media as being cool and as the path to being treated with respect.

We hear from parents and teachers who are worried because girls dress provocatively, often starting at a fairly young age. We also hear stories about pre-teen and teen girls who give sexual favors to popular boys in order to gain acceptance in their middle and high schools – and about boys who are pressured into having sex in order to prove their worth as men. Young people need clear guidelines from their adults that balance their need to express themselves and their right to have sexual feelings with what is safe for them and acceptable in their families and at their schools. Adults tend to be especially concerned that girls will invite sexual attention that might be dangerous to them. It does not work to tell girls, "You are just asking for it if you dress like that. Everybody will think that you are a slut."

The unfair reality is that girls are more likely to be approached and harassed if they dress in a way that is seen as "sexually provocative." They might have to deal with catcalls, being followed, or even having someone grab their arm or their breast. If they know how to deal with this kind of attention by not answering back, leaving assertively, and making sure that they are in places where other people can help them, girls can protect themselves from greater harm most of the time no matter what kind of clothes they are wearing. If they actively solicit and encourage sexual attention by acting provocatively, girls can unfortunately put themselves into situations that are less safe.

We have found that it works best to give factual information with a clear statement about your own expectations and boundaries. For example, adults might say that it is normal to want to be seen as attractive and to have sexual feelings for people you like. It is true that in a perfect world, you should be able to dress how you like, go where you want, and act proud of your body without needing to worry about being bothered or attacked. It is unfair that you have to worry about anyone getting pregnant, getting a bad reputation, or getting a sexually transmitted disease. Unfortunately, the world isn't perfect and life's not fair. That's why we have the safety rules we do.

An increasing area of abuse is through technology. Unfortunately, digital cameras and cell phones make it so easy to share suggestive or explicitly sexual photos and messages in what feels like a very private relationship. Too many young people have been devastated when their trust was betrayed and their private information was given to everyone they know or posted all over the Internet.

In our workshops, we try to be both realistic and truthful in what we tell our teen students. We say that it is not our job to tell them how to dress. We are not going to discuss what kinds of sexual behavior are right or wrong for what they might do with people their own age. That is the job of their parents, teachers, and other adults. As their Teenpower instructors, it is our job to make sure that our students have the skills to:

- Stop and think about what behavior is truly okay with them rather than being on automatic pilot and just going along with something to please other people or to be accepted.
- Set personal boundaries to protect their emotional and physical safety.
- Respect the personal boundaries of others by staying in charge of their behavior no matter what they might be feeling or thinking.
- Get help if someone tries to push against their boundaries or the boundaries of others in ways that are hurtful or unsafe.
- Speak up if a friend seems to be getting into an unsafe situation.
- Defend themselves physically if someone is assaulting them, and they cannot leave and get help.

We remind teens that touch, games, and teasing for fun, play, or affection should be safe, okay with everyone involved, not a secret, and, until everyone involved is legally an adult, allowed by the adults in charge. Even when both are legal adults, we teach young people that consent to sexual activity cannot be given if someone is incapacitated or intimidated. To learn more sexual abuse and assault prevention skills, see the Sexual Harassment section in Chapter 8 on bullying and the Teenpower resources on our website.[9]

It is true that in a perfect world, you should be able to dress how you like, go where you want, and act proud of your body without needing to worry about being bothered or attacked. Unfortunately, the world isn't perfect.

Men as Allies to Children - Answers for Common Concerns

According to John Luna-Sparks, LCSW and clinician working with many children who are sexual abuse survivors[5], "One of the ways to help protect kids from sexual abuse is for them to have healthy relationships with men as well as with women."

A few years ago, I heard this very poignant story from a friend. "When I was a child," she said, "I often had to stay in bed because I had rheumatic fever. A man who was a friend of our family, remembering the isolation and loneliness when he himself had rheumatic fever as a child, used to come up to my bedroom and visit with me, playing games and talking. Recently, I met this man at a party and told him again how much the time he had spent with me while I was sick in bed had meant to me. This lovely man, who is now 88-years-old, said sadly, 'Oh, I'd never dare to do that nowadays. Someone would think I was going to do something wrong."

My friend sighed and added, "Isn't that terrible? What a loss it would have been in my life as a child if I had not had those wonderful visits! Depriving kids of healthy relationships with good men makes them less safe, not more safe!" I completely agree. So many times, I've been approached by men who want to have fun, supportive interactions with the children in their lives, but are afraid of having their intentions misunderstood. Most children have far more opportunities to interact with women than with men. This is a great pity, because both boys and girls often long to do things with men as well as with women.

Although most acts of violence and abuse are committed by men, most men are neither violent nor abusive. In my experience, most men are loving, compassionate, respectful people. However, even when they have very good intentions, both men and women, boys and girls, sometimes do things that are hurtful or upsetting to others. Fortunately, most problems of this kind can be prevented or stopped through better skills and understanding about communication and boundaries with children and their parents.

Below are eight concerns we often hear from caring men about their interactions with children. The answers are based on the experiences of the wonderful men in our organization who use Kidpower skills and strategies to prevent misunderstandings and build strong relationships with the children and parents in their lives.

1. *Concern About Playing: It's gotten so I'm afraid to tickle or rough-house with my grandchildren!* Touch for play like tickling or rough-housing is wonderful as long both the child and the adult like it and the parents are okay with this. Sometimes games like tickling start out okay and then get to be too much. Make an agreement ahead of time that you will stop right away when the child says, "Stop!" and make sure that the child knows how to communicate this message in a way that you can understand.

Even children who can't speak yet have ways of letting you know when they don't like a game anymore. You can build their safety and confidence by paying attention to these cues and helping them develop words to

So many times, I've been approached by men who want to have fun, supportive interactions with the children in their lives, but are afraid of having their intentions misunderstood.

communicate their feelings. For example, you might say to a child who is pulling back, "It looks like your body is telling both of us that you want to stop. Is that right? Thank you for letting me know."

2. *Concern About Lap Sitting: Is it okay to let the child of an acquaintance climb onto my lap?* When in doubt, check with the child's parents. Ask in a way that makes it clear that you will be positive no matter what the answer is. For example, "She looks like she'd like to sit in my lap. I'd love it but only if this is really okay with you. What do you think?" If the parents say that they'd prefer not, be prepared to reply cheerfully, "Thank you for telling me!"

If the child is somewhere without the parents, such as at school, ask the teacher or other adult in charge what the rules are. Again, pay attention to cues like the child starting to wiggle to get down. Rather than trying to coax this child to stay on your lap, encourage the child to do something else when she or he is done sitting with you.

3. *Concern About Watching: My nephew gets upset if I even just watch him too much. What could possibly be wrong with just trying to connect by looking at a child?* People are different, and what bothers one person might be quite enjoyable to another. Some children adore having adults watch them at play. Other children find clear and direct observation to be extremely intense and intrusive and will withdraw from adults who they perceive to be staring at them. The best way to build a connection is to be completely okay with having your nephew not respond to you right away. Instead of trying to push for a direct interaction, do something interesting nearby, possibly related to what he is doing, and let your nephew approach you on his own terms.

4. *Concern About Greetings: I find young children so delightful and really like to say "Hello" when I see them. But often they seem afraid of me because I'm a large man with a loud voice. How can I let them and their parents know that I'm a safe person?* You can show families that you are likely to be a trustworthy person by acting with a great deal of respect towards them. Think about where you are, whether or not other people are around, and how familiar you are to this family. The larger you are, or the more isolated the place is, the more physical space you might need to give in order to not crowd others unintentionally.

If you are a familiar person or in a public place with others around, you can start with a quick friendly greeting, as long as you are completely okay with the parents or children choosing not to respond. Remember that their response has nothing to do with you. Just pleasantly accept the right of others not to greet you.

If the parents are okay with you talking with their child and the child seems interested, try meeting the child where he or she is by getting down to the child's level and making your voice soft and calm. If a child seems uncomfortable even if the adults are okay, the best approach is to ignore the child and have a friendly conversation with the parents. If the parents worry about their child not seeming polite to you, let them know that you are fine and prefer that children not be pressured to interact with you. If you

Some children find clear and direct observation to be extremely intense and intrusive and will withdraw from adults who they perceive to be staring at them.

Healthy relationships help protect kids from abusive ones

keep running into this family, your friendly respectful greetings are likely to have a positive effect after a while.

5. Concern About Protecting: What if I am in public and I see a child I don't know who is lost or about to do something dangerous? If a mother sees a strange man approaching her child, she might panic, but I don't want to stand by and do nothing when a child is at risk of coming to harm. In Kidpower, we teach families that the safety rules are different in emergencies and that, if a child is having the kind of emergency where she or he cannot check first, the safety rule is to get help, even from a stranger.

If possible, try to help or protect the child while keeping your distance. Suppose that you see a young child wandering somewhere with no adults close by. Often it works to say in a very calm way, "Where's your mom? Please take me to your mom!" You can follow the child to her or his adults and say, "I was worried because you seemed so far away from your child." If this doesn't work, you can try to get help by staying near the child while you call 911 or by walking with the child to the nearest checkout counter, security guard, etc.

Suppose that a child is at immediate risk of getting hurt - perhaps by a car, an animal, or another person or because of a cliff, pond, or busy street. Remember that the safety of a child is more important than anyone's embarrassment, inconvenience, or offense. This is a time when you might need to physically stop the child. You can help prevent problems for yourself by calling out to the world over and over to explain what you are doing as you do it. For example, "I am stopping this girl from running into the street. Please help me!"

Be prepared that the child's parents might see your intervention as being threatening or offensive. Remember that you took this action because the safety of a child comes first. If a parent does get upset, you can say something reassuring and leave. For example, "I am sorry I upset you. I just wanted to make sure your child was safe. I will leave now." If you are worried that a parent might make a complaint about your stepping in, you can contact the security guard, store manager, or police yourself to explain what happened.

6. Concern About Hugging: As a male teacher, I've become afraid to hug a child or hold hands. Yet so often my young students crave physical affection, especially if they are upset. How can I make sure this is going to be okay? What a sad and lonely world it would be if children could never be touched with affection by the adults who are caring for them! Develop a written school policy about physical affection that is known to the administration, parents, and teachers. Affection should be age-appropriate, not forced, offered equally to those children who want it, not distracting to educational activities, and never a secret. Within those boundaries, affection at a level you feel good about should be offered joyfully and with confidence.

7. Concern About Forcing: What if I have to make children do something that they really don't like? I'm afraid they will accuse me of child abuse!

One of Kidpower's boundary principles is that, although we each belong to ourselves, some things are not a choice. For example, you might need to stop a child physically who is about to throw a rock through a window or hit another child. You might need to overrule a child who does not want to leave the park or playground or force a child to get stitches, use a car seat, or wear a bike helmet.

Touch for affection or play should be the choice of the child as long as it's okay with each person involved, safe, and allowed by the adults in charge. Touch for health or safety or to move a child when necessary is often not the child's choice – but any kind of touch or any kind of problem should never have to be a secret.

If a child is upset with you, you can acknowledge the child's feelings, explain that this is not a choice, offer what choices you can, and encourage the child to tell everyone about what happened. For example, "I understand that you are sad that we have to go inside. It is okay to feel unhappy. But it is raining and I don't want to get wet. You can walk on your own or I can help you. You can tell your mom and dad that I picked you up to get us both out of the rain."

8. *Concern About Joking: I like to joke a lot. My niece used to think my teasing was wonderful but now she gets offended. What am I doing wrong?* There are two issues here. One is that, as adults, we want to be careful to model using humor respectfully. In other words, even if children laugh, we want to be careful to avoid humor that puts others down for how they look, for their abilities, or who they are or that makes being mean seem funny. The other is that, as children get older, a joke that once seemed hilarious might now seem embarrassing. Your niece is giving you a wonderful opportunity to get to know and understand her better. Ask her what kinds of jokes she likes or doesn't like and why. She might even be willing to help you find jokes that both of you enjoy. Or, she might prefer to have a relationship with you that does not involve teasing at all for a while.

With good boundaries and clear communication, men can be tremendous allies to children and give them the joy of having caring men as active players in their lives

As children get older, a joke that once seemed hilarious might now seem embarrassing.

Making Relationships With Kids Work Safely and Well for Everyone

The People Safety skills that Kidpower teaches are useful in building positive relationships regardless of gender, age, or abilities. Here are ten key points for adults to remember in interacting with children to build relationships that will work safely and well for everyone:

1. **When in doubt, check first with parents or other caregivers and listen to the answers.**

2. **Never try to overrule a child's parents unless there is an urgent safety issue.**

3. **Make agreements with the adults in charge about what is and is not okay in different situations.**

4. **Remember that affection should be a choice, not a requirement.**

5. Meet children where they are in terms of connection and let them come to you.

6. Notice and respect each child's boundaries and be prepared for these boundaries to change.

7. Never ask a child to keep gifts, favors, treats, touch, activities, games, or problems a secret.

8. Be clear and public when something is not a choice.

9. Be careful with humor and teasing, pay attention to everyone's reaction, and be open to changing joking and playing habits in order to strengthen your relationships.

10. Put safety first, even if someone might get upset with you.

Listening Power Safety Sign

Kidpower Research Study

Thanks to funding from the Ruddie Memorial Youth Foundation, Shattuck Applied Research + Evaluation conducted a rigorous research study in 2010 with 238 third-grade students in Santa Cruz County. The results demonstrate that the Kidpower Everyday Safety Skills program produced an immediate and sustained contribution to students' safety knowledge in four competency areas that reduce risk factors for victimization from most bullying, molestation, abuse, violence, and abduction.

On the post-test three months after their workshop, the number of students who gave correct answers to many of the multiple-choice questions in the survey rose significantly compared to the number on the pre-test. For example:

- "If a person you liked a lot asked you to keep a problem a secret, what would you do?" Correct answers rose from 14.8% to 63.3%, a 45.5% gain.
- "If you have a safety problem and your grownups are busy, what would you do?" Correct answers rose from 18% to 81.3%, a 63.3% gain.
- "If someone you like a lot feels upset or sad because you do not want to be hugged or kissed, what would you do?" Correct answers rose from 39.8% to 66.4%, a 26.6% gain.

Chapter Ten

Protecting Kids from Abduction and Teaching Stranger Safety

On a very personal level, I know how quickly a situation can go from safe to dangerous - and how abruptly an assault can occur. As described in Chapter One, I do this work because, in 1985, in the middle of the day, in a public place with people standing all around, I stopped a man who was threatening to kidnap a group of young children, including my own daughter and son. Afterwards, the kids were fine, but I was haunted with questions. What if he had knocked me down? What if I had not been there to protect them? Would they have known what to do? What about the unprotected children this man probably went on to assault? Searching for answers to these questions was the inspiration for my starting Kidpower.

The knowledge and skills explained throughout this book can keep kids safe most of the time. This chapter will discuss what adults need to understand about abductions, actions we can take to help protect our kids, and how we can prepare young people to protect themselves. The September 5, 2010 edition of *The Washington Post* published an article titled, "*Child Abduction Study Finds Capable Kids are Their Own Best Defense*." The study, conducted by the National Center for Missing and Exploited Children, analyzed 4,200 cases of attempted but unsuccessful abductions and found that 84% of the children escaped through their own efforts by recognizing a bad situation and avoiding it or by screaming and kicking to draw attention and get away. 16% of the time, an adult intervened to help them.[1]

Many adults have told me about abduction attempts they remember from their childhood.

When I was about five, I got lost in the store. As I was wandering around, a lady grabbed my hand and started marching me out of the store. To this day, I don't know what would have happened if my Mom hadn't suddenly caught sight of us. As soon as my Mom called out to me, the lady ran away. I can still feel the hand of this woman pulling me away and my little feet following her obediently.

When I was thirteen, my dad dropped me off in the parking lot of the mall so he could go to a store and meet me later. A man started following me in the parking lot, calling out to me that he needed help. I was about to go over to him, but suddenly felt afraid and ran into the mall. When I told my dad about the man, he called the police.

A study analyzed 4,200 cases of attempted but unsuccessful abductions and found that 84% of the children escaped through their own efforts by recognizing a bad situation and getting away from it or escaping it by screaming and kicking to draw attention.

"As soon as I was in the car, I knew I'd made a big mistake."

When I was eight, I was walking to school. It started to rain hard. A man who I thought I knew driving a nice car pulled up and told me I'd better get into the car. I was used to following directions from adults so I did what he said. As soon as I was in the car, I knew I'd made a big mistake. I jumped out of the car at a stoplight, even though the car was still moving a little.

When it comes to child safety, including abduction, a fatalistic "it doesn't happen that often and there's nothing you can do anyway" attitude is not the right answer -- and, neither is overprotecting kids so that they become anxious, never get to do anything on their own, or don't learn take charge of their own safety. Lecturing kids about "stranger danger" just makes them worried without making them safer.

Fortunately, realistic safety plans and positive practice of skills for being safe when you are out in the world both with strangers and people you know can increase confidence, reduce anxiety, and prepare kids to make choices that will protect them from dangerous people most of the time.

When discussing how to protect children and teens from abduction, we must always remember that violence and abuse are caused by people who act in destructive ways towards others. Crime is NOT caused by the victims of these crimes. Parents might sometimes lack the knowledge they need and deserve to help protect their kids from harm, and at the same time, it is *never* the parent's fault or the child's fault if they don't have this knowledge.

We must always remember that violence and abuse are caused by people who act in destructive ways towards others. Crime is NOT caused by the victims of these crimes.

The reality is that not all attacks can be prevented – and that, unfortunately, though the justice system has had great successes, it has also sometimes failed to protect children and communities from dangerous people. I am all in favor of laws that give our law enforcement officers better tools and resources for keeping child predators out of our communities and for acting quickly and effectively when a child is reported missing. However, the focus of this book is on what each of us can do as individuals to protect the children in our lives.

Upsetting Realities About Kidnapping That Adults Need to Know

Sometimes Kidpower is asked to conduct workshops for a family, a school, or a community after children have been abducted and murdered. I can never forget the photos of smiling, bright-eyed girls and boys whose lives have been cut tragically short or the heartbroken voices and faces of their loved ones.

I feel deeply troubled when some people try to minimize the risk of abduction by saying, "Oh, the chance of a child being abducted by a stranger is statistically really small."

The horror and heartbreak caused by the abduction of each child are immeasurable. The ripple effects are terrifying for everyone around that child and for every caring person who hears the story. At Kidpower, we vividly remember the story of twelve-year-old Polly Klaas who was kidnapped from her home in the small town of Petaluma, California, in 1993.[2] Children as young as five kept asking our instructors, "Can you stop what happened to Polly from happening to me?"

Even an attempted kidnapping can be traumatic. "My eight-year-old daughter did everything right," her mother told us. "She was waiting for me outside after her dance class. When a very friendly man she didn't know tried to get her into his car, she ran back in the building to get help from the adults in her class. But months later she is still having nightmares and sleeping in my bed at night."

According to U.S. Department of Justice studies, children are most likely to be seriously injured or murdered when the kidnapping is done by a stranger. Usually, this happens within the first three hours of abduction and within a few miles of where the child was taken. Most abductions of this kind are done by someone luring children to a vehicle rather than by forcing them physically at first. About half of children stolen are from four to eleven years old, and the others are twelve or older. Seventy-four percent are girls.[3]

Law enforcement experts define kidnapping in three different categories: kidnapping by a relative of the victim or "family kidnapping" (49 percent), kidnapping by an acquaintance of the victim or "acquaintance kidnapping" (27 percent), and kidnapping by a stranger to the victim or "stranger kidnapping" (24 percent). A kidnapping by someone who is well known to the child can be dangerous and terrible, but is much less likely to result in murder. It is estimated that between 50 to 150 children a year are murdered in the United States in "stranger kidnapping."[4]

A victim of abduction can be a person of any age. The Justice Department data indicates that the risk of abduction by a stranger is relatively low for preschoolers, but increases through elementary school and peaks at age fifteen. Teen-age girls are considered most vulnerable. A high percentage of "acquaintance kidnappings" involve teens in sexual assault and dating violence situations.[5]

According to the U.S. Department of Justice statistics from a 2002 study quoted on the website of the National Center for Missing and Exploited Children[6] (NCMEC):

- 797,500 children (younger than 18) were reported missing in a one-year period of time resulting in an average of 2,185 children being reported missing each day.
- 203,900 children were the victims of family abductions.
- 58,200 children were the victims of non-family abductions.
- 115 children were the victims of "stereotypical" kidnapping. These crimes involve someone the child does not know or a slight acquaintance who holds the child overnight, transports the child 50 miles or more, kills the child, demands ransom, or intends to keep the child permanently.

No matter who the perpetrator is or what the outcome is, an abduction of any kind is an assault and an act of violence. Although having a child vanish is our greatest fear, most young people who have been kidnapped even for a short time have had a traumatic experience that has often included being molested. Even one child harmed is one child too many - and the numbers of attempted and successful abductions are NOT small!

Children as young as five kept asking our instructors, "Can you stop what happened to Polly from happening to me?"

Even one child harmed is one child too many – and the numbers of attempted and successful abductions are NOT small!

Showing young people videos of kidnappings or visiting spots where a child was stolen does not prevent children from being abducted.

Tragic Lessons

The footage captured on the surveillance camera at a car wash in Sarasota, Florida, on February 1, 2004, shows one unbearable story of what the above statistics can represent. A pretty pre-teen girl is standing on the sidewalk. She keeps standing still as a man comes up to her and says something. Within a few seconds, she goes without resistance as the man leads her away to his car. She might have been fooled by the fact that his shirt looked a bit like a uniform or maybe she was intimidated by what he said. We will never know.

What we do know is that the man shown on the tape, multiple sex offender Joseph P. Smith, eventually showed police where he had hidden the body of twelve-year-old Carlie Jane Brucia, who had taken a short cut on her way to meet her stepfather.[7] Heartsick while watching this tape, we want to shout warnings to Carlie like, "Watch out! Don't go with him! Pull away! Yell! Don't believe what he tells you! Hit him! RUN!"

What happened was not Carlie's fault or her parents' fault. She was taken by surprise and didn't know what to do. Her parents did not have the knowledge about how to prepare her and probably thought she was safe because she was in an area with so many people close by.

Many parents showed the tape of Carlie's abduction to their young teen daughters over and over, in the hope that they would learn not to let this happen. Often parents react to a kidnapping by visiting spots where a child was stolen and piling up toys and candles both to honor the child who was taken and to try to protect their own children. Unfortunately, this approach makes kids anxious but is not likely to prevent them from being abducted.

We cannot bring back the young people who have lost their lives, but we can honor them by using the tragic lessons learned to help protect other kids.

Young people need to know:

• *When and how to be impolite, disobey adults, make a scene, lie, break their promises, and fight back.* Children are normally taught to trust what adults say, to be respectful, to be honest, and to do what they're told. They need to know that, if someone unexpectedly tries to approach them or to take them away, they are safest leaving immediately and going to where more people are. They need to know how to make a scene to attract the attention of bystanders and to hit and kick if need be in order to escape. They need to know that they have the right to lie and break their promises to be safe.

• *To project an attitude of awareness when they are out in public.* No matter how they feel inside, kids are less likely to be selected by someone who is looking for an easy victim if they show awareness and confidence when they are out in the world. A child who is not alert is more vulnerable to being attacked.

• *Not to automatically trust someone who seems to be wearing a uniform.* A high school girl in my town was approached by a man who said he was a plain-clothes police officer and showed her his badge. When she got in his car, he molested her. Abductors have tricked children by saying, "You *have* to come with me. I'm the security guard, and you'll get in trouble if you don't." One twelve-year-old girl was sexually abused in the gardening section of a large department store. She had gone with a man in what she thought was a uniform who had told her that he had seen her shoplifting and that she had to go with him. She was so shocked that she didn't know what to do. Fortunately, someone saw them and stopped the assault.

- *Not to believe what an attacker says.* Abductors coerce kids into going with them by threatening their loved ones and lying about their intentions. Imagine a child being told, "I won't hurt you or your family if you'll just do what I say. I just want money. I promise." Children like twelve-year-old Polly Klaas have bravely cooperated with a kidnapper because they believed that they must in order to keep their families from harm.[2]

- *How to make safer choices when the unexpected happens.* As described in Chapter Seven about self-defense, predatory attackers seek to gain privacy and control. Abductors often take advantage of opportunities to identify and approach a potentially vulnerable person - and then deliberately use tactics that confuse, trick, or intimidate their intended victims into making less safe choices. Being prepared to recognize potential danger and to prevent an attacker from getting more privacy or control can make a huge difference to your safety at any age.

As Gretchen, who is a police officer, told me, "We live on a rural road. Before I let either of my sons walk down the road to the bus stop, I made sure they were prepared. I taught them that, unless they knew the driver very well, if a car slowed down or tried to approach them for any reason, they should immediately run away from the car in a different direction than the car was traveling and start yelling. We also agreed on four neighbors with whom they had permission to get rides without telling me first. During the eight years we lived there, each of my sons had someone in a car try to approach them as they were walking alone. They did what we'd practiced and, each time, the driver left quickly. We all believe that these were dangerous people and that running away saved my son's lives. "

- *To run away, yell, scream, hit, and kick even if the attacker has a knife or a gun.* Being threatened by someone who has a weapon is very dangerous and there are no guarantees, but most of the time people are safer doing their best to escape. Allowing an attacker to tie you up, gag you, or take you away gives the attacker more privacy and more control, which makes the danger bigger. The mystique of weapons is so large that young people need very specific information because otherwise they are likely to freeze. Two teen girls were taken in a car and sexually assaulted by a man who just *said* he had a gun, even though they never saw it. One girl was walking home from school. Suddenly, a man pointed a gun at her and said, "Get in this car!" She turned the other way and ran away screaming for help and he left.

- *What to do if you notice unsafe behavior, even from a woman, someone who seems familiar, or someone you know.* Although most kidnappers and child molesters are men, women have also abducted and abused children

Not paying attention is less safe out in public

We cannot bring back the young people who have lost their lives, but we can honor them by using the tragic lessons learned to help protect other kids.

and, most of the time, children and teens are assaulted by people they know. In addition, a man might have a woman helping him to convince a child into thinking it is safe to be with him. If *anyone's* behavior seems unsafe, young people need to know how to avoid or get away from this person and how to get help.

Being prepared to take action can protect kids from many kinds of danger. One of my most terrifying memories as a twelve-year-old was when the driver of one of the cars on a Girl Scout outing, who was my friend's mother, got progressively more intoxicated as the day went on. I had no idea what to do during our trip or how to explain to my parents what had happened. In our workshops, we sometimes have older kids practice setting boundaries by refusing to go with a family friend who was supposed to give them a ride home from a party and is acting drunk.

Taking Preventative Action Rather than Making Decisions Through Denial or Fear

Our job as adults is to take realistic balanced precautions to protect young people and ourselves from abduction and other dangers. Instead of either denying potential danger or using scare tactics, we can give children and teens clear safety rules to follow and opportunities to practice how to keep themselves safe. In addition, there are other important preventative actions that we can take to increase the security of our families.

Lock the Door. One simple prevention action that adults often neglect is to lock the doors and secure the windows of their cars and homes. Remember that most break-ins are usually walk-ins. Adults can teach children to lock the door and to follow their Safety Rules about opening it to someone. We want to be able to decide who can easily get into our homes or cars, instead of letting chance choose for us.

This simple action would prevent many crimes. To take just one example, a ten-year-old girl in my town was molested at night by a man who was a complete stranger to this family. He had walked in through an unlocked back door in her home. He found her bedroom as he walked down the hall, while her parents slept across the way. Thankfully, this girl managed to yell, and the attacker ran away.

Supervise Children Until They are Old Enough, Big Enough, and Skilled Enough to Protect Themselves. Children and youth need their adults to protect them from danger until they are able to be in charge of their own safety. Young children have been kidnapped within a few feet of their adults or when left for just a few minutes in car, yard, or store - and of course, they are also vulnerable to being harmed in many other ways. The problem is that adults are often lulled into complacency by what I call the "Illusion of Safety."

Once while I was taking a walk with my husband, we saw a three-year-old girl who was at the bottom of her garden, by the street, while the adults with her were almost out of sight at the top of the garden by the house. We stopped, worried that she might wander into the street or meet someone who was not a safe person. The little girl smiled and showed us the spider under the bushes that she was playing with. Her adults had no clue what this child was doing. We were afraid to leave this little girl alone, so I said, "Go get your Mom so you can show her the spider!" The little girl ran happily up the stairs to get her mother.

I have seen a crying baby left alone in a stroller while his family was playing in the water at the beach. I have seen a toddler in a pink dress lagging way behind the two women caring for her on a forest trail. I have seen a preschooler slip through the slats in a fence bordering a cliff while his babysitter was heading with a baby towards home. Each time, I have made sure that the child was returned to the care of the adults who were supposed to be in charge. Each time, I have worried about what might have happened to that child if I hadn't been there. I am sure that the adults with those children loved them and would have been horrified if anything bad had happened to them.

Unsupervised children often do not follow directions or act in ways that adults expect them to. In 2005, a two-year-old who was killed by a train in San Jose. He had climbed out of his stroller and followed his babysitter across the tracks instead of waiting for her to come get him as she had told him to do.[8]

Adults need to remember that no matter how busy or distracted we are, we must make sure that younger children are watched closely and that the people who we trust to care for our children have the same standards that we do.

Make sure that older kids are fully prepared before making them responsible for younger kids. Leaving younger siblings in the care of older siblings or having a teen babysitter can be enormously convenient and a benefit for everyone IF this young person is truly capable of handling this responsibility. A babysitting class such as that taught by the Red Cross[9] plus a self-defense class can prepare a teen to handle most emergencies. When she was fourteen years old, Chantal took her younger brother and cousins to the neighborhood park. Even though it was mid-day, the park was completely deserted. Suddenly, Chantal noticed a man staring at them. When no one else came to the park and the man kept hanging around, she pulled the younger children off the slides and swings and, despite their protests, kept them close to her and brought them home.

Put a child's safety ahead of a child's wishes. Just because your child wants to do something without you does NOT mean that your child is prepared to handle different kinds of safety problems. Decisions about when to allow a child more independence should be made consciously based on a realistic assessment of the child's capabilities and on the specific situation. Just as kids shouldn't go into the pool without an adult next to them until they know how to swim, or walk down the street alone until they know how to stay out of the way of cars, children should not be allowed to be anywhere without adult protection until they are ready to handle potential problems with other people.

When his mother Revé wanted to shop for lamps in a department store, six-

Unsupervised children often do not follow directions or act in ways that adults expect them to.

A child's safety is more important than a child's wishes

Remember that bad things can happen to anyone, anywhere, even in familiar surroundings. It is so much safer to give a false alarm than to ignore a true warning.

year-old Adam Walsh asked her to let him keep watching some older boys playing video games. Since she was only going to be gone a few minutes and was only a few aisles away, she left him. During the seven minutes Revé was gone, a security guard told the boys to leave the store. Adam did not know how to tell the security guard that he was supposed to wait right there for his mother and went outside as ordered, making him vulnerable to the man who captured and killed him.[10]

Don't assume that your child is safe because someone is a woman or because of where you live. Eight-year-old Sandra Cantu often walked on her own and visited neighbors in her mobile home park in Tracy, California. But on March 27, 2009, she never came home. Melissa Huckaby, who was convicted of kidnapping and murdering her, was the mother of Sandra's five-year-old friend, a teacher, and the granddaughter of a minister.[11]

Residents of the Orchard Estates Park did not know that Melissa had previously been questioned by police about possible arson in Northern California and about taking a seven-year old girl from the park in Tracy for several hours without permission a few months earlier. The mother of this girl reported that the hospital emergency room found that her daughter had been drugged with a muscle relaxant.[12]

Your own mobile home park, cul-de-sac, or neighborhood can seem so contained and safe, and neighbors you meet and see coming and going can seem like people you know. But you can't trust someone to be alone with your child unless you spend enough time to get to know this person well. Listen to what this person is saying. Don't ignore or explain away discrepancies. Pay attention to your intuition. Stay connected with this person. Sometimes people who seem trustworthy can have hidden problems that might cause them to become unstable and do something dangerous.

Notice and act on warnings of potential danger. In 1991, the week before twelve-year-old Jaycee Dugard was kidnapped, her friend Amelia Edwards was followed by a car with a man and a woman on her way home from school. Terrified, Amelia ran home and told her parents. They thought Amelia was being "overly dramatic" and took no further action. Although not understanding how to address this issue was neither Amelia's nor her parents' fault, this family later must have been devastated when they realized that this car and couple were very similar to the descriptions of Jaycee's kidnapping.[13]

Remember that bad things can happen to anyone, anywhere, even in familiar surroundings. If a child mentions being followed or approached by someone who is behaving unsafely, call the police and inform other parents, even if it seems unlikely. It is so much safer to give a false alarm than to ignore a true warning. If children's fears seem irrational, try to understand what's going on for them. Instead of just reassuring them, ask caring questions to see if you can get a clear picture of the situation. Doing this helps children develop the habit of telling you about their problems.

Tell children to speak up about anything that worries or bothers them –

and to keep asking until they get the help they need. Imagine what might have been different if Amelia's family had had this knowledge. The school, police, and newspaper could have warned the community. Very likely Jaycee's stepfather or mother would have driven her to school. Maybe law enforcement officials would have caught this couple before they kidnapped Jaycee or another young person.

Teach kids what to do if they get lost or bothered in public. Kids need a safety plan for getting help everywhere they go. If they get lost, they need to know how to find someone who will help them without going with someone who might be a danger to them. If they get bothered, they need to know how to get away from someone who might be insulting or threatening them without getting into a fight and how to get help.

Not knowing how to get help when he got lost in public cost eight-year-old Leiby Kletzy his life. He had begged his parents to let him walk the seven blocks home from day camp through the Brooklyn neighborhood where he'd lived all his life. Even through they'd done a dry run together, Leiby didn't know to go into a store and call his parents if he got lost and didn't know how to avoid being tricked by someone who was acting kind and friendly. On July 11, 2011, the surveillance cameras of stores on Leiby's way show him getting off the route home and then being joined by a kind-looking man who probably offered to help him find his way home. Leiby even waited for this man outside the dentist office before getting into his car and being kidnapped and killed. [14]

Set Up a Neighborhood Watch program. Part of what makes all kinds of crime including home invasions and abductions possible is that people are so focused on minding their own business that they fail to pay attention to suspicious behavior in the world around them. In the US, most police departments are happy to send representatives to help set up a Neighborhood Watch[15] program. Even without an official program, neighbors can help prevent kidnapping and other crimes by reporting unknown people who seem to be hanging around their streets or parks or to be acting in ways that might be unsafe.

Too often, adults will say after an attack has occurred, "I was a little worried about that guy, but I didn't want to be paranoid." In my experience, most police officers are deeply committed to public safety and would far rather be asked to check out what someone is doing in a neighborhood than to deal with the consequences of a crime.

Prepare an ID Kit. Our goal is to prepare and protect children so that they would never have to be in a position where an ID kit would be necessary. However, adults should still make it a habit to keep an updated ID kit, with fingerprints and recent photos of their children. Prepared ahead of time, an ID kit can help searchers find and identify a missing child. Having an ID kit with you when you take children to a public area can also be very useful in helping to find a lost child more quickly. Showing a recent photo works much better than describing the color of a child's clothing. Often in the United States, such kits are made available for free by police or sheriff departments or insurance companies.

Part of what makes all kinds of crime possible is that people are so focused on minding their own business that they fail to report suspicious behavior.

There is no point to teaching children safety skills about strangers until they really understand what a stranger is.

Teaching Stranger Safety - Not "Stranger Danger"

How I wish that the word "stranger" rhymed with "safety" or "awareness" rather than with "danger"! Believing that the world is full of dangerous people called "strangers" is emotionally unhealthy for kids. Too many children believe that, "A stranger is a bad guy who takes you away, and you never see your mommy or daddy again." Although we want to teach young people to be safe with strangers, we also want to teach them to be excited and joyful rather than frightened about meeting new people and having new experiences.

In our classes, we tell our students, "In Kidpower, we believe that most people are good. This means that most strangers are good. A few people in the world might do bad things, but you don't need to worry. You just need to follow your Safety Rules."

Another challenge in teaching kids about strangers is that what it means to "not know" someone can be very confusing. One father brought his daughter to Kidpower after she explained to him, "If I met a stranger, Dad, I could ask his name because then he wouldn't be a stranger anymore! ... Right?" There is no point to teaching children safety skills about strangers until they really understand what a stranger is!

Here are some ways we help young people of different ages understand about strangers.

Baby Simba. At a school assembly of six- and seven-year-olds, I got the students all to repeat with me, "A stranger is someone you don't know! A stranger can look like anybody!"

I then picked up a puppet designed from a character in the movie, *The Lion King*. "Who is this?" I asked.

"BABY SIMBA!" yelled sixty enthusiastic children.

I held my Baby Simba puppet up high so everyone could see. I made his little paw wave at the kids and said in a squeaky voice, "Hey! Come play with me!" Then I asked the children in my normal voice, "If you don't know me and I am with Baby Simba, am I still a stranger?"

Almost all of the kids shouted, "NO!"

A wave of intense anxiety rushed through the parents and teachers who were with the kids in the multipurpose room. "This is why we practice," I reassured the adults.

The students watched raptly while the principal of their school pretended to be a child. As my "Baby Simba" puppet called out to her, she walked over to another adult pretending to be her mother to ask if it was okay to play with me.

What's a Stranger? In classes with younger kids, we often go through a dialogue using leading questions to help build understanding. As the instructor, I start by asking in a cheerful voice, "What's a stranger?"

Especially after another frightening story has hit the news, my students' little faces are worried and their answers make me sad.

- *"A stranger is a bad guy who hurts kids."*
- *"A stranger will steal you and you will never see your mommy or daddy again."*
- *"A stranger gives you poison candy."*

I smile and say reassuringly, "Those are some scary pictures in your mind about worries you have about strangers. But what's a stranger?"

Sooner or later, a child who is frantically waving his or her hand will announce, "A stranger is just someone you don't know well."

"That's right!" I say. "So can a stranger be a man?"

"Yes!" the children say.

"What about a woman?" I ask.

"Yes!" they say again.

Then I ask, "Am I a stranger?"

Some children are unsure, so I ask, "Before today, did you know me?"

"No," they say.

"So," I say, "since a stranger is just someone you don't know well, am I a stranger?"

"Yes," the children agree.

"Now why is it okay for you to be with me here today?" I ask.

"Because you are teaching us to be safe," some children will guess.

I give an example by saying, "I would never do this, but suppose I met you on the sidewalk next week and I said, 'Hi, I'm Irene from Kidpower, remember? How about you come with me to learn more about safety?' Would that be a safe thing to do?" I shake my head no to give them the answer.

"No," my students agree.

"So why is it okay for you to be with me today?" I ask again.

"Because our grown-ups said it was okay!" the children will say.

"That's right!" I say. "Now I have one more tricky question. Are you a stranger to anyone?"

Especially after another frightening story about strangers has hit the news, our students' faces are worried and their answers make me sad.

*Ask leading questions such as, "Are **you** a stranger to anyone?"*

Talk about all the interesting strangers

Most younger children, even after all this dialogue, look doubtful and shake their heads. They have never thought of themselves as being strangers. Finally I ask, "Are there people in this world who don't know you?" As my students think about this, I add, "Maybe even millions and millions of people?"

As the children nod their heads, I sum it up, "Right. You are strangers to all those people and they are strangers to you. Because a stranger is just someone you don't know!"

Animal strangers. With younger children, we sometimes introduce Stranger Safety by talking about animals, explaining, "Most dogs are friendly. But a few dogs might bite or jump on you even if they wag their tails. So you Check First both with your grown-up and then with the dog's person before you play with a dog you don't know." We sometimes practice by having preschoolers pretend to be playing at a park. We approach the kids with a very cute toy dog or bird and coach them to Move Away and Check First with their teacher.

Interesting strangers. As soon as children can speak well enough to understand, we recommend that their adults start using the word "stranger" often in conversations in a fun way. As you walk down the street or look at books, point out all of the interesting strangers. You can also show children photos of all kinds of wonderful strangers doing interesting things – perhaps a firefighter, a kid, a family, a teacher, an ice cream vendor, and a clown.

Pictures in your mind. As kids get older, they get really tired of being warned about strangers. Instructor Mike asks a group of pre-teens, "How many of you have been told never, ever to talk with a stranger?"

Mike's students roll their eyes and raise their hands in a bored "I've heard this a million times" fashion.

Next Mike asks, "So how many of you *have* talked to strangers?"

This time, his students smile back and raise their hands cheerfully, interested in what comes next.

Mike explains, "The problem is that, even though we know better, most people, including adults, have pictures in our minds about the kind of strangers we might worry about. Let's be honest. Suppose someone is telling a story about someone who is alone in a parking lot and a stranger suddenly walks up. What would this stranger look like in your imagination?"

Being honest, his students answer, "A creepy guy. In a raincoat. With a gun." Mike then points out that these negative pictures in our minds about strangers can cause us to fail to notice the potentially dangerous behavior of someone we don't know who seems nice but isn't.

Stranger at the Door Story. We sometimes tell this true story in workshops to show how even someone with a lot of experience can make a mistake. One night, my twelve-year-old daughter Chantal and I were home alone. There was a knock at the door. "Who is it?" I called.

A very sad voice begged, "Please let me come in."

I was about to open the door when Chantal slapped my hand off the doorknob and said, "That's a stranger, Mom!"

My daughter was right so I yelled through the door, "What do you need? Can I make a call for you?"

Instead of answering, the woman wandered to my neighbor's house. Even though there were several adults with my neighbors, this woman had so many problems that they had to call the police in order to get her to a place where she could be helped.

Chantal was indignant. "Mom," she scolded. "You go all over the world telling people that a stranger is just someone you don't know and you were going to break our Stranger Safety Rules because you felt sorry for this woman!"

Acting nice is not the same as being trustworthy. Even as adults, we still make mistakes about trusting someone who acts nice. Logically, we know that we cannot tell from the outside whether someone is a potential danger or not. We can't judge a book by its cover. We don't always know from the outside if an apple will be good or bad. But it's hard not to make assumptions about people based on their appearance or superficial behavior.

Someone's "nice" behavior is not a useful way to decide whether or not this is a safe person. Violence expert Gavin de Becker in his best-selling book, *The Gift of Fear,* describes the tactics that rapists use to get women they

Although most people are good, a few people pretend to be nice because they are trying to trick you.

Children need to understand that their Stranger Safety Rules apply unless their adults tell them differently or until they really know someone quite well.

don't know to lower their guard. A few of these include acting charming, making unasked-for promises, labeling, and ignoring the word "no."[16]

Often people who have been assaulted will be bewildered and say, "But at first he seemed so nice." Both adults and kids need to remember that, although most people are good, a few people pretend to be nice because they are trying to trick you.

When Does Someone Stop Being a Stranger? Children need to understand that their Stranger Safety Rules apply unless their adults tell them differently or until they really know someone quite well. For younger children, it is important to be very specific. "You can stop treating someone like a stranger when I say that you can."

As they get older, children can learn assessment skills for figuring out when they should follow their Stranger Safety Rules and when they don't have to. When in doubt, their job is to ask their adults. Children can learn that it makes a difference whether they have spent time with someone in a public setting such as a park, the sidewalk, a bus, an airplane, or a store – or a more personal setting such as a home or their classroom.

You can ask children to finish this sentence. "You can stop treating someone like a stranger when _____." Possible answers might include:

- "My grown-ups have had this person take care of me."
- "I have seen this person lots of times in different places and know lots about this person."
- "I know this person's family and where he or she lives."

Discuss examples from the child's daily life. Ask questions such as:

- "Is our mail delivery person a stranger? How well do we know each other? Do we visit with this person only at the mailbox or post office or at other times and places?"

- "What about the nice lady who walks her dog? I have given you permission to pet her dog and talk with her in the park. She talks a lot and we know each other's names. But would it be following our Stranger Safety Rules for you to go into her yard to pet her dog?"

- "What about the owner of our corner grocery store? You can go the store without me and it's okay to eat the treat he always has for you. But have we ever spent time with him outside of the grocery store? Would it be following our Stranger Safety Rules for you to accept a ride home from him without checking with me first?"

As young people become more independent, they can make more distinctions such as:

1.　　　*Strangers* – people I don't know at all.

2.　　　*Acquaintances* – people I know somewhat, but not well enough to be sure that they are okay to be with outside of the ways we normally see each other.

3.   *Friends and family* – people I think I really know and can trust unless they start behaving in an unsafe way. (If there is a person you want to exclude from this category, you can tell the child to treat this person like a stranger.)

Helping Children Understand About Strangers

With younger children, look at pictures in magazines, look around their world, and talk about all the wonderful strangers there. Be sure to discuss current popular human or cartoon characters on TV or the movies – people they may feel that they know a lot about but who are still strangers to them.

1   With older children, discuss how well they know the different people in their lives. Explain that just seeing someone all the time, knowing the person's name, or petting the person's dog is not enough. Until we know someone really well, this person is still pretty much a stranger. Asking questions helps children to sort out this complicated idea.

2   Keep reminding children, "Most people are good. That means most strangers are good. Yes, a few people do bad things. But you don't have to worry. You just need to follow your Stranger Safety Rules."

3   Tell older children about a time you have forgotten that someone was a stranger or tell them the story above about my mistake with the stranger at the door. Kids are corrected so constantly that they often enjoy stories about adults doing the wrong thing.

Together or On Your Own?

Adults often give children very mixed messages about what is and is not safe with strangers. On the one hand, we tell children not to take anything from a stranger, not to talk to a stranger, and never, ever to go anywhere with a stranger. On the other hand, we direct children to greet people they don't know at neighborhood gatherings; eat food served to them by people they don't know in restaurants; go in cars, buses, or airplanes driven by people they don't know; and even stay in classrooms or homes in the care of other adults who are strangers to them.

Kids need to understand that their Stranger Safety Rules are different when they are with adults who are responsible for their safety and when they are on their own. This is because adults are better able to decide whether a situation is safe or not.

Here are some ways to build understanding.

Who Is the Only Person With You All the Time? In a Kidpower workshop, our instructor Anne asks her students, "Who is the only person who is with you all the time?"

The first answer most younger children will give is, "My mom," whether their mother is present or not.

Kids need to understand that their Stranger Safety Rules are different when they are with adults who are responsible for their safety and when they are on their own.

Being together means being with your grown-up, not just with your dog and not just with other kids.

Anne asks again, "Suppose your mom is not here right now? Who is the only person with you all the time?"

The second most common response is, "My dad," even if their father is out of town.

As Anne keeps asking, children will say, "My teacher ... my grandpa ... my babysitter." Again, children will say this even when none of these people are around. In the worldview of younger children, their important people always seem to be with them.

Anne gives her students some hints if need be until they can figure it out. "Who is the only person who is with you all the time – whether you are at home or visiting someplace else with friends or all by yourself in your room? That's right – the only person who is with you all the time is yourself! Your grown-ups are here to help you if you have a safety problem, but you are the only person in charge of you all of the time."

Sometimes children will argue, "But God is with me all the time!"

The answer for this that has worked well in Kidpower is, "You are right. God is with you all the time. However, we've asked leaders from a lot of different religions and they all agree that when only God is with you, God wants you to follow the safety rules as if you are on your own!"

We explain to children that understanding the difference is important because, "The safety rules are different when you are together with the grown-ups in charge of you or when you are on your own. Being together means being with your grown-up, not just with your dog and not just with other kids."

The Grocery Store Demonstration. In a workshop, our instructor Phil selects six-year-old Roberto and his mother to help him show the difference between being together and being on your own. "Roberto," Phil jokes, "Let's pretend that you are a kid, and this is your Mom."

"But," Roberto giggles, "I *am* a kid and this *is* my Mom!"

"Oh, that's right!" Phil says, pretending to be surprised. "Now, suppose that the two of you are in the grocery store and you are trying to talk your Mom into buying the marshmallow fudge strawberry breakfast cereal. Are you together with your Mom or are you on your own?"

"We are together," Roberto says.

Phil enlists another adult in the class to help. "Suppose that Lucia here is a stranger, and she wants to give you a free sample of this yummy cereal."

The Kidpower rule for children who are approached by a stranger when they are with their adult is to Check First. As Lucia approaches Roberto holding out an imaginary tray to offer a sample, Phil coaches Roberto to ask his mother, "May I have some?"

Roberto's Mom says, "Good job of checking first. Go ahead."

Roberto pretends to grab the sample, and stuff it into his mouth. His mom says, "Tell the nice lady, 'Thank you.'"

"Thank you," Roberto says dutifully.

Phil turned to the class and points out, "Roberto is eating food from a stranger. And he is talking to a stranger. Why is it okay?"

"Because he is together with his mom, and he asked first," say our students.

Phil moves Roberto's mom to stand a few feet away from Roberto and look in the other direction. He explains, "Now let's suppose that Roberto's mom is picking out some healthy oatmeal, and Roberto is looking longingly at that wonderful marshmallow chocolate breakfast cereal that his unreasonable mother refuses to buy. Roberto, are you together with your mom or are you on your own?"

"On my own," Roberto decides.

Phil points out that even if Roberto and his mom are only a little ways away from each other, if they are doing different things and looking away from each other, then he is on his own. The Kidpower rule for children who are approached by a stranger when they are on their own is to Move Away, go to their adult, and Check First.

Phil directs Lucia to come over again offering the sample. As she does, Phil asks Roberto, "If a stranger comes over now that you are on your own, is it safer for you to take the sample or to Move Away and go over to your mom so you can Check First?"

Lucia approaches with her tray, calling out invitingly, "Try my yummy free samples!"

Phil coaches Roberto to move away from Lucia, to go over to his mom, and to ask again, "May I have some more, please."

Roberto's mom says, "Thank you for checking first. We'll go together."

Learning When Situations Change From Being Together to Being On Your Own. You can act out different examples relevant to each child's specific situation, such as:

- Suppose you and your grandma are in the front yard, and a delivery person comes to bring a package. You want to be the one to take the package. Are you together with your grandma or on your own? (Together.) What do you do? (Ask first.) Now, suppose the delivery person comes into the yard while your grandma is in the house talking on the phone. Are you together or on your own? (On my own.) What do you do? (Move away, go to your grandma, and Check First.)

Practicing checking first

- Suppose you are at the park. Your father is pushing you on the swing, and an older kid wants to play with you. Are you together with your dad or on your own? (Together.) What do you do? (Ask first.) Now, suppose that another grown-up starts to visit with your father. While they are talking, a kid you don't know comes up to play with you. Are you together or on your own? (On my own.) What do you do? (Move away, go to my dad and Check First.)

- Suppose that we are riding the bus, and we meet a person who I seem to know, but you don't. Suppose that this person wants to shake hands with us. Are you together with me or on your own? (Together.) What do you do? (Ask first whether it is okay to shake hands.) Now, suppose that I start talking on my cell phone to someone and a man behind us on the bus reaches through the crack by the wall and tries to hold your hand. If I am not paying attention to what is happening with you, are you together with me or on your own? (On my own.) What do you do? (Move away, get your attention, and Check First.)

- Suppose you and your best friend's family are at the beach. All of you are building a sandcastle together, and a nice stranger comes up to offer an extra shovel. Are you together with your friend's grown-ups or on your own? (Together.) What do you do? (Ask first.) Now, suppose your friend has to go to the bathroom and he goes with his mother for just a minute. Suppose that while you are still building that castle, the nice stranger comes again to offer a pail. Are you together or on your own? (On my own.) What do you do? (Move away, go to my friend's mom, and Check First.)

Assessing situation safety by Thinking First. Instructor Raymond explains to his pre-teen students, "Your job when you are not with adults you can check with is to Think First about whether or not a situation is safe."

Raymond shows how this works by selecting twelve-year-old Sasha to help him. Raymond has Sasha stand in a spot where she is close to lots of other students and explains, "Sasha, let's imagine that you are downtown. The stores are open. There are lots of people walking around. Let's suppose that I'm from the ice cream shop handing out coupons for free ice cream cones to everyone who walks by."

Raymond pretends to hand out coupons to the crowd by offering imaginary coupons to the people in the class near Sasha. "Here's one for you, one for you, and one for you." Raymond approaches Sasha and hands her the coupon. Then, he shifts roles and asks, "Is it safe for you to take a coupon if you want to?"

"Yes it is," Sasha says. "Because I am together with lots of people who can help me if I have a problem."

Next, Raymond asks Sasha to stand in an empty spot in the room. "Now suppose it's another time of day or you are in another part of downtown. Most stores are closed and very few people are around. If I try to hand you a coupon, are you safer taking the coupon or moving away from me?"

Sasha says, "Move away and go to where more people are. Because I am on my own in an isolated place." As Raymond pretends to be the ice cream store employee offering the coupon in a very friendly way, Sasha moves with awareness towards the other people in the room saying cheerfully, "No, thanks!"

Teaching Children the Difference Between Being Together And Being on Their Own

1 Explain to children that their Stranger Safety Rules are different when they are together with their adults or when they are on their own. Act out the grocery store example for a younger child or the downtown demonstration for an older child who is out in public independently as described above.

2 Discuss how situations change using examples from the child's daily life. When a child goes to a new place, review what "together" means and what "on your own" means in terms of that situation.

3 Ask younger children, "Who is the *only* person with you all the time?" (Hint: the answer is, "I am!")

4 Encourage older children to tell you about times when they were approached by strangers and to explain how they decided whether or not this was safe. Try to validate what they did right instead of lecturing. If need be, you can let them tell you what they might do differently another time.

Stranger Safety Rules for When You Are On Your Own

Most abductions from strangers can be prevented if children are prepared to leave a situation immediately and to follow their safety plan for getting help as soon as someone they don't know starts paying attention to them. Knowing what to do and how to do it helps to protect kids most of the time.

Younger children should not have to worry about deciding whether something a stranger wants to do is safe or not. Instead of giving them a lot of "don'ts" about strangers, adults can teach them that their first Stranger Safety Rule is to move away and Check First with their trusted adults if a stranger approaches them when they are on their own. Be sure to remind them that "on their own" can mean anytime that their grown-ups are not paying attention to them.

When children are old enough to go out on their own without an adult to take care of them, their first Stranger Safety Rule is to Think First before letting someone they don't know approach them. Where are they? Are there lots of people close by who can help them if they have a problem? Are they in a more isolated place?

As adults, we can do our best to be vigilant but children are safer when they understand how to take responsibility for their own well-being.

Here is how we explain the safety rules to our students.

Check or Think First before letting a stranger get close to you. As discussed in Chapter Four on self-protection, and Chapter Seven on self-defense, most

Most problems with people who are potentially dangerous can be prevented by moving away from them.

Thank you for checking first!

There's a stranger at the door with flowers.

Check First before you open the door

problems with people who are potentially dangerous can be prevented by moving away from them.

As soon as they realize that they are by themselves and being approached by a stranger, younger children are safer if they immediately Move Away and go to their trusted adults to Check First. As soon as they notice that they are being approached by a stranger in a place where no one to help them is close by, older children are safer if they Think First, Move Away, and go to where there are more people. Opening the door is letting the person on the other side get closer to you, so Check First.

In crowded public places such as a movie line, a store, a bus, or a busy sidewalk, it is impossible not to be close to strangers some of the time. Children who are old enough to go out independently can learn to notice that the situation changes if someone starts paying inappropriate attention to them, starts trying to get closer, or makes them even a little uncomfortable. In that case, their Safety Plan is to go to where there are more people and to get help from a store clerk, ticket-seller, or bus driver if need be.

"Check First Before Talking to Strangers" Rule for Younger Children.
In Kidpower, we have found that younger children have a hard time remembering that someone they are talking with is still a stranger. We recommend teaching children eight years of age or younger to move away and Check First with their adult before talking to strangers when they are on their own.

"No talking" for younger children also means not shaking or nodding their heads or using other body language to communicate information.

In our workshops, we show the problem about talking to strangers using two instructors, Peter and Sandra. We do not do this role-play using children to demonstrate, because it would be too scary and because they learn more from watching. We show no negative consequences to the person pretending to be the child. These are just two people who don't know the Safety Rules.

Peter pretends to be a child playing on the sidewalk in front of his house. Peter might get down on his knees to make his role as a child very clear. Sandra pretends to be a stranger to Peter. She starts far away from him and slowly approaches in a very kind way during the following conversation.

Sandra as the stranger waves, takes a few steps towards Peter as the child, and says in a friendly happy voice, "Hi there! I just moved into the green house across the street. Is this your house?"

Peter, looking shorter on his knees, waves back and says, "Hi! Yes, I live here."

Sandra slowly keeps walking towards Peter and says, "I have a little boy just your age. Would you like to come over and visit some time?"

Peter looks happy and says, "Yes, I would!"

By now, Sandra is right next to Peter. She leans down, holds out her hand to shake his, and says, "My name is Sandra. What's yours?"

As Peter takes Sandra's hand, Sandra shifts out of the role-play and into instructor mode. She asks, "Does this look safe?"

Of course, everyone in the room says, "NO!"

A stranger CAN know your name! In a 2010 Kidpower research project done with third graders, most of the children surveyed prior to our training answered, "No" to the question, "Can a stranger know your name?" After our training, most of them answered correctly, that, yes, a stranger can know your name.[17]

"How could a stranger know your name?" I ask my students.

Usually kids say, "By seeing it on my shirt or backpack, maybe?" and then look unsure.

"Suppose," I explain, "that I am a kid at the park and my mom calls out, 'IRENE!' Will everyone who can hear her know my name?" We then have children practice moving away from a stranger calling their name.

"But what if the person really does know me?" The very first time we did this practice was long ago with my daughter Chantal at age eight. We told Chantal to imagine that she was sitting in our front yard and that Timothy was a stranger.

Timothy walked towards Chantal calling, "Hi, Chantal! Don't you remember me? I'm a friend of your mom."

As directed, Chantal immediately stood up and walked over to me saying, "Mom, a stranger knows my name!"

Both Timothy and I cheered, "Perfect!"

My daughter looked up at me and wondered, "But, Mom, what if he really was your friend and I had forgotten. Wouldn't it be embarrassing if I just walked away from him like that?"

"Well," I asked Chantal. "What's more important, not being embarrassed or following the Safety Rules?"

"Following the Safety Rules!" my daughter said. Then she asked for reassurance, "So if I did that, and the person got upset, you'd still hug me, right?"

"Right!" I said, hugging her then and there.

We still do the same practice in workshops now, coaching children to get up right away and go to their adults as an instructor approached, pretending to be someone they don't recognize calling their name. We coach adults to say, "Thank you for Checking First."

Most of the children surveyed prior to our training answered, "No" to the question, "Can a stranger know your name?

Every family is different, and a rule that is right for one child might not be right for another.

Sometimes the "Stranger" complains to the adult, "Your child just walked away from me. He must have forgotten me!"

We coach adults to say to the child, "You did a good job of following our Safety Rules!"

Think First Before Talking to Strangers if You Are Nine or Older and Don't Give Personal Information. The exact age that a child might be out without an adult will differ in different families. Some parents say, "But I am not ready to give my nine-year-old permission to talk to strangers. He needs to be older."

Other parents say, "In our small town, it just doesn't make sense not to let my younger child greet people in passing, even if she doesn't know them."

We tell children that their parents are the ones to decide how old they have to be before it is okay to talk to strangers when they are on their own. However, in our experience, children who are nine or older are usually able to follow this more advanced Safety Rule.

In a class with a mixed group of ages, instructor Karl asks, "How many of you are nine or older? Please raise your hands." As all the people over nine in the room, including the adults, raise their hands, Karl continues, "Your job is to Think First before you talk to strangers when you are on your own. Remember that you do not *have* to talk to strangers if you don't feel comfortable, and that your safety rule is that you do not give out personal information. So, what is personal information?"

Karl's students call out different answers, including: "My name, my family's name, my school, where I live, how old I am, my phone number, or my e-mail address."

Thinking First before talking with a stranger means:

• Deciding whether or not it is safe to talk to this stranger;
• Not giving personal information unless there is really an important reason to do so;
• Paying attention to what that person is saying and doing, to how far you are from the person, and to where other people are;
• Keeping moving on your way if you are walking; and
• Changing your plan to get to where there are people who can help you if someone is acting in a way that makes you uncomfortable.

Karl shows how the Thinking First Rule works by asking twelve-year-old William to help him demonstrate. He says, "Imagine that William is waiting here for the bus, and that I am a Stranger. He can choose to talk to me, as long as he doesn't give personal information."

Karl starts the role-play by standing near William as if waiting for the bus. He looks around and says, "Nice day, isn't it?"

"Yes," William says.

Karl asks, "Do you know what time it is?"

William says takes a quick glance towards his arm while keeping most of his awareness on Karl and says, "3:10"

Karl reaches his hand towards William as if to shake hands and says, "My name is Karl. What's yours?"

William Thinks First. He realizes that his name is personal information and that this man, who probably means well and who often comes to the bus stop, is still a stranger. He decides to ignore the hand and steps back so that he can keep out of Karl's immediate reach. He changes the subject by saying, "The bus always seems to take such a long time to get here."

A little hurt, Karl says, "I asked what your name is!"

William says, "I don't want to talk about that. Don't you just hate it when the bus is late?" (William could also say, "I don't want to give personal information.")

Going back into his instructor mode, Karl points out that William also has the choice of not saying anything at all or of getting up and moving away if he doesn't feel safe. As long as William feels safe and comfortable, he can change the subject to not give out personal information as well as to decide what he does and does not want to talk about.

Practicing Using Awareness, Following the Talking Rule, and Moving Out of Reach. We give children practice in class by telling them to think of a place they might be walking on their own. This might be playing at the park, going to the store, going to a neighbor's house, or walking home from school.

In a workshop, our instructor Jennifer picks ten-year-old Nikki to help her demonstrate. She coaches Nikki to stand on one side of the room and asks another person to be Safety on the other side of the room. She says, "Nikki, let's imagine that you are walking from home to school, and I am a stranger."

Jennifer stands directly in Nikki's path so that Nikki has to veer around her to move out of reach. As Nikki goes by, Jennifer waves and calls out in a kind cheerful voice, "Hi!"

Nikki says, "Hi!" She waves back, but remains calm, moves out of reach, and keeps walking with awareness and confidence.

Still pretending to be the Stranger, Jennifer leans towards Nikki and says, "Isn't that your school? My daughter just started here."

Because where she goes to school is personal information, Nikki chooses not to answer. Instead, she keeps walking, glancing back to keep track of where Jennifer is standing, until she gets to the person who has been identified as Safety.

Adults then do the same practice with their own children. They are not

Sometimes people who harm children take advantage of their attachment to their possessions or their pets by using a child's own things to get close.

pretending to be a dangerous person, but just a Stranger who does not know the Safety Rules. Adults coach older children to use their awareness, to move out of reach, to decide whether or not to talk, to keep going even if they say something, to be okay with not answering if they don't want to, and to decide accurately when to not answer. They coach younger children to do the same practice without answering the Stranger at all.

Adults pretending to be the Stranger call out friendly remarks like: "Hi! ... Don't you remember me? ... What time is it? ... I'm a friend of your Dad. ... I have a little girl just like you. ... What a nice shirt! ... Where do you live? ... Isn't this your school? My son goes here too ... Can you help me? I'm lost!"

For many children, doing this practice correctly the first time is difficult. Children are trained to be polite and to answer questions from adults. If they don't get it right the first time, their adults let them practice the skill again, acknowledging what they did right. "You did a great job being aware. Now I want you to practice again and this time remember not to say anything to me, even if I ask you a question."

Check or Think First Before Taking Anything From a Stranger, Even Your Own Things. One of the tricks that kidnappers use is to distract children by trying to hand them something. This might be by showing them a map while asking for help to find a place or the photo of a lost child or pet. Remembering to stay away from someone who is trying to hand you something, especially if it belongs to you, is hard for adults too.

Sometimes people who harm children take advantage of their attachment to their possessions or their pets by using a child's own things to get close. Without practice, many children have a hard time walking away from their possessions. Kids are afraid they'll get in trouble if they lose something, and they don't want anything to happen to their pets. As adults, we often reinforce this idea unintentionally. How many times do we adults tell children, "Don't take anything from strangers – not even your own things," compared to how many times that we tell them, "Take care of your things!"?

In one first grade classroom, I pretended to be a stranger offering a boy we'll call Jules his new Game Boy, which was a hand-held video game. Instead of moving away to Check First, Jules came towards me and said in a horrified voice, "Not my Game Boy!! You did not mean these safety rules for my Game Boy!!"

Rather than telling Jules that he was wrong, I asked him, "What's more important? You or your toys?"

This six-year-old boy looked thoughtful and said in a wondering voice, "Hmm. What's more important, me or my toys?" His teacher, the other students, and I waited in suspense to see what his answer would be.

To our relief, suddenly Jules laughed and said, "Why, me, of course." Every five minutes during the rest of my presentation, no matter what the rest of the class was doing, this child repeated to himself, "What's more important? Me or my toys? ... Why me of course!" And then he'd laugh again. Whatever else he might have learned that day, I figured that this was what Jules needed to know the most.

During a workshop, instructor Sterling introduces this idea by handing a child a ball and showing that the child cannot stay out of his reach and still take it from him. Sometimes the child will say, "You could throw it to me. Or, I could knock it out of your hands with a long stick."

Sterling explains, "If I am a Stranger who is trying to hand you something and you are on your own, your Safety Rule is to move away rather than trying to get the ball away from me."

Next, Sterling has seven-year-old Isabelle help him. He sets the stage by having Isabelle imagine that she is sitting in her front yard playing in the grass. Safety is a few feet away, with her grandpa in the house. Sterling then asks Isabelle, "Please tell me what might be a thing or a pet precious to you that it would be hard for you to leave."

"My kitten," Isabelle decides.

Sterling stands a few feet away from Isabelle and strokes the air as if it is the back of a kitten near his feet on the ground. He says, "Let's imagine your kitten here has wandered outside your yard and that I am a Stranger." In the Stranger role, Sterling pretends to pick up the kitten and says, "Is this your kitten?"

Not answering him even by nodding her head, Isabelle immediately stands up and moves away.

"Hey, why are you walking away like that? Come back!" the Stranger calls.

Isabelle keeps going until she gets to the person pretending to be her grandfather in the house. "Grandpa, a stranger has my kitten," she says.

Isabelle's grandpa says, "Thank you for checking first. Let's go together."

Sterling as the Stranger hands the kitten to Isabelle's grandpa, saying, "I was afraid it would get hit by a car. Your little girl just walked away from me."

Grandpa tells Isabelle, "You did a good job of checking first."

All the adults then practice with their children. They set the stage by picking where they are – in front of the school, at the park, or in the front yard. They identify where Safety is, even if it is just a spot on the wall representing the child's Grown-up in the house. They let children pick something precious to them to walk away from – a blankie, a favorite teddy bear, a new sweater, a bike, a ball, a puppy, a bunny, a kitten, etc.

Children nine and older who have permission to talk to strangers can ask, "Please put it down." If they do, their job is still to keep their awareness, be standing up, and move away rather than letting this person come close. If a stranger doesn't listen, the child's Safety Plan is to leave rather than trying to rescue his or her things.

Check First Before You Go, Even With People You Know. With both someone they know and someone they don't, young people are safest if they Check First before they change their plan about going with this person. Remember that most of the people who harm children are not strangers, but people they know.

To avoid confusion, adults can make a habit of reviewing the plans for the day about where the child is going, with whom the child is going, and what the child will be doing. Children should be encouraged to ask questions and double-check even if it is an adult they know very well who is telling them to change their plans.

Once I brought my daughter's eleven-year-old friend, Julia, home with us after school. Unfortunately, I had gotten confused about what day of the week she was supposed to come over. Chantal and Julia played happily without a care in the world. Suddenly, Julia's frantic mother appeared at our door, saying, "Please tell me she's here! I looked all over the school and this was the only place I could think of where Julia might go without telling me."

Guilt-stricken, I reassured Julia's mother and then, worrying about what might have happened if she hadn't been able to find Julia, we threw our arms around each other. Questioned later, Julia said practically, "Well, I was pretty sure it was the wrong day. But I didn't want to say anything because I figured you must know what you're doing!"

Suppose that your plan is for your child to go with someone he or she doesn't know. You can explain this by saying, "Today, I can't pick you up so you are going home with Paul's mother. You don't know her so she is a stranger to you, but it's okay with me and you do know Paul."

Double-check by asking children to repeat the plan, just to make sure that everyone understands each other. If there is a change of plan, be sure that both of you repeat it in order to double-check that you both understand and agree on the changed plan.

Make sure that anywhere you leave your children also has a policy of Checking First. Most child care centers and schools have parents fill out cards that say who may pick up their children. In the child care center of a health club, a nice looking man came to pick up two-year-old Niko, explaining that he was Niko's uncle who was just back after a long trip. Although this man was very charming and knew everyone's names, he was not listed on the authorization card. The child care center teacher told the man to wait while she sent someone into the health club to find Niko's mother. By the time Niko's mother came out, the man was gone.

Niko's mother, thankful that her son was safe but alarmed at the incident, said that Niko didn't have any uncles. The police figured out that this man must have seen Niko walking into the health club with his mother and then seen their names on the register where they signed in.

In situations that are less familiar for the child, review the Safety Rules. Adults can prepare children for different experiences by discussing what is going to happen and being clear about expectations. For example, "We are going to a neighborhood party where there are lots of people you don't know. They are strangers to you, and you are a stranger to them. I think that they are very nice people. It's okay for you to talk with them as long as you stay in the yard where the party is so that I can see you. Before you leave the yard, Check First to make sure that you let me know. Because I might be distracted talking with someone, be sure that I am looking at you and repeat what you are telling me before thinking you have permission to go somewhere else."

In situations like a party, remind children that they can be close to and even say "Hi" to people who seem like strangers to them. If a child checks unnecessarily, praise the child for double-checking instead of guessing. When in doubt, children are safest if they do check with their adults. We want them to have a clear plan in mind that agrees with our idea of what they should do.

Trips. Travel is another time when the rules get murky. If a child takes a long trip alone on an airplane or bus, be clear about what is and is not okay. Keep in mind the abilities of this child and the potential risks in this specific situation.

Before a young person goes on an airplane alone, you can explain, "On an airplane, you are in a place where there are lots of people who can help you if you have a problem. If the person sitting next to you seems friendly, it is okay to visit and to give a little personal information. You can tell this person your first name and talk about the kinds of things that you like to do or where you go to school. Do not tell someone your last name, telephone number, or address. Do not go with this person after you get off of the airplane. In this situation, talking to the person sitting with you is a choice. You can say that you'd rather read or play video games. If the person makes you uncomfortable, get up and tell the flight attendant right away."

A child who is thinking about this might ask, "But what if the seatbelt sign is on?" You can encourage the child to brainstorm with you how to make a decision about whether the safest choice is to get up anyway, set a strong boundary with the person, or push the call button. Things to take into account include what exactly the person is doing that is uncomfortable and how bumpy the airplane is.

The older and more independent a child is, the bigger the unclear zone will become. This is why it is so important to keep updating our agreements and Safety Rules as a child matures.

What if what the stranger has my little sister or brother? Older siblings sometimes worry about this very frightening question. Nine-year old Natasha's eyes got big as she told me this story in class. "One time, our Mom left my little brother and me in front of the grocery store for just a few minutes. A man with puppies in his car stopped by the store and asked if we'd like to pet the puppies. I knew better but my little brother started to

> *Whether someone is a stranger or someone the child knows, children are safest if they Check First before they change their plan about going with that person.*

> *The older and more independent a child is, the bigger the unclear zone will become. This is why it is so important to keep updating our agreements and Safety Rules as a child matures.*

run over to see the puppies. I grabbed my little brother and made him come with me into the store to find our Mom. What if my brother had gotten into the car, and the man was going to take him away?"

When kids ask hard questions like this, they need truthful and hopeful answers. "You did the right thing!" I told Natasha. "You grabbed your little brother before he got close to the man, and you took him with you to get help. But if someone gets your little brother, the best way you can save him is NOT by going with him. Remember that a bad guy does not want to get caught and is more likely to let another kid go if you can describe him. You can start to yell out to everyone that this person is taking your little brother. You can yell everything you notice about what this person and the car look like, including even part of the license number. And remember that you did the best thing of all - you protected your little brother by noticing trouble and stopping him right away from getting close to it."

Practicing Using Stranger Safety Skills For When Children Are on Their Own

The Kidpower Stranger Safety Rules are:

1. Check First with your adult or Think First before you let a stranger GET CLOSE to you.
2. Check First with your adult or Think First before you TALK to a stranger.
3. Check First with your adult or Think First before you TAKE anything from a stranger, even your own things.
4. Check First with your adult or Think First before you GO anywhere with a stranger.

Here's how to practice these rules.

1   For younger children, pick places where they are likely to encounter strangers. Give the child the chance to practice by telling her to imagine that she is in that place and that you are a stranger. Approach her and have her practice moving away and checking first. Remember, you are not pretending to be a dangerous person, just a Stranger who does not know the Safety Rules. This both avoids scaring children and is realistic because many abductors trick children by approaching them with warmth and kindness.

2   Have the child practice standing up and moving away to Check First when the Stranger knows her name, has her favorite toy or pet, is ordering her to come over, or is asking her for help.

3   For older children who might be out without an adult, discuss the difference between answering general questions or replying to casual greetings and giving out personal information or letting someone come too close physically. Make a game of greeting each other and asking each other questions. The other person can reply when it is NOT personal information but not answer when it is.

4   Help older children develop assessment skills for noticing when environments change. You can do this by discussing what to pay attention to – who else is around, the behavior of the person, etc.

5   Give an older child practice by picking a situation where it would make sense for him to move away, whether this is waiting somewhere or walking around. Agree on where Safety - someone who can help you - would be if there were to be a problem. Pretend to be a Stranger who is acting friendly but who might be unsafe. Coach the child to stay calm, aware, and confident while moving away from the Stranger and going to a safer place before letting this person get close to him, talk to him, give him anything, or take him somewhere.

6 Pretend to be a Stranger standing in line behind the child so that there is a reason to be close. Keep speaking appropriately but start becoming intrusive by putting a hand on the child's shoulder. Coach the child to step back and say, "Please stop touching me." Agree, change the subject, and then reach over and put your hand on the child again. Coach the child to walk to the front of the line and ask the person working there for help.

7 As soon as children can speak well enough to understand, and from then on, get in the habit of discussing what the Plan is for the day. Both you and the child should repeat the Plan to make sure you understand each other. You should also both repeat any changes to the Plan to be sure that the communication is clear. For either of you, just nodding your head and saying, "Okay" is not a fully informed agreement.

8 Until children are old enough to be out on their own, make sure that whoever is caring for them knows to check with you before letting an unauthorized person pick them up instead of you. When children are old enough, make sure that they know to Check First with you even if an adult they trust tells them to change their plan.

9 Remind children that, if someone makes them scared, their Safety Plan is to yell as loud as they can and run for help. If someone is about to hurt them or take them away, this is a time to use their self-defense tools.

The Rules Are Different in Emergencies

Firefighters, rangers, and paramedics have told us that children will hide or run away from them because they have been told, "You must never, ever go anywhere with a stranger no matter what." If children do not understand the exceptions to this rule, they are likely to make themselves less safe in an emergency.

The following story from Maya's mother is typical. "When Maya was seven, we went camping. Even though our campsite was right next to the bathroom, she made a wrong turn and headed out to the woods by accident. "When Maya didn't come right back and I couldn't find her, I was desperate. Thankfully, a ranger told me that he had found my child. Maya was hiding in the bushes away from him because he was a stranger. He and another ranger had to keep tracking her so that she didn't get further lost in her attempt to stay away from them."

The Kidpower Safety Rule for emergencies is: *"If you are having the kind of emergency where you cannot Check First, your Safety Plan is to get help, even from a stranger."*

Here's how we teach children about being safe with strangers in different kinds of emergencies.

House on fire. Two of our instructors, Liam and Claire, take turns playing the role of a child who is having an emergency and the role of a stranger who is an emergency worker. Liam says, "Let's pretend that Claire is a kid and she is in her house. She wakes up, smells smoke, and knows that there is an emergency. First, she tries to follow her Safety Plan for getting out of the house and away from the fire, but it doesn't work. Now let's imagine that I am a firefighter with my whole body covered by a big suit to keep the smoke out. It makes me look and sound weird, sort of like Darth Vader in Star Wars."

The Kidpower Safety Rule for emergencies is: "If you are having the kind of emergency where you cannot Check First, your Safety Plan is to get help, even from a stranger."

When they start the role-play, Claire as the child pretends to look around and be scared. Liam as the firefighter pounds on the door, shouting, "Is there anyone in here?"

Claire says to herself, "That's a stranger!" and pretends to hide in the closet.

Liam goes back into his instructor role and asks, "Is this the kind of an emergency where Claire can check first with her grown-ups before going with a stranger?"

"No," the children say.

"Is it safer for Claire to try to hide from this stranger or to get help?" Liam asks.

"Get help!" our students say.

Liam and Claire repeat the role-play. Claire is in her room smelling smoke. Liam is the firefighter pounding on the door. "Anyone in here?" he shouts.

This time, Claire yells, "I NEED HELP!" Liam breaks down the imaginary door and rescues her.

Lost in the woods. For the next example, Claire narrates as Liam pretends to be the child. "Let's imagine that Liam is lost in the woods where there are no people around," she tells the class. "He was with his family or class and suddenly realized that he couldn't find them. His Safety Plan is to stop and stand tall like the trunk of a tree, to turn his head to look in different directions, to call out for the adults who brought him, and to wait right where he is. If he sees a woman with children or a ranger, he can ask for help. Let's imagine that all of us are a search party full of people that Liam doesn't know."

Liam starts the role-play by walking around the room, looking very lost. Claire says, "Let's imagine that we are all in the search party going through the woods trying to find Liam. Everybody call out Liam's name."
"LIAM!" the whole class shouts. "LIAM!"

"Those are strangers," Liam says to himself. "I'd better hide behind a tree."

Again, Claire points out that this is the kind of emergency in which Liam cannot Check First. The students agree that it is safer to get help than to hide. They repeat the role-play. This time, when the search party calls his name, Liam runs towards everyone with his arms open wide and yells, "HERE I AM!"

Having a broken leg. In the third example, Liam pretends to be an ambulance driver, and Claire pretends to be a child who is riding her bike. She acts out falling down and breaking her leg. When Liam comes up in his ambulance and tries to help her, she starts to crawl away. Again, the students see that Claire cannot Check First and that it is safer for her to get help than to try to crawl away with a broken leg.

We remind children that most strangers are good. If they are having the kind of emergency where they cannot Check First, then their safety plan is to get help. If they are not sure who to ask for help, the safest choice is to look for a woman with children.

"Who Is Having This Emergency? Can I Check First?" One of the ways that kidnappers have tricked children is by wearing clothes that look like uniforms or by pretending that there is an emergency. They have told children that their parents are hurt and that they need to come quickly.

If someone else is having the emergency, Check First!

This is why children need clear guidelines for assessing different situations. The Safety Rule we teach in Kidpower is, "If someone else is having the emergency or you *can* Check First, then your Safety Plan is to move away and Check First with your adults."

After doing the demonstrations with Claire described above, Liam picks a child called Andy to help him, and says, "Andy, let's pretend that I am dressed like a firefighter and you are standing in front of your house. I am wearing a uniform, and you can even see my truck down the street."

Liam rushes up to Andy and says, "Hey, kid, there's a fire down the street. Come and help me!"

Claire asks Andy, "Who is having this emergency – you or someone else?"

"Someone else," Andy says.

"Can you go inside your house to Check First or call 9-1-1?" Claire asks.

"Yes," Andy says. "So I'll move away from this stranger and Check First."

Claire picks Lea as her helper, and says, "Lea, let's pretend that you are camping with your family and playing just outside your campsite. And I am a woman you don't know."

Claire approaches Lea, holding out a photograph. "My little girl is lost," she says in an upset voice. "Can you look at the photo and see if you recognize her?"

Liam coaches Lea to think this through by asking, "Who is having this emergency – you or someone else?"
"Someone else," Lea says.

"Can you go to your family at the campsite and Check First?" Liam asks.

"Yes," Lea says. "So I would move away from this stranger and Check First."

Claire continues the role-play by asking again, "Won't you help me find my little girl?"

Lea moves away to get help from her parents in the campsite.

Finally, Liam chooses Rob to help him and says, "Rob, let's imagine that you are standing in front of your school waiting for your parents to come and pick you up. I look familiar to you, but you don't know me very well. Let's imagine that I come driving up in my car."

Liam pretends to drive up in a car and says urgently, "Rob, your Dad asked me to get you. He got sick and is in the hospital. You need to come quickly."

Claire coaches Rob to think this through by asking, "Who is having the emergency here, you or your Dad?"

Rob pauses and says, "If my Dad is really in the hospital, I am having an emergency too."

"That's true," Claire agrees. "But can you go back into the school and have the office call the hospital to Check First before changing your plan about who you go with?"

"Yes," Rob decides. "Even if I am worried about my Dad, I can Check First!"

Liam continues the role-play by pretending to get out of his car and saying to Rob, "Hurry up! There's no time!" Instead of listening to Liam, Rob moves away to go get help from the school office.

The examples above show that the two questions children need to ask themselves are, 1) "Who is having this emergency – me or someone else?" And, 2) "Can I Check First?" Again, the Kidpower safety rule for emergencies is, "If you are having the kind of emergency where you cannot Check First, your Safety Plan is to get help, even from a stranger. If someone else is having the emergency or if you can Check First, then your Safety Plan is to move away and Check First with your adults."

"What if the Stranger Is Really Hurt?" Sometimes older children will ask, "If a stranger is having an emergency, is it okay to call for help?"

The answer is, "Yes, you can call 9-1-1 or find some adults to help this person, as long as you remember that this person is a stranger."

"But what if it's a little kid?" they ask.

We tell these caring children that, "The best way to take care of a little kid who is hurt is to find adults who can help. If a child is much younger than you are and no adult is around, your wisest choice will depend. If the child can walk, you might take the child with you to get help. If the child can't move and you know first aid, you might decide to stay with that child while you call for help. Ask your adults what they want you to do."

Even for adults, the Red Cross recommends that people get additional help instead of trying to rescue someone on their own.

What if It's Really a Police Officer? Sometimes children ask, "What if the person who wants to take me somewhere is a police officer who says that I have to come or I'll get in trouble?"

We explain that, "Someone in a uniform is still a stranger so you need to be very aware. If a police officer is at your door, you can call 9-1-1 and the operator will tell you why the police officer is there and whether it is okay for you to go with him or her. If the police officer is on the street, you can say that you have to call your parents or 9-1-1 before going with anyone, even a police officer. Most police officers understand that kids are supposed to Check First. A real police officer is going to try to contact your parents as soon as possible."

For older children, we remind them to trust their intuition. If a police officer is acting in a way that doesn't seem safe, their Safety Plan is to move away and go to their adults or go into a store where they can get help.

Teaching Children About Safety With Strangers When They Are Having an Emergency

1   Use the examples above or find your own to discuss different kinds of emergencies with children and whether or not they can Check First. Make sure that children understand that if they are having the kind of an emergency in which they cannot Check First, their safety plan is to get help, even from a stranger. Discuss the different kinds of strangers who might help them - a police officer, a store clerk, a security guard, a person selling tickets or food, a ranger, a firefighter, someone in a rescue party, an emergency worker, or a mother with children.

2   Make sure that younger children know how to call 9-1-1 on different kinds of telephones.

3   Be very specific about the Safety Rules and review when you go into new situations: "If you are having the kind of emergency where you cannot Check First, your Safety Plan is to get help, even from a stranger. If someone else is having the emergency or if you can Check First, then your Safety Plan is to move away and Check First with your adults."

4   As children get older and more independent, help them learn more about how to handle different kinds of emergencies. The Red Cross offers excellent training on first aid, emergency preparedness, and water safety. Use this as a time for your whole family to brush up on their safety skills.

Internet Safety

When we first got Internet access in our home in 1994, our teenaged children were the first people to use it. My husband, Ed, was sure that there was nothing there to interest him until our son Arend showed his father how to find that day's soccer scores for his favorite team in the Netherlands.

Our daughter Chantal showed me a chat-group for teens. "Ah," she said indignantly, "Someone is being rude. I'll just tell him!" Speaking up just as she would in a face-to-face conversation with kids at school, Chantal typed in, "That's sexist. Stop it!"

Immediately, a request came to our e-mail address from a different chat room user thanking Chantal for saying something and asking for a private conversation. I felt a little nervous. "You can say hello but don't give any

Stay aware of what your child is doing on-line

personal information," I advised. We didn't realize that, by signing her note in the chat room with her unusual name, Chantal had *already* given out personal information!

When Chantal replied, the person wrote back with some crude explicit sexual language. Chantal disconnected and went to a different Web site. Within a few minutes of my daughter visiting what seemed to be an innocent place with me standing right next to her, explicit pornographic pictures started popping up onto our computer screen!

The Internet is a tremendous resource for gathering information, for sharing resources, and for finding people who are interested in the same things you are. Texting, e-mail, video-conferencing, and social networking make connecting with people easier than ever, which can be a lot of fun. Much more protection is available than existed when social networking first became popular, but adults still need to be vigilant. Children and youth can be exposed to pornography, solicited, and seduced by molesters pretending to be friends, cyber-bullied by other youth, and tricked into putting private information into a public arena where it might be misused.

According to a 2006 online victimization research report for National Center for Missing and Exploited Children[18]:

• Approximately one in seven youth online (10 to 17-years-old) received a sexual solicitation or approach over the Internet.

• Four percent (4%) received an aggressive sexual solicitation - a solicitor who asked to meet them somewhere; called them on the telephone; or sent them offline mail, money, or gifts.

• Thirty-four percent (34%) had an unwanted exposure to sexual material - pictures of naked people or people having sex.

- Twenty-seven percent (27%) of the youth who encountered unwanted sexual material told a parent or guardian. If the encounter was defined as distressing – episodes that made them feel very or extremely upset or afraid – forty-two percent (42%) told a parent or guardian.

We all need to remember that people we have contact with only through the Internet are strangers. In a workshop, Dave shows how easy it is to pretend to be someone you are not. He sits back-to-back with his student, ten-year-old Sonya. He says, "Imagine that we are each in our own homes on the computer in a chat room for kids."

Dave and Sonya each say out loud what they are writing as they pretend to look at their computer screens and type on the keyboards. "Hi," Sonya types.

"Hi," Dave types back. "I am a ten-year-old girl who wants to find other kids who are worried about global warming."

"I think about that a lot," Sonya types. "I'm doing a report on it for class."

"That's great," Dave writes back. "My fifth grade at Claremont Elementary is doing an e-mail campaign about it to our politicians. Where do you go to school?"

Instead of answering his question, Sonya changes the subject and writes, "I found out that our town will be by the ocean if the ice caps melt."

"How scary," Dave writes back. "I live near New Orleans and my town would be under the ocean. Where do you live?"

Again, Sonya changes the subject and types, "Did you have any damage during Hurricane Katrina?"

Dave types, "I asked where you live. Don't you want to tell me?"

"I don't want to talk about that," Sonya types. Then she decides that this person is a little too pushy and leaves the conversation.

All the Stranger Safety Rules are important on the Internet, especially the rule about not giving personal information about where you live or go to school or about you or your family. This is a time when it is especially important to Check and Think First. Sending your photo to someone you have met only through the Internet is giving personal information.

Young people should not agree to meet anyone they have only communicated with through the Internet without their adults knowing and being with them when they do this for the first time.

You might be unpleasantly surprised if you Google your child's name or check on-line "friend" communities such as Facebook, MySpace, and others. Even if your own child is very careful, he or she might have shared information with a friend who might have connected on a site with insecure privacy settings, causing all of the personal information about friends to become public.

All the Stranger Safety Rules are important on the Internet, especially the rule about not giving personal information about where you live or go to school. This is a time when it is especially important to Check and Think First.

Without proper privacy precautions, a typical profile of a teen girl or young woman might show you or anyone else who wants to know:

• Her name;
• Photos of her and her friends;
• The names and photos of other family members including children; and
• Where she lives, goes to school, plays sports, or hangs out.

Many of the contacts on a teen chat line or an online "friends" web site are men who are prowling the Internet to gain access to young people.

Pornographic web sites with extremely explicit pictures, animations, and videos of every kind of sexual activity imaginable – and some that are hard to imagine – can be accessed by a few clicks of the mouse. If anyone enters your e-mail address in a registration box on these sites, you might start receiving e-mail with sexual pictures in it. The more ethical web sites will at least ask if the viewer is over eighteen.

However, there are pornographic web sites that have deliberately taken names of places that sound very innocent or credible with the intention of fooling children.

Keeping Kids Safe Online

Having children be online is like letting them have interactive access to millions of strangers. Here are some steps you can take to keep kids safe online.

• **Know what your child is doing. Especially if your child is more tech-savvy than you are, insist on co-piloting by watching and staying with your child so you can see what happens when your child cruises the Internet. Law enforcement experts strongly recommend keeping your computer in the living room rather than in a child's bedroom so that adults can monitor what's going on. Taking the time to see what children are doing is the best way to prevent problems.**

• **Keep reminding young people about the difference between the real world and the virtual one. Using a computer gives a false illusion of privacy and connection. Remembering at all times that you really do not know who a person is that you are communicating with through the Internet is difficult. Ask your young people, "Would you hand out flyers with your personal information to strangers walking down the street? Then remember that the Internet is no different than the street – these are still strangers in a public area. In fact, because you can't see them, you have even less information about who they might be on the Internet than you do in person."**

• **Explain to young people that, even if they know someone, they cannot control what that person might do with any information given through the Internet. Tell them, "Once you put something on the Internet, it is available for the world to see. No matter what guarantees are made, it is a mistake to post anything on the Internet that you would not want your parents, teachers, other friends, neighbors, or employers to see."**

• **Have clear rules and consequences. Be firm about the fact that computer access is a privilege, not a right. A logical consequence for breaking a rule might be the loss of computer use for a few days except for doing homework. Young people might not always follow your rules, but you should be clear on what your expectations are.**

- Tell your kids that their job is to *Check First* with you before changing the plan about Internet use. Both in the real world and the virtual world, your kids are safest if you know *what* they are doing, *where* they are going, and *whom* they are with. Tell them that this rule applies to computer use at a friend's house or the library as well as at home.

- Tell children and youth that their rule is to check with you first before they put *any* personal information on the Internet by filling out a survey, registering on a web site, joining a chat group, etc. Personal information includes their photos, where they live, where they go to school, their name, their telephone number, your name, your place of work, the names of their friends or family or teacher, sports team, neighbors, city, or school.

- Be explicit that you expect children and youth to get your permission *before* they accept gifts from, have a telephone conversation with, or make a plan to meet someone they don't already know well, whether they learned about that person through the Internet or anywhere else.

- Understand that it can be hard to say "No" to an interesting friendly person who requests personal information. You can practice this skill by pretending to be a stranger who is initiating an e-mail conversation. To keep trust, tell children from the beginning who you really are and remind them that this is for practicing skills. Make a game of trying to trick the child into giving you personal information so that she or he can say, "Sorry. I don't give personal information on the Internet." The child can also just end the conversation by disconnecting. You could also pretend to be an acquaintance at school who is requesting that the child sends a photo or shares other private information.

- Turn the tables and let the child try to trick *you* into giving personal information or into sharing something that would be embarrassing if it fell into the wrong hands. This practice does *not* need to be scary or creepy. It is a way to show how each one of you could say anything (pretend to be a child or an adult, to live in the same town, to like the same type of things, etc.) and the other person wouldn't know if you were telling the truth or not.

- If children resist practicing, tell them that their ability to demonstrate safety skills on the computer is required before you will have enough peace of mind to allow them on the Internet.

- In order to protect children from exposure to sexual images and language, tell children clearly that, the second that someone starts to initiate sexual or threatening talk or that a Web site starts to show something sexual or graphically violent, children need to stop the contact and let you know. You can tell a younger child, "If you read or see something that looks weird, strange, or scary, get off the computer and tell me." To make young people less of a target when they are exploring the Internet, make sure they use e-mail addresses that do not have their or your name as part of the address.

- To prevent computer problems, have a rule that young people are to check with you before opening or replying to any kind of spam and before opening any kind of attachments. Our experts recommend that spam you don't want should just be deleted. Even if you ask to be unsubscribed, some unethical places will send your address to several other places just because you responded.

- Ask your Internet provider about their resources for screening tools to restrict access to inappropriate language/sites for children. There are also programs that can tell you what websites someone using the computer has visited and other programs that can screen for pornography. However, these are quickly out of date and sometimes stop access to or from many legitimate Web sites and e-mail addresses. In any case, a curious computer-savvy child will probably be able to figure out how to disable or work around whatever screening or monitoring devices you put into place.

- Ask your Internet provider how you should report a person on the Internet who seems potentially dangerous.

- Ask your legislators to support groups that want to take balanced action in making the Internet a safer place for young people. For example, the Children's Online Privacy Protection Act (COPPA)[13] requires Web sites to explain their privacy policies on the site and get parents' consent before collecting or using personal information from a child under 13, such as a name, address, phone number, or social security number. The law also prohibits a site from requiring a child to provide more personal information than necessary to play a game or participate in a contest."

- Finally, the best way to help young people be safe on the Internet is also the best way to help protect them from other dangers – no matter how busy or stressed you are, be a positive person who makes time to talk. You want young people to tell you what they are doing and to ask you about anything that seems confusing or odd to them. Notice when they act stressed, withdrawn, or secretive. Make the time to *listen* and *pay attention* to the children and teens in your life. When they do tell you about an Internet issue, work with them to figure out a solution. Kids may be reluctant to come to their adults if there are going to be strong consequences to them telling. Some behavior does require consequences, but whenever possible reward children for talking to you by working together to find a solution that balances their drive for independence with your responsibility to keep them safe.

Before You Let Your Child Go Alone

In her frightening and inspiring book, *A Stolen Life: A Memoir*, Jaycee Dugard tells her painful and courageous story about how she was assaulted with a stun gun and kidnapped from a country road on her way to catch the school bus at age 11; her 18-year ordeal with kidnappers Phillip and Nancy Garrido; the failures of our justice system to protect her; the way in which she was brainwashed until she became unable to seek help and started to trust her kidnappers more than the outside world; how she held onto her courage, love, and hope in dreadful circumstances; her amazing rescue thanks to two police officers who were paying attention; and her beautiful relationship with her mother, who never, ever stopped longing for and looking for her child.[19]

This was an extremely dangerous situation, and we will never know what would have happened – but it is possible that more knowledge might have helped to prevent or shorten Jaycee's ordeal. Hearing her story, I cannot help but wonder, what if....?

What if Jaycee's mother had been informed about the Illusion of Safety that can lull us into believing that our kids are safe because of where we live and had been given a plan of action for how to prepare her daughter to walk to the school bus on her own?

What if Jaycee had known that a car with someone you don't know well in it, even if there is a woman, might be dangerous to you so that she could avoid getting close to it – perhaps even immediately start yelling and running for safety either to the closest person or in a direction opposite to where the car was going?

What if, when she was being moved from the car to the house, Jaycee had known that an attacker wants privacy and control and that, even if the attacker had told her to be quiet, to try to make a scene to get the attention of other people?

What if Jaycee had known that it is NOT your fault if you cannot get away right away, to keep looking for a new chance to get away, that this is such a big emergency that you can ask for help from ANY stranger, not to believe what a person who takes you tells you, and that your family will always love you and want you, no matter what happens.

With over 100,000 attempted abductions by non-family members in the U.S. every year, we have to assume that people with ill intent are looking for opportunities to steal and harm an unprotected or unprepared child. Children have been abducted from their front yard, riding a bike to the corner mailbox, walking to the school bus, from a department store, and on their way to summer camp. They have been kidnapped when with other kids, in sight of their friends, visiting a neighbor, and from their bedroom in an unlocked house.

On her website, MissingMichaela.com, Sharon Murch describes the November 19, 1988 kidnapping of her nine-year-old daughter Michaela Joy Garecht, and makes a plea for parents to educate their children to prepare them to avoid and escape from a kidnapper. After persuading her mother to let them go on their own, Michaela and her best friend Trina rode their scooters two blocks to the neighborhood grocery store to get some candy and soda. They started walking home, forgetting that they had left their scooters at the store. When they got back to the store, one of the scooters was not by the door where they had left it. Michaela saw her scooter next to a parked car and walked into the parking lot to get it. As her friend Trina watched in horror, a man jumped out of the car, grabbed Michaela from behind, and threw her screaming into the car, and drove off. Despite a massive search that continues to this day, Michaela is still missing.[20]

After each kidnapping, parents are overwhelmed with terror and helplessness, wondering, how can I decide when my child is ready to go somewhere on her or his own? At the same time, we do not want to live in fear or have our children living in fear. Our job is to prepare young people so that they can explore their world with safety, joy, and confidence.

The best way to combat fear and helplessness is with awareness, skills, and preparation. Assess realistically what the safety risks are everywhere your child goes - and your child's ability to avoid those risks. Safety risks include cars, animals, and potentially dangerous places such as ponds as well as people. Until they have the skills to take care of themselves in different situations, children need adults to provide ongoing supervision, guidance, and support. Powerful respectful adult leadership is essential in teaching children to manage peer interactions and other social situations in emotionally safe ways – and in preparing them to negotiate their world in physically safe ways.

Our challenge as adults is to find the right balance between protecting a child from harm and depriving that child of the opportunity for important life experiences. We cannot protect children from all risks in life, no matter how hard we try and no matter how much we wish we could. Children learn and grow from being able to do new things and from meeting new people. It's the adults' job to provide a structure for doing this as safely as possible.

Instead of dwelling on the bad things that sometimes happen, empower children and teens by giving them opportunities for successful practice of the "People Safety" skills described in this book.

We need to be realistic about what situations are more safe and less safe and to plan accordingly. For example, a neighborhood is likely to be safer from crime with lots of people around in the morning than with very few people around in the early afternoon. However, people backing their cars out of driveways in a hurry to get to work might make riding a bike in some places too dangerous until a child is older.

We also need to be realistic about what level of independence is appropriate for each specific child. Children are unique individuals and are constantly changing. What is right for one child will not necessarily be right for another. For example, a child who easily gets lost in thought might take longer to be safe crossing the road alone than a child who is very aware of his or her physical surroundings.

It only takes a moment for something to go wrong, which is why it is so important to take the time to make and practice safety plans with children for "what if" situations (i.e. what if you fell off your bike, what if you got separated from me at the store, what if you got lost? etc.). Don't assume that your child will know what to do or make the same choices you might make. If you are unsure or concerned that your child might not make the safest choice or if you feel that your child isn't ready to do something independently, it is safer to take the time to review skills with him or her or make different plans that provide more supervision and support.

Instead of dwelling on the bad things that sometimes happen, empower children and teens by giving them opportunities for successful practice of the "People Safety" skills described in this book in contexts that are relevant to their lives:

- Walking and acting with awareness, calm, and confidence;
- Checking first with their adults before they change their plan about what they are doing, where they are going, and who they are with, including people they know;
- Moving away and checking first with their adults if they are on their own before they let a person or an animal they don't know well get close to them (or thinking first if they don't have an adult to check with);
- Moving out of reach if something or someone might be unsafe;
- Setting strong, respectful boundaries with people they know;
- Protecting their feelings from hurtful words;
- Making a safety plan for how to get help everywhere they go;
- Being persistent in getting help from busy adults;
- Understanding that the safety rules are different in emergencies where they cannot Check First;
- Shouting for help and running to safety if they are scared; and
- Using self-defense skills to escape and get to safety in an emergency.

As described throughout this book, lead the practice of these skills in the same spirit you might help a young child learn how to fasten his or her seatbelt independently, with your upbeat focus on supporting their success without turning your attention to the bad things that might happen to a person who is not wearing a seatbelt.

If you feel yourself becoming anxious or upset when you are working with your child, take a break and practice again later. Children learn much better when their adults are calm. This is sometimes easier said than done when you are worried about your child's safety, but being able to practice together in a calm way is essential for your child to build his or her People Safety Skills.

Preparing Your Child to Go Somewhere Without Adult Protection

Before you let your child go anywhere without adult protection, follow these steps to prepare:

1   Assess your child's safety readiness and the specific situation, understanding that an attack can take place in seconds, anywhere.

2   Travel the route or visit the place with your child, discussing how your child can get help if he or she has a safety problem such as getting lost or being bothered.

3   Role-play with your child how to interrupt a busy, impatient adult and be persistent in asking for help.

4   Co-pilot by letting your child lead you through the route while you walk or ride behind, asking your child what she or he would do if someone friendly asks for help, if he or she gets lost, if someone familiar offers to take him or her somewhere, if someone acts scary, if someone in a car pulls over, if someone asks for directions etc.

5   Practice until your child stays aware and confident the whole way, rather than daydreaming, acting tough, or acting timid.

6   Identify the store clerk, bus driver, or a woman with children along the way who could be a help. Introduce your child to people who can be a resource

7   Make sure your child knows how to move away quickly from someone approaching her or him, to pull away from being grabbed, yell for help, and run to safety, and hit and kick to escape if need be.

Just in Case! - What Children and Teens Need to Know if They Cannot Get Away at First

Sometimes bad things happen no matter what one does, and we have no way to know if being prepared with skills and information would have helped a child who was abducted to escape or get away later. However, we do know that many kids have escaped – by jumping out of a car, using their teeth or a sharp edge to tear off the ropes or duct tape tying them, screaming for help, appearing to cooperate and then tricking the attacker, or leaving later.

Sometimes kids don't get away because they are too traumatized and are too afraid of the abductor to see opportunities to leave or ask for help from the strangers around them. The Stockholm Syndrome is a psychological phenomena in which hostages develop empathy and positive feelings towards their captors.[21] In the same way, abducted children kept in captivity sometimes come to identify with and trust the person who took them more than the other people in the world around them.

Make a scene if you feel scared

Here are some ideas for helping to prepare children "just in case" they cannot get away at first.

• *Teach Children not to Blame Themselves if Things Go Wrong or They Make Mistakes.* Most of us have had situations when we couldn't do what we thought we should, when something went wrong, or when we made a mistake. Sometimes these situations might result in problems that make us feel upset, stupid, or scared every time we think about what happened. Feeling bad about yourself can get in the way of figuring out what you need to do to get help to solve these problems.

When things go wrong, children are often likely to blame themselves. This is why, as soon as children are able to understand, it is important to teach them, "It's NOT your fault when you couldn't do something, made a mistake, or forgot something. If you have a safety problem, we want you to keep looking for what you CAN do to get the help you need."

• *Address the Issue in an Empowering Way.* In our workshops for children ages 6 or older, after our students have had the chance to practice a number of skills, we answer the question that most children start to ask as they get older, which is, "What if I can't get away at first?" Most children seem relieved to have an answer, because not talking about this issue at all means that it is too terrible to mention, and anything that is too awful to talk about must be truly terrifying.

Even without a workshop, age-appropriate language can put boundaries around this concern for children and give them the bottom line of what they need to know.

• *Practice Skills to Reduce Fear and Build Confidence.* Give children the opportunity to be successful in practicing self-protection and self-defense skills to show them how they can avoid getting kidnapped most of the time. Some child safety programs recommend putting children in trunks of cars and having them practice kicking out the taillights. Most often, kids are in the car rather than the trunk, and, depending on the child, this kind of practice could be traumatic. However, the underlying concept of teaching kids to keep looking for a new chance to get away and practicing how to make a scene even if they feel scared or embarrassed is important.

• *Tell Children Only What They Need to Know*. We want to be truthful, but we don't want to put upsetting details into children's minds that are unnecessary. Don't focus only on strangers, because most of the people who harm children are NOT strangers, but people they know. Tell children that, "Most people are GOOD, and that this means that most strangers are good. However, a few people might try to do dangerous things, which is why it is important to learn how to keep ourselves safe."

• *Focus on What Children Need to Do Rather than on Details of What Could Go Wrong*. In a calm, matter-of-fact voice, explain to a child who is old enough to understand, "If you cannot get away at first from someone who is trying to harm you, it does NOT mean that you did anything bad – just that you had some bad luck. If someone does something that makes you feel bad, this does NOT mean that you are bad. Remember that you might need to lie and break promises in order to get away and that's okay because you are doing this to be SAFE. A lie to give you a chance to get away might be, 'I will do what you say and I will stay right here.' If you cannot get away at first, your safety plan is to KEEP looking for a NEW chance to get away, because your grownups will love you and want you, no matter what. This is such a big emergency that you can run to ANY stranger to get help. And remember that it is never too late to get help and that this problem is never your fault."

In our workshops, we immediately have children practice after this explanation. For example, they might all yell, "I NEED HELP!" while running to Safety and then review some physical self-defense skills. We use the term "Safety" to mean an adult who can help the child.

Because children often feel helpless if there is a weapon, they also need to know, "If someone has a knife or a gun, it would be really scary and you might get hurt. But you can keep yourself safe most of the time if you remember a few things. If you have any room at all, run away and get to Safety. Even police officers, who practice every month, miss a target moving away from them most of the time. If the person has a knife, you can also throw ANYTHING – your backpack, sand, a book – and then run. Remember to keep looking for a new chance to get away. As soon as you can, get away and get help."

• *Tell a Success Story*. Keep the story simple, focusing on what the child did to be safe, not on the attack. Leave out scary details. For example, instead of saying that the person was making threats or being sexual, you could say that the person was "acting scary" or "being weird." Act out or practice what the child did to be successful.

*If you cannot get away at first, **keep** looking for a **new** chance to get away, because your grownups will always love you and always want you, no matter what.*

For example, in Kidpower we might tell children ages 6 or older this story. "When someone is being dangerous, it is okay to tell lies and break promises, because you are doing so to keep yourself safe and you will get help from an adult you trust as soon as possible. One young boy who got taken away promised the guy who took him that he would stay quietly in the motel room while that guy went to the bathroom. Instead, this boy used the telephone in the motel to call 9-1-1. Even though the boy didn't know where he was, the computer could find out from the phone line. The police got there and arrested the man before he got done going to the bathroom! Now, let's practice using different kinds of phones to call 9-1-1!"

We might tell older kids the story of a girl who was kidnapped at gunpoint, said that she was tired and asked if she could sit down on the ground to take off her backpack. While her attacker stood over her, looking around nervously, she jumped up and ran off screaming. The man was so startled that he jumped into his car and drove through a stoplight. He was stopped by the police, who saw his gun on the seat, heard the report about him, and arrested him.

• *Avoid the "Too Much Talking" Pitfall.* When adults are worried, a major pitfall is to talk too much and to get caught up in answering lots of questions, instead of practicing what to do. Suppose that you were to talk to children about a fire drill and to start answering their questions about what happens during a fire. Even if you are being very kind and positive, after a very short time of just talking, most children are likely to start to get very worried about there being a fire. In this case, most questions can be put to rest simply by practicing going outside of the building and walking to the designated place where children are supposed to gather.

The same principle is true with other safety problems. It works best if you give a simple explanation and then redirect children into what they CAN do rather than answering their questions. Just say, "First, let's practice!"

Just in Case for Adults – What if a Child Is Abducted?

In Kidpower, our focus is on doing everything in our power to prevent children from being kidnapped or otherwise coming to harm. However, many parents want to know what they could do just in case. If your child is missing and cannot be found, your job is to get help immediately, persistently, widely, and aggressively.

The Klaas Kids Foundation's excellent web site defines a comprehensive nine-point plan for what to do when your child is missing. They point out that your child's disappearance is a life and death emergency, so you must stay aware and focused rather than escaping into wishful thinking or denial. Be ready to fight complacency and bureaucracy to get help for your child. Don't wait and hope that things will get better.[22]

First, in the United States, if you believe that your child might have been abducted, call 9-1-1, all local police departments, the sheriff's department, and other local law enforcement agencies right away. Tell them that you fear that a predatory abduction has occurred and that you want immediate action.

Be pushy. Go up the chain of command if someone is resistant. Demand that officials institute an Amber Alert, a system created after the tragic 1996 kidnapping and murder of nine-year-old Amber Hagerman in Arlington, Texas. An Amber Alert will notify all officials of the potential kidnapping and will make the public aware to be on the lookout through TV and radio announcements. [23]

When a child is abducted by a non-custodial parent or other family member, many of the same strategies apply. The Vanished Children's Alliance has useful resources for how to get law enforcement officials to be effective in dealing with a "family abduction." [24]

If your child has been kidnapped, never give up hope. Involve volunteers, organizations and others in your search. Thousands of children who were kidnapped have been found and saved from further harm due to the sustained effort of law enforcement officials, volunteers, media, and families working together.

Protecting Children's Emotional Safety When They Learn of an Abduction

Like caring adults everywhere, we at Kidpower are saddened and shocked every time we hear a story about a child who has been abducted or harmed. Children deserve to be safe in our neighborhoods, homes, and schools – and too often they are not. We grieve for the tragic loss of a young life cut short and want desperately to protect other children from harm. At the same time, we do not want to deal with this tragedy in a way that traumatizes children or prevents them from enjoying their lives.

Here are ways to support young people who learn about a child abduction:

1. *Don't Blame the Victims*. When tragedies like this occur, it's tempting to look for some fault on the part of the children or caregivers in order to feel more safe. It's tempting to lecture children to "be more careful so that something bad like this won't happen" to them.

   When faced with a terrifying experience such as an abduction, children and their adults almost always did the best they knew how. A mobile home park or familiar neighborhood can feel almost like an extension of one's home. It is normal for parents and caregivers to believe that a child might safely go down the street to visit a friend's house without adult supervision. It is normal for children to be trusting and caught up in their own worlds rather than using the awareness they might use more commonly outside their neighborhoods.

2. *Take Charge of what Children Are Hearing and Seeing*. Reviewing upsetting details about what happened over and over does not make children safer – it makes them scared and runs the risk of causing avoidable, additional trauma. Years later, our students have told us about how traumatized they were about seeing adults acting terrified and helpless. Make sure that children are not

If your child is missing and cannot be found, your job is to get help immediately, persistently, widely, and aggressively.

overhearing adult conversations, and turn off the news. Be aware of radio or television that might be in the background at some public place like a restaurant, a friend's house, or even an elevator.

As adults, we need to remember how important it is to shelter children and make sure we don't overwhelm them with too much information and our own feelings of shock, fear, and anger. Many children are like sponges and they hear everything even when they don't seem to be paying attention. Be prepared to interrupt an adult who is sharing his or her reaction to this story in the presence of children, especially small children. You can warmly, but decisively, stop the conversation by saying something like, "Let's talk about this later." Act calm in front of children so that they know that you believe that they are safe, even though something very sad happened.

3. *Explain what Happened in a Calm, Reassuring Way.* If children are likely to hear about any upsetting event, it is better that they be able to talk with you rather than just overhearing conversations or getting stories from other children. Avoid graphic details. Focus on what adults are doing to keep everyone safe. If possible, try to create a supportive space for this discussion. At school, kids might be gathered together in a circle. At home, kids might be sitting on a parent's lap or holding hands. Do something comforting afterwards rather than trying to go on with business as usual.

    A simple explanation might be, "A very sad thing happened to a girl at our school (or in our town), and she died. The police are figuring out what happened, and we are all working hard to make sure that everyone stays safe."

    If a child asks if she was kidnapped or stolen, you can say, "Someone took her, and we don't know why. The police are figuring out what happened."

    It can be traumatic for children to dwell on horrifying details. If a child brings up graphic details in front of other children, interrupt the child and say, "Lots of people are talking about what happened, and the police are working hard to figure things out. What I want you to know is that this is a very safe place most of the time and that you are very strong and can keep yourself safe most of the time." If you are talking one-on-one with a child, and she needs to tell you what she heard to help her cope with what she has heard, listen to her supportively, and say, "yes, those of very scary things you heard. It is very sad. I am very sad too." Then bring the focus of the conversation back to the things you can do to stay safe most of the time. Do not add new information yourself as this just gives children more upsetting images.

4. *Give Children Positive Ways to Deal with Feeling Sad and Scared.* As much as we adults want to protect children from being upset, learning how to deal with fear and grief in positive ways is a skill

that can serve them throughout their lives. Children need to have outlets for their own feelings without being burdened by the intense feelings of their adults and without discussing upsetting details.

You can acknowledge children's upset feelings by saying in a very warm, matter-of-fact voice, "This is a very sad and scary thing to happen. It is okay that you feel sad and scared. It is okay to cry and to wish that this had not happened."

You can reassure children by saying, "Lots of people are here to keep you very safe, and we are going to practice safety plans so you will know how to keep yourself safe." If a child is concerned about her or his own safety, you can practice what to do. For example, suppose a child knows that a girl got taken from her bedroom. You could make a game of shouting from different rooms and seeing how you can hear each other and come running to the rescue.

One six-year-old boy was too afraid to sleep in his room after his home had been robbed because he was worried that the robber could come back and get him. After his family practiced shouting for help, getting out of the house, going to a neighbor and asking for help, and using the phone to call 9-1-1, he felt much less afraid.

Help children find positive outlets for grief by doing something to honor the child who was harmed – drawing pictures to send to her or his family, planting a tree in her or his honor, or, if you know this child, writing down memories of good times you've had. Help children find positive outlets for fear by practicing skills such as the ones mentioned below that will keep them safe most of the time.

Different children are likely to deal with upsetting events differently. Wanting just to play or do something else rather than keep talking is not necessarily a sign of denial or a lack of emotional health. Give children permission to show and talk about whatever feelings they have without having an expectation of what those feelings should be.

Depending on the wishes of the child and your relationship to that child, this is a good time for hugs, cuddling, and holding hands. If a child tries to act like a younger child for a while, this is normal. For example, a child who has enjoyed having her or his own room might not want to sleep alone.

If a child continues to stay very upset, this is a good time to seek professional help from a counselor.

5. *Get Support for Yourself.* The murder of a child is absolutely horrifying and we would not be caring people if we did not have feelings such as rage, terror, and grief. Find other caring

Children need to have outlets for their own feelings without being burdened by the intense feelings of their adults and without discussing upsetting details.

Awareness Power Safety Sign

adults to talk with away from your children. If this happened in your community, support police departments by sharing any information that can help them figure out what happened. Take effective action by ensuring that children have the supervision they need, reducing hazards where you can, and teaching children how to explore their world with safety and confidence.

PART FOUR

Conclusion

Chapter Eleven

The Safety of Kids Is Everybody's Business – How to Intervene

What if any of us saw a child about to be harmed? We'd want to do something to protect that child! Our challenge is to understand what to do and when to do it.

The focus in this chapter is on interventions when the child's adults are behaving unsafely or failing to provide adequate supervision, but much of this information can also apply to addressing other safety problems.

Being prepared to take effective action means knowing how to:

1. Recognize a potential safety problem. Does a child look lost or frightened? Is a child about to do something that could hurt her or someone else? Does an adult seem to be acting in an unsafe way towards a child? If something bothers you, make a conscious decision about what you are and are not going to do. Don't assume there is no problem or that someone else will take care of it.

2. Assess the situation and your surroundings. How big is the potential danger to the child? Is it possible something illegal might be happening? Are there other people around to witness the problem or to help? Where is this child's adult? Does the adult seem likely to get physically violent with you or to retaliate towards the child? Do you have someone with you or are you by yourself? Are you providing care for another child? Rather than automatically reacting or not doing anything, having this information will help you to assess what response is best for this specific problem.

3. Put Safety First - ahead of embarrassment, inconvenience, or offense. Some people react poorly to being told that you think their behavior is unsafe. But it is better to have someone yell at you than to have a child get hurt. As one father said, "I told my neighbors that their five-year-old son was too young to walk alone at dusk from the school bus to their home along a rural road. They yelled at me to mind my own business. But I noticed that they didn't have him walk alone there anymore, so it was worth it!"

4. Stay respectful no matter what the other person says or does. Check in with yourself to make sure you are centered and calm. Use the Emotional Raincoat technique of imagining a raincoat protecting you from someone's stormy feelings and words. Even if someone's behavior is outrageous,

It is better to have someone yell at you than to have a child get hurt!

The fact that another adult is paying attention and validating the parent's feelings without agreeing with the behavior can be enough to help a parent regain control.

reacting in a shaming way is likely to make the problem worse. I once grabbed the arm of a young girl to stop her from going over a cliff. She threw herself to the ground and started throwing a tantrum. Her mother, who had been about 100 feet away, came running over and started screaming at me, "You shouldn't have grabbed her!" Rather than arguing, I apologized.

5. **Decide on what actions are going to be best for the child and safe for you to take.** Remember that you have choices. You can stay with the child, explain your concerns very politely to the child's adults, offer to assist an overwhelmed parent, shout for help, report the problem to law enforcement, or, hard as it is, decide that this is a situation where your intervention will not make the child safer. Depending on the other person's reaction, be prepared to keep adjusting your strategies, always putting safety first.

From Witness to Advocate – A Study About Interventions to Protect Kids

From Witness to Advocate[1] is a study about interventions by bystanders to prevent parents from being abusive to their children that was conducted by psychologist Dr. Susan Wilde for her dissertation. Dr. Wilde is also a long-time advisor to Kidpower and was one of the five people on the pilot development team for Kidpower in 1989. In this study, Dr. Wilde interviewed people who had attempted interventions when they saw an out-of-control adult scaring, hitting, or verbally abusing a child in public. She wanted to find out what ordinary people did in such situations and how well it worked.

Wilde found that the most common reasons that people gave for not intervening were:

• They were afraid of making things worse for the child.
• They were afraid of making the parent mad at them.
• They thought that they didn't have the right to "interfere."
• They didn't know how.
• They were afraid of the embarrassment of a "scene."
• They didn't want to inconvenience themselves.

The witnesses interviewed for Wilde's study who did intervene used a variety of methods and techniques. Although all the techniques used by these intervening people did succeed in stopping the physical abuse, some techniques used commands while others used compassion and empathy to help the adults regain control of themselves and shift their behavior.

Wilde found that, when used appropriately, empathic interventions helped to de-escalate the situation and created more safety. Often adults who are at the end of their own rope need kindness, limits, and to feel validated and understood – just like the child. The fact that another adult is paying attention and validating the parent's feelings without agreeing with the behavior can be enough to help a parent regain control.

In more urgent situations, where serious injury seemed immediate, the witnesses in Wilde's study called police or security to help. Several witnesses enlisted the help of other bystanders by giving them clear instructions or asking them to go for more help – just like some of the techniques taught in Kidpower. Setting clear limits always worked to stop the physical hitting that occurred in the situations in the study, whether the adult became calmer or turned their frustration verbally onto the witness instead of the child.

Empathic responses could include offering to help the adult. For example, witnesses could say sympathetically, "It looks like your hands are really full. Can I help you carry that?" Or, they could validate the adult's experience and at the same time, re-frame the situation: "Isn't it difficult shopping with little ones at the end of a long day?" What was most important was the willingness of the witness to try something to change the situation and to shift and adapt strategies when what they tried first didn't seem to work.

A 9-1-1 operator says, "If you feel unsafe, CALL!"

Most of the time, I have found that compassion is the key to keeping an overwhelmed parent from being hurtful to a child. Once, I found a two-year-old boy wandering around our neighborhood and brought him back to his home. His mother was terrified when she realized that he had opened their front door without her realizing that he could or would. She started to raise her hand to slap him. I distracted her by saying very sympathetically and firmly, "I can see that this was frightening for you, but your little one is too young to understand." She didn't hit, looked surprised, and we talked some more.

Calling Authorities for Help in an Emergency

Be sure you know what telephone number to call for emergency help everywhere you go. As soon as they are old enough to understand, be sure to teach this phone number to your children and make sure they know how to use it on different phones.

In North America, the number for getting emergency help is 9-1-1. According to 9-1-1 Dispatcher Melody MacDonald, "If you see something unsafe happening and can't handle it yourself, call for help. We would much rather have a mistaken outcome than a tragic one." Here are some of her tips about what to teach kids and remember yourself about how to get help in an emergency.

1. If you feel unsafe and don't know what to do, CALL. Teach children that they can call and how to do it. 911 dispatchers are trained in how to talk with kids and are happy to speak with them directly when they do not have an adult to help them.

2. If you see something unsafe happening, CALL. Don't assume someone else will do it, or that the problem will go away by itself.

3. Pay attention to and report details like the appearance of the car and/ or person. With a car, in addition to trying to get the license number, notice any dents, tinted windows, stickers, and the color. With a person, notice the color and style of someone's hair, moles, accents, phrases, the shape of someone's mouth, and other features. Write things down as soon as you can. Details like these can be very helpful in identifying someone.

"We would much rather have a mistaken outcome than a tragic one."

4. Know where you are – look for street names, numbers, cross streets. Cell phones, especially if you stay on the line, can help to find your location, but additional information can get help to you more quickly.

5. Call right away – the sooner you call, the more chance emergency services have of being able to do something. Don't wait. Even a few minutes can make a difference.

The same principles apply for other potentially dangerous situations such as seeing someone hitting a child or a child or teen behaving very unsafely. For example, although laws about spanking kids are different in different countries, if you see someone hitting a child in a way that looks dangerous or illegal, treat this as an emergency and call. The police can investigate and determine if there is abuse or not.

If you see a child using a skateboard or bike dangerously and illegally with no adult around and you feel safe doing so, you might try to make a connection and then set a friendly boundary. For example, "I'm glad you are having fun and, where's your helmet?" Or, "... and, please keep control of your skateboard!" Or, "... and, please don't skate or bike on this walking path because someone might get hurt." If you are worried that saying something might turn into an ugly confrontation and that this young person's behavior might lead to someone getting injured, call and ask the police to investigate.

"My Mama Left Me!" - A Personal Story About Taking Action
In a complicated situation, you might need to use a number of different strategies. Late one afternoon, my brother Ken and I were walking on the entry road to Natural Bridges State Park, which goes about half a mile through the woods along the edge of the beach before ending at the parking lot and Visitor's Center. The road bends so that you can't see very far ahead for much of the way, and there are no buildings along it.

Suddenly, Ken and I saw a little girl about seven-years-old walking in the sand on the side of the road towards the parking lot, crying her heart out, saying over and over, "My Mama left me!"

As Ken looked in all directions to see if anyone was around, I asked her, "Where IS your Mama?"

Sobbing non-stop that she wanted her Mama, the child pointed in the direction she was walking. Usually, I stay a little away from a child I don't know, but, in this case, there was no adult in sight. I was worried she might wander into the road in front of a car or panic and run into the bushes, so I started walking next to her and said firmly and warmly, "We'll come with you and help you find your Mama!"

An SUV stopped with a concerned couple who said that another woman had seen this child's mother make her get out of the car by the park entrance and had driven off. We asked them to go to the Visitor's Center and report what happened to the ranger.

As Ken kept looking around, I stayed close to the little girl, reassuring her that we would get help to find her mama, hoping I was telling her the truth, and that what had happened was NOT her fault. She was so upset that I asked if she wanted to hold my hand. She immediately clutched it and calmed down a little.

After a few minutes of walking this way and still seeing no mother or ranger, I asked Ken to call 911. Just as he started, a car came around the curve with two women and a younger child in the back seat who did not appear to me to be in a car seat or seatbelt.

The car screeched to a halt and a woman glowered at me out of her open window. "Do YOU want THAT?" she asked me in a disgusted voice, glaring and pointing at the little girl.

THAT? I thought. What an awful way to talk about your child!

"Is this your mother?" I asked the little girl, who nodded her head, let go of my hand, and eagerly got into the back of the car.

As she did, I told her mother, "This wasn't safe!"

The girl's mother and her friend started justifying, saying, "She was MISBEHAVING ... She WANTED to get out ... How ELSE could she learn?"

I was worried about letting this child go, even though I was definitely planning to report what happened. If she had seemed at all frightened or as if she had been physically harmed, I would have tried to keep her until we got to some law enforcement officials. However, she looked glad to see her mother, and I did not think I had the right to stop her.

I felt like yelling at this mother for shaming her child. Knowing this was a bad idea, I put those feelings aside and wondered if she might be open to talking so we could make a connection and discuss some safer ways of parenting. In the past, I've sometimes been able to do this in intervening with upset parents. Unfortunately, my sense was that this woman was so defensive, especially with her friend egging her on, that she would take anything I said or asked as another reason to be angry with her daughter and that this child's safety needed to come ahead of my need to fix things.

Instead, I looked carefully at the license plate as they turned the car around to head back into the park, repeating the numbers and letters aloud over and over until Ken typed it into his cell phone. The couple in the SUV who had gone for help drove back to see if the little girl was okay, and we asked for their contact information so that there would be other witnesses. Then two rangers drove up, and we all made our report. The rangers headed back to the park and were approaching the family as Ken and I walked past the parking lot. These were official rangers who are also law enforcement officers with full jurisdiction when anything happens in the park.

Ken and I were still concerned about the situation, but we were not sure what else we might do right then. Later, I called Child Protective Services

I told her mother, "This wasn't safe!"

Always put safety first

"Your child is too young and too precious to be left here even for a second!"

and found that the rangers had already made a report. In retrospect, in addition to getting the license plate number, my brother or I could have used our cell phones to take a photo.

I really believe that this mother would have been devastated if her daughter had gotten hurt, and hope that this experience will lead to their family learning safer ways of dealing with conflict.

"Not Even for a Second!" – A Personal Story About Putting Safety First

When you use "Put Safety First" as your guide, other decisions often become much easier to make. Once, my husband Ed and I took a vacation in an area full of beautiful mountains and a great deal of wildlife. One afternoon, I left Ed sitting by a trail and went back to the parking lot to get something for our hike. Suddenly, I noticed a small child of less than two-years-old sitting alone on a picnic table, next to a sign warning about this being an active bear area. She had rosy cheeks, a very pink dress stained with what might have been apple juice, and no adults with her. I could hear voices of people and splashing in the direction of the river where she was looking intently, but no one was in sight.

No part of me could have left this toddler alone there, but, especially with my husband waiting for me, I felt indignant and wished that parks and parking lots would have those signs that many stores do: "Do not leave your children unattended!" Surely, I thought crossly, this reminder is as important as the signs warning not to leave your valuables in your car and not to feed the bears. I waited near this little girl for quite a while, not wanting to alarm her by staring at her or approaching her, hoping that her adults would appear. Understandably, she eventually started to get restless, so I called out towards the river, "HELLO! EXCUSE ME!"

A woman's head peeked out over the edge of the hill and called, "Is she all right?"

"She's fine," I reassured the woman. The woman's head then disappeared, as she headed back to the river. "WAIT!" I yelled. "Please come here!"

The child's mother reluctantly walked up the hill to us. She looked hot and tired and said apologetically, "I was only going to be gone for a second."

"Your child is too young and too precious to be left here even for a second!" I said in a firm, kind voice.

"Really?" the woman asked.

"There are Bears," I pointed out. "And the River. And Cars. And People! You should not leave her in a place like this even for a second."

The woman lifted her child and put her on her hip. "Thank you," she said, doubtfully, and carried her daughter off to join the rest of their family.

Later, Ed and I told our story to a ranger who, with a great deal of emotion, described how children drown every year in that river because people are misled by the serenity of the surroundings into believing that it is safe.

A plan to Put Safety First makes decisions in a situation like this so clear – waiting with a child even if your husband must be wondering why you are taking so long; speaking up even if someone might be upset with you; and being supportive to a tired mother even though you feel frustrated about her lack of awareness.

When Grownups Act Dangerously – What Their Kids Need to Know

Kidpower provides extensive services for families that have experienced domestic violence, mental health problems, and child abuse and for the organizations that help them. However, these issues go beyond the scope of this book. As adults, if we become aware that a family is in crisis, we must be prepared to speak up and, if necessary, seek appropriate professional support and/or legal interventions to protect the children from harm. When parents or other primary caregivers act dangerously towards themselves or others, a cornerstone of their children's security gets knocked out of place. As a friend told me, "When I was a young teenager, my father had a brief breakdown, and I was worried that he was going to kill himself. My feeling of walking on eggshells around him lasted for many years."

As adults, we need to remember that, even though it may seem like things have gone back to normal after a crisis, the feelings of uncertainty and upset could last for a young person's lifetime without help. Having adults act dangerously is so traumatic that most children need professional counseling. They also need caring adults to keep reinforcing the following four messages.

1. If your grownups have problems and do something hurtful to themselves or others, it is NOT your fault. Lots of times kids think a grownup's problems are their fault because they forgot something or did something wrong. But if a grownup acts dangerously, it is ALWAYS a grownup problem, NOT a kid problem, no matter what you did or didn't do.

2. No matter what your grownups might have said or done, you are worthy of love and you are loved. When grownups have big problems, they might do or say things that are very hurtful and scary and that can make a kid feel unloved. Often people with problems say things when they are upset that they forget saying later or don't really mean. It's normal for kids to feel very bad when grownups make mistakes that scare or hurt their kids or each other. Remember that you are loved and important just the way you are.

3. If you feel scared that a grownup might do something dangerous, your job is to get help. It is not safe for kids to try to figure out how to stop the grownup. Instead, kids need to follow their safety plan to get away from the person who is acting dangerously if they can and to GET HELP from other adults who can help their grownup to make safer choices.

4. Remember your safety plan. If they are living in an unstable situation, kids need to know and practice a safety plan that is appropriate for their

If a grownup acts dangerously, it is ALWAYS a grownup problem, NOT a kid problem.

We use the word "safety" generously to mean not only "protected from harm" but also having the confidence, knowledge, and skills to create safety within ourselves and for everyone in our lives.

age, understanding, and life situation for how to get help. Going to a neighbor, calling 9-1-1, an advocate, or another family member might all be part of a safety plan.

Again, these complex issues go beyond the scope of this book. However, we can each make sure that the kids in our lives understand that they are not responsible for their grownup's behavior, that they are loved no matter what, that their job is to get help if any grownup is acting unsafely, and that remembering their safety plan for getting help is important to us.

Taking Action For Child Safety in Ways Large and Small

At Kidpower, we truly believe that the safety of kids *is* everybody's business. We use the word "safety" generously to mean not only "protected from harm" but also having the confidence, knowledge, and skills to create safety within ourselves and for everyone in our lives.

If all of us keep our minds and hearts open, we will find countless times where a few words or simple actions can make a profound difference. Here's a story about a ripple effect that lasted for years from our long-time supporter Cheri Haft:

When my kids were in Junior High School, I used to park my car on a side street around the corner so they wouldn't be embarrassed. One day after school, as I was waiting for them, I saw three boys picking on another kid, shoving him into a wall and verbally assaulting him. I watched for a moment or two. Not one parent got out of their cars!

I couldn't stand it. I got out of my car and stopped them. My kids were sooooooo mad at me! My response to them, so they could save face, was if anyone makes fun of you, just tell them your mom is mentally ill and sometimes she can't help herself. Ironically, at one point later in high school, my son stood up for a girl who was being harassed by other boys! I'd say he got the message. That lesson has stuck with both my sons who are now 26 and 27. I give a lot of credit to Kidpower for giving me this training and belief for myself and both my kids!

Cheri needed only a few moments to step in and stop the bullying she witnessed. In addition, she found a creative way of respecting her kids' discomfort while showing with her behavior that doing nothing was not an option for her.

Whether an intervention takes a few minutes or much longer, each action we take to make the safety of a child our business can have a lasting impact in their lives.

Chapter Twelve

One Million Safer Kids – A Call to Action From Kidpower

If we all take the actions described in this book, think of the misery and tragedy we can help to prevent! And think of the kids we will be able to empower with "People Safety" skills so they are better prepared to take charge of their safety, build healthy relationships, and develop enough confidence to get the most out of their lives.

Life's more fun when it's safe - and we believe that *everyone* has the right to be safe!

After providing twenty-two years of grassroots education through Kidpower, we've seen again and again how a few simple ideas and skills can stop most attempts of bullying, violence, and abuse. We are proud that we have shared Kidpower knowledge with over two million people worldwide, on every inhabited continent in the world. When we say, "Kidpower is for everyone," we mean it!

We also realize just how much work we still have to do. No matter how long I do this work, my heart still breaks each time I hear of a child who has been harmed by any kind of emotional or physical violence. We must reach far more children, families, and caring adults with our core messages and skills.

The tragic increase in "bullycides"; the much greater awareness about child abuse because of recent scandals in schools, universities and churches; and the reforms taken to address these issues have created a watershed moment in our culture. Countless caring adults are talking about how to protect kids from violence and abuse and are looking for answers at a level that we have not seen before.

On July 1, 2011, Kidpower started an ambitious, interactive, worldwide project called One Million Safer Kids. Our goal is simple: to make one million young people safer from bullying, violence, and abuse through greater awareness, action, and skills.

We will do this through greatly expanding our online and media outreach, distance learning, books, and already-extensive library of articles. Our in-person training will still be as central to our mission as it has always been, and we will enhance it with new offerings that we can share worldwide. We are eager to capitalize on our growing ability to connect with caring adults no matter where they live, both people who have used Kidpower training and

No matter how long I do this work, my heart still breaks each time I hear of a child who has been harmed by any kind of emotional or physical violence.

*We invite you to join us by taking action in your home, school, neighborhood, and community. What can **you** do to help a young person be safer? How can Kidpower help?*

resources over the years and people who have yet to hear of us.

As a core element of the One Million Safer Kids campaign, Dr. Amy Tiemann[1] and I are co-authoring a new project and book called *Doing Right by Our Kids: Protecting Child Safety at All Levels of Society*[2]. The "Protecting Child Safety at All Levels of Society" theme is a natural extension of what we have been doing at Kidpower for many years. Amy and I will show how to apply Kidpower principles and skills to overcome obstacles to social change necessary to "Put Safety First" and will showcase other best practices from exceptional people and organizations. We will be sharing new and innovative resources for parents, teachers, and community leaders online through **www.DoingRightByOurKids.com**.

One Million Safer Kids by June 30, 2016 or sooner is our goal. We invite you to join us by taking action in your home, neighborhood, and community. What can you do to help a young person in your life be safer? How can Kidpower help? If you let us know how you are using Kidpower, we will count your efforts, as we reach the next million kids, and the million after that.

Here are three actions you can take right now to join Kidpower in creating One Million Safer Kids.

1. Keep learning. Please go to our website at **www.kidpower.org** to visit our online Library and Store. Subscribe to our free *Kidpower News and Resources, Bullying Solutions*, and/or *Kidpower Connect* e-newsletters so you can stay informed about our progress and receive new materials.

2. Share knowledge and resources. Teach the ideas and skills in this book to all of the young people in your life. Give a copy of this book to leaders at your school and to family members. Use your social network to send out Kidpower articles and safety tips through Twitter, Facebook, school newsletters, newspapers, company newsletters, and parenting blogs so that more people can learn about the resources Kidpower has to offer and can in turn help Kidpower to further our vision.

3. Stay in touch. E-mail us at **safety@kidpower.org** to tell us your experiences about how both this book and Kidpower have served you and to recommend any improvements we might make. Talented martial artists make a commitment to "keeping a beginner's mind" because, no matter how accomplished they are, they know there is always more to learn. In Kidpower, we also are committed to keeping a beginner's mind. We are always looking for ways to improve our program and will welcome your questions, ideas, stories, examples, and suggestions.

We look forward to hearing from you! With your help, we can work together to create cultures of caring, respect, and safety for everyone, everywhere.

Footnotes

Note: We have attempted to document references as thoroughly and accurately as possible, but a few references are missing because, after so many years, we could not find them. Please contact safety@kidpower.org if you have any additions or corrections.

Chapter One

1. Matt Thomas and Model Mugging (13)

2. Van Der Zande, Irene. 1993. *1,2,3...The Toddler Years: A Practical Guide for Parents and Caregivers*. Toddler Center Press: 2nd edition, www.sctcc.org. (14)

3. Bass, Ellen and Davis, Laura. 1994. *The Courage to Heal – Third Edition – Revised and Expanded: A Guide for Women Survivors of Child Sexual Abuse*. New York: HarperCollins Publishers, Inc. (15)

Chapter Two

1. Finkelhor, D., Hamby, S., Omrod, R., Kracke, K. and Turner, H. 2009. "Children's Exposure to Violence: A Comprehensive National Survey". *U.S. Department of Justice, Office of Justice Programs, Office of Juvenile Justice and Delinquency Prevention*. (22)

2. U.S. Department of Justice. 2008. *Criminal Victimization in the United States, 2008 Statistical Tables*. U.S. Department of Justice, Office of Justice Programs, Bureau of Justice Statistics. (22)

3. Finkelhor, D., Hammer, Heather and Sedlak, Andrea J. 2002. "Nonfamily Abducted Children: National Estimates and Characteristics." *U.S. Department of Justice, Office of Justice Programs, Office of Juvenile Justice and Delinquency Prevention, NISMART*. (22)

4. Bass, Ellen and Davis, Laura. 1994. *The Courage to Heal – Third Edition – Revised and Expanded: A Guide for Women Survivors of Child Sexual Abuse*. New York: HarperCollins Publishers, Inc. (22)

5. Finkelhor, D., Hammer, Heather and Sedlak, Andrea J. 2008. "Sexually Assaulted Children". *U.S. Department of Justice, Office of Justice Programs, Office of Juvenile Justice and Delinquency Prevention*. (22)

6. Center for Disease Control and Prevention. 2010. Youth Risk Behavior Surveillance - United States, 2009. *Surveillance Summaries, 2010. MMWR 2010;59* (22)

7. Bryant, A. L. 1993. "Hostile Hallways: The AAUW Survey on Sexual Harassment in America's Schools". *Journal of School Health, Vol. 63 Is. 8* (22)

8. David-Ferdon C., PhD. and Hertz M. F., M.S. 2009. "Electronic Media and Youth Violence: A CDC Issue Brief for Researchers". *U.S. Department of Health and Human Services: Centers for Disease Control*. (22-23)

9. Sendak, Maurice. 1963. *Where the Wild Things Are*. New York: Harper & Row Inc. (24)

10. Mayer, Mercer. 1968. *There's a Nightmare in My Closet*. New York: Dial Press. (24)

11. Bacon, F. Sir. 1561-1626. He was Western philosopher and pioneer of the scientific method during the scientific revolution. (24)

12. Stone Elizabeth. is the author of *Black Sheep and Kissing Cousins: How our Family Stories Shape us* and *A Boy I Once Knew*, journalist, and a professor of English, Communication, and Media Studies at Fordham University's College at Lincoln Center in Manhattan. Stone is the author of quotes widely used in parenting programs. (24)

13. Kraizer, Ph.D., Sherryll. is a pioneer in documenting through research that practicing skills is the most effective way of teaching safety skills to children and was an early advisor to the Kidpower program. Author of *The Safe Child Book: A Commonsense Approach to Protecting Children and Teaching Children to Protect Themselves*. (1985) New York: Delacorte Press. *The Safe Child Book* provides parents with successful, non-threatening techniques for keeping their children safe. The book is based on the author's education workshops that cover safety topics such as sexual abuse, abduction, leaving children alone, surfing the Internet, and school safety. www.safechild.org (28)

14. Gerber, Magda and Johnson, Allison. 1997. *Your Self-Confident Baby*. John Wiley & Sons, Inc. Outlines a parenting philosophy based on respect and treating a baby as a competent person, communicating with him or her, and providing the room for a baby to explore. (29)

15. Angelou, M. (45)

Chapter Three

1. Search Institute. http://www.search-institute.org (49)

2. Covey, Sean. 1989. *The 7 Habits of Highly Effective People*. New York: Fireside. (49)

3. Frankl, Viktor E. 1984. *Man's Search for Meaning*. New York: Pocket Books. (49)

4. Bronson, Po and Merryman, Ashley. 2009. *Nurture Shock: New Thinking about Children*. Hachette Book Group New York: New York. (50)

5. Kraus, Robert. 1971. *Leo the Late Bloomer*. Windmill Books: New York. (50)

6. Seligman, M. E. P. Ph.D. 1998-2006. Founder and Director of the Positive Psychology Center at the University of Pennsylvania. http://www.ppc.sas.upenn.edu/positivepsychologyresearch.htm (55)

7. Hazleton, Lesley. 1985. *The Right to Feel Bad*. Ballantine Books. (59)

8. Aron, Elaine N. 2002. *The Highly Sensitive Person: How to Thrive When the World Overwhelms You and The Highly Sensitive Child: Helping Our Children Thrive When the World Overwhelms Them*. New York: Broadway Books. (60)

9. Brown, Frederic. 1961. *The Mind Thing*. Bantam. (61)

10. KGO San Francisco, ABC Radio, Associated Press. Aug. 14, 2011. *Girl, 8, Escapes Captor*. ABC News. http://abcnews.go.com/US/story?id=96145&page=1 (64)

11. Brown, Brené, Dr. Ph.D. 2010. *The Gifts of Imperfection: Let Go of Who You Think You're Supposed to Be and Embrace Who You Are,* Hazelden: Center City, Minnesota. (68)

Chapter Four

1. Few, Roger. *The Atlas of Wild Places: In Search of Earth's Last Wildernesses*. Washington D.C. Smithsonian Books, 1994. Describes the Tiger Story. (78)

2. De Becker, Gavin. *The Gift of Fear: Survival Signals That Protect Us from Violence*. New York: Dell Publishing (a division of Random House, Inc., 1540 Broadway, New York, NY 10036), 1997. Describes the warning signs of a violent attacker and the importance of recognizing them before an attack can occur. De Becker shows the importance of listening to your fears and intuition that a situation or person might be dangerous, in order to avoid becoming a victim. www.gavindebecker.com/books-gof.cfm (81)

Chapter Six

1. The Media Awareness Network in Canada has a wealth of lesson plans for different grades on how to teach Media Awareness Skills. In their section on gender stereotypes and sexual assault, they have lessons that include asking what it means to "act like a man" and "be a lady," how this affects the students' images of themselves, and how this relates to violence. They also have lessons on diversity and violence, including homophobia and racism. www.media-awareness.ca/english/index.cfm (136)

Chapter Seven

1. Leisey, Kim Ph.D. *The meaning of self-protection through the voices of early adolescent girls: Toward a grounded theory*. Doctoral dissertation, University of Maryland, 2002. Research demonstrated that the process of self-protection is based on the categories of safety, fears, help, and staying safe. The fifth key category and central category was identified as being confidence; a process of knowing what to do, feeling strong, and having a choice. The category of staying safe was comprised of six dimensions; listening to self, verbal defense, avoidance, mental defense, awareness, and physical knowing. (165)

2. CNN. April 20, 1999. *Gunmen Open Fire at Colorado School; Some Students Trapped*. http://edition.cnn.com/US/9904/20/school.shooting.03/ (194)

3. http://today.msnbc.msn.com/id/35794401/ns/today-today_people/t/boy-who-saved-family-thanks-dispatcher/#.TwI9BU0Q3sk . (200)

Chapter Eight

1. Herner, Tom. National Association of State Directors of Special Education (NASDSE) President, Counterpoint 1998. (208)

2. Rigby, Ken Ph.D *"What Harm Does Bullying Do?"* presented at the Children and Crime: Victims and Offenders Conference in 1999. Presented research to address beliefs that bullying is natural, character building or unimportant and to describe the real harms of allowing bullying to continue. Rigby is the author and co-author of many other books on bullying, and is an international consultant in the field. www.aic.gov.au/conferences/children/rigby.html (210)

3. National Education Association (NEA) is a volunteer-based organization on the local, state, and national level. The mission of the NEA is to improve the quality of education for all children in America despite their family income or place of residence. www.nea.org (210)

4. *"Walk in Another's Shoes- Teens Speak out About Bullying"* by Teen Advisory Board of Kidpower of Colorado (213)

5. Alsop, Peter, Child Psychologist (216)

6. Rose, Lillian Roybal, Cross cultural communications expert (218)

7. Mate, Gabor, and Gordon Neufeld. 2005. *Hold On to Your Kids: Why Parents Need to Matter More Than Peers*. Ballantine Books. Provides a guide and warning for parents who are becoming disconnected from their children. Illustrates how the connection of a parent and child is crucial to healthy development even when the influence of peers competes for attention. www. drgabormate.com/ (220)

8. *Kidpower Tools for Creating a United Front Against Bullying, Harassment and Violence*. www.kidpower.org (221)

9. Wikipedia is a Web-based, free-content encyclopedia written collaboratively by volunteers and sponsored by the non-profit Wikimedia Foundation. www.wikipedia.org (225)

10. School Mediation Associates has a mission to transform schools into more effective and safer institutions through mediation, facilitation, and training services. Provides educational materials and training. www.schoolmediation.com (235)

11. Perkins, B. K. 2011. *Where We Learn: The CUBE Survey of Urban School Climate*. Council of Urban Boards of Education: National School Boards Association. (240)

12. Peck, Scott M., M.D. 1998. *A Different Drum: Community Making and Peace*. New York: Touchstone. This book describes the process of creating healthy communities. www.mscottpeck.com (248)

13. Scott, Sharon. 1997. *How to Say No and Keep Your Friends: Peer Pressure Reversal for Teens and Preteens*. Amherst: Human Resource Development Press, Inc. (22 Amherst Road, Amherst Massachusetts 01002). This book presents suggestions and effective skills for teenagers dealing with negative peer pressure. www.sharonscott.com (261-262)

Scott, Sharon. *Peer Pressure Reversal: An Adult Guide to Developing a Responsible Child*, 2nd Ed. by Sharon Scott, L.P.C., L.M.F.T. Copyright 1997, Sharon Scott. Available from HRD Press, 22 Amherst Rd., Amherst, MA 01002, 800-822-2801. www. hrdpress.com/SharonScott. A comprehensive lesson plan for parents, counselors, and teachers to teach peer pressure reversal to youth from ages five to eighteen. The text offers tips on how a teacher or parent can reinforce skills, discipline, help their children select appropriate friends, parent networking, and how to reinforce good decision-making. (262)

14. The American Association of University Women (AAUW) promotes equality for women in areas such as civil rights, education, and the work place through the sponsorship of research programs and publishing research on women, girls, and education. www.aauw.org (264)

15. *Harassment-Free Hallways: How to Stop Sexual Harassment in Schools* is a response to the research report *Hostile Hallways*, which revealed the need for a transformation in our nations schools. *Harassment-Free Hallways* is a resource guide for parents, students, schools, and school districts created by a task force of educators, researchers and experts on school-based sexual harassment. The guide provides assistance in assessing strengths and weaknesses of existing sexual harassment policies, developing user-friendly policies from the existing ones, understanding the rights and responsibilities that a school has to report and respond to sexual harassment, and how to take a strong leadership role in preventing sexual harassment cases. This guide is available for free at www.aauw. org (264- 265)

16. The U.S. Department of Education's Office of Civil Rights. *Sexual Harassment: It's Not Academic*. In an easy-to-read question-answer format, this pamphlet outlines the rights of students and the responsibility of educators to protect their students against sexual harassment. www.ed.gov/index.jhtml (265)

17. *Webster's Online Dictionary* (265)

18. The Media Awareness Network in Canada has a wealth of lesson plans for different grades on how to teach Media Awareness Skills. In their section on gender stereotypes and sexual assault, they have lessons that include asking what it means to "act like a man" and "be a lady," how this affects the students' images of themselves, and how this relates to violence. They also have lessons on diversity and violence, including homophobia and racism. www.media-awareness.ca/english/index.cfm (266)

19. *Communication Technology Youth Safety Contract* www. kidpower.org (278)

20. Faber, Adele and Elaine Mazlish. 1999. *How to Talk so Kids Will Listen and Listen so Kids Will Talk*. New York: Quill. Provides a very practical and positive step-by-step approach to improve parents' ability to talk and problem-solve with their children. www. fabermazlish.com/ (283)

21. Faber, Adele and Elaine Mazlish. 1998. *Siblings Without Rivalry*. New York: HarperCollins Publishers. Offers tips for parents with multiple children on how to be a better parent by treating their children as individuals and not comparing. Also gives tips on how to respond to arguments between siblings and how to reinforce new positive behaviors. (283)

22. *Kidpower Safety Comics* www.kidpower.org (284)

23. The Positive Coaching Alliance is a nonprofit organization dedicated to providing youth and high school athletes with a positive, character-building youth sports experience. www.positivecoach.org/ (287)

Chapter Nine

1. Bass, Ellen, Co-Author of *The Courage to Heal* and *I Never Told Anyone*. (292)

2. Konigsburg, E.L. 2000. *Silent to the Bone*. Atheneum Books for Young Readers: New York. (292)

3. Child Abuse Prevention and Treatment Act provides federal funding to states in support of prevention, assessment, investigation, and prosecution of child abuse. www.acf.hhs.gov/programs/cb/laws_policies/cblaws/capta/index.htm (293)

4. U.S. Department of Health and Human Services. Abuse, Neglect, Adoption & Foster Care Research National Incidence Study of Child Abuse and Neglect (NIS-4). (2004-2009) http://www.acf.hhs.gov/programs/opre/abuse_neglect/natl_incid/index.html (294)

5. Luna-Sparks, John, Kidpower Senior Instructor and Clinician at the Child Protection Center in Children's Hospital and Research Center in Oakland. (294)

6. Hammel-Zabin, Dr. Amy. 2003. *Conversations with a Pedophile: In the Interest of Our Children*. Barricade Books: New Jersey. (296)

7. Isenstadt, Paul L.C.S.W., has specialized in correctional mental health evaluation, treatment, and program administration and has served as the Director of Programming at ComCor, a community corrections program in Colorado Springs. www.comcor.org/index.htm (297)

8. Child Protective Services is a governmental agency in many states in the United States that investigates reports of abuse and neglect of children, offers services to children and their families, places children in foster homes or adoptive homes, and helps foster children make the transition into adulthood. (319)

9. Teen resources on Kidpower website http://www.kidpower.org/who-we-serve/teens.html (326)

10. Shattuck Applied Research + Evaluation, 2010, *The Effects of the Kidpower Everyday Safety Skills Program on Third Grade Students in Santa Cruz County*, http://www.kidpower.org/about-us/evaluations.html#shattuck (331)

Chapter Ten

1. St. George, Donna. 2010. *"Child-abduction study finds capable kids are their own best defense."* Washington Post http://www.washingtonpost.com/wpdyn/content/article/2010/09/04/AR2010090403226.html (332)

2. Newsweek Magazine, The Daily Beast. 1993. *"The Sad Case of Polly Klaas"*. Dec. 12. http://www.thedailybeast.com/newsweek/1993/12/12/the-sad-case-of-polly-klaas.html (333)

3, 4, 5. U.S. Department of Justice. Office of Justice Programs. 2002. "Nonfamily Abducted Children – National Estimates and Characteristics". Office of Juvenile Justice and Delinquency Prevention, National Center for Missing and Exploited Children. (334)

6. U.S. Department of Justice. Office of Justice Programs. 2002. "National Estimates of Missing Children: An Overview". Office of Juvenile Justice and Delinquency Prevention, National Center for Missing and Exploited Children. http://www.missingkids.com/missingkids/servlet/PageServlet?LanguageCountry=en_US&PageId=2810 (334)

7. Carlie Jane Brucia Abduction, http://www.youtube.com/watch?v=tJolD7VwRtM (335)

8. Two-year-old killed by train, http://abclocal.go.com/kfsn/story?section=news/local&id=3674873 (338)

9. Red Cross babysitting course: http://www.redcross.org/portal/site/en/menuitem.53fabf6cc033f17a2b1ecfbf43181aa0/?vgnextoid=5ced914124dbe110VgnVCM10000089f0870aRCRD (338)

10. Adam Walsh http://en.wikipedia.org/wiki/Murder_of_Adam_Walsh (339)

11. Sandra Cantu http://www.latimes.com/topic/crime-law-justice/crimes/crime-victims/sandra-cantu-PECLB004581.topic (339)

12. Melissa Huckaby http://www.people.com/people/article/0,,20273817,00.html (339)

13. Friend of Jaycee followed http://www.examiner.com/headlines-in-salt-lake-city/childhood-friend-of-jaycee-dugard-saw-phillip-garrido-s-car-before-kidnapping (339)

14. Leiby Kletzy http://www.nytimes.com/2011/07/14/nyregion/arrest-made-in-brooklyn-killing-of-leiby-kletzky.html?pagewanted=all (340)

15. *Neighborhood Watch* http://www.usaonwatch.org/ (340)

16. De Becker, Gavin. 1997. *The Gift of Fear: Survival Signals That Protect Us from Violence*. Dell Publishing: New York. (344)

17. Shattuck Applied Research + Evaluation, 2010, *The Effects of the Kidpower Everyday Safety Skills Program on Third Grade Students in Santa Cruz County*, http://www.kidpower.org/about-us/evaluations.html#shattuck (352)

18. U.S. Department of Justice. Office of Juvenile Programs. 2006. "Online Victimization of Youth: Five Years Later". Office of Juvenile Justice and Delinquency Prevention, National Center for Missing and Exploited Children (365)

19. Dugard, Jaycee. 2011. *A Stolen Life: A Memoir.* Luna Lee, Inc. (369)

20. Michaela Garecht http://www.missingmichaela.com/ (370)

21. Stockholm Syndrome (372)

22. The Klaas Kids Foundation was established to honor the memory of Polly Klaas, who was kidnapped and murdered when she was twelve-years-old, through their mission to prevent crimes against children. They give information to parents about what to do if your child is missing and lobby for government agencies to make prevention, protection, and prosecution a high priority. www.klaaskids.org/ (375)

23. Amber Alert, a program that established alliances between the police departments and the broadcast organizations to report abductions in order to mobilize the community to make sure the child is returned safety to the family. http://www.missingkids.com/missingkids/servlet/PageServlet?LanguageCountry=en_US&PageId=4319 (376)

24. The Vanished Children's Alliance assists law enforcement and families of missing children and educates on a local, national and international level about abduction prevention. www.vca.org (376)

Chapter 11

1.Wilde, Dr. S. *From Witness to Advocate.* Ongoing data collection and analysis for multicultural-grounded theory study of witness interventions in observable child maltreatment situations. www.wildelife.com/research/w2a (383)

Index

Kidpower in Practice

Acknowledgements

You can learn more about the remarkable people who have built and keep building our organization through our website and annual report.

Kidpower is a tapestry of many different threads woven by many different hands. This book has grown from the ideas, questions, teaching, feedback, and stories of countless people since I first started learning about personal safety and self-defense in 1985.

I want to express my appreciation to each of our Kidpower instructors, board members, honorary trustees, senior program leaders, center directors, workshop organizers, advisors, volunteers, donors, parents, students, funding partners, service partners, family members, advocates, hosts, and office staff. Thank you for the thought, care, time, and generosity that you have given to bring Kidpower Teenpower Fullpower International to where we are today. I feel honored to have you as colleagues and as friends.

Writing each person's story would be a book unto itself. You can learn about the remarkable people who have built and keep building our organization by reading *A Tapestry Woven By Many Different Hands* on our website at http://www.kidpower.org/about-us/tapestry.html.

I want to give special acknowledgement to the people who have made publication of *The Kidpower Book for Caring Adults* possible.

Kristen Calcatera of Big Sky Creative contributed an enormous amount of her time and expertise to design the cover and layout of the advance reader's edition of this book, making it far more professional and attractive than any of our books had been up until that time. Thank you also to long-time supporter Lynda Leonard and former board member Laurel Miranda for donating countless hours to edit my early drafts, greatly increasing the book's clarity and accuracy.

For this official first edition, Cornelia Baumgartner, Amanda Golert, Kelly Goodwin, Chantal Keeney, Marylaine Léger, Erika Leonard, and Kathy Pavlik all contributed extensive editing and feedback, resulting in this book becoming better-written, more complete, and easier to use. Thank you also to Jan Isaacs Henry, Carla Lemmon, and John Luna-Sparks for their valuable input on the chapter about protecting kids from sexual abuse.

Ian Price of Price Watkins Media created the beautiful book cover, design, and accessible layout – and our wonderful Kidpower logo.

The photographs are thanks to Catherine Arnold, Nicole Barbara, Allegra Doriss, Cate Gaffney, Amanda Golert, Alice Keeney, Erika Leonard, Lynda Leonard, Claire Laughlin, Juliana Schweidzon Machado, Laurel Miranda, Eugene Tanner, Shmuel Thaler, Phung Bich Thuy, Zaida Torres, and Pat West. Amanda Golert drew the cartoons, and most of the drawings were given to us by children.

Research, footnotes, and indexing are thanks to Andrew Carl and Jessica Yazmin Herrera.

Kidpower® Services for All Ages and Abilities

Workshops. Through our active centers and travelling instructors, Kidpower has conducted workshops in over 40 countries spanning six continents. Our programs include: Kidpower Parent/Caregiver Education seminars; Parent-Child workshops; Weekend Family Workshops; classroom and teacher training programs; Teenpower self-defense workshops for teens; CollegePower for young people leaving home; Fullpower self-defense and boundary-setting workshops for adults; SeniorPower for older people; programs for people with special needs; training for professionals; and workplace violence prevention and communication programs.

Coaching, Consulting, and Curriculum Development. Long-distance coaching by video-conferencing, telephone, and e-mail to family members and professionals allow our services to be accessible worldwide. We consult with organizations and schools on how to best adapt our program to meet their needs and develop new curriculum to increase the "People Safety" knowledge of different groups facing difficult life challenges.

Free On-Line Library. Our extensive on-line Library offers over 100 free "People Safety" resources including articles, videos, webinars, blog entries, and podcasts. We regularly send new resources directly to our subscribers through our *Kidpower News* and *Bullying Solutions* e-newsletters. Free downloads are available of our *Kidpower® International Safety Signs*, our *Kidpower® 30-Skill Challenge*, a coloring book, and most articles. In addition, we give permission to organizations, blogs, and media sources to use and share these materials without cost for charitable purposes that meet our criteria.

Publications. Our online Store has a variety of affordable publications for sale. Our cartoon-illustrated *Kidpower® Safety Comics* and *Teaching Kits* make it fun and easy to discuss and practice safety skills with people of different ages and abilities in individual and group settings. *Bullying – What Adults Need to Know and Do to Keep Kids Safe* provides a comprehensive overview and specific tools on how to address bullying in a positive, effective, and empowering way. The *Relationship Safety Handbook* helps professionals teach teens and adults to create safe and strong relationships.

Instructor Training and Center Development. Our very comprehensive training program prepares qualified people to teach our programs and to establish centers and offices for organizing services in their communities under our organizational umbrella.

For more information, please visit www.kidpower.org!

About the Author

Irene van der Zande is an international expert in personal safety, prolific author, and inspiring trainer. As the founder and executive director of Kidpower Teenpower Fullpower International®, known as Kidpower® for short, Irene has been a tireless leader in protecting and empowering children, teens, and adults around the world for more than two decades. Through in-person workshops and educational resources, Kidpower has reached over 2 million people since being established as a nonprofit organization in 1989. Irene has personally taught well over 30,000 students of all ages and abilities how to take charge of their safety, build better relationships, develop greater confidence, and take action to prevent most bullying, abuse, abduction, and other violence.

Irene has also written many training manuals, books and articles, and has been blogging and building an extensive library of resources to bring "People Safety" knowledge into the daily practices of individuals, families, schools, organizations, and communities. Her publications include *1,2,3... The Toddler Years*; *Bullying – What Adults Need to Know and Do to Keep Kids Safe*; the *Kidpower Safety Comics Series*; the *Kidpower and Fullpower Teaching Kits*; the *Kidpower and Teenpower/Fullpower Comprehensive Program Manuals*; *Kidpower Safety Signs for Individuals With Limited Speech*; *One Strong Move: Introductory Self-Defense Lessons*; and *The Relationship Safety Handbook*. Adaptations of her work include the *SeniorPower Workbook* with Marylaine Léger of Pleins Pouvoirs KIDPOWER Montréal in Canada and the *Healthy Relationships Interactive Resources for Adults and Older Teens with Intellectual Disabilities* with Cornelia Baumgartner of the Kidpower Teenpower Fullpower Trust in New Zealand.

Irene is currently working on a book with co-author Dr. Amy Tiemann called *Doing Right by Our Kids®: Protecting Child Safety at All Levels of Society*. She is also collaborating with Beth McGreevy on developing ProPower®, an online training program for professionals.

Kidpower Teenpower Fullpower International®, known as Kidpower® for short, is a global nonprofit leader in personal safety education, which has served more than two million people of all ages and abilities across six continents, since its founding in 1989. Instead of using fear to teach young people about violence prevention, the Kidpower Method™ makes it fun to learn to be safe, building habits that increase the skills and confidence of kids and the whole family that can last a lifetime.

In 2011, Kidpower launched our *One Million Safer Kids initiative*, which has one simple goal: to make at least one million young people safer from all forms of violence through education, awareness, and skills by July 2016. We hope *The Kidpower® Book for Caring Adults* will be a transformational resource for caring adults who want to help kids be safer, healthier, and happier.

For more information:
Write to *safety@kidpower.org* to share your stories about how you are using ideas and skills from the Kidpower program to help kids, teens, and adults - and have your efforts be counted toward our next One Million Safer Kids.

Visit *www.kidpower.org* and *onemillionsaferkids.org* to learn more about our services, books, and extensive free on-line Library and you can get involved.

Sign up for our free *Kidpower News and Resources* and *Bullying Solutions* e-newsletters.

Like us on Facebook and/or follow us on Twitter.
Write to Kidpower, P.O. Box 1212, Santa Cruz, California 95061

18845944R00228